The Blackwell Guide to the
Philosophy of
Religion

Edited by

William E. Mann

Blackwell
Publishing

BLACKWELL PUBLISHING
350 Main Street, Malden, MA 02148-5020, USA
108 Cowley Road, Oxford OX4 1JF, UK
550 Swanston Street, Carlton, Victoria 3053, Australia

First published 2005 by Blackwell Publishing Ltd

Library of Congress Cataloging-in-Publication Data

The Blackwell guide to the philosophy of religion / edited by William E. Mann.
p. cm. — (Blackwell philosophy guides ; 17)
Includes bibliographical references and index.
ISBN 0-631-22128-X (hardcover : alk. paper) — ISBN 0-631-22129-8 (pbk. : alk. paper)
1. Christianity—Philosophy. 2. Religion—Philosophy. I. Mann,
William Edward, 1947– II. Series.

BR100.B49 2004
210—dc22
2003026163

A catalogue record for this title is available from the British Library.

Set in 10/13pt Galliard
by Graphicraft Limited, Hong Kong
Printed and bound in the United Kingdom
by MPG Books Ltd, Bodmin, Cornwall

For further information on
Blackwell Publishing, visit our website:
http://www.blackwellpublishing.com

Contents

Contents

Notes on Contributors

William P. Alston is Professor Emeritus of Philosophy at Syracuse University. His main work has been in philosophy of religion, epistemology, and philosophy of language. Among his recent books are *Epistemic Justification* (1989); *Divine Nature and Human Language* (1989); *Perceiving God* (1991); *A Realist Conception of Truth* (1996); and *Illocutionary Acts and Sentence Meaning* (2000).

Alfred J. Freddoso is John and Jean Oesterle Professor of Thomistic Studies at the University of Notre Dame. His most recent work focuses on the relation between faith and reason and on scholastic metaphysics. His books include translations, notes, and introductions to Luis de Molina, *On Divine Foreknowledge: Part IV of "The Concordia"* (1988); Francisco Suarez, *On Efficient Causality: Metaphysical Disputations 17, 18, and 19* (1994); and Francisco Suarez, *On Creation, Conservation, and Concurrence: Metaphysical Disputations 20–22* (2000).

Philip Kitcher is Professor of Philosophy at Columbia University. His areas of specialization include philosophy of science, particularly philosophy of biology, and philosophy of mathematics. His recent books include *The Advancement of Science* (1993); *In the Lives to Come: The Genetic Revolution and Human Possibilities* (1996); *Science, Truth and Democracy* (2001); and *In Mendel's Mirror: Philosophical Reflections on Biology* (2003).

Brian Leftow is Nolloth Professor of the Philosophy of the Christian Religion at Oxford University. His research has concentrated on philosophical theology, metaphysics, and medieval philosophy. His books include *Time and Eternity* (1991); *God and Necessity* (forthcoming); and *Aquinas on Metaphysics* (forthcoming).

William E. Mann is Marsh Professor of Intellectual and Moral Philosophy at the University of Vermont. He specializes in philosophical theology and medieval philosophy. His publications include essays on "Augustine on Evil and Original Sin" (2001); "Duns Scotus on Natural and Supernatural Knowledge of God"

(2003); "Abelard's Ethics" (forthcoming); and "Divine Sovereignty and Aseity" (forthcoming).

Gareth B. Matthews is Professor of Philosophy at the University of Massachusetts, Amherst. He works in the areas of ancient and medieval philosophy. He is the author of *Thought's Ego in Augustine and Descartes* (1992) and *Socratic Perplexity and the Nature of Philosophy* (1999), and the editor of *The Augustinian Tradition* (1999) and Augustine's *On the Trinity (Books 8–12)* (2002).

Hugh J. McCann is Professor of Philosophy at Texas A&M University. He specializes in action theory, philosophy of religion, and related problems in metaphysics and ethics. His published works include *The Works of Agency* (1998); "Divine Sovereignty and the Freedom of the Will" (1995); and "The Author of Sin?" (forthcoming).

Derk Pereboom is Professor of Philosophy at the University of Vermont. His research areas include history of modern philosophy, especially Kant, philosophy of mind, metaphysics, and philosophy of religion. His publications include *Living Without Free Will* (2001); "Self-Understanding in Kant's Transcendental Deduction" (1995); "Kant on God, Evil, and Teleology" (1996); and "Robust Non-reductive Materialism" (2002).

Philip L. Quinn is John A. O'Brien Professor of Philosophy at the University of Notre Dame and was formerly William Herbert Perry Faunce Professor of Philosophy at Brown University. He is the author of *Divine Commands and Moral Requirements* (1978) and numerous journal articles, book chapters, and reviews in philosophy of religion and other areas of philosophy. He is also coeditor of and contributor to *A Companion to Philosophy of Religion* (1997) and *The Philosophical Challenge of Religious Diversity* (2002).

William L. Rowe is Professor of Philosophy at Purdue University. He has written extensively in the philosophy of religion, especially on the cosmological argument and on the problem of evil. His books include *Religious Symbols and God* (1968); *The Cosmological Argument* (1975); *Thomas Reid on Freedom and Morality* (1991); and *Philosophy of Religion* (2001).

Elliott Sober is now Professor of Philosophy at Stanford University, having taught for many years at the University of Wisconsin, Madison. His interests are mainly in philosophy of science and philosophy of biology. He is the author of *Philosophy of Biology* (1993) and coauthor, with David Sloan Wilson, of *Unto Others: The Evolution and Psychology of Unselfish Behavior* (1998).

Peter van Inwagen is John Cardinal O'Hara Professor of Philosophy at the University of Notre Dame. His main work has been in metaphysics and philosophical theology. His books include *An Essay on Free Will* (1983); *Material Beings* (1990); *God, Knowledge and Mystery* (1995); *The Possibility of Resurrection and Other Essays in Christian Apologetics* (1997); and *Metaphysics* (2002).

William J. Wainwright is Distinguished Professor of Philosophy at the University of Wisconsin, Milwaukee. His chief area of research is in philosophy of religion. His books include *Mysticism* (1982); *Reason and the Heart* (1995); and *God, Philosophy and Academic Culture* (1996). He is currently working on a book entitled *Religion and Morality.*

Linda Zagzebski is Kingfisher College Chair of the Philosophy of Religion and Ethics at the University of Oklahoma. Her research interests are in philosophy of religion, ethics, and epistemology. Her recent books include *Virtues of the Mind* (1996) and *Divine Motivation Theory* (2004). She is also coeditor of *Virtue Epistemology* (2001) and *Intellectual Virtue* (2003).

Preface

Whether one applauds it, deplores it, or is puzzled by it, the fact is that religious belief has survived any number of historical and cultural upheavals that had been thought to signal its demise. In similar fashion the philosophy of religion is alive and healthy despite attacks on its integrity from positivism, postmodernism, and deconstructionism. The essays contained in this volume amply attest to the vigor – and rigor – with which the philosophy of religion is presently being practiced. They have been written to be accessible to advanced undergraduate and graduate students and to members of the educated public. The authors, pre-eminent scholars in the field, not only provide an overview of their respective topics, but also further scholarly reflection on those topics. The next few paragraphs provide an overall sketch of the structure and content of the volume.

Part I The Concept of God

The major theistic religions, Judaism, Christianity, and Islam, acknowledge the existence of a supreme being. This being, God, is generally thought by these religious traditions to be responsible for the creation and conservation of the world. More than that, God is supposed to care about his creatures, to know their innermost thoughts, joys, and sorrows, and to desire their flourishing. God is thus thought to be *personal*, inasmuch as he has a mental life consisting of beliefs, desires, and intentions. At the same time, however, theists insist that God is a *deity*, a status they emphasize by claiming that unlike humans, God is omniscient (all-knowing), omnipotent (all-powerful), and perfectly good. Many theists claim, further, that although humans live in space and time, God in some way transcends these dimensions of human existence. These assertions about God's nature have undergone extensive philosophical examination.

In Chapter 1 Linda Zagzebski examines the implications of supposing both that God is omniscient and that some of our actions are genuinely free, thus actions for which we are responsible. It would seem that if God is omniscient, then he knows in advance every detail of what we will be doing, long before we do it. But if God already knows now, for instance, what you will be doing one year hence, there seems to be no possibility that you will be able to do otherwise than what God now knows you will do. Thus, your actions a year from now – for that matter, at *any* time in the future – appear to be unfree if God already knows them. Zagzebski probes these and related issues.

Hugh J. McCann, in Chapter 2, discusses a series of problems that arise from the supposition that God is omnipotent. As McCann puts it, it seems that "to the extent that we maximize God's power in creating the world, we tend to minimize the powers of the things he creates." Consider, for example, the action of a cue ball striking the eight-ball. If God's power is required to keep the created world in existence from one moment to the next, are we not simply mistaken in thinking that the cue ball is the cause of the eight-ball's moving? Or suppose that we think that squares have four sides "by definition." Could it be, nevertheless, that omnipotent God has the power to create a five-sided square?

Brian Leftow's chapter examines the philosophical implications of the Biblical conception of God as existing "from everlasting to everlasting" and the related claim that God is immutable. Most theists agree that God exists at every moment of time. But beneath that surface agreement there lurks a fundamental disagreement about whether God is "in" time, as creatures are, progressing from past to present to future, or whether what we creatures regard as past, present, and future is all simultaneously present to God. Leftow sheds new light on these issues.

Part II   The Existence of God

One undertaking is to define the concept of a thing. Another is to determine whether anything exists that fits the concept. A Greek mythologist can specify precisely what a gorgon is without believing for a moment that there are, or ever were, any gorgons. Even if we were to converge on a uniform conception of God, it would still be an open question whether God, as so conceived, exists.

Some philosophers have sought to prove God's existence by showing that, unlike the case of the gorgons, God's existence is entailed directly by the concept of God. For these philosophers no empirical investigation is necessary or appropriate: reason unaided by facts about the world can demonstrate the necessity of God's existence. Arguments that purport to accomplish this feat are called ontological arguments. The most famous one was the earliest, formulated by Anselm of Canterbury (1033–1109). Anselm claims that anyone who reflects adequately on the notion of God as "something than which nothing greater can be conceived" should come to realize that God must exist. Anselm's argument has fascinated and outraged philosophers since its inception. It receives a thorough examination in Gareth B. Matthews's chapter.

Various versions of the so-called cosmological argument for God's existence take as their point of departure the question, "Why is there something rather than nothing?" Cosmological arguments appeal to the intuitions that the universe might not have existed, that the explanation for its existence does not seem to lie within the universe itself, and that the cause of the universe should be something that cannot fail to exist. Interest in the cosmological argument has been rekindled in the light of the success of "Big Bang" theories about the origin of our universe. In Chapter 5 William L. Rowe explores some of the important historical and contemporary versions of the argument.

Big Bang theories have also stimulated a reexamination of arguments from design for God's existence. Before the twentieth century, design arguments focused their attention on the structural complexities and functional capacities of living organisms, arguing that it was extremely improbable that such organisms came to be by chance. But if not by chance, then by design, and design implies a designer, who must be God. In the second half of the twentieth century physicists came to realize that it is also extemely improbable that the Big Bang should have produced a universe that was suitable for life. So once again a designer has been suggested to explain the fact that the universe is "fine-tuned" to be receptive to life. Elliott Sober examines both types of argument in Chapter 6.

The ontological, cosmological, and design arguments are all attempts either to prove God's existence or to make God's existence seem probable. Stacked up against them is the problem of evil. Stated briefly, the problem is this. If God is omniscient, omnipotent, and perfectly good, then God knows about all the suffering in the world, has the power to prevent or eliminate it, and wants to prevent or eliminate it. Why, then, is there suffering? Strong versions of the problem allege that the presence of evil disproves the existence of God. Weaker versions maintain that the presence of evil makes it improbable that God exists. In Chapter 7 Derk Pereboom surveys different versions of the problem, important theistic attempts to respond to it, and critical issues raised by those attempts.

Part III Religious Belief

Although many theists place some stock in one or another of the arguments for God's existence, many of them do not base their faith on the arguments. Hence they are relatively unperturbed by criticisms of those arguments. And few believers abandon their faith upon finding themselves unable to give a definitive solution to the problem of evil. Aware of these phenomena about the fixedness of religious belief, non-believers accuse believers of cognitive irresponsibility. The intensity of religious belief, it is said, is nowhere near to being matched by the clarity of the evidence. Theists sometimes respond by claiming that not all beliefs must be backed by evidence, and that non-believers themselves inescapably harbor some such beliefs. The essays in this section focus on various dimensions of the notion of religious belief.

Judaism, Christianity, and Islam converge on some beliefs – that the world is governed by a wise, powerful, and good God, that Abraham is a pivotal figure in God's relationship to humankind – but diverge on others. There is divergence among them, for instance, concerning the importance of a *bar* (or *bat*) *mitzvah*, or of baptism, or of making a pilgrimage to Mecca. How might one assess the intellectual responsibility of these kinds of religious belief in particular?

In Chapter 8 Alfred J. Freddoso points out that one way to go about such an assessment is to articulate a set of standards of rationality that would pass muster by reasonable people's lights and then show that an individual religious belief conforms to or violates those standards. Freddoso's approach is somewhat different. His strategy is to explore a whole network of beliefs constituting a particular faith, Christianity, "from the inside, so to speak," showing how its various metaphysical, ethical, and psychological elements fit together.

William P. Alston's chapter is an examination of the claim, made by some theists, that their beliefs are grounded or supported by their experiential awareness of God. Such awareness is sharply distinguished from ordinary sense perception, since the latter is confined to material objects while the former is alleged to be of a purely immaterial being. Alston explores in some detail the credentials of the claim for perceptual awareness of God by comparing it to the case that can be made for basing beliefs on ordinary sense perception of physical objects.

In the final chapter in this section, William J. Wainwright confronts the issue of how to appraise the phenomenon of religions whose beliefs do not merely diverge from the beliefs of other religions, but are incompatible with them. Wainwright assesses some responses that discount the alleged incompatibilities. He also discusses the prospects for "exclusivist" strategies, that is, strategies that maintain that one religious tradition is correct; thus, any religion incompatible with it is at least partially mistaken.

Part IV   Religion and Life

Try to imagine a religion that has nothing to tell us about our origins, our purpose in life, our destiny, and that is equally silent about what is right and what is wrong, about how we should conduct our lives, and why. Among theistic religions perhaps the closest approximation to this stripped-down position was *deism*, a religious movement centered in England in the seventeenth and eighteenth centuries. Deism rejected all religious teachings purporting to be based on any kind of divine revelation, maintaining instead that everything we can know about origins, purpose, and destiny must be based on and confined to our natural, empirical knowledge of the world. Similarly, deism claimed that our know-ledge of right and wrong did not depend on any specific divine revelation. Deists claimed that a benevolent God would see to it that all people at all times could come to know by natural means the principles necessary for their happiness.

As the natural sciences became more successful in the explanation of all sorts of phenomena, many thinkers came to harbor the suspicion that there was nothing left over for theistic religions to explain. And if each of us is naturally fit to uncover the ethical principles necessary for human happiness, then there seems to be no distinctive educational task that can only be carried out by religious authorities. In retrospect, then, deism appears to have sowed the seeds of its own demise.

The major theistic religions have insisted that deism is not enough. To the extent to which they claim, however, that there are important questions left unanswered by science and secular morality, they raise issues about the place of religion in scientifically enlightened, democratic societies. The essays in this section address some of the most salient of these issues.

Biologists estimate that over 99 percent of all species that have ever existed on earth are now extinct, and that the average lifespan for a species is approximately 4 million years. Judaism, Christianity, and Islam have maintained that you and I are immortal. How can these religions be right if, as seems extremely likely, our species will become extinct? In Chapter 11 Peter van Inwagen discusses issues related to this question, devoting special attention to a fascinating argument, the "Doomsday Argument," pertaining to what our expectations should be con-cerning species survival.

Deism was, at heart, an attempt to make room for religion within a scientific world-view. It thus offered the comforting prospect of peaceful coexistence for two enormously influential fashioners of human thought. In Chapter 12 Philip Kitcher questions whether any attempt to reconcile the two can succeed, and mounts a campaign on several fronts in favor of a scientific world-view.

Religions have been and continue to be pervasive in shaping the moral attitudes and institutions of their adherents. Some of those attitudes and institutions have been pernicious, fostering practices like racial and ethnic exclusivism and coloni-alism. Other religious attitudes and institutions have had undeniable beneficial effects. But could those beneficial effects have been brought about just as well by purely secular means? In other words, are there any values that are distinctively religious? In order to be in a position to answer that question we may need to grapple with another one: "What are the differences between a secular ethical outlook or system and a religious ethical system?" In Chapter 13 I explore a generic sort of theistic normative ethical theory, one that lays emphasis on divine commands, in particular, commands to love God and neighbor.

In the final chapter Philip L. Quinn probes two political ideals that can seem to pull their advocates in opposite directions. On the one hand liberal societies stress the value of religious toleration. On the other hand many defenders of liberal democracy argue that political arguments based solely on religious principles should be discounted in a liberal society's debate over public policy. Quinn concludes that the cases hitherto made for religious toleration and for an exclusionary principle in political deliberation are fragile at best.

The aim of this volume is to present its reader with a number of talented philosophers examining a number of topics central to the philosophy of religion. It will have served its purpose if it provokes its readers to reflect further on these topics. As a guide to further reflection, at the end of each essay there is a list of suggested further readings, over and above those discussed in the texts of the essays.

Part I

The Concept of God

Chapter 1

Omniscience, Time, and Freedom

Linda Zagzebski

Introduction

Consider the possibility that there is a being who has infallible beliefs about the entire future, including your own future choices. Suppose also that this being did not acquire these beliefs at this moment. He or she had them at some time in the past, say yesterday, or a hundred or a million years ago. That supposition, when combined with some very strong and quite ordinary intuitions about time and what it takes to act freely, leads to the conclusion that nobody acts freely. That is the main topic of this paper. It is not the only topic, however, because our exploration of the dilemma of foreknowledge and freedom will reveal a dilemma of foreknowledge and temporally relative modality that has nothing to do with free will.

The relevance of the foreknowledge dilemma to those who believe there actually exists a being who has infallible beliefs about future choices is obvious; the relevance to those who have no commitment to the existence of such a being but who think one is possible is less obvious, but no less real because the problem is one of conflicting possibilities. No matter what we think about the existence and nature of God, the dilemma of freedom and foreknowledge forces us to rethink prior intuitions. Most people who reflect about this problem for long realize they have to give up something. To use Quine's metaphor, most of us have to give up something in our web of belief, and that means, of course, that a portion of the web will unravel. I will not presume to tell the reader which part of your web should unravel because I do not know where these beliefs occur in your web, but I hope to convince you that something has to break.

Here is the problem in the clearest terms I know. Suppose that tomorrow you will decide to perform a simple act, the type of act you would describe as freely chosen, if anything is. Perhaps you will decide what to drink with your lunch. Either you will decide to have tea or you will not decide to have tea. The law of excluded middle rules out any other alternative. Suppose that you will decide to have tea. That means it is true that you will decide to have tea. If it is true, a being who now knows the entire future now knows that you will decide to have tea, and if that being had the same knowledge yesterday or a hundred years ago, then he knew then that you would decide to have tea tomorrow. And since his belief occurred in the past, there is nothing you can do now about its occurrence. Suppose also that that being knows in a way that is perfect. He not only is not mistaken, he cannot be mistaken in his beliefs; he is infallible. If so, he could not have been mistaken in the past about what you will do tomorrow. So when tomorow comes, how can you do otherwise than what that being infallibly knew you would do? And if you cannot do otherwise, you will not make your decision freely. By parity of reasoning, if you will decide differently, the same conclusion follows. No matter what the infallible foreknower believed about what you will do tomorrow, it appears that you cannot help but act accordingly. And if that being knew everything you and everybody else will do, nobody does anything freely. This is the problem of theological fatalism.

Let us now make the argument more precise. Since much hinges on the way the problem is formulated, I will aim to identify the strongest valid form of the argument for theological fatalism in order to consider which, if any, premises can be rejected. I will make any principles of inference used in the argument other than substitution and *modus ponens* premises in order to make the validity of the argument transparent. I will then consider whether any premise can be weakened without threatening the argument's validity. This is important because even if one or more premises of a typical strong argument for theological fatalism is false, we should be on the alert for the possibility that a weaker and more plausible premise can lead us to the same conclusion, or perhaps the premise is not needed at all. And, of course, it is also possible that validity requires interpreting the premise as stronger than it is generally thought to be.

An inspection of the informal argument just given shows that theological fatalism arises from the conjunction of the assumption that there is a being who has infallible beliefs about the future and three principles: the principle of the necessity of the past, the principle of alternate possibilities, and a transfer of necessity principle. Here is a more careful formulation of the fatalist argument, making all four of these components explicit.

Basic argument for theological fatalism

Let B be the proposition that you will choose to drink tea with your lunch tomorrow. Suppose that B is true. Let "now-necessary" designate temporal necessity, the type of necessity that the past has just because it is past. Let "God" designate a being who has infallible beliefs about the future. It is not required for the logic of the argument that this being be identical with the deity worshiped by any religion.

(1) Yesterday God infallibly believed B. [Supposition of infallible foreknowledge.]

(2) If E occurred in the past, it is now-necessary that E occurred then. [Principle of the necessity of the past.]

(3) It is now-necessary that yesterday God believed B. [(1), (2) substitution, *modus ponens.*]

(4) Necessarily, if yesterday God believed B, then B. [Definition of infallibility.]

(5) If p is now-necessary, and necessarily (p → q), then q is now-necessary. [Transfer of necessity principle.]

(6) So it is now-necessary that B. [(3) and (4) conjoined, (5), *modus ponens.*]

(7) If it is now-necessary that B, then you cannot do otherwise than choose tea tomorrow. [Definition of necessity.]

(8) Therefore, you cannot do otherwise than choose tea tomorrow. [(6), (7), *modus ponens.*]

(9) If you cannot do otherwise when you act, you do not act freely. [Principle of alternate possibilities.]

(10) Therefore, when you choose tea tomorrow, you will not do it freely. [(8), (9), *modus ponens.*]

This argument is logically valid. The next task is to investigate the extent to which its premises can be weakened without losing validity. The weaker and more plausible the premise, the stronger the argument. Perhaps this procedure will also show us where the argument is vulnerable.[1]

The Premise of Omniscience

Let us begin with the premise that there is a being whose beliefs are infallible. Infallibility is connected with a time-honored attribute of the Christian, Jewish, and Muslim God: omniscience. To be omniscient is to be all-knowing. To be all-knowing includes knowing the truth value of every proposition. It may include more than that if there are forms of knowledge that are non-propositional, but it includes at least this much: there is no true proposition an omniscient being does not know, and an omniscient being does not believe any false proposition. Like other divine perfections such as omnipotence, omniscience has traditionally been thought to be a component of the divine nature. If so, God is not only omniscient, but essentially omniscient. The latter, of course, is stronger than the former. Essential omniscience entails infallible knowledge of the truth value of all propositions. A being who is essentially omniscient is one who cannot be mistaken in any of his beliefs, and for every proposition, he either believes it is true or believes it is false.[2]

Notice next that essential omniscience is sufficient for infallibility in a particular belief but is not necessary, whereas omniscience is neither necessary nor sufficient for infallible belief. Omniscience is not necessary because a particular belief or set of beliefs can be infallible even if the knower does not know the truth value of all propositions. It is not sufficient because a being who knows the truth value of all propositions may not know one or more of them infallibly unless infallibility is included in the definition of knowing. As long as it is possible to know without knowing infallibly, there is nothing in being omniscient that entails knowing infallibly. Essential omniscience is sufficient for infallibility because an essentially omniscient being knows the truth value of all propositions infallibly. Essential omniscience is not necessary for infallibility in a particular belief, however, because there might be a being who has some infallible beliefs, but who also has some beliefs that are not infallible.

These considerations show that the problem of theological fatalism arises from infallible foreknowledge, not simple omniscience. Infallible foreknowledge is entailed by essential omniscience, and essential omniscience is no doubt the doctrine that motivates the supposition that there is a being who has infallible beliefs, namely, the God of the major monotheistic religions, but essential omniscience is stronger than is required to generate the problem. As we can see in the argument above, infallibility with respect to belief B is sufficient to get the conclusion that the agent is not free with respect to B. Widespread infallibility generates widespread lack of freedom, and infallibility with respect to all future acts of created agents is sufficient to generate the conclusion that no such agent acts freely.

So far, then, we see that the first premise of the fatalist argument cannot be weakened to a premise that merely refers to the omniscience of the postulated foreknower, but it need not be so strong as to refer to the essential omniscience of such a being. Infallible believing is the crucial concept.

Can the first premise be weakened in some other way without threatening the validity of the argument? What about the attribution of beliefs to the being postulated in that premise? It has sometimes been proposed that God does not have beliefs; beliefs are mental states that only finite beings can have. That is because an ancient tradition in philosophy going back to Plato makes knowing (*episteme*) and believing (*doxa*) mutually exclusive states, the latter being inferior to the former. If so, believing is not possible for a perfect being. But even so, a perfect being is presumably cognitively perfect, and cognitive perfection involves being infallible in grasping reality outside of himself, including that part of reality consisting in human acts. Whether those states are properly called instances of belief is not important for the argument. Readers who find the term "believes" problematic need only reword the fatalist argument, using whatever word they think accurately designates mental states that can be infallible.

There is still one important way the first premise can be weakened without harm to the argument. Consider the modal status of each premise in the basic argument. The principles of the necessity of the past, alternate possibilities, and transfer of necessity are thought to be necessary truths, so premises (2), (5), and (9) are necessary, as are the other two premises, (4) and (7), which are definitions.

The logic of the argument shows that with these premises in place, infallible foreknowledge is inconsistent with free will in the sense of having the ability to do otherwise. If infallible foreknowledge is possible, free will is impossible. So the dilemma is generated from the mere possibility of an infallible foreknower; an actual one is not required. That is the reason theological fatalism is not only a problem for committed theists.

The Premise of the Necessity of the Past

The necessity of the past is critical to the fatalist argument. The idea that the past has a kind of necessity simply in virtue of being past is expressed in the aphorism "There is no use crying over spilt milk." This idea is one side of a wider intuition that there is a modal asymmetry between past and future. The fixity of the past is understood in contrast with the non-fixity of the future. We will explore this intuition further in later sections, but for now the question is whether this premise can be weakened. Suppose that God, or the infallible foreknower, is not in time. Of course, if such a being is not in time, he cannot be a *fore*knower. Nonetheless, he could have the cognitive perfection of infallibly knowing everything. This idea is one of the oldest proposed solutions to the fatalist dilemma, going back to Boethius in the early sixth century and endorsed by Aquinas in the thirteenth,[3] but I think that even though this move is normally understood as a way out of theological fatalism, it simply alerts us to a way that problem can be broadened.

In earlier work I argued that the existence of infallible knowledge of what is future to us threatens fatalism whether or not the infallible foreknower is in time.[4] I am not suggesting that the generality of the problem can be demonstrated in a single argument, however. For a timeless knower, we need a different premise in place of (2) that refers to the necessity of eternity rather than the necessity of the past:

(2′) Timeless states of affairs are now-necessary.

(3) then becomes:

(3′) It is now-necessary that God timelessly believes B infallibly.

I recognize that (2′) is not a common principle. Nonetheless, it seems to me that if there is an intuition that leads us to think that we can do nothing about what is past, a similar intuition would lead us to think that we can do nothing about what is eternal. A timeless realm would be as ontologically determinate and fixed as the past. Perhaps it is inappropriate to express this type of necessity by saying that timeless events are *now*-necessary. Even so, we have no more reason to think that we can do anything now about God's timeless knowledge than about God's past knowledge. If there is no use crying over spilled milk, there is no use crying over timelessly spilling milk either. Of course, the nature of timeless eternity is elusive, so the intuition of the necessity of eternity is probably weaker than the intuition of the necessity of the past. Perhaps, then, the view that God is timeless puts the theological fatalist on the defensive. It is incumbent upon him to defend the principle of the necessity of eternity, which, unlike the necessity of the past, does not have the advantage of being deeply embedded in ordinary intuitions – I presume that most people's intuitions about eternity are thin at best. Nonetheless, when we consider candidates for timeless truths such as truths of logic and mathematics, they are truths that are unaffected by anything we do. Clearly we have no power over mathematics. Whether we can do nothing about it because it is timeless or because it is mathematics is another issue, of course. But it is illuminating to notice that, leaving theological truths aside, every instance of a timeless truth is one over which human beings are powerless.

Premise (2′) might then be modified to make it clear that it is not ascribing a temporal modality to a timeless proposition:

(2″) We cannot now do anything about timeless states of affairs.

And (3′) becomes:

(3″) We cannot now do anything about the fact that God timelessly believes B infallibly.

With (2″) and (3″) in place, we can generate an argument for theological fatalism that parallels the basic argument. I do not think there is a more general premise than (2) or (2″) that covers them both, and certainly not a weaker one. They are just different modal principles. Their connection is not in content, but in a common picture of modal reality and its relation to human power. I think, then, that (2) cannot be weakened or broadened, but it can be shifted to a premise that applies to timeless knowing. The foreknowledge dilemma and the timeless knowledge dilemma therefore ought to be treated separately. In most of the rest of this paper I will concentrate on the foreknowledge dilemma because it is the classic problem.

The Premise that Freedom Requires Alternate Possibilities

Let us now look at premise (9), a form of the principle of alternate possibilities (PAP). It is possible simply to define freedom by PAP, in which case the conclusion that nobody acts freely follows by definition, but not by everybody's definition. However, PAP can be defended by an argument that the existence of alternate possibilities is entailed by agent causation, the type of causation libertarian freedom requires. If that claim is right, the conclusion of the fatalist argument is that nobody has libertarian free will, the kind of free will incompatible with determinism. Since those who think the kind of freedom we have *is* compatible with determinism are not threatened by the argument anyway,[5] the claim that PAP is entailed by libertarian freedom is a significant defense of the important premise (9).

Several writers on PAP have argued that libertarian freedom does not require alternate possibilities, and I am among them.[6] The crux of the argument is that the kind of power required for libertarian freedom is agent causation, and the thesis that human agents exercise agent causation is a thesis about the locus of power. PAP, in contrast, is a thesis about events in counterfactual circumstances. My position is that it is possible that an act is agent caused even when the agent lacks alternate possibilities. Or, to be more cautious, perhaps we should say that it might be possible. That agent causation and alternate possibilities can come apart is illustrated by so-called Frankfurt cases, or counterexamples to PAP originally proposed by Harry Frankfurt.[7] Frankfurt intended his examples to give aid and comfort to determinism, but I believe he succeeded in showing PAP is false without showing anything that should lead us to reject libertarian free will. This issue is currently one of the most hotly disputed topics in the free will literature, and I will not attempt to engage directly with that literature here. Instead, I want to use the distinction between the thesis of agent causation and the thesis of alternate possibilities to show the fundamental irrelevance of PAP to both sides of the dispute over theological fatalism. This will permit the defender of our basic argument to give up premise (9) and still have an equally plausible fatalist argument.

Here is an example of a typical Frankfurt case used to show that an agent can act freely even when she lacks alternate possibilities:

> Black, an evil neurosurgeon, wishes to see White dead but is unwilling to do the deed himself. Knowing that Mary Jones also despises White and will have a single good opportunity to kill him, Black inserts a mechanism into Jones's brain that enables Black to monitor and to control Jones's neurological activity. If the activity in Jones's brain suggests that she is on the verge of deciding not to kill White when the opportunity arises, Black's mechanism will intervene and cause Jones to decide to commit the murder. On the other hand, if Jones decides to murder White on her own, the mechanism will not intervene. It will merely monitor but not affect her neurological function. Now suppose that, when the occasion arises, Jones decides to kill White without any "help" from Black's mechanism. In the judgment of Frankfurt and most others, Jones is morally responsible for her act. Nonetheless, it appears that she is unable to do otherwise since if she had attempted to do so she would have been thwarted by Black's device.[8]

Most commentators on examples like this agree that the agent is both morally responsible for her act and acts freely in whatever sense of freedom they endorse.[9] They differ on whether she can do otherwise at the time of her act. Determinists generally interpret the case as one in which she exercises compatibilist free will and has no alternate possibilities. Most libertarians interpret it as one in which she exercises libertarian free will and has alternate possibilities, contrary to appearances. I interpret it as a case in which she exercises libertarian free will but does not have alternate possibilties.

For the purposes of the foreknowledge issue I am not going to address the standard Frankfurt case above. Instead, I want to begin by calling attention to a disanalogy between the standard case and the situation of infallible foreknowledge. In the standard Frankfurt case the agent is prevented from acting freely in close possible worlds. That is not in dispute. Black's device is counterfactually manipulative even if it is not actually manipulative. In contrast, infallible foreknowledge is not even counterfactually manipulative. There is no close possible world or even distant possible world in which foreknowledge prevents the agent from acting freely. Of course, if theological fatalism is true, nobody ever acts freely, but my point is that there is no manipulation going on in other possible worlds in the foreknowledge scenario. The relation between foreknowledge and human acts is no different in one world than in any other. But it is precisely the fact that the relation between the Frankfurt machine and Mary's act differs in the actual world than in other close worlds that is supposed to make the Frankfurt example work in showing the falsity of PAP.

To make this point clear, let us look at how the standard Frankfurt case would have to be amended to make it a close analogy to the situation of infallible foreknowledge. The device implanted in Mary's brain would have to be set in such a way that no matter what Mary did, it never intervened. It is not even true that it *might have* intervened. Any world in which she decides to commit the murder is a world in which the device is set to make her commit the murder should she not decide to do it, and any world in which she does not decide to commit the murder is a world in which the device is set to prevent her from deciding to do it if she is about to decide to do it. Now of course you may say that this is a description of an impossible device. Perhaps that is true. But the point is that it would have to be as described to be a close analogy to the foreknowledge scenario. And I propose that our reactions to this amended Frankfurt case are very different from typical reactions to the standard Frankfurt case.

In the standard case it at least appears to be true that the agent cannot do otherwise, whereas in the case amended to be parallel to the foreknowledge case there is a very straightforward sense in which the agent can do otherwise because her will is not thwarted by Black in any possible world. The machine is ready to manipulate her, but it does not manipulate her, nor might it have manipulated her since it does not even manipulate her in counterfactual circumstances. We might describe the machine as a metaphysical accident – an extraneous addition to the story that plays no part in the sequence of events in any world. My interpretation of the amended story is that Mary is not prevented from exercising agent causation in any world because of the Frankfurt device, and, by analogy, neither is she prevented from exercising agent causation because of foreknowledge.

Furthermore, the amended story is plausibly interpreted as one in which Mary does have alternate possibilities. I do not insist on that, however, since, as I have said, my position is that it is possible to lack alternate possibilities even when exercising agent causation. My point is that whether or not she has alternate possibilities, she exercises agent causation and hence is free in making her choice.[10]

This means that even if I am right that libertarian freedom does not require alternate possibilities and premise (9) is false, we are not yet in a position to reject the theological fatalist's argument. What the Frankfurt cases and my amended Frankfurt case show, I think, is that the existence of alternate possibilities is subsidiary to what is actually required for free will, namely agent causation.[11] And that means the argument for theological fatalism can be recast. Here is roughly the way the argument should go.

(i)   Yesterday God infallibly believed I would do A tomorrow.
(ii)   I have no agent power over God's past belief or its infallibility.
(iii)   Therefore, I do not have the power to agent-cause my act A tomorrow.

Looking back at the basic argument for theological fatalism, the place where the argument goes off the track is premise (7). I suggest that the defender of the argument can bypass the dispute over PAP by changing (7) to:

(7′) If it is now-necessary that B, then you do not agent-cause your act of choosing tea tomorrow.

(8) then becomes:

(8′) You do not agent-cause your act of choosing tea tomorrow.

And (9) becomes the much more plausible:

(9′) If you do not agent-cause your act, you do not act freely.

Now we have an argument for fatalism that does not rely upon PAP. Whether it is sound depends upon the kind of necessity possessed by the necessity of the past and (7′) becomes the crucial premise. (7′) is true only if the necessity of the past is a kind of necessity that prevents the power needed to exercise agent causation. I believe (7′) is plausible, but probably somewhat less so than (7).

The Premise of the Transfer of Necessity

The final problematic premise is premise (5), the transfer of necessity principle. This principle says that the necessity of the past is closed under entailment.

Variants of this principle are part of every system of modal logic, so an attack on such a principle is unlikely to succeed without attacking the coherence of the type of necessity transferred. That means that the principle of the necessity of the past and the transfer principle ought to be considered together.

What exactly is the alleged necessity of the past? It is intended to be a type of necessity that the past has simply in virtue of being past. It is therefore a temporally relative kind of necessity; the past has it and the future does not. The intuition that the past is closed or fixed or necessary is therefore one side of a single intuition, the other side of which is the intuition that the future is open or unfixed or contingent. It seems to me that one side of the intuition is threatened by a defeat of the other because they are two aspects of the same idea, that time is modally asymmetrical. Now it could be argued that the intuition that the past is fixed is firmer than the intuition that the future is open, and that is possible, but notice that if it turns out that the future is fixed in the same sense as the past is fixed, the necessity in question cannot be a temporally relative one. The past could not then have a kind of necessity simply in virtue of being past if the future has the same kind of necessity.

Consider for a moment the reverse foreknowledge argument.

Reverse foreknowledge argument

Let B be the proposition that you will choose tea tomorrow. Let "now-contingent" designate the contingency of the future, the type of contingency that the future has now just because it is future. To say that it is now-contingent that B is to say that it is now-possible that B and it is now-possible that not-B.

(1r) B.
(2r) If E is a future state of affairs, it is now-contingent that E. [Principle of the contingency of the future.]
(3r) It is now-contingent that B.
(4r) If q is now-contingent and p is now-possible and necessarily (if p then q), then p is now-contingent. [Transfer of contingency principle.]
(5r) It is now-possible that God infallibly believed B yesterday.
(6r) Necessarily, if yesterday God infallibly believed B, then B.
(7r) Therefore, it is now-contingent that yesterday God infallibly believed B.

And, of course, (7r) is no threat to human freedom.

This argument is generated from the other side of the intuition that time is modally asymmetrical, the side that maintains that the future is temporally contingent. The reverse argument does not rely upon any notion of a free act. What drives the argument is a variation of what I'm calling the transfer of contingency principle, which can be derived from the Transfer of Necessity principle as follows.

(1) nec (p → q) → (nec p → nec q) [transfer of necessity]
(2) nec (~ q → ~ p) → (nec ~ q → nec ~ p) [(1), substitution]
(3) nec (p → q) → (~ nec ~ p → ~ nec ~ q) [(2), contraposition]
(4) nec (p → q) → (poss p → poss q) [(3), definition of "possible"]
(5) nec (~ q → ~ p) → (poss ~ q → poss ~ p) [(4), substitution]
(6) nec (p → q) → (poss ~ q → poss ~ p) [(5), contraposition]
(7) nec (p → q) → [(poss p & poss ~ q) → (poss q & poss ~ p)] [(4), (6), sentential logic[12]]
(8) [nec (p → q) & poss p] → [(poss ~ q & poss q) → poss ~ p] [(7), exportation]
(9) [nec (p → q) & poss p] → [(poss ~ q & poss q) → (poss ~ p & poss p)] [(8), tautology]
(10) [nec (p → q) & poss p] → (q is contingent → p is contingent) [(9), definition of "contingent" (transfer of contingency)[13]]

This pattern of argument can be used to derive a transfer of contingency principle for contingency of type Φ from a transfer of necessity principle for necessity of type Φ. In particular, the transfer of temporally relative contingency – premise (4r) of the reverse argument – can be derived from the transfer of necessity for temporally relative necessity – premise (5) of the basic argument for theological fatalism – by the above argument. It follows that an upholder of the transfer of temporally relative necessity is committed to the transfer of temporally relative contingency. The principles are logically related.

We now have two arguments: the basic fatalist argument and the reverse counterfatalist argument. Both begin with one side of the intuition that time is modally asymmetrical and argue by way of a transfer of modality principle to the conclusion that time is not modally asymmetrical. According to the basic argument, if the past is necessary, so is the future. According to the reverse argument, if the future is contingent, so is the past. Which of the two arguments do we choose? One answer is "neither." The conclusion of each of these arguments undermines the intuition supporting the modality generating the argument – either the necessity of the past or the contingency of the future. The future cannot be as necessary as the past if the type of necessity the past has is supposed to be temporally relative. Similarly, the past cannot be as contingent as the future if the type of contingency the future has is supposed to be temporally relative. Both arguments are problematic, but since the reverse argument is as well supported as the standard argument, there is no more reason to adopt the one than the other. These arguments should make us suspect a problem in the notion of temporally relative modality. And perhaps we should have realized that even in the absence of the reverse argument, since the conclusion of the basic fatalist argument undermines the intuition supporting premise (2). It appears, then, that these arguments show that if infallible foreknowledge is possible, the modal asymmetry of time can be maintained only at the cost of giving up both transfer of modality principles. However, I will argue next that even giving up the transfer principles is not enough. In the following section I will argue that the possibility of essential omniscience directly conflicts with the modal asymmetry of time.

The Dilemma of Foreknowledge and the Modal Asymmetry of Time

Have we now pared down the basic argument to the minimum necessary to get the fatalist conclusion? We have retained the premise of infallible belief about human future free choices, the necessity of the past (with worries about its temporal relativity), the transfer of necessity principle, and the principle that the necessity of the past is incompatible with agent causation. But the argument can be pared even further. Here is a dilemma I have proposed in earlier work that eliminates any premise about freedom, agent causation, or alternate possibilities, and that does not use a transfer of modality principle. The argument combines some features of the basic fatalist argument and the reverse argument. In one respect the argument uses a stronger premise than the basic argument since it arises from the premise that there is an essentially omniscient and necessarily existent foreknower. However, we will consider whether this premise also can be weakened.

Argument establishing the dilemma

Again, let B be the proposition that you will choose to drink tea tomorrow. As in the reverse argument, to say that p is now-contingent is to say that it is now-possible that p and it is now-possible that not-p.

> (1t)   There is (and was in the past) an essentially omniscient foreknower (EOF) who exists necessarily.

The principle of the contingency of the future tells us that:

> (2t)   It is now-possible that B and it is now-possible that not-B.

Since the EOF is necessarily existent, B is strictly equivalent to *The EOF believed before now that B*. (1t) and (2t) therefore strictly imply:

> (3t)   It is now-possible that the EOF believed before now that B and it is now-possible that the EOF believed before now that not-B.

From (1t) and the law of excluded middle we get:

(4t)   Either the EOF believed before now that B or the EOF believed before now that not-B.

From the principle of the necessity of the past we get:

(5t)   If the EOF believed that B, it is not now-possible that he believed that not-B, and if he believed that not-B, it is not now-possible that he believed that B.

(4t) and (5t) entail:

(6t)   Either it is not now-possible that he believed that B or it is not now-possible that he believed that not-B.

But (6t) contradicts (3t).[14]

There are a number of things to notice about the strength of this argument. Free will does not enter into it at all. In fact, we can make the event in question a contingent event that is not a human act, if there are any. So denying any premise about alternate possibilities or agent causation will not get us out of this dilemma. Second, no transfer of modality principle is used, so it will not help to reject those either. The problem here is deeper than a problem about fore-knowledge and freedom. It is a problem about foreknowledge and time.

The dilemma of foreknowledge and time does not have a reverse argument because no transfer principle is used. That means that the fatalist argument cannot be matched against a counterfatalist argument like the reverse fore-knowledge argument given in the previous section. That also makes this new dilemma particularly strong.

Let us now consider whether the first premise of the new dilemma can be weakened without harm to the validity of the argument. That premise affirms the existence of an essentially omniscient and necessarily existent being. We have already seen one way that premise can be weakened in our discussion of the basic argument: The premise need only affirm the possibility of the existence of such a being. Actual existence is not required. But the premise can be weakened further. The foreknower designated in the first premise need not be essentially omniscient and necessarily existent. He need only have complete and infallible beliefs in some range of knowledge that includes propositions about the contingent future, for example, the food and drink choices of humans. In fact, the property of the foreknower that generates the problem can be limited to his relation to a single proposition. Let us consider a being who satisifes the following condition with respect to a future contingent proposition p:

Necessarily (Alpha knows p if and only if p).

Let us say that any being Alpha who satisifes this condition is *essentially epistemically matched* to p. Being essentially epistemically matched to p includes satisfying the following conditions:

Necessarily, if Alpha believes p then p (Alpha is infallible in believing p)

and

Necessarily, if p then Alpha believes p.

If Alpha is essentially epistemically matched to p then Alpha exists in every possible world in which p is true, but necessary existence is not required.

We can demonstrate that the existence of a being who is essentially epistemically matched to a proposition p is incompatible with p's having temporal modality by a modification of the dilemma of foreknowledge and temporal asymmetry. The argument proceeds as follows.

(1t′) There is (and was in the past) a being who is essentially epistemically matched to B.

(2t) It is now-possible that B and it is now-possible that not-B.

B is strictly equivalent to *The being essentially epistemically matched to B believed before now that B*. (1t′) and (2t) therefore strictly imply:

(3t′) It is now-possible that the being essentially epistemically matched to B believed before now that B and it is now-possible that the being essentially epistemically matched to B believed before now that not-B.

From (1t′) and the law of excluded middle we get:

(4t′) Either the being essentially epistemically matched to B believed before now that B or the being essentially epistemically matched to B believed before now that not-B.

From the principle of the necessity of the past we get:

(5t′) If the being essentially epistemically matched to B believed that B, it is not now-possible that he believed that not-B, and if he believed that not-B, it is not now-possible that he believed that B.

(4t′) and (5t′) entail:

(6t′) Either it is not now-possible that he believed that B or it is not now-possible that he believed that not-B.

But (6t′) contradicts (3t′).

This is the strongest foreknowledge argument I know. It shows that there is an inconsistency between the existence of a being essentially epistemically matched to a contingent proposition B and the assumption that the belief-states of such a being and the event that B is about possess temporally relative modality. Clearly, parallel arguments can be given that apply to propositions other than B, in fact, to any proposition about which it is possible that there is some being essentially epistemically matched to it. Together they generate a strong attack on the compatibility of the existence of any such foreknowers and the modal asymmetry of time.

Before examining our options in responding to the arguments of this section, let us look at an even more radical way of attempting to eliminate a premise without affecting the validity of the argument. The most ancient of all fatalist arguments holds that fatalism follows internally from the nature of time itself; it does not appeal to any premise about a foreknower. This is the argument of logical fatalism.

Logical Fatalism

Arguments for logical fatalism do not use any premise about infallible knowledge or essential omniscience. The logical fatalist argument does, however, use the transfer of necessity principle as well as the principle of the necessity of the past. Here is a typical strong argument for logical fatalism that parallels our basic argument for theological fatalism.

Argument for logical fatalism

As before, let B be the proposition that you will choose tea tomorrow.

(1l)   Yesterday it was true that B. [Assumption.]
(2l)   It is now-necessary that yesterday it was true that B. [Necessity of the past.]
(3l)   Necessarily, if yesterday it was true that B, then now it is true that B. [Omnitemporality of truth.]
(4l)   If p is now-necessary, and necessarily (if p then q), then q is now-necessary. [Transfer of necessity.]
(5l)   So it is now-necessary that it is true that B. [(2l), (3l), (4l), conjunction, *modus ponens.*]
(6l)   If it is now-necessary that it is true that B, then B cannot be false. [Definition.]
(7l)   If B cannot be false, then you cannot do otherwise than choose tea tomorrow. [Definition.]

The most interesting feature of arguments for logical fatalism in contrast with arguments for theological fatalism is that almost everybody finds the former unsound, whereas many more think the latter is sound. That means that the logical fatalist argument cannot be construed as an attempt to *strengthen* the basic argument for theological fatalism by reducing the number of premises or weakening them. Instead, most people find something fishy in logical fatalism, and it can be illuminating to try to identify what makes logical fatalism seem fishy whereas theological fatalism does not.

Previously I have suggested that (2l) is much less plausible than (2).[15] The past truth of a proposition is not the sort of thing that is a plausible candidate for possessing the necessity of the past, whereas the past belief of a being is the sort of thing that ought to have the necessity of the past, if anything does. A past belief is like spilled milk; the past truth of a proposition is not. In the logical fatalist argument the proposition said to possess the necessity of the past obviously depends upon a future event, and that is one obvious source of the suspiciousness of the premise. But it is hard to make the analogous move that a proposition asserting that a foreknower had a belief in the past is future-relative in the same way, although some have tried, most famously, William of Ockham.[16] I am not suggesting that it is impossible to make a case for the position that a past infallible belief about the future lacks the necessity of the past, but at a minimum it requires considerable argument. In contrast, the parallel claim that it is not now-necessary that what was true in the past was true requires hardly any argument at all. In short, logical fatalism is suspicious because it collapses truth into necessity. It purports to show that if a proposition is omnitemporally true, it is omnitemporally necessary. To reject logical fatalism we need only deny that the pastness of the truth of a proposition confers temporal necessity on that proposition. That is compatible with the more fundamental modal asymmetry of temporal events. In contrast, it is not so easy to deny that the pastness of an occurrence of a belief confers temporal necessity on that occurrence.

Recently, Ted Warfield has given an interesting argument that theological fatalism is equivalent to logical fatalism. He argues that it is widely agreed that propositions such as the following are consistent:

(1) It was true in 1950 that LZ would do θ in 2010.
(2) LZ freely does θ in 2010.[17]

If God is essentially omniscient and exists in all possible worlds, then (1) is logically equivalent to:

(3) God knew in 1950 that LZ would do θ in 2010.

But if two propositions are logically equivalent and one is consistent with some third proposition, so is the other. Hence, (2) is consistent with (3).

It seems to me that Warfield's argument does not show that the basic argument for theological fatalism is sound just in case the basic argument for logical fatalism is sound. What it does show is that a theological fatalist must maintain that propositions (1) and (2) are inconsistent in that there is no possible world in which both are true. That is a perfectly coherent position for them to take since their position is that there is no possible world in which (2) is true. It means that (1) and (2) are inconsistent in the sense in which 2 + 2 = 4 and *God is evil* are inconsistent according to traditional theism. But, of course, it is not the truth of one that makes it impossible for the other to be true. They are independent in content.

One moral of Warfield's argument is that we cannot trust metaphysically untutored intuitions in determining which propositions are necessary, which contingent, and which impossible, and for the same reason we cannot use those untutored intuitions to determine logical consistency, implication, and equivalence. But this result is a two-edged sword. We have been using our intuitions all along, and some of them may be misguided. The theological fatalist who is not a logical fatalist must deny the common intuition that (1) and (2) of the preceding paragraph are consistent. I have urged that the new dilemmas of the previous section show us that we must give up the common intuition that essential omniscience and the modal asymmetry of time are consistent. At this stage of our analysis our argument has outrun our intuitions. I think we need to take stock and assess our metaphysical options.

Rejecting the Modal Asymmetry of Time

The arguments concerning the dilemmas of foreknowledge and time are the strongest fatalist arguments I know. These arguments are strong in that there are fewer premises than in the basic argument, and hence fewer ways out, and the only premises other than the foreknowledge premise express the intuition that there is temporally relative necessity and contingency, an intuition that is deeply embedded in the way most of us think of the past and the future. This reduces our options considerably. As far as I can see, there are four possible responses:

(1) It is logically impossible that there is a being Alpha who is essentially epistemically matched to any future contingent proposition p.
(2) Alpha's past state of believing p has the same contingency of the future as does p.[18]
(3) p has the same necessity of the past as does Alpha's past state of believing p.
(4) Temporal modality with respect to p and/or Alpha's past state of belief is incoherent.

Options (2), (3), and (4) all require giving up at least part of the modal asymmetry between past and future. Options (2) and (3) might appear to be safer than (4) since they require more modest rejections of the asymmetry, but that appearance is deceptive. Option (2) was vigorously defended by Ockham and his recent supporters, but is notable for its lack of success. Option (3) is the fatalist option. I have already said that if we say that some significant part of the future is as necessary as the past, or that some significant part of the past is as contingent as the future, we are undermining the idea that temporally relative modality exists at all. It is hard to see the justification for retaining a belief in temporally relative modality when the intuition is undermined to the degree required for (2) or (3).

Option (4) has the advantage of avoiding the difficult, perhaps impossible task of defending temporal modal asymmetry for some propositions and not others. According to this option, the solution to all fatalist arguments that rely upon the alleged modal asymmetry of time is simple: they are based on a confusion. In the next section I will offer a conjecture on the source of the problem – the confusion between temporal and causal modalities. If I am right, option (4) is less radical than it appears.

Temporal versus Causal Modality

So far I have argued that the dilemmas of foreknowledge and temporal asymmetry lead us to the conclusion that either it is impossible that there is (and was in the past) a being essentially epistemically matched to contingent propositions about the future, or modal temporal asymmetry is incoherent. I believe, though, that a major reason for thinking that temporal modality must not be given up is that it is easy to confuse with causal modality. Recall that the alleged necessity of the past is the necessity the past has simply in virtue of being past; the alleged contingency of the future is the contingency the future has simply in virtue of being future. If an event has the necessity of the past, then there is no longer anything anybody can do about it; it is beyond our power. If an event has the contingency of the future, then there is nothing about its temporal status that prevents it from being such that we can do something about it. But it does not follow that if an event is temporally contingent we can, in fact, do something about it, since the event might be beyond our power for some other reason; for example, it might be causally necessary or – and this is not the same thing – it may be too late to cause it.

To see the extent to which temporal and causal modalities are independent, let us first look at how a tempting way to make them dependent will not work. An innocent-looking suggestion would go as follows. To say that p is now causally necessary is to say that p is now causally closed; nobody now or in the future can do anything to cause p, to bring about its truth. To say that p is now causally contingent is to say that p is now causally open; somebody now or in the future can do something to cause the truth of p. Given the assumption that we have no causal influence over the past, it seems to follow that the entire past is causally necessary even if some parts of the future are causally contingent. If so, there is a significant correspondence between causal and temporally relative modality. But the compatibility of the existence of an infallible foreknower and causal modality as just described can be refuted by an argument exactly parallel to the arguments of the section on foreknowledge and time.

(1t) There is (and was in the past) a foreknower who is essentially epistemically matched to B, a contingent proposition about the future.

The principle of the causal contingency of the future tells us that:

(2t) It is causally possible that B and it is causally possible that not-B.

B is strictly equivalent to *The being essentially epistemically matched to B believes B*. (1t) and (2t) therefore strictly imply:

(3t) It is causally possible that the being essentially epistemically matched to B believed B before now and it is causally possible that the being essentially epistemically matched to B believed not-B before now.

From (1t) and the law of excluded middle we get:

(4t) Either the being essentially epistemically matched to B believed B before now or the being essentially epistemically matched to B believed not-B before now.

From the principle of the causal closure of the past we get:

(5t) If the being essentially epistemically matched to B believed that B, it is not causally possible that he believed that not-B, and if he believed that not-B, it is not causally possible that he believed that B.

(4t) and (5t) entail:

(6t) Either it is not now causally possible that he believed that B or it is not now causally possible that he believed that not-B.

But (6t) contradicts (3t).

This argument shows that under the assumption that an infallible epistemic agent as defined above is possible, it is impossible that the entire past is causally necessary whereas some part of the future is causally contingent. And as we saw in the previous section, there are four responses. The parallel to option (4) is that causal necessity and contingency as defined above are incoherent. If that is right, and I suspect it is, it means that the causal necessity or contingency of an event has nothing to do with whether it is past or future. And that in turn means that causal necessity and contingency cannot be modalities that change over time. Instead, an event must possess causal necessity or contingency in virtue of its enduring relations to other events. An event cannot be causally contingent up to a certain moment of time whereupon it becomes causally necessary. To think so is to fall prey to the same problem that infects temporally relative modality. If, in addition, it is a metaphysical law that causes precede their effects, then an event's causal necessity or contingency is determined by its enduring relations to events previous to it. But whether or not causes must precede effects, the causal modality of an event is not temporally relative. That is the lesson of the dilemmas of foreknowledge and time.

But, someone will reply, it *does* make sense to say that we no longer have any causal power over events that have already occurred even though it also makes sense to say that we had causal power over (some of) those events before they occurred. Indeed, it does, but we must be careful how we express that fact. There is a difference between lacking causal power over an event because it is a causally necessary event and lacking causal power over an event because it is now outside the realm of causes due to the metaphysical law that causes precede effects. An event does not become causally necessary once it occurs, although it may none-theless be true, indeed, a law, that nobody can any longer do anything to cause it.

It follows that temporal and causal modalities are independent. If there is temporal modal asymmetry, then any event in the past is temporally necessary even if that event is a causally contingent event. Similarly, an event in the future can now be causally necessary even though it is now temporally contingent.[19] More importantly, this independence means that if temporal modality is incoherent, it need not drag causal modality into incoherence with it. As we have seen, it does drag one way of understanding causal modality into incoherence – the one just given above, but there remains a notion of causal modality that does make sense. It may be true that we have no causal power over the past even though we have causal power over the future, not because the past is past and the future is future, but because of the metaphysical law that causes precede effects. The aphorism "There is no use crying over spilt milk" should not be interpreted to mean that we cannot do anything about the past just because it is past. Certainly, it means that we cannot do anything about the past, but that is because doing something about the past requires a cause to come after its effect and that is ruled out by the causal arrow. It follows that if temporal modal asymmetry collapses, our power over an event has nothing to do with its pastness or futurity per se; it depends upon laws of causality.

It is my position that temporal modal asymmetry is incoherent. I have argued that even if that is the case, we can save the arrow of time most important in science and ordinary life: the causal arrow, or the earlier-to-later direction of causes and effects. But temporal modality is not an arrow of time in addition to the causal arrow.

Is Essential Omniscience Possible?

For those people convinced of the modal asymmetry of time and unwilling to make the timelessness move, there remains only the option of rejecting the possibility of an essentially omniscient and necessarily existent being, as well as rejecting the possibility of a being who is essentially epistemically matched to any contingent future proposition. Most of the literature on omniscience and infallible foreknowledge has focused on theological reasons for either keeping or giving up the assumption that such a being is possible. I have already remarked that the thesis that the Christian God is essentially omniscient is a central part of the traditional conception of God. Recently, the so-called "free will theists" or "open God" advocates have argued that the God of Christianity is a God who takes risks, one of which is the risk of giving humans freedom at the cost of denying himself infallible foreknowlege. But the arguments of the section on foreknowledge and time have nothing to do with freedom, so God's motive in "giving up" infallibility in belief cannot be love of human creatures. Moreover, there is nothing to give up because being essentially epistemically matched to a proposition about a future human choice is metaphysically impossible. Of course, those who have theological reasons for denying that God is essentially epistemically matched to propositions about their future choices may also be willing to deny it for reasons arising from their beliefs about the metaphysics of time. Generally, however, one's theological beliefs and one's beliefs about time occupy different places in one's web of belief. The epistemic consequences of giving up the possibility of a perfect epistemic agent are quite different from the consequences of giving up the modal difference between past and future, and I have said only a little about what those consequences might be. The implications of the choice are not always easy to determine. It is not simply a matter of deciding which belief is more important or is one to which we are more deeply committed. Both the belief that a perfect epistemic agent is possible and the belief in the modal asymmetry of time have deep implications about what is possible and what is impossible that may ramify into seemingly unrelated areas of the metaphysics of modality. I would not be surprised, then, if the choice is frustrating even for non-theists.

I conclude that either essential omniscience is impossible or time is not modally asymmetrical. I do not think we can determine which of the two takes precedence without determining other metaphysical truths. If time was created by a being with infallible knowledge, then there is no contest. Even an omnipotent being cannot create something with modal properties inconsistent with his own. But if time, with its modal asymmetry, is metaphysically necessary, then it is metaphysically impossible that there is an essentially omniscient being. The moral is that we cannot solve the dilemma of foreknowledge and time using logic alone. We need to make metaphysical choices. Logic can tell us what the choices are, but we still need to make them. I see no way that can be done independently of background beliefs on the relations among God, time, and the structure of modality.[20]

Notes

1   The literature on this argument or some variation of it is enormous. For a survey of work in the last couple of decades, see my "Recent Work on Divine Foreknowledge

and Free Will," forthcoming, in *Oxford Handbook on Free Will*, ed. Robert Kane (New York: Oxford University Press). The paper contains a substantial bibliography.

2   I am making the common assumption that every proposition has a truth value.

3   Boethius, *The Consolation of Philosophy*, 5; Aquinas, *Summa theologica*, 1, 14, 13.

4   Linda Zagzebski, *The Dilemma of Freedom and Foreknowledge* (hereafter *DFF*, New York: Oxford University Press, 1991), pp. 60–3.

5   For an example of a compatibilist take on the dilemma, see Anthony Kenny, "Divine Foreknowledge and Human Freedom," in *Aquinas: A Collection of Critical Essays*, ed. A. Kenny (New York: Anchor Books, 1969).

6   I argued for the position that libertarian freedom does not require alternate possibilities in *DFF*, chapter 6, and most recently in "Does Libertarian Freedom Require Alternate Possibilities?" *Philosophical Perspectives*, 14 (Action and Freedom), ed. James E. Tomberlin (Oxford: Blackwell, 2000), pp. 231–48. Eleonore Stump has defended this position in "Libertarian Freedom and the Principle of Alternate Possibilities," in *Faith, Freedom, and Rationality*, ed. Jeff Jordan and Daniel Howard-Snyder (Lanham, Md.: Rowman and Littlefield, 1996), pp. 73–88. David Hunt is another proponent of the position. See "On Augustine's Way Out," *Faith and Philosophy*, 16, 1 (January 1999), pp. 3–26. Another incompatibilist who denies PAP is Derk Pereboom in "Alternative Possibilities and Causal Histories," in *Philosophical Perspectives*, 14 (Action and Freedom), pp. 119–38.

7   Harry Frankfurt, "Alternate Possibilities and Moral Responsibility," *Journal of Philosophy*, 66 (December 1969), pp. 828–39.

8   This adaptation of Frankfurt's example using a neurological device is similar to some of the cases described by John Martin Fischer. An early use of this type of example appears in his "Responsibility and Control," *Journal of Philosophy*, 89 (January 1982), pp. 24–40.

9   A recent exception is David Widerker in "Frankfurt's Attack on the Principle of Alternate Possibilities: A Further Look," *Philosophical Perspectives*, 14 (Action and Freedom), pp. 181–202.

10   I made this point in *DFF*, chapter 6, section 2.1.

11   I pursue the way human agency in obtaining knowledge and the satisfaction of counterfactual conditions can come apart in "Must Knowers Be Agents?," in *Virtue Epistemology*, ed. Abrol Fairweather and myself (New York: Oxford University Press, 2001), pp. 142–57.

12   The inference from (4) and (6) to (7) can be easily demonstrated in sentential logic by indirect proof.

13   Notice that unlike the transfer of necessity principle, the transfer of contingency principle requires the assumption that p is possible. That is because an impossible proposition implies every proposition, including a contingent proposition q. I thank James Hawthorne for discussion about the transfer principles.

14   I first presented this argument in the Appendix to *DFF*.

15   *DFF*, chapter 1, section 3.

16   See William of Ockham, *Predestination, God's Foreknowledge and Future Contingents*, trans. Marilyn McCord Adams and Norman Kretzmann (Indianapolis: Hackett Publishing, 1969).

17   Warfield is using a libertarian notion of freedom.

18 More precisely, Alpha's past state of believing p has the contingency that is transferred from the contingency of p via the transfer of contingency principle. Presumably, it is the same kind of contingency that is transferred since it is hard to see how the transfer principle could produce a new kind of contingency. The parallel point applies to option (3).

19 And even if every event is causally determined, that is because of the truth of a metaphysical thesis, not because temporal necessity entails causal necessity. In any case, causal contingency does not entail temporal contingency.

20 My thanks to Fritz (Ted) Warfield for helpful comments on an earlier draft of this paper.

Suggested Further Reading

Bobzien, Susanne (1998) *Determinism and Freedom in Stoic Philosophy.* Oxford: Clarendon Press.

Fischer, John Martin (ed.) (1989) *God, Foreknowledge, and Freedom.* Stanford, Calif.: Stanford University Press.

Chapter 2

Divine Power and Action

Hugh J. McCann

It is natural to think of God as a being supreme in power and influence, whose creative will and sovereign authority extend to all that exists, and whose loving providence governs the universe in every dimension. The moment we take such characterizations seriously, however, a number of problems arise. For example, suppose we agree with theological tradition that God's creative action is needed not only to put the world in place but also to sustain it, so that he is as much responsible for the present existence of things as for their existing at all. If this is so, it is reasonable to think God is also responsible for things having the properties they do, since the idea that he might create utterly propertyless entities is exceedingly suspect. But if God is responsible for the properties of things, then what role is there for natural causation in the operation of the universe? If, when the cue ball strikes the object ball, the latter's acceleration is owing to God's activity as creator, then what, if anything, is owing to the action of the cue ball? On a somewhat different front, consider our activity as moral agents. If God's creative fiat produces all of our properties then it must also produce our actions. But if that is so then what becomes of free will and the power of human agency? And how does God escape responsibility for moral wrongdoing?

These concerns are as daunting as they are familiar, but in fact they are only the beginning. Think of the injunctions of morality, which in scripture are presented to us as divine commands. In advancing these commands, is God simply passing along to us information that exists independent of his will, or is he doing what the air of authority suggests – i.e., actually creating morality? If the former, then God's authority is limited, and his actions are no doubt hemmed in by moral rules, just as ours are. On the other hand, if the laws of morality come to no more than a set of arbitrary dictates, then regardless of their pedigree they appear to lack rational force: murder, robbery, and incest could as well have been right as wrong. A similar problem pertains to the conceptual order. In giving existence to the world, does God create only things, or their natures as well? That is, does he create only such things as triangles and humans, or does he also create things like triangularity and humanity, the universals that define creaturely natures? If not the latter, then God is subordinate to the conceptual order: his options as creator are bound by what universals happen to be available. But if he creates natures as well as things, it looks as if anything goes – as if we might have had three-and-a-half-sided triangles, perhaps, or two plus two equal to five. Finally, consider those universals that pertain to the divine nature, things like perfect wisdom, goodness, and omnipotence. Might God also create those, and what would be the implications of that?

A common thread runs through these dilemmas: to the extent that we maximize God's power in creating the world, we tend to minimize the powers of the things he creates. In the natural order, if God's power as first cause is all-embracing, there is a danger that very little power may be left to creatures, to physical bodies and human wills. In the moral and conceptual spheres, if God is the source of moral imperatives and abstract natures, then moral imperatives may wind up with little persuasive force, and the abstract natures of things may prove incapable of structuring reality. We can, of course, escape such dilemmas by restricting God's power and hegemony, by holding that the moral and conceptual orders exist independently of anything he does, and by confining God's creative activity to putting the natural world in place "in the beginning," together, perhaps, with an occasional foray of miraculous intervention. But that would accord neither with piety nor with traditional theology, which sought to understand God's power and action in a way that would maximize his sovereignty, yet also keep intact the power and significance of what is created. Let us consider how well such an enterprise might succeed.

The Natural Order

Traditional theology holds that God's creative activity alone is responsible for the entire existence of the universe. He does not just put things in place "in the beginning," assuming there was one; rather, he must conserve the world through its entire history, for it is not self-sustaining. Lacking God's creative support, it would simply cease to be (Aquinas, *ST* 1, 104, 1, 1945, vol. 1, pp. 962–5). There is scriptural backing for such a view (e.g., Heb. 1:3), and it fits well with other claims about creation. For example, theists would argue that even if the universe has always existed it must still have been created by God, since otherwise we would have no explanation for the fact that it is this universe that exists, rather than some other or none at all. Now if indeed God has created a world whose history is infinite, it is plausible to think his creative activity is equally responsible for every moment of the universe's existence. The alternative would be to say he sustains things only up to a certain point, and then introduces a self-sustaining feature that takes over from there. But if such a feature is possible, why delay creating it? And what could be the reason for introducing it at one point in time rather than any other? The arbitrary introduction of a power of self-sustenance would be a violation of the principle of sufficient reason, which it is fitting for a perfect God to observe. Better, then, to say that God is equally and directly responsible for the entire existence of such a world, in all its infinite history; and to say that is, of course, to say that the universe is sustained in existence by the creative power of God, not by any power of its own.

The situation is less clear if we understand the universe to have had a temporal beginning, for then it might be thought that although the universe is indebted to God for the first moment of its existence, it sustains itself thereafter. God may intervene occasionally to perform some miracle, but otherwise the world operates entirely under its own power, not just for the changes it undergoes but also for its continued existence. We might even think a power of self-sustenance has scientific credentials, being called for by laws for the conservation of mass and energy. When we try to describe how such a power might function, however, we are at a complete loss. Science does not detect, nor does metaphysics describe, any operation by which either the universe or its contents somehow bootstrap themselves into the future. Indeed, it is not even possible to imagine such a thing. Nor can we imagine how the operation could contrive to be efficacious in the future – that is, at points in time later than its own occurrence, which must necessarily be at a temporal distance from it (Kvanvig and McCann, 1988, pp. 42–3). If, on the other hand, we discard the idea of an operation, and think of self-sustenance as just a pure disposition of things to survive, we find that the supposed disposition boils down to nothing beyond the phenomenon to be explained. Such a disposition could not supervene on anything else in the structure of the world, for if it did we would need another disposition to explain how that supervenience base persists. And again, we really cannot imagine what the basis for such a disposition might be. But then the sole manifestation of the alleged disposition to survive has to be the very thing we were trying to explain – namely, the fact that the universe does persist in being. There is no difference between that kind of disposition and no disposition at all. No matter how we seek to conceive of a power of self-sustenance in the world, therefore, we are forced to conclude that it does not exist.

If this is correct, then whether the world is finite or infinite in duration, the fact that it endures can only be explained by the creative power of God, whose fiat holds all things in being. Nor should this be taken as somehow contradicting scientific law. Laws of conservation do not speak of a pure power of things to persist; rather, they tell us that in all natural processes, the quantity of mass-energy in the world remains the same. But that is the equivalent of saying precisely what is argued above: that there are no natural processes that account either for the existence or for the persistence of things – which, rather than being explained, is in fact presumed in our descriptions of the operations of nature. In this much, then, there is no conflict between the claims of natural theology and those of science. But what about the operation of natural causes? If God's creative activity is alone responsible for each moment of every entity's existence, then it ought to be responsible for the existence of every property as well. Malebranche, for one, claimed it is impossible for God to create an entity and not create it in a particular place, in a particular state of rest or motion, etc., and he drew from this the conclusion that physical entities have no natural powers (Malebranche, 7, 1980). It is not possible for the cue ball to move the object ball; rather, the cue ball coming into contact with the object ball is the *occasion* for God to impart motion to the latter, which he does according to the orderly principles we refer to as "laws of nature." A similar explanation would be in order for any property a thing might have. Moreover, there is at least some firm metaphysical ground here. For if God were to create things with no properties at all, the products of creation would be bare particulars – entities with no determinate nature, that could as well turn out to be quarks, atoms, frogs, or humans, depending on how natural causes operate. There is no plausibility to that idea. Yet it seems equally implausible to hold that natural causation is a mere illusion, and natural laws nothing but a record of God's constancy in producing a regularly ordered world.

How, then, is it possible to preserve the insight that God alone is responsible for the existence of all of nature without lapsing into Malebranchian occasionalism about natural processes? The key is to realize that natural causation is not a matter of existence conferral. We tend to suppose it is – to think, for example, that when the cue ball strikes the object ball, that event somehow generates or necessitates (*ex nihilo*, one might say) the succeeding event of the object ball's motion. If this is our paradigm, we will think of natural causation as another bootstrapping operation: a grand process by which, in accordance with a few fundamental scientific laws, the universe propels itself into the future, with each successive state conferring existence on the next. In fact, however, this picture is deeply problematic. Classically, at least, scientific laws are not diachronic. There is nothing in Newton's laws that gets us from one moment to the next. Rather, Newton's laws speak of simultaneous action and reaction: an object not acted upon by a net force at t is at rest or in uniform rectilinear motion *at* t; if subject to a net force, it is under acceleration *at* t. That is all. We only get to the future by extrapolating from this: that is, by *assuming* the masses and energy in question will continue to exist, and then inferring their future dynamic situation from the present one. If we have the physics right, we will predict that future correctly. But as Hume famously pointed out, there is nothing either in law or in observation that necessitates its occurrence (1959, pp. 160–5). We see nothing that counts as the past conferring existence on the future, nor does a proper understanding of science call for such a thing.

Once this is realized, the temptation to treat natural causation as a matter of existence conferral disappears. Rather, causation should be viewed as a process in which conserved quantities, such as mass, energy, momentum, and the like, enter into new configurations, which emerge from the past as natural outcomes of ongoing dynamic interaction. Thus, unlike what classical occasionalists claimed, the cue ball really does operate on the object ball. When the two come into contact kinetic energy is transferred from the former to the latter, so that the latter accelerates. But the acceleration, though a new event, is not in any useful sense "created" by the collision. It just *is* the absorption of additional kinetic energy by the object ball. The only creating is done by God, who conserves in existence all of the participants in the operation. Understood in this way, there is no conflict between God's activity as creator and the operation of natural causes. Neither God nor the cue ball duplicates the effort of the other, for the operation of the two is entirely different. God is solely responsible for the existence of everything; he conserves the cue ball and the object ball *in* their interaction, and so is responsible for the existence of the event which is the object ball's acceleration. Nevertheless, that event occurs as a natural outcome of the collision with the cue ball, and so has the collision as its physical cause.

Human Agency

If the above account is correct, God is able to exercise complete sovereignty over the operations of nature without detriment to those operations themselves. Properly understood, natural causes are fully efficacious, even though God is responsible for the existence of all. Can the same be said for the operations of human agents? Many think not, especially if, as is often supposed, the decisions and actions of rational creatures are free in the sense of not being determined by causes analogous to the natural forces of physics – things like preponderant motive, or strongest desire. Theists have good reasons for claiming we enjoy such freedom. For one thing, creatures able to choose an authentic moral destiny for themselves represent an enhancement to creation. They are made in the image of God, who we assume also enjoys free will. We shall eventually have to examine that assumption, but most believers would be surprised if it turned out that creation represents not a spontaneous outpouring of divine love, but rather the work of a God passive in the face of all options, because he is compelled to do what is best. We do not think God is driven by motives, and neither do we think we are. Indeed, we generally feel that this so-called "libertarian" freedom is necessary for meaningful moral appraisals of action. Lacking it, a person could not have done otherwise, and so is not responsible, no matter what wonders or horrors he might perpetrate.

The most attractive dimension of libertarian freedom for many theists, however, concerns its implications regarding the problem of evil. Opponents of theism are fond of arguing that the evil the world contains is not compatible with the existence of the God of traditional belief, a God who is supposed to be all-powerful, all-good and all-knowing. How, they ask, is the existence of such a God to be maintained in the face of the holocaust, child abuse, or the sufferings of burn victims and those dying of cancer? If God is omniscient he must, in creating the world, have known such things were portended; if he is omnipotent he could have prevented them; and if he loves us he would have wanted to do so. Surely, then, any God that exists must have a nature far from what theologians take it to be, and there may well be no God at all. It is here that free will enters the discussion. A prominent reply to the argument from evil is that at least when it comes to moral evil – that is, evil owing to the operations of creaturely freedom – God is not to be faulted. Instead, we creatures are to blame for moral evil, for it is we who cause it (Plantinga, 1974, pp. 29–30). God does, of course, risk the occurrence of moral evil, by creating creatures with libertarian freedom. But moral evil comes to pass only when we exercise our freedom wrongly, and that is our doing, not God's. Moreover, God was fully justified in risking moral evil, due to the great value of a universe that includes creatures with free will. Only in such creatures is God's image truly manifested, and only such creatures can come to a loving relationship with God by their own choice, rather than through some form of manipulation or coercion.

It should be noted that the free will defense addresses only moral evil, whereas a great deal of human suffering seems to arise from strictly natural causes, such as disaster and disease. Even in the case of moral evil, however, the antitheist can claim the defense fails. It is part of the concept of free will that any particular act that is freely performed need not have occurred. A free agent might always have done otherwise. It seems possible to imagine, moreover, that there be rational agents who possess free will but who never sin, who always decide and act rightly. But then, if God is all-powerful, he should have been able to create a world entirely composed of such creatures – of beings who, though possessed of free will, always exercise it for good (Mackie, 1955, p. 209). If what the free will defense claims about the relationship between divine power and creaturely freedom is correct, however, to create such a world falls within God's power only in the rather weak sense that he can set things moving in that direction. The desired outcome might occur, but only if we free creatures choose to bring it about, which obviously we have not done. This level of power is far below that of the Judeo-Christian God – who, the prophet says, has wrought all our works in us (Isa. 26:12), and who works in us both to will and to do of his good pleasure (Phil. 2:13). Such a God must exercise complete sovereignty over all outcomes – including, paradoxical though it may seem, any that occur through free will. The free will defense does not accord God this sovereignty, thus it diminishes his power.

The free will defense also threatens God's omniscience. For if he has no control over how we exercise our freedom, how can God know what we will do? As creator, at least, it seems he cannot, because how we act depends entirely on how we decide, which we cannot do until we are on the scene. The Spanish Jesuit Luis de Molina claimed otherwise (Molina, 1988). He held that for every free creature God might create, and each set of circumstances in which that creature might be placed, God knows prior to creation how the creature would behave in that situation. Some contemporary philosophers have taken up this view – holding, for example, that God knew in creating the world that if I were given the opportunity to contribute an article to this volume I would (freely) do so, and was able to adjust his creative decisions accordingly. But knowledge requires more than true belief, even on God's part. It demands justification, and in this case there is none. It is only a contingent fact that given the opportunity I would decide to write this article, so there is no basis for God to deduce this truth a priori. And any actual activity of mine has no ontological standing prior to God's decision to create me, and so can provide no evidence. Indeed, to have such evidence would only further undermine God's creative autonomy, since that would amount to his being presented, prior to any creative decision, with the fait accompli that he was *going* to create me in the circumstances he did, and that I was going to decide as I have. So if God has no control over the decisions and actions of free creatures, there is no basis for him to know as creator what they will be. He is in the dark until, in the wake of creation, he is able to observe what we do.

If these arguments are correct then the free will defense, at least in its normal deployment, is not a satisfactory strategy for exonerating God for the existence of moral evil. It hardly follows, however, that we should give up the claim that rational agents enjoy libertarian freedom. The claim that such creatures enhance creation has force, and it may well be that this sort of autonomy is crucially involved in the plan of salvation. The only obstacle lies in the supposition that libertarian freedom is incompatible with divine sovereignty, that our exercises of will must, to be free, outreach God's creative fiat. Traditional theology asserted the opposite. Aquinas, in particular, holds that God is the first cause even of those acts in which we sin (*ST* 1–2, 79, 2, 1945, vol. 2, pp. 653–4). But he sees no conflict between God's action as creator and ours as free creatures. On the contrary: he holds that as first cause, God is actually the cause of our freedom, since he moves us in accordance with our voluntary nature, just as he moves natural things in accordance with their nature (*ST* 1, 84, 1, 1945, vol. 1, pp. 786–8). Can we make sense of this idea?

We can, if we avoid two common misapprehensions. The first is that when we behave freely, we confer existence on our own acts of will. It is natural enough to think we do, for we think that when we behave freely what we do is entirely "up to us," and what could this mean except that we are responsible for the existence of our willings? In fact, however, we do not confer existence on events any more than natural causes do. For consider again my act of deciding voluntarily to write this paper. If it was I who conferred existence on it, then I had to do so either through a separate act or as an aspect of the decision itself. If it was through a separate act, then my decision appears to have been caused rather than free. So if I was free at all, my act of conferring existence on my decision must have been the true locus of my freedom. But if it can be rendered voluntary only by postulating yet another act, we are headed for a vicious regress. Might I, then, have conferred existence on my decision as an aspect of the decision itself? Again no, for until my decision was on hand it would have been impossible for that dimension of it to do its work, and once the decision was present there was no work to be done. Whatever voluntariness consists in, then, it is not a matter of bringing our acts of will into existence. If exercises of creaturely freedom have any cause at all, that cause has to be God, who must create us *in* our decisions and willings, just as he creates us in all else that we do or undergo.

Here, however, there is a second mistake to be avoided. We tend to think of God as creating things by employing commands as causal means: He says *Fiat lux*, and his doing so causes light to exist. Applied to our example, this would mean God issues an edict that I decide to contribute to this volume, and this in turn causes me to decide. That is, he acts upon me, producing my decision through an independent event that determines its occurrence – just the sort of thing we see as ruling out libertarian freedom. But this view of God's action as creator is misguided. Even if we think that, unlike other events, God's commands have existence-conferring power, the actual operation of that power could not occur with logical necessity. It would constitute an event-causal relation, and such relations are contingent. But then whatever nexus we might think binds God's command to my decision must itself have been created by God, and if that takes another command we are headed for another vicious regress. The only way to avoid the regress is to hold that God *directly* creates the causal connection in question, without employing a command as means. If God's will can be directly efficacious in that task, however, it can be equally efficacious in producing my decision. There is no need, therefore, for a causal nexus to explain the efficacy of God's creative will, nor is there any causal distance at all between God's will and either us or our behavior. Rather we and all that we do have our being *in* God, and the *first* manifestation of his will regarding our decisions and actions is not some imagined command, but those very acts themselves.

If this is correct, then libertarian freedom can be a reality even though God's sovereignty over our actions is complete. God is not an inhabitant of the created world, interacting with entities within it. Rather, our relationship to God is rather like that of characters in a novel to their author. The characters have their being first in the author's creative act; but they are not acted *upon*, nor (if the author is any good) are they manipulated. On the contrary: they may be as free and as authentic as the author creates them. And so it is with us. Our actions are willed by God, but not as an external, determining cause. Quite the contrary: assuming God's own will is free, there is no event in heaven or earth that is independent of my decision to contribute to this volume, and which caused that decision. My act of deciding just *is* God's will made manifest. The decision is still mine as to ownership, however, and as such it can have all the legitimate features of voluntariness. I do not confer existence on it, but I could not do that in any case. I do, however, act in complete freedom from all secondary causation, and I am fully identified with my act. Indeed, all decisions are intrinsically intentional: it is not possible to decide something inadvertently or accidentally. When I decide to contribute to this volume, therefore, I do so with complete spontaneity and moral authenticity, notwithstanding the fact that I do so only under God's creative sovereignty. There is, of course, something that cannot happen: it is not possible for God to will as creator that I decide to write this paper, and for me to forebear deciding, or to decide something else. But that is not because were I to try it, I would find myself in a losing battle with God's efficacious will. Just the opposite: were I to try, that would have been God's will. Yet I would have acted with complete voluntariness and all legitimate freedom, just as I did in making the decision I did make.

Divine Freedom

If this view is correct, then God exercises full power and authority over every dimension of creation, and knows the world completely simply by knowing his own intentions as creator. Yet our decisions and actions can still be free, because the relationship between his will and ours is not that of cause to effect, but instead analogous to that between mental act and content in the case of human authorship. The difference is that in God's case the content of the act of creation is real: my act of deciding to contribute to this volume is the content, and hence the first expression, of his creatively willing that I so decide – a relationship, interestingly enough, too intimate to damage my freedom. The price of this view is that the standard free will defense, which places our wills outside God's creative authority, must be given up. Based on what we have seen, however, this is not much of a price, and while the matter can hardly be taken up here, we need hardly despair of an effective theodicy. God's willing that I perform the actions in which I sin no more makes him a sinner than his willing that a billiard ball have velocity puts him in motion. Indeed, the position of God vis-à-vis the evil in the world is little different on this view from what it would be on any other account that has him knowingly and willingly creating a world that contains sin and suffering.

There is, however, a potential difficulty to be faced. The view described makes both divine sovereignty and creaturely freedom depend on God's having free will. The first is obvious: without freedom, God's control over creation would be as hollow as that of any determined agent over his behavior. His sovereignty would come to nothing, because it could be exercised in just one way. Equally, however, we would lack freedom if God did, since our actions are expressions of his will as well as ours. Thus, if God's creative decisions were the product of some deterministic process having to do with his choices as creator, our freedom would be undone, by causes we could neither observe nor control. And it is easy to think of a scenario on which this might be so. God is supposed, after all, to be perfectly good; indeed, this is usually claimed to be an essential trait of his – one of the things that makes him God. This fact promises trouble if we combine it with what we might call the *deliberational model* of creation. According to the deliberational model, God is presented in advance of creation with a complete set of descriptions of all the countless ways things might go. That is, God has complete knowledge of all possible worlds, where a possible world is just an exhaustive description of some universe logically eligible for creation. Suppose, then, that there is a best of all possible worlds – that is, a single world description such that none other equals it in goodness. It seems obvious that this is the world a perfectly good God would choose to actualize in creation. But if perfect goodness is an essential trait of God would he not be compelled to do so? Would he not be driven by the attractiveness of that world to prefer it over all others? And if so would not his will, and by proxy our own, be unfree after all?

One strategy for heading off this problem is to question whether, in deliberating over creation, God is faced with exactly one best alternative. Perhaps there are many. Maybe if we arrange worlds in order of perfection more than one will be found to occupy the top level. There could even be an infinite number of worlds which, though they outstrip inferior competition, are nevertheless on a par with each other, each being of unsurpassable value. If so, then although God may be compelled to choose a world from this top tier, he would still have the luxury of many alternatives. Or, it may be that *no* world is unsurpassable, that when we rank them according to perfection worlds simply ascend to infinity, each surpassing all that go before it, yet surpassed by all that come after (Adams, 1972, p. 317). Then, God's goodness would not compel him to create any one of them, since an infinity of better alternatives would always be available. Yet he might still select some very excellent world to create, since this would presumably be better than creating nothing at all. This selection could presumably be made freely, since no available candidate is dictated by perfect goodness.

Upon reflection, however, this strategy appears heavily flawed. For one thing, neither of these suggestions for generating multiple creative options may be viable. Believers maintain that the concrete world of daily experience, the one God actually chose to create, is headed for an eventual transformation, in which the bodies of the saved will be glorified, heaven and earth will be renewed, and those destined for it will enjoy a life of eternal bliss, in which no good thing will be denied them. Now we may not often think of it this way, but the fact is that this new heaven and new earth would have to count as part of God's present creative project, and hence as belonging to the possible world he has chosen to actualize. But if this is so then it may well be that the present world is infinite in both the quantity and the variety of goods it contains. That would preclude there being any better worlds, and it is not clear how a world held to be distinct but equal might actually differ from it.

But even if these ways of multiplying God's alternatives should prove conceptually viable, they are unsatisfactory theologically. Multiple unsurpassable worlds might secure a modicum of divine liberty, but only at the expense of rendering it pointless. They place God in a Buridan's ass situation as creator, where he is free only because there is no meaningful decision to be made. Of course, God might still select a world to create, assuming it is better to have some unsurpassable world than to have a lesser one, or no world at all. But in these respects God's choice would still be determined, if our original assumptions were correct. His freedom would concern only which of the ideal options he selects. And in this task freedom is useless, even irrational, since there could be no sufficient reason for preferring any option over its competitors. The situation in which God faces an ascending infinity of creative options is even worse. According to traditional theology, God is pure act: that is, his nature involves no unrealized potency or disposition, but rather is fully realized in what he is and does. Applied to our present problem, this means that God's goodness cannot be measured by any desire on his part to do good, for he has no desires in the passional sense; it has to be measured entirely by what he does. Assume, then, that for any world God might choose to create, there is an infinite, ascending hierarchy of better worlds. If so, then whatever world God chooses, he would have been a better God had he aimed higher (Rowe, 1993, pp. 228–9). Moreover, since the succession of higher worlds is endless, God could have been infinitely better than he is. That is an unacceptable price for theology to pay for securing divine freedom.

We can, however, secure divine freedom if we abandon the deliberative model, and there is every reason to do so. Suppose that, instead of designing the Sistine Chapel ceiling out of his artistic imagination, Michelangelo had in fact painted it from a set of pastel drawings, perfect in every detail, that he chanced to find on the ground in the Vatican gardens. Would we then call the Sistine Chapel ceiling a creation of Michelangelo's? Hardly. Michelangelo, we would say, was only the manufacturer; the true creator was whoever produced the drawings. Suppose, however, that the drawings were actually left in the gardens by God, who had simply selected them as the best alternative from a complete catalog of all possible chapel ceilings, which he happens to possess a priori. Who is the creator now? Obviously, no one, at least so far. Only the creator of God's catalog would qualify, and we have yet to locate that individual. But then why call God the creator of heaven and earth, if all he does is select the world he will actualize from a complete set of exhaustively described alternatives given in advance? We might think the title is deserved because creation is *ex nihilo*, which is often naively be taken to mean the created world is produced out of some prior nothingness. As long as the plan is given a priori, however, even this is a task only for a conjuror, not a creator. A true creator produces the plan as well as the product – often in the very same effort, as with poetry, improvisational music, and a lot of sculpture and painting.

The lesson of this example is obvious: there is no plan from which the world is created. What would be the point, to guard against error? If God is anything like we take him to be, he requires no such precaution; nor is it necessary for him to deliberate over blueprints – or indeed even to form an advance intention – in order to assure quality control. Rather, God creates as the perfect artist: spontaneously yet with total mastery, able to accomplish in a single movement of his will the production of a world flawless in each minutest detail. To be sure, such a world, if only we were able to comprehend it, could readily be mistaken for a product of exquisite planning. Nothing would be out of place, nothing wanting, nothing redundant. If we understand what creation truly is, however, we will see that the measure of God's perfection as creator is precisely that all of this is accomplished with no deliberation whatever. The deliberational model is, then, mistaken; its home is in the realm of moral decision-making, not creation. And once it is abandoned, any threat to God's freedom disappears. There is no danger that he will be carried away by the attractions of any particular world model, driven by any mandate, or determined by any disposition of spirit. Creation is not a matter of evaluating alternatives, or of following instructions, and God has no dispositions. He simply does what he does, with full authority and power, and that alone constitutes his character. Thus, he can act with absolute spontaneity and complete freedom; indeed, if God has no dispositions then no cause can act upon him, for there is nothing in him to be set in motion.

Divine Commands

Our attention so far has been directed to the domain of the actual – to the world of substances and events, and to human and divine acts of will. Our argument has been that everything in this realm is subject to God's power and authority as creator. But what about the conceptual world, that of universals, propositions, and commands? It appears, at least, to play a powerful role in structuring reality. Universals encapsulate the natures of things. The propositions we frame in terms of them often record facts about reality, as when I state that my desk is rectangular. Some propositions do much more: they record the boundaries of *possible* reality – as when we say that a rectangle must have four sides, and that if my desk is to have fewer sides it must be triangular, since there is no two- or three-and-a-half-sided figure it can display. In large collections, as we have seen, propositions can encode entire possible worlds. And besides the possible and impossible, there is the permissible and impermissible: what we may and may not do, which gets formulated in the commands and injunctions of morality. How much of all this can reasonably be claimed to be put there by God? Does it all fall under his creative sovereignty, or are there things belonging to the conceptual order that God is simply stuck with, just as we are?

A good place to begin this discussion is with divine command accounts of moral obligation, which, commencing with Adams (1973), have appeared in several formulations in recent years. It was mentioned earlier that the laws of morality are given in scripture as commands that proceed directly from God. This raises the possibility that there is no intimate or direct tie between ethical rules and the descriptive nature of agents and their actions, that God simply superimposes morality on the world in the wake of creation, perhaps to foster human solidarity, or to assist us in exercising an otherwise bewildering free will. Such a situation would not be without appeal. For one thing, it promises help with the notoriously difficult problems of moral epistemology. Rather than having to find a ground for ethics in human nature or the demands of rational agency, we would insist that it arises immediately from the expressed will of God: what he commands is required, what he permits is permissible, and what he forbids must not be done. Moral quandaries, when they occur, are to be resolved solely by consulting his will, whether in scripture, the messages of contemporary prophets, or our own religious experience. No more sophisticated method is either necessary or possible. But divine command ethics also holds promise for our present discussion, for it seems to offer a handy way of extending God's sovereignty (Quinn, 1990). If ethics is strictly a matter of heavenly mandate, then it has no existence prior to divine injunction. In effect, God creates morality by issuing orders as he pleases. This may help settle a lingering doubt about his freedom as creator. Not only is there no prior plan of creation; there are no moral strictures God must follow, either. And this approach to ethics provides a ready explanation of divine impeccability – that is, of the fact that God cannot sin. For if morality is nothing but what God wills it to be, then his will would have to transcend morality, and so be exempt from it. How could God's commands be binding on his own will, if by that same will any obligation can summarily be revoked?

But divine command ethics also faces profound difficulties. The most obvious is arbitrariness. If morality is simply superadded to the world, and in no way tied to the nature of things, it is in principle possible that anything might be permitted or forbidden. God could as well have made killing the innocent, theft, or adultery right as made them wrong; he could alter the moral worth of any type of action as he pleases with no attention to setting and circumstance; and he could give conflicting commands to different groups of agents, demanding of some the very conduct he forbids to others in situations exactly alike. This is offensive to our intuitions about what morality should be, and removes any possibility that ethics might be given a rational foundation. It also appears to trivialize an idea believers take to be profoundly important: namely, that God himself exhibits moral qualities, such as justice, benevolence, and mercy. A second problem with this approach to ethics is its potential for fostering a certain kind of elitism. Ordinary people often find their experience of the world morally compelling: we see the sufferings of the poor, or the desolation of war, and feel we must do something about it. Simply formulated, however, divine command ethics does not allow God to speak to us through the world. His commands must be given independently, either in religious experience or through communication with others. And the danger then is that a special class of messengers will develop, an elite corps of moral experts who claim God's special guidance, and on that basis insist on our obedience. The idea that there is such a thing as moral sensitivity, and that each of us is required to develop it, would have little or no purchase in that kind of setting.

By far the greatest problem with divine command ethics, however, has to do with God's authority as commander. When I tell my young son to be in by midnight my command has the effect of obligating him, because he and I both know that independent of anything *I* say, he is required to obey me. As to how that general obligation arises, we may allow that it is based in a command from God – "Honor your father and your mother," perhaps (Ex. 20:12). Notice, however, that we cannot make the same move in God's case. Suppose that when he was commanded to go to Nineveh, Jonah had taken an even more reckless course than he did, and replied to God, "Where do you get off, giving me orders? What right have you to demand obedience from me?" No doubt, God would have found an effective reply; but it certainly would not have consisted in issuing a second command, enjoining Jonah to obey his first one. When someone's authority to issue commands is at stake, it cannot be rescued by another command from that same person. And since in God's case there is no higher authority, this means that our obligation to obey his commands cannot be grounded in his or anyone else's verbal insistence. It has to supervene on the nature of the case, to be grounded in the relationship between creator and creature, wherein we owe God our complete loyalty in return for his loving providence. Once we make this concession, however, any crude form of the divine command theory is in trouble. For if Jonah's obligation arises from the relationship between creator and creature, why does my son's not arise from the bond between parent and offspring? That, after all, is the way obligations are normally understood – as grounded in the way things are, not superimposed externally – and this perspective offers the hope, at least, that morality will finally be found to have a rational basis. We might as well hang on to that hope, as well as avoid the other problems of a naive command theory, since the view that obligations are simply decreed requires a fundamental exception anyway.

If we take this approach, we give up the false dream of a quick and effortless solution to the problems of moral epistemology, and recognize that these must be solved on their own ground. Somehow, we have to be able to discern what is right and wrong through ordinary experience of the world itself. If we could not, the assistance of religion would do no good, because the moral force of a divine command would be imperceptible to us. But we need not surrender entirely the view that morality is a matter of divine injunction, and there are good reasons not to. As we have seen, God's autonomy and sovereignty as creator are increased if he is the source of moral duties. Moreover, the idea that the content of morality is to be formulated in imperatives has an honored history, and commands make no sense without a commander. The problem only comes when God's role as commander is separated from his role as creator – that is, when we take the decrees of morality as a kind of divine afterthought, superimposed on the world rather than built into it. Instead, we have to think of moral import as essentially tied to the descriptive nature of things, so that right and wrong cease to be arbitrary, and learning what is morally required of us becomes part and parcel of understanding our own nature, and that of the world over which, in the religious perspective, we are given dominion and stewardship. We can think this way and still maintain that ethics consists in commands that come from God. All we have to claim is that God is the creator not just of the entities that make up the domain of the actual, but of their natures as well.

Absolute Creation

If we hold that the injunctions of morality supervene on natures created by God, we make it possible for the force of those injunctions to be felt through our experience of the world, while at the same time placing them under the creative sovereignty of God, and therefore retaining a form of the divine command theory. To make God creator of the natures of things is, however, a bold and controversial step, because it amounts to claiming that God is the creator not just of the actual world, but of the domain of necessity and possibility as well. That would represent a huge extension of divine sovereignty. We are prone to assume that necessary truths constitute a kind of a priori framework *within* which creation occurs: particular triangles have three sides because it is logically necessary that a triangle have three sides; tigers are mammals because they cannot be anything else; and two plus two is four because it has to be that way. There is no suggestion, usually, that any of this is up to God. But if this is so then the defining natures of substances and events, what we call "universals," and the necessary truths determined by them also define the limits of God's creative authority. His ability to create triangles depends on the prior availability of the nature of triangularity, and he must create particular triangles according to the specifications this universal imposes. The same goes for any other entity God might create, and any features it might have. Suppose, however, that in creating particular triangles God also creates triangularity itself. Then the direction of dependency is reversed. By creating triangularity, it is God who determines that such a nature shall be, that the sum of the angles will be 180 degrees, etc. Similarly, in creating tigers he wills that a tiger shall be a mammal, and thereby makes it so; and by creating entities as individuals he determines their mathematical nature, and thus sets up the principle that twice two must be four. In the same way, he is creatively responsible for any principles that supervene on the natures of things, as we have suggested the commands of morality must.

To adopt this view is to espouse *absolute creation* – the theory that everything that exists in any way has its being grounded in the creative will of God. If the understanding of God's creative freedom suggested earlier is correct, moreover, an especially economical form of the theory can be upheld. One need not maintain that *abstracta* are created by God as an independent realm – a sort of Platonic heaven in which the formal principles of the world find reality independent of anything concrete. Indeed, such a claim would be highly problematic. A realm of Platonic entities would be of no use to us in understanding the world, for we would have no access to it. And far from helping God, it would be an actual impediment to him: to create it would only impose prior limitations on himself as creator – something which, if he is truly omnipotent, he need not and cannot do. Rather, what is fitting is that God create the plan with the production, as the more mundane artists of our common experience do. Absolute creation fits nicely, then, with the view of God as a consummate artist, who fully creates and thoroughly understands all that has being simply by exercising his conscious will. But it also faces two serious lines of objection, one having to do with the very nature of necessary truth, and the other with the universals we understand to pertain to God's own essence. The first will be considered in the remainder of this section, and the second in the section to follow.

Absolute creation makes the existence of necessary truths depend on God's will. He creates them by creating the natures of things, and he creates those natures simply by creating the things that display them in the world of actuality. But that seems to have two untoward consequences. First, it suggests that the existence of *abstracta* has a temporal beginning – for example, that prior to the existence of the first actual triangle there was no such thing as triangularity, or any truth that triangles must have three sides. The same would go for all universals having to do with the created world, and the necessary truths that go with them. But we are accustomed to think of *abstracta* in more Platonic terms, as being eternal. Second, to hold that necessary truths depend on God for their existence is to suggest a view with which Descartes seems at least to have flirted – namely, that the truths of logic, mathematics, and other conceptual disciplines are not really necessary, or at least that other necessary truths were possible (Plantinga, 1980, pp. 95–107). But surely this kind of claim, sometimes called *universal possibilism*, is unacceptable. It implies that it might have been true that triangles have two sides, or three and a half – or, to cite an even more egregious example, that God might have made it true both that he exists necessarily and that he does not exist at all (Plantinga, 1980, p. 127). If philosophy, and human knowledge in general, are to have anything resembling a rational foundation, consequences like these cannot be allowed.

These doubts can, however, be allayed. On the matter of temporality, the version of absolute creation stated above denies that abstract entities exist at all in separation from the world of the actual. Thus, it denies any being to triangularity apart from particular triangles, and the conceptions of beings who understand what a triangle is. Accordingly, defenders of this view need maintain only that particular triangles, and the conceptions of triangles held by created intellects, have a beginning in time – which, of course, is true. As for God's conception of triangularity, whether it has a temporal beginning depends on whether God himself is a temporal being. Space does not permit discussion of that issue here, but there are good reasons for thinking God is not a temporal being (McCann, 1998), and while the machinations of Molinist and other deliberational accounts of creation may suggest otherwise, the account of God's power and action defended in this paper does not. It is entirely consistent with the idea that all of heaven and earth are both created and sustained in a single, timeless act on God's part, an exercise of power in which the universe in all its history is both given existence and comprehended. If that is so, then God's conception of triangularity has no temporal beginning: it is part of the timelessly eternal content of his knowing will. Similar observations apply to necessary truths. Propositions, on the present view, have no temporal beginning, because in themselves they have no independent existence. Only particular conceptions of them count as real, and in God's case even that is not temporal. This allows us to treat propositions as timeless abstractions, and so to hold that principles such as *Triangles have three sides* or *Twice two is four* are eternally true.

As for whether absolute creation implies universal possibilism, there is a persuasive argument by Morris and Menzel (1986, pp. 356–7) that this is not the case. What makes it seem otherwise is the thought that if the relationship between triangularity and three-sidedness, or between numbering twice two and numbering four is owing to God's creative activity, then it must have been possible for things to go differently, that it was possible for God to make triangularity a matter of having three and a half sides, or to make two plus two equal five. This, however, overlooks the fact that the entire range of possibilities as to what a triangle might be is completely determined by the nature that God creates when he creates triangularity. That nature is created with complete spontaneity, and apart from it there simply are no possibilities or impossibilities to be considered. The modal facts appear only with triangularity itself. The fact that it includes three-sidedness makes the entailment between the two a matter of necessity, and that is all there is to the matter. Similarly, it is owing to the nature of two, four, and the addition and equality relations that two plus two is four. And because this truth is owing to the natures involved, it is a necessary truth. There is no other possibility. Universal possibilism is therefore false. But this is not a limitation on God's power or sovereignty; on the contrary, possibilism fails for no other reason than that God chooses to create the universe as it is, with legitimate natures involving real entailments.

Creation and the Divine Nature

The challenge having to do with God's own nature is more difficult. Traditional theology associates a number of perfections with the divine essence. Some are moral in character: God is held to be perfectly loving, just, merciful, and so forth. Others, such as omniscience and omnipotence, reflect God's absolute sovereignty over all things. Still others try to get as close to the core of God's being as we can: he is held to be pure act, to exhibit absolute simplicity, to exist by his very nature. Now because these universals pertain to God's own essence, they threaten his sovereignty far more than those that characterize only created things. For if they have reality independent of his creative will, then God is dependent on them for his very life and being: he is able to be all-good and all-knowing only because of the a priori availability of these properties, and he can come to exhibit them only by behaving as they require. Thus, his autonomy and power are compromised. But if we attempt to rectify this situation, we court far worse trouble. If the universals that define God's nature arise only from the creative exercise of his will, it begins to appear that in fact God has no nature (Plantinga, 1980, pp. 7ff.).

We creatures, after all, have a choice only about characteristics that are accidental to us – about our careers, for example, or whether to marry. The attributes that are essential to us are with us all along; indeed, if they were not, we would not be here to do any choosing, since our existence depends on their presence. Why should it not be the same for God? But if it is, then his instantiating those universals that pertain to his nature must be ontologically prior to any choices God makes. Moreover, if God has a choice about whether to display an attribute, it would seem that he need not have displayed it, in which case it cannot be essential (Plantinga, 1980, p. 126). Finally, we need to remember that God is unique among all beings, in that his existence belongs to his essence. Indeed, many would say this is his most important defining attribute – that God is *ipsum esse subsistens* – being itself subsistent. And surely, it will be urged, we cannot claim this aspect of his nature is owing to God's creative will, for to say this is to suggest God is somehow self-creating. That is unacceptable; no being can confer existence on itself.

It will not do to bail out at this point. One could try to draw a line, claiming that while most *abstracta* owe their reality to God's creative will, those that pertain to his own nature do not. Such a distinction has an arbitrary ring, however, and it is hard to see how universals that are independent of God's will could ever influence his nature. Alternatively, one might try arguing that God's nature is completely impenetrable to us, so that questions about the origin of the universals that populate our pale descriptions of him are entirely moot. But while there is some plausibility to this stance, neither revealed nor natural theology has tended in the main to be so radical. True, the divine nature may finally escape literal description, but our efforts in that direction are generally allowed to convey some understanding, however dim and analogical. To the extent they succeed, it is fair to accept talk of God as having properties, and to seek to square that idea with the complete sovereignty tradition accords him as creator. What sense can be made, then, of the idea that the properties that define God's own nature owe their reality to his creative will?

We can begin by recalling the point mentioned in discussing God's freedom, that he is supposed to be pure act. The import of that claim is that there is no potentiality in God, that the attributes he exemplifies do not consist in dispositions to behave in various ways, but instead are fully realized in what he is and does. Consider, then, those attributes of God that are moral in import, such as complete goodness, and perfect justice and mercy. These are not propensities on God's part to act virtuously. Rather, they accrue to him entirely as a result of his action, as intrinsic to the very operation of his will in which, with complete freedom and spontaneity, he does all things well. God's having these properties is therefore entirely a matter of his will and action. Furthermore, since on the present view universals have no being apart from the actual events in which they are instantiated or understood, the universals that encapsulate the excellence of God owe their being to the operation of his will. Omnibenevolence, perfect mercy, and the like have reality entirely due to the fact that God creatively wills the actuality of everything that displays these perfections – an act which, remember, he performs without the aid of a plan. Accordingly, these universals can be said to be created by him. Furthermore, it is clear that the same would apply to every universal that God displays because he acts as he does. That covers an awful lot, perhaps even everything. For example, it includes the sovereignty and providential care with which God governs the created order, as well as the omnipotence and omniscience that go with them. All of these attributes too accrue to God in light of his pure actuality, for they are manifested entirely in the knowing will through which he creates, sustains, and governs all things.

There is more to the story, however. The situation described above is not that strange, really, because it has a close analog in the human setting. Not all brave acts are performed by courageous people, nor all acts of kindness by the good. Rather, we come to possess moral virtues largely through our actions, and we can be momentarily brave or kind even if we lack an abiding disposition to be that way. So apart from the fact that God acts without prior guidelines, the situation in which the present view places him is not unfamiliar. There is, however, a major difference. In our case, attributes we come to possess through our own will are always accidental. In part, this is simply because we have free will, and so can always behave differently, in ways that would gain us other attributes. But there is also the fact that we, as agents, are ontologically prior to our actions. We exist before they do, and we take advantage of our essential features, our intellect and will, in undertaking to act as we do. Now if God's freedom is analogous to ours, should things not be the same within him? And if it is, then are we not faced with the situation alluded to above, in which God has little or nothing by way of a nature? Properties like omniscience and omnibenevolence are usually thought to be essential to God. How can this be so if he gains them through the exercise of his will?

The solution to this difficulty is to be found in another traditional doctrine, that of divine simplicity. According to this teaching, the reality that is God is completely simple – he cannot be analyzed into elements of any kind. He has no parts, and there is in him no composition, whether of matter and form, potency and act, or substance and attribute. This last pair is the one most important to the present discussion, for if there is no composition of substance and attribute in God, then, unlike us, he is not ontologically prior to the action in which his attributes are expressed. Rather, he must be held to be *identical* with the action in which his perfections are manifested (Mann, 1982). So the actual reality in which God's perfect goodness is manifested – we might call it God's acting with perfect goodness, or his being perfectly good – turns out to be nothing other than God himself. The same goes for the other attributes we have been discussing. God is identical with his being perfectly merciful, with his being omniscient, with his being absolutely sovereign, and so forth – all of which turn out, as a result, to be exactly the same actuality: the single, timelessly eternal act through which God both knows and creatively wills all that exists. Notice this is not, as is sometimes thought (Plantinga, 1980, pp. 52–3), a view on which God turns out to be an abstract entity. God's creating the universe is not an abstraction but an action, just as Lindbergh's crossing the Atlantic was, and his being perfectly good is as much a reality as my cat's being friendly. So this account of divine simplicity reflects the view that *abstracta* have no reality independent of concrete actuality. We should observe too that nothing said here demands that God ever *become* good, merciful, sovereign, or the like. Rather, we can understand God as having these attributes in timeless eternity, by virtue of a single creative act in which he undergoes no change. Finally, we need to see that, if this account is correct, then the attributes made real through God's creative activity are indeed essential to him.

We can do so by considering some human act of virtue – say, Mother Teresa's tending the sick. Saintly though she was, goodness was only an accidental feature of Mother Teresa. Indeed, she need not have done anything virtuous. But if goodness supervenes on the descriptive aspects of acts of tending the sick, then even though it was accidental to Mother Teresa, goodness was essential to her action. In the same way, moral traits such as perfect justice and mercy have to be essential to God's action in creating and governing the universe: they have reality only in that he acts as he does. The same goes for omnipotence, which God has precisely in virtue of his activity as creator, and for omniscience, since he can only will what he conceives, and therefore knows. Now according to the simplicity doctrine God is unlike us, in that he is identical to the single action in which his various attributes – his omnipotence, omniscience, perfect justice, and so forth – are displayed. But then, since those attributes are essential to his action, they are essential to him, even though they owe their being solely to his creative will. Moreover, since these attributes owe their reality solely to God's behaving as he does, there is no point to talk of alternative possibilities. Thus, just as by creating triangles God makes them necessarily three-sided, so also by creating for himself the essential attributes of perfect goodness and the like, God makes it the case that he is necessarily good.

This account depends, of course, on a number of assumptions, most notably the claim that God is pure act, and the version of divine simplicity that has been adumbrated. But if these are granted, the upshot is that God is indeed the creator even of his own nature – at least in so far as the attributes that characterize him can be held to find reality solely through his creative willing. Can all of his attributes be brought under this rubric? We may suspect that some will prove recalcitrant: perhaps pure actuality and simplicity themselves, or necessary being. Or, we might pick on the trait we have relied on most: that God is manifested in his very willing. Could the aspect of God's nature that consists in his willing as he does find reality only as a matter of his willing? These are difficult questions, and this article is now well beyond its word limit. But none of these potential problem-cases should cause us to throw up our hands. Simplicity and pure actuality may find reality simply in the fact that God intends to create the world as he does, in a single, eternal act that is truly creative, rather than a product of planning and deliberation. Necessary being is more difficult, for while there is plenty of reason for thinking God has this trait, we do not really understand it. This much, however, can be said: to tie God's necessary existence to an eternal act of will with which he is in fact identical would not involve our saying that God confers existence on himself, in the sense of bringing himself into existence. That would not be possible for a timeless God. What it would mean would be something more like this: that God is pure act not just in the sense of being actual, but in a sense that incorporates the features of voluntary agency. This is implicit in the doctrine of simplicity anyway, and it may prove very important. For consider the last of our potential problem children, the attribute that consists in God's having a will. By the simplicity and actuality doctrines, this attribute is not exemplified as it is with us, through a latent faculty God possesses; it arises out of God's being identical with the very act in which he wills all that he does – everything, let us say. If this act has the features of voluntariness, then it is completely spontaneous, and intrinsically intentional. Just as we cannot engage in an act of will or decision without meaning to will exactly as we do, so God must intend to be exactly what he is, and that intention is carried out in the very act to which it is intrinsic, the act which, as it turns out, is God himself. Thus, while God does not confer existence on himself, he does intend to exist, and indeed to exist necessarily, and that intention is carried out in the very act which is his existing, and therefore existing necessarily. A difficult and mysterious nature, no doubt. But still a coherent one, and if the poor description given here may be forgiven, perhaps even a nature appropriate to the creator of heaven and earth.

References

Adams, Robert M. (1972) Must God Create the Best? *Philosophical Review*, 81, 317–32.

Adams, Robert M. (1973) A Modified Divine Command Theory of Ethical Wrongness. In Gene Outka and John P. Reeder (eds.), *Religion and Morality* (pp. 318–47). Garden City, N.Y.: Anchor Books.

Aquinas, Thomas (1945) *Summa theologica*. In A. C. Pegis (ed.), *Basic Writings of St. Thomas Aquinas*, 2 vols. New York: Random House. Excerpts. Original work written 1265–72.

Hume, David (1959) *A Treatise of Human Nature*, ed. L. A. Selby-Bigge. New York: Oxford University Press. Original work published 1739–40.

Kvanvig, Jonathan L. and McCann, Hugh J. (1988) Divine Conservation and the Persistence of the World. In Thomas V. Morris (ed.), *Divine and Human Action* (pp. 13–49). Ithaca: Cornell University Press.

Mackie, John L. (1955) Evil and Omnipotence. *Mind*, 64, pp. 200–12.

Malebranche, Nicolas (1980) *Dialogues on Metaphysics*, trans. W. Doney. New York: Abaris Books. Original work published 1688.

Mann, William E. (1982) Divine Simplicity. *Religious Studies*, 18, 451–71.

McCann, Hugh J. (1998) The God Beyond Time. In L. P. Pojman (ed.), *Philosophy of Religion* (pp. 242–56). Belmont, Calif.: Wadsworth.

De Molina, Luis (1988) *On Divine Foreknowledge: Part IV of "The Concordia"*, trans. Alfred J. Freddoso. Ithaca: Cornell University Press. Original work published 1588.

Morris, Thomas V., and Menzel, C. (1986) Absolute Creation. *American Philosophical Quarterly*, 23, 353–62.

Plantinga, Alvin (1974) *God, Freedom, and Evil.* New York: Harper & Row.

Plantinga, Alvin (1980) *Does God Have a Nature?* Milwaukee, Wis.: Marquette University Press.

Quinn, Philip L. (1990) An Argument for Divine Command Ethics. In M. D. Beaty (ed.), *Christian Theism and the Problems of Philosophy* (pp. 289–302). Notre Dame, Ind.: University of Notre Dame Press.

Rowe, William (1993) The Problem of Divine Perfection and Freedom. In E. Stump (ed.), *Reasoned Faith* (pp. 223–33). Ithaca: Cornell University Press.

Suggested Further Reading

Curley, Edwin M. (1984) Descartes on the Creation of the Eternal Truths. *The Philosophical Review*, 93, 569–97.

Mann, William E. (forthcoming) Divine Sovereignty and Aseity. In William J. Wainwright (ed.), *The Oxford Handbook of Philosophy of Religion*. New York: Oxford University Press.

Quinn, Philip L. (1983) Divine Conservation, Continuous Creation, and Human Action. In Alfred J. Freddoso (ed.), *The Existence and Nature of God* (pp. 55–79). Notre Dame, Ind.: University of Notre Dame Press.

Chapter 3

Eternity and Immutability

Brian Leftow

Western theists agree that God is eternal. But Western theists disagree on what being eternal is. "God is eternal" makes a claim about what kind of life God has. Some see it as claiming that God lives through all past and future time. Others see it as claiming that God's life is wholly atemporal. Still others see being eternal as something between these two extremes. Thinkers from Augustine to Duns Scotus denied God's life most or all temporal properties. Scotus began a retreat from this; today most treat God's life as fundamentally temporal. I first show that views of God's eternality must meet a condition Western scripture sets. I then lay out some views of God's eternality, noting how they do or don't meet this condition. I next show how the doctrine of divine immutability factors into the discussion of God's eternality. Finally I consider some arguments for and against the claim that an eternal God's life is "timeless," i.e. without location in time.

Beginning with Scripture

Ultimately, all Western views of what it is for God to be eternal have Western scripture as their touchstone. For the concept of God has its home in religion, not philosophy. So however far Western philosophy moves in the end from Western scripture's language, it succeeds in talking of God, not some purely philosophical construct, only if there is some connection between what philosophy says of its deity and what scripture says of its God. Thus I begin with a look at some scriptural statements about God's eternality.

Many Old and New Testament texts call God eternal. But bare use of the word "eternal" does not tell us just what it is for God to be eternal. More informative is the Psalmist's "Your years will never end."[1] If God's years (a metaphor for his life) never will end, they never did begin: being endless pastward seems as fully part of being eternal as being endless futureward. Some Old Testament authors assert that God is eternal by saying that

(1)   God exists "from everlasting to everlasting."[2]

This confirms that being endless pastward matters. So scripture has it that

(2)   God's life neither begins nor ends.

(1) has still more content. To some, (1) asserts that

(3)   God exists, has existed through all past time, and will exist through all future time.[3]

But if (1) asserts just (3), (1) would be true even if there has been only a finite amount of past time or will be only a finite amount of future time, so long as God existed and will exist through all of it.[4] And this does not seem so. Intuitively, a life with a finite past is not "from everlasting," and one with a finite future is not "to everlasting."

Given this, one might suggest that (1) asserts

(4)   God exists, has existed through a non-finite past time, and will exist through a non-finite future time.[5]

But (4) does not capture (1)'s force either. God could exist through infinite past time (for instance) without existing through all past time, if the sequence of (say) past minutes had the structure of the series 1, 3, 5 . . . 2, 4, 6 . . . , in which one infinite series begins after another. Were there an infinite past time before God existed, then even if he himself existed for an infinite past time, it would not seem apt to say that he had existed "from everlasting." Rather, it seems part of the phrase's force that God has existed *from forever* – i.e. through *all* past time.

Thus (1)'s force might be that

(5)   God exists, never began to exist, has lived through all of a non-finite past time, will live through all of a non-finite future time, and will never cease to exist.

But (5) says too much (and of the wrong sort) to be what (1) intends. Gen. 1:1–5 speaks of there being a first "day," a first time-period of some sort. And perhaps harking back to this, New Testament texts assert that time began. (Of this more anon.) But apart from this, it is doubtful that Biblical authors want to make or imply claims about the nature of time. They were not "doing" cosmology. For the most part, they simply assumed the cosmology they had at hand, and within it used temporal talk to make claims about God. Had their milieu offered a different cosmology, they would have used *its* resources to make the same claims about God, correcting *it* as their view of God dictated and otherwise not bothering with it.

If (1) asserts (5), there is a Biblical doctrine of the extent of time, one as binding on theists who take the Old Testament as authoritative as the very claim that God is eternal. There is no such doctrine.[6] Save for the exceptions just noted, if what Biblical writers say has implications about time's nature or structure, these implications are part of the medium, not the message.[7] So (1) does not assert (5). Some conjuncts of (5) are not really part of (1)'s content. One can better read (1) as asserting just that

> (6) God exists, and his life never began, will never cease, and is not finite pastward or futureward.

Unlike (5), (6) makes claims only about God's life.

(1) may also assert that God exists from and to further away than we can temporally measure. This is in any case something scripture wants to say. Thus Job: "How great is God – beyond our understanding! The number of His years is past finding out."[8] Job also gives us a spatial parallel: "Can you probe the limits of the Almighty? They are higher than the heavens – what can you do?"[9] Our spatial measures can reach only to the heavens, for the Biblical authors. What is "higher than the heavens" goes beyond our ability to measure distance. "From everlasting to everlasting," I suggest, does in temporal terms what "higher than the heavens" does in spatial terms. It asserts *inter alia* that God's life goes beyond our ability to temporally measure. In doing so it may hark back to Genesis 1, which depicts God as acting (and so living) temporally before he establishes the natural phenomena by which we measure time: only on the fourth "day" does God say "Let there be lights in the expanse of the sky to separate the day from the night, and let them serve as signs to mark seasons and days and years."[10] So either (1) asserts that

> (7) God exists, and his life never began, will never cease, is beyond temporal measure, and is not finite pastward or futureward

or (7) is at any rate part of the overall "mind of scripture" on God's life. There is still more to the latter, though. In the Pauline corpus we read: "we speak of God's secret wisdom . . . that God destined for our glory before time began."[11] "This grace was given to us in Jesus Christ before the beginning of time . . ."[12] "God . . . promised us eternal life before the beginning of time."[13] There is no "before" the beginning of time. If a time t has something temporally before it, t is *ipso facto* not time's beginning. Whatever we make of talk of acting before time began, such talk certainly implies that time's limits somehow do not limit God's life and activity. Thus "the mind of scripture" on God's eternal life is at least that

> God exists, and his life (a) never began, will never cease, is not finite pastward or futureward, (b) is beyond temporal measure and is not limited by time's limits (if any).

This statement makes no claim about time's nature or structure – though it may imply some in conjunction with further premises. Its (a)-clause asserts that God's existence is permanent. Its (b)-clause asserts that God's life in some way transcends time.

Scripture also asserts that God's relation to time is unique: "I am the first and I am the last . . . Who then is like me?"[14] "He is before all things."[15] "God . . . alone is immortal."[16] If God's relation to time is unique, God's life also has a unique relation to time.[17] Now consider again the Pauline "before time began." This suggests that God was there first, before time, and then time began. If God has the sort of power and authority Western theists typically claim for him, it seems inconceivable that time should begin against his will. If time cannot begin against God's will, he is able to prevent its beginning. So if God was there before time began, God has power over whether time begins. If time begins, time begins to exist. So if God has power over whether time begins, God has power over whether time exists. Gen. 1:1–5 may even depict God creating time. Evening, morning, and the first "day" are clearly things he brings to be; it is not implausible to take his doing so as his causing time to begin.[18] Moreover, scripture has it that God created "all things" . . . in heaven and on earth, visible and invisible."[19] Arguably whatever begins to exist is enough of a "thing" to fall under this.

So "the mind of scripture" on God's life seems to be that

> (8) God exists, and his life (a) never began, will never cease, is not finite pastward or futureward, (b) is beyond temporal measure and is not limited by time's limits (if any), and (c) has a unique relation to time, (d) transcending time in that God has power over whether time exists.

The power in (d) may go so deep as to make God time's creator, and clearly does go so deep that whether time exists depends on whether God does, and not vice versa. Philosophical treatments of God's eternality, then, can claim to be theories about the God of Western religion only if they adequately embody (8). I now introduce three sorts of account of God's eternality.

Temporal Eternality

Pure temporalism is the view that God is "in time" as we are, but unlike ours, his life is both omnitemporal and infinite – as in (5). One finds this at least in process philosophers like Charles Hartshorne.[20] This view has a problem squaring God's eternality with current cosmology's suggestion that time is finite in extent.[21] More to the present point, it is hard to see how pure temporalism can handle

(8b). One move would be to say that what is infinite is as such immeasurable. But this would then imply that (time being infinite) time itself extends beyond temporal measure.[22] And this is just wrong: one can measure infinite time in years, and there are numbers of years infinite time could have, e.g. $\aleph_0$. For pure temporalism, God exists through time as we do. So counter to (8b), his life is not beyond temporal measure, and any limits time has are limits within which he toils. As to (8d), process philosophers, at least, are emphatic that God has no power over time as such,[23] that he is caught up in a temporal flow which is either as ultimate metaphysically as he or more so.[24] More generally, any thesis about God which satisfies (8d) will entail that his relation to time is non-ordinary, and so push a temporalist view away from being pure.

If (8) represents what scripture has to say about eternality, pure temporalism won't do, particularly in its "process" version. What gives God's life a unique relation to time cannot be just its extent. A viable temporalist position must claim that God's life relates to time in some *way* ours don't.

Atemporality

All temporal events either are first present and then past, or are first future and then present, or have parts of which one of these is true. They either are before or after other events or have parts which are. Thus they *ipso facto* have positions in some time-series.[25] If an event has a part which is later than another part, earlier–later relations order its parts. Thus the event also has intrinsically a non-spatial direction. Pure atemporalism denies the items which make up God's life these and any other attributes typically associated with temporality. Maimonides and Schleiermacher may hold this view.[26] Both profess faithfulness to Western scripture. Asked for their reading of (1), they might reply that its real point is that what time it is is irrelevant to whether God exists. Certainly, if God is wholly atemporal, God never began or will cease to exist. If a wholly atemporal God is alive, his life is beyond temporal measure, not finite pastward or futureward, and not limited by time's limits (if any). An atemporal God is well placed to have power over time: He can create it, or refrain.[27] But an atemporal God's relation to time is unique only if there are no atemporal abstract entities. Further, Western scripture's God is "the living God."[28] Lives consist of events. Can anything wholly atemporal be an event?

Intermediate Temporalisms

Many views are possible between the extremes of pure temporalism and atemporalism, each distinguished by which set of properties typically associated with temporality it ascribes to God's life. Let's say that a view calls God timeless if (whatever else it holds) it denies God's life location in time, and let's call a view temporalist if (whatever else it holds) it locates God's life in time. New forms of temporalism, then, dot the current scene. On each, God exists in time, but his life has some property no other temporal life has. So each seeks a middle ground between claiming that God is ordinarily, "purely" temporal and claiming that God has no typically temporal properties at all. Lucas and Swinburne propose that

(9)   Before the universe existed, God lived alone in unmetered time, time such that there is no fact about how much of it has passed; once he institutes laws of nature which set a metric for time, creating facts about how much time has passed, he lives in metered time.[29]

Padgett suggests instead that

(10)   God lives in unmetered time both before and while the universe exists.[30]

Padgett, Craig, and Senor assert that

(11)   God is contingently temporal: he could have been timeless instead.[31]

Craig adds that

(12)   God's life actually has both a timeless and a temporal phase.[32]

(9)–(12) let temporalism satisfy (8b). On (9), God's life is beyond temporal measure. God's life in metered time has a definite length, but his life in unmetered time has none, since there are no definite temporal lengths there. The sum of a definite length and an indefinite one is an indefinite length, one which cannot be measured. And on (9), God's life extends at least beyond the limits of measured time. On (10), God lives outside ordinary (metered) time – which amounts to his life's escaping ordinary temporal measurement.[33] On (11), God need not exist in time at all, which makes him wholly free of time's limits.[34] On (12), God initially did not live in time. This again makes him free of time, and as with (9), entails that God's life as a whole has no definite temporal length.

But (9)–(12) face questions. I first show the troubling nature of Swinburne's unmetered time, then suggest that his (9) runs foul of the "no beginning" requirement.

As Swinburne sees it, in empty unmetered time before the universe, "every period ending with the beginning of the universe would be identical with every other."[35] If they're all identical, there is just one. If there is just one, it has no sub-periods ending with the universe's beginning. Nor has it distinct sub-periods beginning or ending elsewhere. For Swinburne, periods are distinguished by the actual or possible events ending or beginning where the periods begin or end.[36] So on his view, empty time before the universe has parts begin or end elsewhere than in the universe's beginning only if other events actually or possibly begin or end these parts. Nothing actually occurs in empty time. Each period of it can host instances of the same set of event-types: beginning of a universe of type 1, type 2, etc. There could be distinct possible token events to distinguish these periods only if these tokens' possible times of occurrence distinguished them. But if one needs distinct periods to have distinct possible event-tokens, one can't appeal to distinct possible event-tokens to ground the distinctness of periods. So on Swinburne's terms, there is nothing to render sub-periods of pre-universe empty time distinct. There is just one period of it, period. Further, for Swinburne, instants are distinct only by beginning or ending distinct periods.[37] So if there is just one period of empty time, without sub-periods, it does not even contain distinct instants. This period has the internal structure of a single instant.[38]

Putting God into this picture changes it only slightly. Instead of empty unmetered time there is unmetered time filled by God's having a single qualitatively changeless thought, which does not begin, and ends when God makes a universe.[39] As God's thought is qualitatively changeless, nothing in it marks off one period of unmetered time from another. God's unmetered time is as homogenously filled as empty unmetered time. The events which might end God's period of unmetered time are not comings to be of universes but God's making them come to be or having a new thought. But as in the empty-time case, the same set of event-types can be instanced at any point within this period, and so here too there are no sub-periods, and so (on Swinburne's terms) no distinct instants either. Thus it is not surprising that to Swinburne, the only referent for a token of "now" during God's life in unmetered time is the whole period of unmetered time:[40] it is all just one "now." Here too, it is hard to see why Swinburne's period of unmetered time is not just an instant. If it contains neither distinct parts nor distinct instants, how can unmetered time be extended? Swinburne replies that

> I do not hold that it has distinguishable parts, but I do hold that something could have happened during that period which would have produced distinguishable parts . . . it has potential parts, in the sense that it might have been divided – although there would be no difference between it being divided in one place and it being divided in another . . . We can individuate a period by what actually happened, and then consider what could have happened during such a period so individuated . . . assume that God had one qualitatively undifferentiated thought until he created the universe. We now have a fixed point – the creation of our universe, and we can consider what could have happened before it. If he had had a second thought before he created the universe, then that period before the universe would have consisted of two parts: and so (given that he didn't have the second thought) it now consists of potential parts. (There are of course no different actual instants at which his second thought could have begun.) . . . if we mean non-distinguishable parts, it has an infinity; if we mean distinguishable parts it has none.[41]

"It now consists of potential parts" seems to mean that it now is extended, and because it is, it can be divided into parts. It is not actually parted. It contains no distinct instants, but could. It has the internal structure of an instant, but need not have. So the question remains, in virtue of what is it actually extended? It would be hard doctrine indeed to hold that a period of time is actually extended due to what might have happened during it, but did not.[42] For this would be to hold that time passed during that period due entirely to what could have occurred then.[43] So perhaps Swinburne's answer is best taken as: its being extended is a primitive fact about it, in virtue of which it is divisible. The same will be true of God's mental event too, for if this had any internal part-structure, this would provide internal structure for the period in which it occurs.

This leads to a fundamental question. Why is a supposed extension with neither instants nor periods within it a form of time at all? It's not clear that Swinburne's unmetered time contains before–after relations. For it does only if something bears them. But in empty time there are neither events, periods, nor instants to bear them. In unmetered time filled with God's homogenous mental event, this event as a whole cannot be before or after itself, and it has temporal parts to bear them only if the time during which it occurs does. (Merely possible events have no actual attributes at all, and so don't stand in relations.) But again, there are no distinct periods or instants here. The best Swinburne can say is that there could have been. So as things actually are, Swinburne's divine unmetered time has nothing to stand in before–after relations. And so it seems to contain none. But an extension in which nothing is before anything else is not a form of time.

Again, it's not clear that Swinburne's unmetered time *passes*. If a period of time passes, then as time goes on, more of it has passed than had passed earlier. If this is true, the period contains distinct sub-periods: there is the period up to now, and then later there is the period up to a later now.[44] There is a present edge to the period, forging into future. "Now," tokened within the period, can refer to that present, not the whole interval, and the "now" moves within that period.[45] None of this depends on the claim that the period has a metric, and none of it is true of Swinburne's unmetered time. So Swinburnean unmetered time seems an extended pure present: one extended "now." This is just what Stump, Kretzmann, and others take to be Boethius's description of God's non-temporal mode of existence.[46] So it's just not clear why what Swinburne describes is a period of *time*. In any case, just why is God's unmetered time supposed to pass, if there is no change in the divine life to (as it were) power its passage? If God's single thought never in any way alters, why does it *continue* to exist, rather than simply exist, in a Boethian *nunc stans*?[47] If this is imposed on God from without, then God seems time's prisoner; it, not he, has the ultimate say.[48] Perhaps this is a function of his nature: but then we must ask whether a perfect being's nature would imply temporal passage or Boethian stasis. Moreover, if this is a function of his nature, then while God is responsible for there being time – it depends on his being, and not vice versa – his *power over it* is only as great as his power over his nature. It gives God greater sway to hold that God literally creates time, and can refrain – that time passes because God so chooses, not because of what he is or as an aspect of his being.

If there is just one partless period, one "now" before metered time's beginning, God's life has a unique first segment (of indefinite length). This segment (says Swinburne) does not itself begin.[49] All the same, a unique smallest unpreceded segment which is a proper part of a life is that life's beginning.[50] That the segment does not begin does not entail that God's life does not begin *with* it – so too, if God's life began with a single instant of time, that instant would not begin, but God's life would begin with it.[51] In fact, having no beginning makes unmetered time more, not less, like an initial instant.[52] If one asks whether starting with a segment of unmetered time is the *sort* of beginning (2) wants to rule out, the answer rests with whether one would say that Swinburne's God exists "from everlasting." A finite life in metered time plus a segment of indefinite length do not seem to add up to existing "from forever." (10) parallels (9) for the period prior to creation, and so does no better. (12) may also fail here. The timeless "phase" of God's life – at best an oxymoron – would clearly count as its beginning. And if a timeless "phase" has no duration at all, there seems no relevant difference between a life with a finite temporal past but no first instant in time, "preceded" (!) by a timeless phase, and a life with a finite temporal past and a first temporal instant.[53] Neither seems to count as existing "from forever."[54]

Padgett and Senor hold that God chose to be temporal.[55] But when? Says Padgett, "this choice . . . must always have been made."[56] That is, every time is one at which it already *has been* made; none is a time at which it *is being* made. But this can't be true. If something *has* occurred, then at some time it *is* occurring. Nothing gets into the past save by being at some time present. So let's ask just when and how God could choose this. He couldn't do it while he's temporal, one would think. If he already is, it's too late to choose to be. If God chooses this while he's timeless, then he's first timeless, then (!) temporal. This is (12). There is a third option: perhaps God's choice *makes itself* temporal. Perhaps a God who could have been timeless chooses to be temporal by initiating time. Because God decides to make time, there came to be events or times later than this decision. So the decision comes to *have been* temporal, and so God's decision accounts for his being in time. But there is a problem with this: the decision is not temporal till there are events after it. The decision comes to have been temporal, though "while" it was occurring it was *not* temporal. So its being temporal is past without having been present. Further, the decision will presumably lack temporal extent. (Having events after it presumably could not alter its length.) So its time will be the first instant of God's life, giving it a beginning. I take it, then, that if God lives in time, this is by nature, not choice, unless (12) is viable. I suggest below that (12) is not.

An Intermediate Timelessness

The claim that God's life is not located in time entered Western theism with Philo Judaeus and became well-nigh universal by Augustine. Some deride this as kowtowing to Platonic fashion in philosophy.[57] Another view would be that early Jewish and Christian thinkers saw in Platonism a powerful, plausible theory of "eternal" truths which grounded them on real eternal truthmakers ("Forms"), and wanted to reconcile that theory with their belief that only God is truly eternal. They did so by taking God as the locus of all Plato's Forms, making some aspects of His being, others ideas in His mind. In so doing, they ascribed to God some traits of Forms which fit them for their role as truthmakers for "eternal" truths, including immutability and timelessness.

Philo wrote that in God's life "there is no past or future, but only present existence."[58] Boethius gave this claim its most influential exposition. Boethius wrote that "our now, as it were running, makes time . . . God's now, permanent and not moving . . . makes eternity."[59] Talk of "now" moving suggests an image, that the now – presentness – alights on ever-later events like a spotlight moving down a row of buildings, the events being present when the light hits, past when it passes on.[60] Behind the image is the fact that temporal events are present and then past. For Boethius, this is what "makes" events temporal.[61] According to Boethius, God's "now" does not "move." The spotlight of the present stands still on events in God's life. They are present but never are past, or over. Nor are their parts (if any), for these would just be smaller events in God's life. No part of any event in God's life is ever over. This is not to say that these persist forever. They do not persist at all. For an event to persist is for ever-new parts to continue it as earlier parts end. So only events whose parts end persist. Events in God's life simply occur. They do not continue to occur. Nothing about them is imperman-ent, while temporal events achieve the only sort of permanence open to them only by surmounting their parts' impermanence. Temporal events are permanent if *some part of them* is always there. Eternal events are permanent because the whole of them is always there. All of this courts an objection: "but the Israelites' crossing the Red Sea was an event in God's life, and all of its parts are over." Reply: this was *not* an event in God's life. One's life is the sum of the events that happen to one – acting, being acted on, and being, oneself, in various states. The Israelites' crossing happened to the Israelites, not God. Parting the Red Sea and being aware that the Israelites are crossing it happened to God. Boethius would cheerfully grant that both happen to God permanently.[62]

Temporal events pass away. Events in God's life do not. They are permanent features of reality. And so for Boethius events in God's life are not temporal. Boethius instead calls them eternal; God is eternal because such events make up his life. For Boethius, events in God's life have at least one property typically associated with temporality – being present – yet are not temporal. So for Boethius, being present is not always or necessarily a property of temporal events, though it is typically so.

Boethius and Scripture

For Boethius, God's being eternal is its being the case that

(13) All events in God's life are permanently present.

Boethius would say that (13) fits (1)'s intent. For (1)'s intent is surely to say *inter alia* that God's life is a permanent feature of things. In (1), Biblical authors try to point, as best they can, to the greatest *sort* of permanence possible. Boethius claims that the permanence of being everlasting in time is just a pale imitation of the permanence (13) involves;[63] on (13), events in God's life are (as it were) too permanent to need to persist. Boethius's account fits (8) perfectly. Boethius's God exists "from everlasting to everlasting" if (as some claim)[64] Boethius also ascribes a sort of infinite non-temporal duration to God. Without this note, one can still say that Boethius's God will exist timelessly as long as time endures (endlessly, to those who believe in an endless afterlife): at each moment, it will be true to say that timelessly, God exists. One can also define a sense in which Boethius's God exists before time. To ease exposition, suppose that time had a first instant. We would not want to say that "God timelessly exists" *becomes* true at that instant. For this would have been true even if time never existed. If so, it seems that we should say that at that instant it is already true that God timelessly exists. If we should say this at the first instant, then of course we should say it at every later instant. The first-instant "already true" has roughly the force "is true, and would have been true even if time had not existed." At each later instant, a further note is added, that it *was* true earlier. But while "already true" does not entail at the first instant all that it entails at later instants, its meaning may well be the same. For all t, a proposition is already true at t just in case it is true at t and would have been true had time never reached t. At an instant after the first, this implies that the proposition was true at an earlier time. At the first instant, it does not.

Taking "already true" as suggested, "God exists" was already true when time began. We can then say that "God existed before time" simply means that "God exists" was already true when time began. "From before time" is (I submit) an acceptable reading of "from everlasting." (The Pauline texts quoted earlier may even *be* readings of "from everlasting.") Without (12)'s claim that God ceases to be timeless, so that his timeless existence becomes one terminus of a temporal life, existing before time does not render God's timeless existence a beginning of his life.

Boethius's view faces questions. Craig suggests the most basic when he writes that "to ascribe presentness to a timeless being in any literal sense is . . .

self-contradictory, for if a timeless being had presentness, it would exist now, at the present time."[65] But there could be time-series discrete from ours, i.e. series no times in which occur before, after, or while any time in our own time-series occurs.[66] If there were, there would be a present in another time-series. Yet what is present in that time-series would not exist *now*, i.e. in our series' present. Times in a time-series discrete from ours have no temporal relation to our times at all. Nor does the present of Boethius's God. But if it is coherent to claim that there is a second time-series, the claim that some present does not occur now is coherent. Some might object instead that whatever has a present must be temporal, even if its present is not ours. But this raises large further issues: what is it to be temporal, exactly, and *why* is presentness supposed to carry temporality with it?

There is much more to say about all these views of God's eternality. But let us turn to divine immutability.

Divine Immutability

The doctrine of divine immutability (DDI) has it that God cannot undergo intrinsic change.[67] Intrinsic changes are changes like learning or expanding, which (roughly) occur entirely within the changing item. As a first pass at a more careful account of intrinsic change, let's say that an item is discrete from A just in case it has some part A lacks, and that being F is intrinsic to A if and only if

(a)   for no property G does A's being F entail that something discrete from A has or lacks G or
(b)   that something has or lacks G before or after A is F,

and being F is extrinsic to A just in case it is not intrinsic to A.[68] If F meets condition (a), then in mereological terms, A's being F is wholly internal to A: it has no implications for items not wholly contained by A. So to speak, A could have F even if the universe ended at A's skin. If F meets condition (b), then in temporal terms, A's being F is wholly internal to A's being F. It has no implications for times not contained by the time A is F; so to speak, A could be F even if the spacetime universe ended at the spatiotemporal skin of A's being F. I say, then, that a change is intrinsic just if it is the gain or loss of an intrinsic property; otherwise it is extrinsic.

While Western scripture clearly has a doctrine of divine eternality, it may not teach complete divine immutability. The Old Testament depicts a God of raging emotion, who makes humanity and then is grieved to have done so,[69] whose anger at Israel flares and then is replaced by longing and forgiveness.[70] The New Testament depicts a God who first was not incarnate in Christ and then became so: "the Word became flesh."[71] On the other hand, much that scripture says of God is clearly metaphorical, and defenders of DDI are not slow to show that change-involving Old Testament texts could be.[72] And metaphysicians partial to DDI parse even the incarnation in ways which avoid divine intrinsic change.[73] Standard Western theism clearly excludes many sorts of change in God. For Western theists, God is a spirit, without body.[74] If he is, God cannot change physically. Western theists deny that God can begin or cease to be, and so rule it out that he changes with respect to existence. So it is not clear that the Western God could undergo changes other than mental changes – changes in knowledge, will, or affect.[75] Further, scripture amply supports the claim that God is somehow perfect. In conjunction with certain other scriptural claims, God's perfection seems to rule out many sorts of mental change.

If perfect, God is all-knowing. If God learns something new, then before that he was not all-knowing, unless the new item could not have been foreknown. Only free beings' future actions and states of affairs dependent on these are even prima facie beyond God's foreknowledge.[76] But scripture is full of claims that God foreknows our free actions. So if God is necessarily perfect, he is largely unchangeable in knowledge, on what are largely scriptural grounds. The one sort of divine knowledge which might nonetheless change is knowledge of contents involving temporal indexicals ("now", etc.) and tenses. It isn't clear that God can know beforehand what we know when we know that it is now noon. For "it is now noon" is true only at noon. If it is not true till then, it cannot (one would think) be known till then. Can God know that it is now noon without having changed from a prior state of knowing that it is now 11:59:59?

If God changes his plans, either he was not perfectly wise in making them, or he is not perfectly wise to change them now. This claim does not suppose that God can foreknow what would lead him to change his mind. It requires only that a perfectly wise God could work out in advance all contingencies his plan ought to take into account and either avoid them altogether or build into the plan a perfect response to each. God need not have foreknowledge to work out his plans so perfectly as never to need to change them. He need only be omniscient with regard to what is possible, and able to make up his mind what he would do in response to each possible situation. So if God is necessarily perfectly wise, God *cannot* change his plans. God's plans consist of some unconditional intentions (e.g. to create a world) and his conditional intentions for every circumstance ("if the Israelites disobey, I will exile them to Babylon"). God will not change any intention involved in a perfect plan; the plan is perfect only if this is so. If God necessarily plans perfectly, God cannot change such intentions. The only change that might occur in God's intentions, then, is the forming of *new* intentions as time passes. Now if God's plan is perfect, the intentions which constitute his adopting it already include intending unconditionally or conditionally to do every act which might count as a response to anything creatures might do. So the only room his plans leave for new intentions is that God might will to execute *now* whichever phase of his plans creaturely developments bring into play. But would a perfectly wise God really wait on developments before acting? A wise guardian pre-empts problems, starting to make sure his/her plans are not thwarted before obstacles actually arise. So a perfectly wise God acts preemptively, triggering his response to all possible contingencies, so that the arrival of one particular event brings its response from God without further divine effort (as it were). When Moses speaks, God replies. But he was making his reply from the beginning of time; when Moses finally spoke up, he finally heard what God had always been saying to him. And so perhaps a necessarily perfectly wise guardian cannot act otherwise. Could God change in affect? A wise God would so change only if he came to know something affecting which he did not previously know. *Per* earlier argument, this could only involve temporally indexical facts, e.g. that Christ is *now* suffering on the cross. But if God had more to react to in the "sight" of the actual event than he had in foreknowing it, he would not have perfectly fore-known its concrete character.

So scriptural considerations at least suggest a God much less changeable than we, one changing only in ways for which time's passage alone accounts. But the roots of the full DDI are also philosophical. Plato asserted that a god is "the . . . best possible" in virtue (perfection of mind) and beauty (non-mental perfection). If so, he reasoned, a god cannot change for the better. But being perfect includes being immune to change for the worse – too powerful to have it imposed without permission and too good to permit it. Thus a god cannot improve or deteriorate.[77] Plato ignores changes which neither better nor worsen. But there may be some. If one first knows that it is 11:59:59 and then knows that it is noon, is one the better or the worse for it? If the best possible state of mind includes omniscience, then perhaps it includes constant change in respects which neither better nor worsen God, e.g. in what precise time God knows it is. Plato's argument does not rule out such changes, and so does not deliver full divine immutability. Later writers based DDI not directly on divine perfection but on broader metaphysical theories about God (themselves largely motivated by intuitions about God's perfection).[78] Aquinas, for instance, argues it from God's "simplicity," "pure actuality," and infinity.[79]

Immutability and Some Other Divine Attributes

Immutability is not impassibility. The doctrine that God is impassible claims that God cannot have negative affects (e.g. sadness, anger), or else that nothing external has an emotional or causal impact on God. Nor does DDI entail divine impassibility. An immutable God could be unchangeably sad about something outside himself, and be aware of it by being unchangeably causally dependent on its occurrence. Nor does the doctrine of divine impassibility entail DDI. An impassible God could grow ever more cheerful as time passes, for reasons entirely of his own.

DDI does not directly rule out beginning and ceasing to exist. An item changes only if it exists at both the beginning and the end of the change in question, and so these are not changes in the things which begin or cease. But if DDI entails timelessness and a timeless being cannot cease to be timeless – i.e. (12) is imposs-ible – DDI also rules out beginning and ceasing to exist.[80] For no timeless being can begin or cease to exist; these are events which take place at some time or other. So if a timeless being cannot cease to be timeless, it cannot cease to be unable to begin or cease. But DDI rules out ceasing to be timeless if being temporal is an intrinsic property, for then change with respect to being temporal is an intrinsic change. And being temporal does count as intrinsic. Any temporal substance could be the only temporal substance – its being temporal is settled entirely "within its skin." Recurring to (a) and (b), an item A's being temporal does not entail that there is anything discrete from A. Some temporal thing could be the only temporal thing or include all other temporal things. So being tem-poral satisfies (a). Nor does A's being temporal entail that anything has attributes at times beyond when A is temporal. Time itself is temporal, and nothing has attributes temporally before or after this is so. So being temporal satisfies clause (b). Thus if DDI entails both being timeless and being unable to cease to be timeless, DDI rules out beginning and ceasing to exist – by a slightly circuitous route.

Immutability and Timelessness

Augustine and Aquinas thought that DDI does entail divine timelessness.[81] It would be easy to show that it does were growing older an intrinsic change. For then DDI would entail that God does not grow older – which is so only if God either exists for only an instant of time or does not exist in time. The concept of God rules out the former. But growing older is gaining and losing temporal attributes such as having lived 44 years. I am 44 years old only because certain attributes were had *before* I was 44 years old (e.g. those of being Leftow and being born). So being 44 flunks clause (b) of the definition of "intrinsic" above. It is not an intrinsic attribute. So growing older is an extrinsic change. Coming at this another way, growing older is gaining new temporal relations – becoming 44, for instance, is gaining the temporal relation of being 44 years separated from one's birth. Most would call change with respect to non-causal relations extrinsic.

Aquinas argued from DDI to divine timelessness this way:

(14)　A thing is temporal only if it can change intrinsically, or change its place, or has parts which can change places, or can begin and cease to exist.[82]

(15)　Whatever is essentially not in space cannot change place or have parts which do.

(16)　So whatever is intrinsically immutable, not in space, and without beginning or end of existence is not temporal.

(17)　God is essentially not in space.[83]

(18) Whatever is intrinsically immutable does not begin or cease to exist.[84]
(19) God is intrinsically immutable.
(20) So God is not temporal – his life is not located in time.

(15) is clear, and standard Western theism accepts (17). Aquinas's arguments for (18) are not his best, but he does not need them: scripture rules out the claim that God begins or ceases to exist. All turns, then, on (14). Aquinas's thought may be that a thing is temporal only if some of its life is located at a time, and some of its life is located at a time only if it does or can change intrinsically or it or its parts can move spatially at that time. I'd expand this a bit further, to two claims:

(c) A thing exists at a time only if an event can happen to it or its parts then, and
(d) Only intrinsic changes, spatial movements, and comings and ceasings to exist are events.

(c) seems correct, *modulo* a suitable parsing of what events are. (d) is certainly plausible. (d) does not intend to rule causings out. Rather, on Thomas Aquinas's Aristotelian theory of causation, the causing of an event of these types is identical with the event caused.[85] (d) denies event-status to being and continuing to be in mere states and undergoing purely relational, extrinsic changes like becoming admired by Zeno. I'd rather rule the first in, but must confess that a wall's being or continuing to be pink is not our ordinary idea of a happening. On the second, it's plausible that if one becomes admired by Jones, nothing really happens to one – not least because Jones can come to admire Sherlock Holmes (not knowing that Holmes is fictional), even though Holmes is not there to *have* anything happen to him. Again, suppose that someone in China breaks a dish. Then I gain an extrinsic property: I come to coexist with the broken dish. But is coming to coexist with the dish really something that *happens* to me? Our intuitions about events rebel at this. Xanthippe is a wife extrinsically, since her being so entails that someone is a husband. If Socrates dies, he loses the property of being Xanthippe's husband, and so Xanthippe ceases to be a wife, becoming instead a widow. But surely the only real event here is Socrates' dying. If "Xanthippe's becoming a widow" refers to an event at all, it refers to (and describes) Socrates' dying. On the view I'd prefer, any event is as such possibly a primary causal *relatum*, something which can cause or be caused due entirely to its own character, not due to some other event's character. Extrinsic changes other than changes of place flunk this requirement. My coming to coexist with the broken dish can have no independent place in the world's causal skein. Its causes can only be those of the dish's breaking. It cannot cause anything at all. What cannot be causally connected to something in its own right is not really part of the world.

As (c) is true and (d) plausible, (14) is at least plausible. So (14)–(18) make a plausible case that if God is immutable, he is also timeless.

Aquinas also takes it, correctly, that if something's life has no parts and does not occupy a single temporal instant, it is timeless.[86] Now suppose that God exists alone. Time's passing either would or would not entail intrinsic change in God. If it would, then if God exists alone and DDI is true, time does not pass: time does not exist. So if time's passing would change God intrinsically and God exists alone, DDI entails divine timelessness. If time's passing would entail only extrinsic change in God, things are a bit more complex. A life divides into parts only if something new happens within it. For if and only if a new event e happens in it, there is the part up to e, and the part from e on. If God is intrinsically immutable, nothing new can begin purely within God's life. So there cannot be such a thing as the place in God's life where something new would begin purely within God: there can be no intrinsically determined boundaries between parts of God's life, and so no intrinsically determined parts. We must inquire, then, about extrinsically determined parts. Suppose that time t ceases to be present and time t* comes to be present, so that God first coexists with t and then coexists with t*, a purely extrinsic change. Isn't there then first the part of God's life where t* hasn't come, then the part where t* has, and so doesn't t* partition God's life? There is a new part in God's life only if a new event happens in God's life. So t* partitions God's life only if coming to coexist with t* is a new event in God's life. But (again) the acquiring of a purely extrinsic property is not really an event. If I come to coexist with a broken dish, nothing *happens* to me. So if God exists alone, even if time's passing changes him extrinsically, DDI still entails divine timelessness. But if God coexists with temporal creatures, matters are no different: the extrinsic change of coming to coexist with a broken dish is an event for him no more than for me. So DDI entails that God's life has no parts, *simpliciter*. So given that the concept of God rules out God's existing at just a single temporal instant, DDI entails that God is timeless. In any case, that A and B coexist entails merely that both exist. It doesn't entail that they exist at the same time unless both exist in time. You needn't coexist with me where I coexist with you: I am here, you are there, and though separate we coexist. So too, God needn't coexist with Bertrand Russell when Russell coexists with God. Russell coexisted with God in 1960. If God is timeless, God coexisted with Russell timelessly. So first God timelessly coexisted with Russell, and then God timelessly coexisted with his absence. "First" and "then" are to be parsed entirely with reference to Russell's times, not God's. This does not entail that God timelessly both coexists and does not coexist with Russell. When Russell existed, God timelessly coexisted with him, *simpliciter*. When Russell did not, God timelessly did not coexist with him, *simpliciter*. Speaking timelessly, God is such that first Russell coexists with him and then Russell does not.

Another argument broadly along Aquinas's lines runs thus. If God is intrinsically immutable, there are no intrinsically distinct phases of his life such that some other event could occur before or after that particular phase. As we've just seen, the acquiring of an extrinsic property is not really an event, and so there are no "extrinsically distinct" parts of God's life, parts made distinct from other parts by what they coexist with. So there are no parts in God's life at all, and so no temporal event can stand before or after any part of God's life. If God's life is in some sense everlasting, no other event is before or after the whole of it. So if God is immutable and everlasting, neither the whole nor any part of his life stands before or after any event. This seems good reason to say that such a life is not located in time; whatever is in time either is before or after something or has parts which are. Thus (I submit) there are promising routes from DDI to divine timelessness where Aquinas thought. I now offer one more along Anselm's lines.

Were God temporal and immutable, he would seem oddly frozen. We pity rather than admire Lot's wife; immutability would not seem a perfection in a temporal being.[87] If God must be maximally perfect, then the claim that God is immutable entails that a maximally perfect being is immutable. If a temporal immutable deity would be less perfect a temporal deity than one who is mutable, a being is both maximally perfect and immutable only if it is not temporal. In short, *divine* immutability may entail *divine* timelessness.

The claim that DDI entails timelessness courts objections. The most basic begin from the fact that DDI lets God undergo extrinsic changes. Extrinsic change, some argue, is truly change. Whatever can change is in time.[88] So whatever can change extrinsically is in time. So if an intrinsically immutable being can change extrinsically, it is in time: DDI does not imply timelessness. I've already disputed the first premise: if extrinsic changes are not events, they are not really changes in their subjects, either. But let's consider some arguments.

Wolterstorff asks us to "Consider . . . my act of referring to [God] . . . my referring to [God] is a temporal event. It both begins and ends . . . The event of my referring to [God] is identical with the event of [God]'s being referred to by me,"[89] whence God undergoes an event which begins and ends, and so is temporal. Wolterstorff is right that there is just one event here. But as the only event involved in Xanthippe's widowing is the one better described as Socrates' dying, the only event involved in God's being referred to is one better described as Wolterstorff's referring. As we saw above with Sherlock Holmes, changing only extrinsically and relationally at a time t does not entail existing at t. This is true even of items which do tenselessly exist. Consider posthumous predication: Socrates dies at t_1, Zeno comes to admire Socrates at a later time t_2, and so posthumously a new predicate, admired-by-Zeno, comes to apply to Socrates. Speaking tenselessly, Socrates exists, even after he dies. For after he dies, it is true tenselessly that Socrates exists – that is, it is true that Socrates did, does, or will exist.[90] But though it is true tenselessly at t_2 that Socrates exists, and Socrates undergoes extrinsic change at t_2, this does not entail that Socrates exists (present tense) at t_2, or even that his tenseless existence is located at t_2. Socrates exists tenselessly entirely due to an existence which ended at t_1. A timeless God, too, tenselessly exists and is referred to without existing at the present time.[91]

Craig writes that "in creating the world God . . . undergoes an extrinsic change. For at the moment of creation, God comes into the relation of . . . co-existing with the universe . . . in which He did not stand before . . . (since there was no 'before') . . . He . . . undergoes an extrinsic change . . . which draws Him into time . . ."[92] But if there was no before, there was no change. A subject changes, even extrinsically, only if it is in one state and then in another.[93] If it is a change in God to come to coexist with the universe, even though it is not the case that he had earlier not coexisted with it, then it is equally a change in the universe to come to coexist with God, even though it is not the case that it had earlier not coexisted with him. But what was not there, was not there to change.

In short, one can (I think) defend the claim that DDI entails timelessness, or at least that DDI plus some plausible premises do so. Still, the hefty metaphysical premises it takes to get to DDI make it a fragile reed on which to rest any further claim, including the claim that God is timeless. So it is perhaps unsurprising that DDI figures in debate about God and time today mostly as a consequence one must accept if one holds the (to some) more appealing claim that God's life is not located in time.

Divine timelessness may in turn entail DDI. While timeless, God cannot change intrinsically. For an item changes intrinsically only if at some time it has an intrinsic attribute F and at a later time it lacks F, and what exists timelessly has an existence not located at any time. If a timeless God could become temporal, as (12) envisions, then perhaps by doing so he could become able to change intrinsically. If so, God would count as intrinsically mutable even while timeless, in virtue of being able to become temporal. But if being temporal is intrinsic, as suggested earlier, then, while timeless, God cannot become temporal, and so divine timelessness does entail DDI. Thus, too, if being temporal is intrinsic, (12) is impossible.

Let's return to God's relation to time.

What View of Eternality?

Any intermediate view of eternality seeks to hold that God's life has some but not all attributes typical of temporal lives. While many combinations of such attributes are possible, the most influential has been Boethius's, on which God lives in a non-passing present not located in time. The claim that God has a present seems inseparable from the claim that he is a free agent. For if he is free, he acts when he will – and acts then because he has some intention including in its content to "do it *now*." So if we understand God as a free agent, we understand him to intend to act now, for some now. But God cannot form an inappropriate intention. If he intends to act now, he has a now, a present. Thus the claim that God has a present of some sort may be inescapable. On the other hand, it is not hard to see why one might want to claim that God, a perfect being, has no past or future. Boethius writes that any temporal being "does not yet grasp tomorrow" and "has now lost yesterday."[94] We no longer live past parts of our lives. We cannot even remember their future parts. If one's life is through-and-through good, why would one want to cease to live any part of it? Surely a perfect life (one may think) would have no parts one is better off not living, and so the most perfect way to live it would be one with no past or future.[95] Thus the Boethian package has a natural appeal. But a present with no past or future is not any present in our time. And were it simply a present in some *other* time, God would still have a past he has lost and a future yet to come. So a present without past or future is timeless, not located in time.

The Boethian package is attractive. But is it true, or can it be? That (12) is impossible pushes us in its direction. For I've suggested that (9) and (10) collapse into (12). There is obviously more to say on that subject, but if they do, they fall with (12), leaving no intermediate form of temporalism to compete with Boethius's intermediate atemporalism.

Arguments for Timelessness

There are many arguments for divine timelessness.[96] I've just given Boethius's; I expand on it elsewhere.[97] Another worth mentioning is that the standard, Minkowskian reading of special relativity entails that whatever is in space is in time. No orthodox theist holds that God is in space. So the claim that God exists outside of time should be precisely as plausible as the standard reading is.[98] Augustine held that God is beyond time not just as a consequence of DDI, but because he held that

(21)   God has created time.

(21) let Augustine deflect the question "what was God doing before he created the universe?" (Augustine's move: time was created with the universe, and so there *was* no before for him to occupy.)[99] But (21) is appealing independently. Western theists face the scriptural constraint that God must have power over time. Further, they wish to see God as transcendent, free of and superior to even the most basic conditions of our lives. It makes God awesomely free of time to be its creator, and so master – and being time's free creator would give God maximal power over it.

Suppose that time exists only if God creates it, and God is free not to create time. Then God is at least possibly timeless, and had he not created time, he would have been so. Suppose too that creating time would not immerse God in it.[100] Then if God is free to exist without time and has created it, God's life is timeless, not located in time.[101]

Arguments against Timelessness

There are also many arguments that God cannot be timeless.[102] Some argue that a timeless being could not act: actions are events, and events (they say) must occur in time. But God acts. Again, some argue that we must take at face value scriptural passages which depict God changing intrinsically, or that God must change intrinsically if (as Christians believe) he became incarnate. If God changes intrinsically, however, God is in time. Some argue that God cannot truly interact with or respond to us if he is timeless, and that for this among other reasons a timeless God could not be a person.[103] An argument some find particularly force-ful begins from the fact that a timeless God must be both immutable (because timeless) and omniscient (because God).[104] If God is omniscient, they say, God knows what time it is now. What He knows, then, is constantly changing, since what time it is now is constantly changing. But surely knowledge of what time it is is intrinsic to God. So it seems that God cannot be intrinsically immutable, nor then timeless.

One reply is that knowing the correct time is *not* an intrinsic state of God's. Intrinsic states are those settled entirely within one's own skin. But then unless p is a truth entirely about matters within one's own skin, knowing that p is not an intrinsic state, for that one knows that p rather than believes falsely that p is settled by matters outside one's own skin. But when it is now is not a matter settled within God's own skin. What time it is now is not a fact about God alone.[105] But then knowing that it is now t has entailments beyond God's own skin, and so again is not an intrinsic state. More carefully, for any time t after the first instant (if there was one), knowing what time it is involves knowing the temporal distance between t and some other time, and so entails that there was some time other than t.[106] Thus it entails that *being a time* was exemplified at some time outside the period in which God knows that it is now t. Knowing what time it is at any time after the first instant thus flunks (b) above. It is not an intrinsic state.[107] And if this is so, it is hard to see why even knowledge that it is time's first instant would be. So change with respect to knowledge that it is t does not count as intrinsic change. So if God's cognitive state with respect to what time it is changed, it would not follow from this that he is not *intrinsically* immutable.

This result may seem a bit hard to swallow. One wants to know *how* a change in knowledge could fail to be an intrinsic change. Well, in knowers who can err, cognitive states can go from being knowledge that it is now t to not being knowledge that it is now t without any intrinsic change in the knower. If I maintain too long my belief that it is now noon, the belief goes from being knowledge to being error just due to the change of time.[108] But this is not a change in the content I affirm, and the change from believing that it is now t to believing that it is now some other time *is* a change in content believed. Suppose, then, that I believe that the present moment is *this one*. Then as the time changes, what I believe changes, as which moment "this one" picks out changes (assuming that "this" functions to make the time to which it refers part of the content of my belief). Intuitively, this involves no intrinsic change in me. I always believe a truth, and what truth I believe changes, but the change in content consists entirely in changes outside my skin. So it's possible for a change in content one affirms not to involve intrinsic change. Perhaps God's knowledge that it is now t is something like a compound consisting of God's inner cognitive state and t – like my belief that the present moment is this one. If it is, perhaps the only change involved when God first knows that it is now t and then knows that it is now t* (≠ t) is the change from t to t*.[109]

Another objection has it that God is timeless only if there is no ontological difference between present and future.[110] But there is such a difference: the present is real, the future not. Now if anything is yet to occur for God, he has a future (a part of his life when what is yet to occur finally occurs) and so is not timeless. So for a timeless God, nothing is yet to occur. For any event e in our present and event e* in our future, the part of God's life in which e occurs is the part in which e* occurs. In God's life, e and e* are real at once.[111] If God is timeless, he has no future. The question, though, is whether there being a God with no future really would entail that there is no future *simpliciter*, i.e. wipe out the ontological distinction between present and future.

I think not. A rough analogy: it's possible that there be two discrete temporal series, two series of times ordered as earlier and later, such that no instant of one occurs before, after, or during any instant of the other. So suppose that there are two, and consider an event e in series 1. What is its temporal relation to series 2? Those in series 2, were they to learn of e, would certainly have to grant that e occurs – using "occurs" entirely without tense. But e has to every part of series 2 exactly the same temporal relation: none. So the part of 2 at which it is true that e tenselessly occurs will simply be all of 2. The same will apply to any event e* which occurs later than e in series 1. We can suppose that the future is wholly unreal, so that while e is present, e* in no way exists. This changes nothing, for none of series 2 occurs while e is present. Despite the real difference between present and future in series 1, the part of series 2 at which e occurs equals the part of series 2 at which e* occurs. And series 2 is temporally related to series 1 just as a timeless God is to us, for 2 has no temporal relations to 1 at all.

Granting that the present is real but the future is not, suppose that *our* time is series 2, and consider an event e which is present in series 1 and is not to be 1's last. Then in series 1 there will be but as yet are not events later than e. But now let those of series 2 ask: are any 1-events later than e part of reality? The question asks us, in our present, what it is now correct to say, and it seems that the possible answers are yes, no, and not yet.

"Not yet" locates these events in our time-series, for it says that in the future – *our* future – they will happen. If the two series are discrete, this is impossible: no 1-event is in our present, past, or future.

If we answer "no," we raise a further question: will this "no" eventually change to "yes"? If it will, then before "no" changed, these events were in our future. The series' discreteness rules this out. If we say it won't, then we say that these events never happen – which is false. They happen at some time in series 1.

So all we can say (I submit) is "yes" – these events are part of reality, whether or not they have happened yet in series 1. That is, it is *now* the case that they are part of reality, though the "now" at which we say this has no temporal relations to 1-events. Series 1 is tenselessly there as a whole relative to us. "Tenselessly" does not deny that there is a real present/future difference in series 1. It entails only that *relative to us*, distinctions of tense in series 1 – past, present, future – do not exist. Now just as series 1 has no temporal relations at all to us, we have no temporal relations to a timeless God. So even if the future is unreal, all of time is tenselessly there for a timeless God.

Notes

1 Ps. 102:27. This and all quotations are from the New International Version.
2 Pss. 90:2, 103:17; Neh. 9:5. For "from everlasting" on its own, see Ps. 93:2, Hab. 1:12.
3 Thus Swinburne: "God is everlasting . . . He exists now; he has existed at each moment of past time; he will exist at each moment of future time. This is, I believe, the view explicit or implicit in Old and New Testaments . . ." (Richard Swinburne, "God and Time," in *Reasoned Faith*, ed. Eleonore Stump, Ithaca: Cornell University Press, 1993, p. 204).
4 Swinburne might object that God's being everlasting rules it out that time is finite or has an end point in either direction, and so this is illicit. But if this is true, that God is eternal asserts more than (3). And I suggest below that with one exception, scripture does not really make claims about the structure of time.
5 So Pike: "God is . . . described as existing 'from everlasting to everlasting' . . . this appears to be the claim that the life of God has unending duration both forwards and backwards in time" (Nelson Pike, *God and Timelessness*, New York: Schocken Books, 1970, p. 184). In one sense, a finite time open pastward and futureward is unending, but this does not seem Pike's intent. Pike suggests that this "apparent" view is correct (ibid. pp. 184–7).
6 That time began does not entail that it is finite pastward unless

   (a) Necessarily, no two times are separated by an infinite expanse of time (if two times can be so separated, the beginning of time can be infinitely long ago), and
   (b) Necessarily, there has been no unmetered time (if there has been some, then even if time began, it is neither finite nor infinite pastward).

   The Bible does not imply (a) or (b). So even the claim that time began does not give us a *Biblical* doctrine of time's past extent.

7   This claim obliges me to say why time's having begun is part of the message, not the medium. This may be because it is part of the message that only God is in any sense eternal: if time never began (and will never end), it would be in some way eternal. In fact, if time is non-finite pastward and futureward, one can make a case that it would satisy (a)–(c) in (8) below.

8   36:26.

9   11:7–8.

10   Gen. 1:14.

11   1 Cor. 2:7.

12   2 Tim. 1:9.

13   Titus 1:2.

14   Isa. 44:6.

15   Col. 1:16.

16   1 Tim. 6:15–6.

17   At a minimum, these texts suggest that God's life stretches further into the past than any other.

18   In which case "in the beginning" (v. 1) denotes the beginning of time as well as the world, and heavens and earth (v. 1) are among the things by creating which God brings time to be.

19   Col. 1:16.

20   So, e.g., Charles Hartshorne, *The Divine Relativity* (New Haven: Yale University Press, 1947). For Whitehead, process philosophy's founder, God is in an important respect atemporal. So, e.g., A. N. Whitehead, *Religion in the Making* (New York: Macmillan, 1926), p. 88; and see William Christian, *A Study in Whitehead's Metaphysics* (New Haven: Yale University Press, 1964).

21   The most obvious move is simply to go antirealist about the cosmology: what general relativity tells us is finite, one can argue, is just time as certain verificationist assumptions make it appear, not real time. So Quentin Smith, "Absolute Simultaneity and the Infinity of Time," in *Questions of Time and Tense*, ed. Robin Le Poidevin (New York: Oxford University Press, 1999), pp. 135–83. But then theists (not Smith!) face charges of theologically motivated special pleading. A whiff of fallacy also hangs about this argument. "p plus verificationism implies q and verificationism is false" does not imply "q is false."

22   Aquinas accepts both premise and conclusion at *Summa theologica* (henceforth *ST* 1), 10, 4. But his reasoning rests on a denial (universal in his day) that there are infinite numbers.

23   Though he can guide the particular events of which time consists.

24   In this they just echo Whitehead. For the key passages in Whitehead, see Donald Sherburne, ed., *A Key to Whitehead's "Process and Reality"* (Bloomington, Ind.: Indiana University Press, 1975), pp. 31–4.

25   If an event has parts and contains before–after relations but does not as a whole stand in any, its position is "coextensive with the whole of time."

26   Moses Maimonides, *The Guide for the Perplexed*, trans. M. Friedlander, second edn. (New York: Dover Publications, 1956), 1, chapter 57, pp. 80–1; Friedrich Schleiermacher, *The Christian Faith*, trans. H. R. Mackintosh and J. S. Stewart (Philadelphia: Fortress Press, 1928), p. 203. For more detail on their views, see my "The Eternal

Now," in *God and Time*, ed. Gregory Ganssle and David Woodruff (New York: Oxford University Press, 2002).

27 Craig and Padgett argue that an atemporal God could create only "tenseless" time, time containing earlier–later relation but no moving "now," presentness, pastness, or futurity (William Lane Craig, "God and Real Time," *Religious Studies*, 26 (1990), pp. 336–7; Alan Padgett, *God, Eternity and the Nature of Time*, New York: St Martin's Press, 1992, pp. 74–6). I show that the argument they share fails at *Religious Studies*, 30 (1994), pp. 247–9.

28 See e.g. 1 Sam. 17:26; Ps. 84:2; Hos. 1:10.

29 John Lucas, *A Treatise on Time and Space* (London: Methuen, 1973), pp. 311–12; Swinburne, "God and Time," pp. 204–22. Dean Zimmerman defends this view's coherence in "God Inside Time And Before Creation," in Ganssle and Woodruff, *God and Time*.

30 Padgett, *God, Eternity and the Nature of Time*, pp. 125–30.

31 Padgett, *God, Eternity and the Nature of Time*, pp. 56–62; Thomas Senor, "Divine Temporality and Creation Ex Nihilo," *Faith and Philosophy*, 10 (1993), pp. 87–9; William Lane Craig, "Divine Timelessness and Necessary Existence," *International Philosophical Quarterly*, 37 (1997), p. 223.

32 William Lane Craig, "Timelessness and Omnitemporality," *Philosophia Christi*, 2 (2000), p. 33.

33 Padgett, *God, Eternity and the Nature of Time*, pp. 126, 129.

34 Perhaps this also defines some sense in which his life is immeasureable.

35 Swinburne, "God and Time," p. 211.

36 Swinburne, "God and Time," p. 209.

37 Richard Swinburne, "The Beginning of the Universe and of Time," *Canadian Journal of Philosophy*, 26 (1996), p. 170.

38 It also does not begin (Swinburne, "God and Time," p. 219). As to whether it has a last instant, when the universe begins, there is either a first instant of metered time or a last of unmetered, but not both, due to time's continuity. Swinburne holds that there is "no content to" the distinction between open and closed periods (Swinburne, "The Beginning," p. 171), and so is in no position to plump for the claim that unmetered time has a last instant. So he cannot distinguish unmetered time from an instant by way of its (supposed) boundaries. Those who believe that there *is* a difference between an open and a closed period and who also find appealing the notion that the universe had a first moment of existence will hold that unmetered time before it had no last.

39 Swinburne, "God and Time," p. 218.

40 Swinburne, "God and Time," pp. 220–1.

41 Swinburne, e-mail, December 5, 2000.

42 Though this may be what Swinburne holds; see Richard Swinburne, *The Christian God* (New York: Oxford University Press, 1994), p. 78.

43 Or perhaps because "laws of nature operate during such a period" (Swinburne, *Christian God*, p. 78). But it's hard to see how the bare obtaining of laws could make time pass either, and in any case, there are no laws in unmetered time.

44 If the whole period is one now, there are no later nows within it.

45 Zimmerman claims that this first period can satisfy all requirements of instanthood laid down by (say) a set-theoretic construction of instants, yet be internally enduring

(Zimmerman. "God Inside Time and Before Creation"). But does it really make sense to talk of an instant with a moving now within it?

46 Eleonore Stump and Norman Kretzmann, "Eternity," *Journal of Philosophy*, 78 (1981), pp. 429–58. I argue this reading in *Time and Eternity*, pp. 112–46. What I say below about Boethius is neutral on this issue; I take him to say that an eternal being is too permanent to need to persist as temporal beings do, but make no claim as to whether Boethius thinks God endures in another sense. Further: if Swinburne's unmetered time is a single now somehow containing earlier and later, it sounds rather like what I call quasi-temporal eternity. But that is arguably not a form of time either.

47 Swinburne answers, in correspondence, "because I can give no sense to anything happening unless it happens over time, and also because it can be interrupted." But many do not share Swinburne's skepticism about literally instantaneous events, and one can even make a case for events which do not count as temporal. (See my "The Eternal Now," in Ganssle and Woodruff, *God and Time*) And while I endorse Swinburne's sufficient condition of being temporal – it amounts to claiming that the period or part of it cease – I'm not sure Swinburne's answer will do here. What we want to know is what categorical base underlies this modal property, since what Swinburne describes *seems* to be something whose categorical character would not.

48 Despite Swinburne's assurance, "God and Time," pp. 205–6.

49 Swinburne, "God and Time," p. 219.

50 Though not on Swinburne's conception of a beginning. See his "The Beginning of the Universe and of Time," *Canadian Journal of Philosophy*, 26 (1996), pp. 169–89. Unmetered time is the smallest segment beginning God's life because it does not actually have any parts to be smaller.

51 Swinburne has objected in correspondence that "if a period of time [God's unmetered time] has no beginning, then anything which lasts as long as [or includes] that period also has no beginning." But again, if an instant A has no beginning, a period of time including A nonetheless will, if A is the period's first instant.

52 If Swinburne's unmetered time *is* just an instant in the end, his God has a finite past, and (again) God's life has a beginning.

53 Also, on Craig's version of (12), God cannot create a backwardly infinite time. For as Craig sees it (see below), God first is timeless, then enters time by creating it. This entails that God begins to be temporal. If the existing of time makes God temporal and God begins to be temporal, then time begins to exist – in which case the past was not infinite. Now it would not bother Craig to hold that God cannot create a backwardly infinite time, for he holds that there can be no such thing (William Lane Craig, *The Kalam Cosmological Argument*, New York: Macmillan, 1979). But his arguments on this are less than persuasive. If it *is* possible that a time have an infinite past, we ought to hold that God, being omnipotent, can effect this. So it would be better to hold a view of God's eternity which does not deny him the power to bring this about. Given that there is time, God's life has an atemporal part only if there can be a time God does not enter – i.e. only if God can create time without entering it. So to hold both (12) and that God can create a backwardly infinite time, one must hold that creating time would not automatically render God temporal.

54 There is a sense in which existing timelessly counts as existing forever, but this does not apply if the timeless existence ends.

55 Padgett, *God, Eternity and the Nature of Time*, p. 123; Senor, "Divine Temporal-
    ity," pp. 88–9. Padgett adds that if this is so, even if time's passing depends on
    God's being, God is time's free source and creator.

56 Ibid., 123.

57 Pike, *God and Timelessness*, p. 189.

58 Philo, *On the Immutability of God* 6, 32, in *Philo*, trans. F. Colson and G. Whitaker,
    vol. 3 (Cambridge, Mass.: Harvard University Press, 1960), p. 27.

59 Boethius, *De trinitate* (henceforth *DT*) in *Boethius: The Theological Tractates*, ed.
    H. F. Stewart and E. K. Rand (New York: G. P. Putnam's Sons, 1926), chapter 4,
    ll. 71–4, p. 22. My translation.

60 So C. D. Broad, *Scientific Thought* (London: Routledge and Kegan Paul, 1923),
    p. 59.

61 Boethius, *Philosophiae consolationis* (henceforth *PC*), in Stewart and Rand, *Boethius*
    5, 6, p. 422, ll. 12–3, pp. 22–4).

62 "But how can God be aware that the Israelites *are crossing* – present tense – when
    the crossing is long over?" We do this too. Sense perception is cognitive contact
    with the very states of affairs which cause our perceptions. When we see a star in the
    night sky, we see a star emitting light – present tense – even though that particular
    event is much further removed in time than the Red Sea crossing.

63 *PC* 5, 6, p. 424, ll. 40–56.

64 So Stump and Kretzmann, "Eternity," and my *Time and Eternity*, pp. 112–46.

65 William Lane Craig, "On the Alleged Metaphysical Superiority of Timelessness," in
    Essays on Time and Related Topics, ed. L. Nathan Oaklander (Boston: Kluwer,
    forthcoming).

66 See *Time and Eternity*, pp. 21–31.

67 Such friends of DDI as Augustine and Aquinas are explicit that an immutable God
    can undergo extrinsic changes. See e.g. Augustine, *De trinitate* 5, xvi, 17; Aquinas,
    ST 1, 13, 7.

68 (a) and (b) take off from claims in Dean Zimmerman, "Immanent Causation,"
    Philosophical Perspectives, 11 (1997), pp. 462–3, and Rae Langton and David Lewis
    "Defining 'Intrinsic'," *Philosophy and Phenomenological Research*, 58 (1998),
    pp. 333–45. Further complications are needed here, but I forego them due to space
    constraints; they do not (I think) affect the uses to which I put (a) and (b).

69 Gen. 6:6–7.

70 Hos. 11:8–9.

71 John 1:14.

72 See e.g. Philo, *On the Immutability of God*.

73 See e.g. my "A Timeless God Incarnate," in *The Incarnation*, ed. Steven Davis, Daniel
    Kendall and Gerald O'Collins (New York: Oxford University Press, forthcoming).

74 So e.g. John 4:24.

75 Changes in moral character traits reduce without remainder to change in disposi-
    tions of will and affect. Changes in non-moral character traits would have to be
    functions of changes of other sorts in God. The changes left over once divine
    perfection has ruled out what it rules out are not obviously such as to prompt these.

76 Some might want to add truly random quantum fluctuations. But any means God
    could have for knowing future free acts would likely cover these too, and in any case
    I am not sure I believe in true randomness here.

77 *Republic*, 2, 381b–c. Consider any improving quality F. If God can give himself F, he can make himself better – but it would be better still to have F sooner, and so best to have F without any temporal delay, i.e. initially and from himself.

78 For discussion of such "perfect being" thinking about God and of some relevant intuitions, see my "Concepts of God," *Routledge Encyclopedia of Philosophy* (New York: Routledge, 1998), vol. 4, pp. 93–102.

79 *ST* 1, 9, 1.

80 Were (12) possible, then *per* earlier argument, his timeless "phase" would seem his existence's beginning.

81 Augustine, *83 Different Questions*, 19; Aquinas, *ST* 1, 10, 1–2.

82 *ST* 1, 10, 1 and 10, 3 *ad* 3. That is temporal, in short which can move or be in temporary intrinsic states. If I both begin and cease to exist, I exist temporarily – even if I begin to be at time's first instant and cease to be at its last.

83 *ST* 1, 8.

84 *SCG* 1, 15.

85 So Aquinas, *In III Physica*.

86 *ST* 1, 10, 4. Here I ignore complications about angelic "time."

87 Perhaps the main reason for this is that we think that a temporal being ought to be able to respond at once to what goes on around it. So to the extent that my earlier arguments toward the complete immutability of God have force, they move us toward divine timelessness as well.

88 Or else – if (12) is possible – is atemporal but able to become temporal. But I show below that (12) is not possible.

89 Nicholas Wolterstorff, "God Everlasting," in *Philosophy of Religion: A Guide and Anthology*, ed. Brian Davies (New York: Oxford University Press, 2000), p. 501. So too Quentin Smith, *Language and Time* (New York: Oxford University Press, 1993), pp. 209–10.

90 My point can be stated equally well in terms of a more radical sort of tenselessness, which consists not in a disjunction of tenses but in a complete absence of ordinary tense.

91 A timeless God exists completely without ordinary tense – his existence is not in our past, present, or future. If our timeless God is Boethian, he has his own present, and so it is false that his existence is disjunctively tenseless, if one includes the extra tense the eternal present requires in the disjuncts.

92 Craig, "Timelessness and Omnitemporality," p. 29.

93 Craig notes this at "Tensed vs. Tenseless," p. 222. Yet later in the same paragraph, he again calls this an extrinsic change.

94 *PC* V, 6, p. 422, ll. 15–6.

95 This argument is resistable. One question worth asking: if there is no qualitative difference between any part of God's life and any other, *why* is it better to possess it all? Why not say instead that God's life passes, but God loses nothing because he continues to have qualitatively the same experience?

96 For a full treatment, see my *Time and Eternity*, pp. 267–82.

97 See my "Eternity," in *The Cambridge Companion to Philosophy of Religion*, ed. Philip Quinn and Charles Taliaferro (New York: Cambridge University Press, 1997), pp. 258–9.

98　Some philosophers do challenge the standard reading. See e.g. Michael Tooley, *Time, Tense and Causation* (New York: Oxford University Press, 1997), pp. 335–72; Smith, "Absolute Simultaneity."

99　Augustine, *The Confessions*, 11.

100　I think this is true, and what I've said against (12) supports this. But I cannot argue it fully here, as a full discussion would have to delve into deep metaphysical issues. Craig and Padgett argue that if God creates "tensed" time, God *ipso facto* becomes temporal. I show that Padgett's argument fails in *Religious Studies*, 30 (1994), pp. 247–9. Craig's argument is essentially that by coming to coexist with tensed time, God undergoes an extrinsic change, and whatever does so is temporal (Craig, "Tensed vs. Tenseless," esp. pp. 222–3. So I've already dealt with it in my treatment of extrinsic change and timelessness. But Craig's full case includes discussion of the nature of real relations, the relations between time and eternity and other matters of metaphysics, which are indeed important here. Again, Craig's position implies that God is contingently temporal. I think whatever is temporal is necessarily so: again, a matter too deep to argue quickly here. If I am right about this last, incidentally, then if God creates time and is free to live without it, it again follows that God is timeless.

101　Senor raises the suggestion that even if creating time would not necessarily immerse God in it, a timeless God could choose to be made temporal by creating time ("Divine Temporality," p. 88). But this just brings us back to the "when did he choose" problem discussed earlier.

102　For full discussion, see my *Time and Eternity*, pp. 283–359, with the literature cited therein. More appears in my "Eternity" and William Lane Craig, *God, Time and Eternity* (Dordrecht: Kluwer, forthcoming).

103　So e.g. Pike, *God and Timelessness*, pp. 121–9.

104　The contemporary *locus classicus* is Norman Kretzmann, "Omniscience and Immutability," *Journal of Philosophy*, 63 (1966), pp. 409–21. The argument was first discovered by al-Ghazali.

105　This is clearly so if time is God's creature or if God is "purely temporal," simply "in" time like the rest of us. Padgett and Deweese (Garrett Deweese, "Atemporal, Sempiternal, or Omnitemporal," in Ganssle and Woodruff, *God and Time*) hold that some intrinsic passage within God is the foundation of all time, and so might dispute this. But they would not dispute that what *metered time* it is now is not a fact about God alone, and the argument from knowledge of what time it is now has always been put in terms of metered time. It's an interesting question whether if God alone existed, in unmetered time, he could himself know what time it is now. Swinburne would say that the only "now" involved is that of the whole of unmetered time, and so he can. But Swinburne also insists that unmetered time passes, and surely if time is passing, when it is now is changing. If the now of unmetered time changes, can even God pick out distinct instants of it, to know what time it is now (*pace* Swinburne's claim above that it does not actually contain distinct instants)? On Swinburne's account, no changes occur in unmetered time to distinguish one period of it from another. Nor have periods there any definite length to distinguish them. So God could pick out one period from another only if he could pick out their bounding instants, individuating one as the period t–t* and another as the period t–t**. But how could God pick out distinct instants? It's not clear that he could do so via (say) set-theoretic constructions from intervals "centering" on those instants, for he'd first have to pick out the intervals, and if no event occurs which distinguishes any one interval from another, how could he? It seems he'd have to grasp the instants directly, via non-relational individual essences, where an individual essence e of an instant i is a property which only i possibly bears, and e is non-relational just in case i could bear e even if only i and God existed. But it's not clear that instants have such essences. (Swinburne does not believe in them – see his "The Beginning of the Universe")

106 At least, this is so if it is not the case that

(H) "t" expresses a haecceity of the time t, an individual essence which the instant would bear even if it were the only instant of time, and this haecceity is non-relational (i.e. is not a property like *being the instant which ends period p*).

If (H) is true, knowing that it is now t is in effect knowing something of the form "essence e is now exemplified," which makes no reference to other times or distances from them. But (H) is (to put it mildly) debatable.

107 For that matter, if – as some hold – an isolated instant of time is impossible, and every instant must be the boundary of some extended stretch of time, then even knowing that it is the first instant of time is not an intrinsic state. For the occurrence of any instant of time entails the occurrence of others.

108 This assumes that if I believe at noon that it is now noon and believe a millisecond later that it is now noon, *what I believe* has not changed. This is plausible intuitively, though some analyses of such beliefs might not support it. Some analyses which do support it take it that belief that it is now noon amounts to belief that noon is present. Given this, on "presentism," on which only what is present is real, what I believe is that a particular event e involving a clock-process is uniquely real, or perhaps (simply) occurs. On "growing block" views, on which both past and present are real, my belief amounts to belief that e is real and no later event is real, or that e occurs and no later event has occurred. On either analysis, I can maintain the same belief while time's passage takes it from truth to falsehood.

109 Ockham briefly suggests some such view of divine knowledge in e.g. his *Treatise on Predestination, God's Foreknowledge and Future Contingents.*

110 So Padgett, *God, Eternity and the Nature of Time*; Craig, "Tensed vs. Tenseless." The argument goes back at least to Duns Scotus, *Lectura* 1, d. 39, q. 5.

111 Read 'at once' here purely mereologically, as "in the same part."

Suggested Further Reading

Ganssle, Gregory E. and Woodruff, David M. (eds.) (2002) *God and Time: Essays on the Divine Nature.* New York: Oxford University Press.

Kenny, Anthony (1969) Divine Foreknowledge and Human Freedom. In Anthony Kenny (ed.), *Aquinas: A Collection of Critical Essays* (pp. 255–70). Garden City, N.Y.: Anchor Books.

Mann, William E. (1983) Simplicity and Immutability in God. *International Philosophical Quarterly*, 23, 267–76.

Mann, William E. (1987) Immutability and Predication: What Aristotle taught Philo and Augustine. *International Journal for Philosophy of Religion*, 22, 21–39.

Part II

The Existence of God

Chapter 4

The Ontological Argument

Gareth B. Matthews

St Anselm's ontological argument is certainly one of the most audacious arguments in the history of Western philosophy; it may even be the most audacious.
It is also one of the most perplexing. Some philosophers have scorned it. St
Thomas Aquinas did. Others have thought they had refuted it. Immanuel Kant
thought he had done that. Many philosophers have tried to ignore it. But it is
difficult for a serious philosopher to ignore the claims of such a daringly elegant
bit of reasoning.

Many philosophers have developed their own version of Anselm's argument.
Some of these versions are quite crude, others are very sophisticated. In the
seventeenth century every self-respecting rationalist philosopher, including
Descartes, Malebranche, Leibniz, and Spinoza, promoted some version or other
of the argument. In the three subsequent centuries the argument suffered periods
of almost complete neglect. But after each period of neglect, the argument has
always been rediscovered, re-defended, and re-criticized.

The ontological argument is certainly not neglected today. No other argument
for the existence of God – indeed, for the existence of anything! – has received
such lavish attention in the last half-century as has the ontological argument. To
be sure, the argument's detractors are more numerous today than its defenders;
but the detractors are not obviously more acute, ingenious, or wise than the
defenders. And sometimes a vocal detractor turns into a defender, or the other
way around.

Bertrand Russell reports this moment of illumination:

> I remember the precise moment, one day in 1894, as I was walking along Trinity
> Lane, when I saw in a flash (or thought I saw) that the ontological argument is
> valid. I had gone out to buy a tin of tobacco; on my way back, I suddenly threw it
> up in the air, and exclaimed as I caught it: "Great Scott, the ontological argument
> is sound."[1]

Although Russell later unconvinced himself of the cogency of the argument, he retained a deep respect for what it attempts to accomplish, if not for what it succeeds in accomplishing. In his *A History of Western Philosophy* he offers this summary of the argument:

> We define "God" as the greatest possible object of thought. Now if an object of thought does not exist, another, exactly like it, which does exist, is greater. Therefore the greatest of all objects of thought must exist, since, otherwise, another, still greater, would be possible. Therefore God exists.[2]

As we shall see in what follows, Russell's précis is not an entirely accurate reflection of Anselm's own version of the argument. Yet it does make vivid an essential part of that version. Russell also makes clear one important reason why philosophers keep returning to the argument:

> The real question is: Is there anything we can think of which, by the mere fact that we can think of it, is shown to exist outside our thought? Every philosopher would *like* to say yes, because a philosopher's job is to find out things about the world by thinking rather than observing. If yes is the right answer, there is a bridge from pure thought to things; if not, not.[3]

Although there are many versions of the ontological argument, it is the original version, the one to be found in St Anselm's little treatise, *Proslogion* (also sometimes referred to by its latinized title, *Proslogium*), that I shall concentrate on here. I have two reasons for paying special attention to Anselm's own version. One reason is simply that it is the original one. Another reason is that it is, in fact, much more interesting than most all the successor versions.

Among the many intriguing peculiarities of the original argument in Anselm is the fact that this argument for God's existence turns up in a work that is not an impersonal treatise on metaphysics, or theology, but rather a sort of philosophical prayer, an "allocution," or address, *to God!* It is surely paradoxical to be addressing a being whose existence one is trying to establish. It is especially paradoxical to be offering the proof as part of a *petitionary* prayer to that very being. There is, to be sure, no formal contradiction in saying to someone (or *as if* to someone), "I hereby offer a proof that you exist," or even, "Help me construct a proof that you exist." But such a procedure is extraordinarily odd. Indeed, the sincerity of one's address to God seems to be undermined by the project of offering a proof of God's existence, just as the sincerity of one's truly needing or wanting a proof seems to undermine the genuineness of the prayer. Nor does paradox or perplexity end there. Why should God, if he does exist, even be interested in one's proof that he exists, especially if God is omniscient? The whole enterprise seems riddled with paradox.

Still, odd as it may seem to be telling God about one's proof of his existence, the project does have important antecedents in Western, especially in Christian, thought. For starters, there is the biblical story of the father who asks Jesus to cure his demoniac son. When Jesus tells him, "All things are possible to him who believes," the father responds, according to the story, "I believe, help my unbelief."[4]

Then there is an important precursor passage early on in Augustine's *Confessions*, which work is also, in its entirety, a prayer addressed to God. "Give me to understand, Lord," Augustine writes, "whether to call on you first or to praise you, and whether to know you first or to call on you. But who calls on you who does not [yet] know you? Not knowing you he could call on another [being] in your place. Or are you rather called on that you may be known."[5]

A reader might think it only a rhetorical flourish for Augustine to suggest that the one who prays might actually, by mistake, be calling on another being, instead of God. But it is well to remember that Augustine was a Manichean learner before he was converted to Christianity. So he could well have thought that some of his own prayers while he was a Manichean were, as it later became clear to him, simply misdirected.

Readers of Plato will recognize in Augustine's puzzle a close relative of what has come to be called the paradox of inquiry, which is to be found in Plato's dialogue, *Meno*, at 80de. There Plato's interlocutor, Meno, asks how it will be possible to inquire into the nature of virtue. Either one knows already what virtue is, so that the inquiry will be a sham; or one doesn't, in which case one will not know at what to aim the inquiry, nor will one recognize it, should one happen upon it.

The application of Plato's paradox of inquiry to Augustine's project of searching for God is obvious. Augustine is searching for God when he asks for God's help in the search for him. So, it seems, his directed search shows, by its very directedness, that it is not a genuine search for something he has not yet found. In addition to Plato's worry about how one can direct a search without already knowing the object of the search and his worry about how one could recognize the object of the search, should one stumble on it, Augustine has another problem. It is the problem of knowing how to direct his request for assistance in his search to the right being, when the being whose assistance he is requesting in the search and the being he is searching for are one and the same.

Eventually Augustine comes to conceive of his search as faith in search of understanding – understanding who it is one has, or should have, faith in. Indeed, this Augustinian phrase, "faith in search of understanding" (*fides quaerens intellectum*) is, Anselm says in his Preface to the *Proslogion*, the first title he gave his own work. Appropriately, Anselm ends Chapter 1 of the *Proslogion* this way: "For I do not seek to understand that I may believe, but I believe in order to understand. For this also I believe – that unless I believed, I should not understand."

This idea, too – as I have already indicated – is clearly Augustinian. Even the wording is taken from Augustine, who uses it in a number of passages. For example, in *Sermon* 43 Augustine admonishes his hearers: "You said, 'I would understand that I may believe.' I said, 'Believe that you may understand.'"

Proslogion 2

In the first sentence of Chapter 2 of the *Proslogion*, where Anselm presents the core of his great argument, he writes: "And so, O Lord, you who give understanding to faith, give [it] to me so that, as much as you know to be useful, I may understand that you exist, just as we believe you do, and you are this [being] that we believe [you to be]." Thus Anselm asks God to give him understanding, specifically, as it turns out, understanding through a rational proof (a) that God exists and (b) that God has the nature Anselm supposes God to have. The proof for (a) is given in Chapter 2; but the proof of (b) occupies Anselm for the rest of his little treatise.

In the second sentence of Chapter 2 Anselm offers a formal characterization of the being he takes himself to be addressing and whose existence and nature he wants to be able to prove. His formal characterization, though brief, is brilliant. It is also somewhat enigmatic. It is this: "You are something than which nothing greater can be conceived." Although this characterization is stated in the second person ("You are . . ."), it functions in the argument as something like a definition of the term "God." Since we will be referring to it often in what follows, let's state it formally and understand it to function in much the way definitions of terms function:

(D)   God is something than which nothing greater can be conceived.

One might think Anselm has sneaked in his conclusion in this, as I shall call it, "quasi-definition." After all, (D) tells us that God *is something*. And that, by itself, could be taken to mean that God exists. Thus we could eliminate almost all of Chapter 2 and see Anselm as presenting this simple argument:

Argument S1

(1)   God is something than which nothing greater can be conceived.
Therefore,
(2)   God is something.
Therefore,
(3)   God exists.

Argument S1 is not only simple, it is also simple-minded. Since what Anselm actually presents in *Proslogion* 2 is neither simple nor simple-minded, we should protect him against the accusation that his argument is, even in its barest bones, simply Argument S1. The best way to do that is to read (D) in such a way that it comes to no more than this:

(D*)   To be God is, or would be, to be something than which nothing greater can be conceived.

Since (D*) is somewhat cumbersome, and (D) is closer to what Anselm actually says in *Proslogion* 2, I shall continue to appeal to (D). But in the further use I make of (D) I shall ask that it be read in such a way that it is equivalent to (D*).

There is another way in which Anselm might be charged, falsely, with begging the question. In modern standard quantificational logic there is a rule called "existential generalization." This rule allows us to infer from "a is F" (i.e., "Fa") that something is F – i.e., $(\exists x)$ Fx. If we add identity to first-order quantification theory, we can infer "Aristotle exists" from, say, "Aristotle is a philosopher." Thus from "Aristotle is a philosopher" (Pa) we may infer "Someone is a philosopher and he is Aristotle" – i.e., $(\exists x)Px.x=a$), which may be simplified to "Someone exists who is Aristotle" – i.e., $(\exists x)(x=a)$.

Having seen how the rule of existential generalization works we may think that any statement about God – whether it is a complex statement, such as "God is something than which nothing greater can be conceived" or something quite simple, such as, "God is wise" – is enough to warrant the conclusion that God exists. Thus we could have this argument, which is almost as simple-minded as Argument S1:

Argument S2

(1) God is a perfect being.
Therefore,
(2) Something is a perfect being and it is God.
Therefore,
(3) Something is God, i.e., God exists.

There is, moreover, nothing special about beginning with the premise that God is a perfect being. We could as well begin with any other claim about God, for example, that he is wise, thus:

Argument S3

(1) God is wise.
Therefore,
(2) Something is wise and it is God.
Therefore,
(3) Something is God, i.e., God exists.

As we shall see, Anselm seems to have thought about such simple-minded arguments; he certainly has a way of making sure we don't confuse them with *his* argument. Thus he distinguishes between existence *in the understanding* (*in intellectu*) and existence *in reality* (*in re*). With this distinction in hand, he can agree that using a proper name, such as "God," in a statement, almost any statement, sets us up for existential generalization. But just because we understnd and accept the claim that Homer wrote *The Odyssey*, or that Hamlet is a prince, or that God is, say, wise, it does not follow that Homer or Hamlet or God exists *in reality*. All that follows is that Homer and Hamlet and God exist in the understanding. We will need something more to prove that they exist in reality.

So (D) doesn't immediately concede what is to be proved simply because something is being said of God and it follows from the fact that God is such-and-such, say, wise, or a perfect being, or whatever, that God exists. Rather, we are going to have to pay attention to the particular "such-and-such" that (D) gives us – that is, to what it is, or would be, to be something than which nothing greater can be conceived, to be justified in concluding that God exists in reality.

Where did Anselm get the idea that a proper noun might succeed in doing its job by picking out something in the understanding that is not anything in reality? That is, where did he get the idea that proper names can function by picking out merely imaginary, or mental, entities, rather than robust dwellers in reality? He doesn't say. But it seems likely, when you stop to think about it, that he was drawing on a response to an ancient puzzle in philosophy. That puzzle concerns a difficulty about how we can ever succeed in making a statement that is both meaningful and true when we say something of the form, "x doesn't exist" (where, it is understood, "x" will be replaced either by a proper name, like "God" or "Hamlet," or by a definite description, such as "the teacher of Aristotle"). To be meaningful, it seems, the proper name or definite description that replaces "x" must succeed in picking out something. But if "the Loch Ness Monster" or "Shangrila" succeeds in picking out something, then what it succeeds in picking out exists, and the statement "The Loch Ness Monster doesn't exist," or the statement "Shangrila doesn't exist," will be false. If, on the other hand, the proper name (say, "Hamlet") or definite description (say, "the teacher of Aristotle") does not pick out any definite person or thing, then our hope of denying existence to the teacher of Aristotle, or to Hamlet, would be dashed by the fact that the putative statement we make would not be a real statement at all. Saying "Hamlet doesn't exist" or "The teacher of Aristotle doesn't exist" would be like saying "Blah doesn't exist."

We can call this puzzle about statements of the form "x doesn't exist" "the problem of negative existentials." It is a puzzle about how intended denials of the existence of putative individuals can ever be both meaningful and also true. The puzzle has been around since the time of the pre-Socratic philosopher Parmenides.

Parmenides thought that we couldn't get away with saying *of anything* that *it* doesn't exist.[6] One way to meet Parmenides' challenge is to distinguish, in the fashion of Anselm, between existence in the understanding, that is, existence in the mind, and existence in reality. We then happily concede that, to succeed in denying the existence of some particular individual or thing, we do need to have that individual person or thing in mind. Thus we concede that that person or thing at least exists in the understanding. But what we are doing, on this proposal, when we deny existence to something or someone we have in mind is to claim that that person or thing exists only in the understanding. Our claim is that something or someone we have in mind does not exist in reality.

After Anselm gives us (and God!) his quasi-definition, that is, (D), his next move is to recruit a stand-up atheist. He gets his stand-up atheist, whom he calls "the Fool," to deny God's existence. Quoting a verse from the Biblical book of Psalms, a verse he expects will be familiar to his readers,[7] Anselm writes: "The Fool has said in his heart, 'There is no God.'"

One might object to labeling an atheist "the Fool," especially in an argument from reason alone aimed at proving God's existence. Doesn't labeling the atheist "the Fool" prejudice the outcome of the reasoning?

Perhaps. And perhaps Anselm does mean to express his disapproval of atheism by labeling the atheist "the Fool." On the other hand, it is essential to the argument he is about to present that either Anselm or someone else deny God's existence. This is essential because the argument he presents is, in form, a *reductio ad absurdum*, that is, an indirect proof or reduction to absurdity. A *reductio* such as this argument works by denying what one wants to prove and then showing that this denial, no doubt with the addition of assumptions thought to be non-problematic and non-question-begging, leads to absurdity. Since a philosopher's favorite kind of absurdity is self-contradiction, the philosopher will try to show that the denial of what is to be proved will lead to self-contradiction. And this is precisely what Anselm tries to do.

Of course, Anselm needn't have recruited some *person*, real or imagined, to deny God's existence. He could have just said, on his own behalf, "Suppose: God doesn't exist." But enlisting the aid of the Fool makes the *reductio* more dramatic. Moreover, since the whole *Proslogion* is in the literary form of a prayer addressed to God, having his resident atheist make the statement Anselm wants to show leads to contradiction saves Anselm the discomfort of having to say, in his prayer, "Suppose you don't exist." Indeed, something more than discomfort is at stake here. There seems to be, if not a formal contradiction, what philosophers have sometimes called a "pragmatic contradiction," in saying, "Suppose you don't exist." Anselm avoids this worry by getting his Fool to say, "God doesn't exist."

The next step in Anselm's argument is to get the Fool to admit the distinction between merely existing in the understanding and existing in reality as well. Having secured that admission from his Fool, Anselm goes on to get him to agree that God exists at least in the understanding. "But certainly even this very Fool," he writes, "when he hears this very thing that I say ("something than which nothing greater can be conceived") understands what he hears, and what he understands is in his understanding, even if he should not understand the thing to exist," – that is, even if he did not understand it to exist *in reality*.

This is the central move in Anselm's ontological argument. It is this move that most clearly distinguishes Anselm's form of ontological argument for God's existence from many other forms of the argument. By insisting that the atheist must agree that God is in the understanding anyway, Anselm opens the way to prove that the atheist is assigning contradictory features to this entity that both he and the atheist have in mind. Thus, whereas Anselm himself supposes that this entity in the understanding, something than which nothing greater can be conceived, exists in reality as well, the atheist supposes that this something than which nothing greater can be conceived is only a mental or imaginary entity.

We can think of Anselm's making the atheist admit that God exists in the mind anyway as establishing a "referential peg" on which to hang his definition-like characterization of God, "something than which nothing greater can be conceived."[8] Anselm is then in position to ask whether this something in the understanding could be both (a) something than which nothing greater can be conceived and also (b) something that fails to exist in reality.

His argument will try to show that assigning both (a) and (b) to this something in the understanding is absurd, and even absurd in the philosopher's favorite sense of being self-contradictory.

Should the Fool ever have allowed Anselm to have his referential peg? Without that peg Anselm would not be in position to argue that atheism assigns incompatible features to something in the understanding. Perhaps the Fool should not have been so accommodating. What could Anselm have said to a fool who had dug in his heels and refused to admit that this something than which nothing greater can be conceived exists even in the understanding?[9]

Presumably Anselm's response would have been something along these lines:

> Oh Fool, if you either claim not to understand the words, "something than which nothing greater can be conceived," or else deny that, having understood these words, you still do not have something than which nothing greater can be conceived in your mind, you will not be able to deny God's existence.

Warming to his topic, he could have gone on in this way:

> For your atheism to amount to anything, your denial of existence must be directed at God, rather than at the Abominable Snowman, or at Santa Claus, or at an old man in the sky. So, when you say, "God doesn't exist," you mustn't mean "There is no man with a long white beard in the sky," or anything of that sort. You must, in fact, have in mind *something than which nothing greater can be conceived* and deny the existence of that.

We shall return in a moment to the question of whether the Fool should have allowed Anselm to have his referential peg so that he could interpret the Fool's atheism in the way he does. But, for now, we can say that Anselm does have a good case for saying that the Fool's atheism consists in saying of something, x, that x is both (a) and (b).

Anselm's final move in *Proslogion* 2 is to argue that saying of anything that it satisfies both (a) and (b) is self-contradictory. The reason is this:

(G)   It is greater to exist in reality as well than to exist merely in the understanding.

We can call (G) "the great-making assumption." Although, as we shall certainly have to admit, (G) is highly controversial, it has a certain immediate plausibility. Persons and things that exist in reality thereby have actuality, something that merely imaginary entities lack. This actuality, it seems quite plausible to say, makes them greater than their merely imagined counterparts. After all, things that exist *only* in the understanding are obviously dependent beings in the relatively straightforward sense that they wouldn't have existed at all if someone hadn't thought of them. By contrast, things that exist in reality are not in this way mind-dependent for their existence. And such mind-independence, it seems plausible to say, is a great-making property.

To see that we are now ready to conclude that God exists in reality, let's rehearse the steps that Anselm has taken so far in *Proslogion* 2. We find at the beginning of the chapter a *definition*-style characterization of the being whose existence is to be proved, namely, God. ("You are something than which nothing greater can be conceived.") Next, we try *assuming the opposite* of what is to be proved, with the aim of showing that it leads to absurdity – ideally, self-contradiction. Anselm's way of assuming the opposite is to quote the Fool from the Book of Psalms: "There is no God." He then reasons that even the Fool, that is, the atheist, must have God in mind when he denies God's existence. Thus the denial of God's existence is to be understood as the claim that something in the mind, namely, God (that is, *something than which nothing greater can be conceived*) *fails to exist in reality*. But now we are to see that what the Fool is claiming is self-contradictory. It is self-contradictory because it is the claim of something in the understanding that it is both (a) something than which nothing greater can be conceived and also (b) something that fails to exist in reality. But anything in the understanding that satisfies (b) will be something than which a greater can be conceived, namely, something that exists in reality. And so the atheist's claim becomes, it seems, a claim about something in the understanding that it is both something than which nothing greater can be conceived and also something than which *a greater can be* conceived, which would clearly be absurd. So God exists in reality, as well as in the understanding.

Objections to the Argument in *Proslogion* 2

1.   A fairly obvious way to reject the argument in *Proslogion* 2 would be to deny the great-making assumption, (G). Why can't a supremely great being be simply a figment of one's imagination? Less grandly, why does, or would, existing in reality make something greater than it would be if it existed only in the understanding?

Norman Malcolm, who shocked many in the American philosophical community back in 1960 by defending a reconstruction of the argument he thought he found in *Proslogion* 3, criticized the argument in *Proslogion* 2 for relying on (G), which he considered a mistaken principle. Malcolm wrote:

The doctrine that existence is a perfection is remarkably queer. It makes sense and is true to say that my future house will be a better one if it is insulated than if it is not insulated; but what could it mean to say that it will be a better house if it exists than if it does not?[10]

Malcolm took himself to be restating a criticism of Anselm's argument to be found in Kant, whom he quoted thus:

By whatever and by however many predicates we may think a thing – even if we completely determine it – we do not make the least addition to the thing when we further declare that this thing *is*. Otherwise, it would not be exactly the same thing that exists, but something more than we had thought in the concept; and we could not, therefore, say that the exact object of my concept exists.[11]

In defense of Anselm, one could say that his argument does not ask us to consider whether *the concept of God as existing* is greater than simply *the concept of God*. What he asks us to consider is whether something in the mind or understanding *that also exists in reality* is greater than something in the mind *that fails to exist in reality*, that is, whether a real F is greater than a merely imaginary F. We might value the house Malcolm has in mind, even if we know it exists only in the mind; but we would pay more money for it if it existed, not only in Malcolm's mind, but also in reality.

2.   A more basic criticism of the argument in *Proslogion* 2 is also to be found in Kant. "'Being' is obviously not a real predicate," Kant writes; "that is, it is not a concept of something which could be added to the concept of a thing."[12] This objection is referred to in the literature as the claim that *existence is not a predicate*.

Again, the criticism does not exactly fit Anselm's statement of his argument. He does not speak of adding the *concept of existence*, or even the *concept of existence in reality*, to the concept of God, or the concept of something than which nothing greater can be conceived. What he does instead is to ask us to compare something existing merely in the understanding with something existing in reality as well. And the latter, he says, is greater.

We might want to know, however, exactly what the terms of comparison are meant to be. Which of these versions of (G) is Anselm assuming?

(G1)   Anything that exists both in reality and in the understanding is greater than anything that exists in the understanding alone.

According to (G1) an existent gnat is greater than a merely imagined giant.

(G2)   Anything that exists both in reality and in the understanding is greater than the otherwise same kind of thing that exists in the understanding alone.

According to (G2), a scrawny and diminutive, but existent, horse, would be greater than the largest, most graceful, and most beautiful, but merely imagined, horse.

(G3) Anything that exists both in the understanding and in reality is greater than the otherwise exact same thing, if that thing exists merely in the understanding.

What (G3) invites one to compare is, for example, some admirable character in what we take to be a novel, and the person we suppose to exist when we are told that the book we had taken to be a novel is, in fact, a biography of a real woman or man.

The text suggests that it is (G3) that Anselm is appealing to. "For if [it] is even in the understanding alone," he writes, "[it] can be conceived to exist in reality as well, which is greater." But, since Anselm doesn't actually state the principle he appeals to, we are left to try to do it on his behalf.

3.   The most famous objection to Anselm's argument in *Proslogion* 2 is usually called "the Perfect Island" objection. It is inspired by a passage the monk Gaunilo, a contemporary of Anselm's, wrote, as he put it, "On Behalf of the Fool." What Gaunilo actually wrote concerns an island allegedly more excellent than all others, rather than a perfect one:

> Now if someone should tell me that there is such an island, I should easily understand what was said, in which there is no difficulty. But suppose that he went on to say, as if by logical inference: "Moreover, you cannot doubt that this island more excellent than all [other] lands, which you do not dispute is in your understanding, exists somewhere in reality. And, since it is more excellent not to be in the understanding alone, but to exist both in the understanding and in reality, for this reason it must exist [in reality]."[13]

Gaunilo's lost island (or "Perfect Island," as it is generally referred to in the literature) is clearly meant to be a parody of Anselm's argument in *Proslogion* 2. With his parody of Anselm's argument Gaunilo presents Anselm with a challenge. Although the parody does not, by itself, make clear exactly what is wrong with Anselm's reasoning, the parody is meant to be so obviously unsatisfactory as an argument for its own conclusion that Anselm is challenged to either (a) explain why the objection one has to the parody does not apply to the ontological argument, or else (b) agree that the ontological argument is also unsatisfactory. Thus Gaunilo's parody produces the conclusion, by reasoning alone, that some lost island exists. But surely we ought not to be able to establish facts about lost islands by merely a priori reasoning, without any empirical investigation at all. Yet if there is something wrong with the lost-island argument, there must equally, it seems, be something wrong with Anselm's argument.

In fact, the reasoning in Gaunilo's parody does not track exactly Anselm's reasoning in *Proslogion* 2. To bring it closer into line with Anselm's argument we should have to characterize the lost island as something than which nothing greater can be conceived. But no mere island could plausibly be thought to be something than which absolutely nothing greater, or more excellent, can be conceived. More appropriately, it might be thought to be an island than which *no greater island* could be conceived. Perhaps Gaunilo should have characterized his lost island that way.

If Gaunilo did characterize his lost island as an island than which no greater island can be conceived, we could reply that islands, like natural numbers, are inherently limited entities. For any specified island, it could be argued, one might conceive one that is bigger and better – perhaps one that has even more palm trees, or bigger beaches, or whatever.[14] Anselm's characterization of God, by contrast, does not claim that God is merely an F such that no greater F can be conceived Anselm's characterization of God is unqualifiedly superlative. God, Anselm supposes, is something than which *nothing greater* (period!) can be conceived. Thus one might agree that there can be no such thing as an *island* than which no greater island can be conceived any more than there could be such a thing as a *natural number* than which no greater natural number can be conceived. But that fact, by itself, does not establish that there can be no such thing as *something* than which nothing greater can be conceived. And so Gaunilo's parody is just that, a parody. It does not undermine the credibility of Anselm's argument.

4.   Another popular attempt at a counterexample to Anselm's reasoning is an argument for the existence of the devil. Can't we prove the existence of the devil, a being than which nothing more *evil* can be conceived, by similar reasoning? If so, again, there must be something wrong with Anselm's reasoning.

One complication this time concerns the idea, perhaps quite plausible to us, that existing in reality ought to make an evil being even more evil, just as existing in reality makes a good, or great, being even better or greater than it would be if it were purely mental. Anselm, however, stands in the Platonic tradition, according to which the scale of being is also a scale of goodness, or greatness. That means that non-existence would be evil. Implausible as it may seem to us, a devil that exists in the understanding, but not in reality, would actually be less good, and so more evil, than one that exists in reality.

5.   Perhaps the most interesting objection that can be made to Anselm's argument in *Proslogion* 2 is what we might call a "meta-objection." It concerns the way Anselm interprets the Fool's claim, "There is no God." As we have seen, Anselm understands this claim, and, by implication, all claims of the form "x doesn't exist," to be claims about something in the understanding. More specifically, according to the Anselmian, each such claim is a claim about something in the understanding that it fails to exist in reality. But, as we know from

twentieth-century philosophy, there are other ways to understand negative existentials besides this.

Bertrand Russell suggested that when we say, "Socrates doesn't exist," we can be taken to have a definite description in mind to replace "Socrates" – maybe "the teacher of Plato." So perhaps "Socrates doesn't exist" means "The teacher of Plato doesn't exist," and what that means is, perhaps, "Nobody fits the description, 'the teacher of Plato.'"

If we don't accept the idea of translating

(1)   Socrates doesn't exist

into a sentence that mentions the English phrase, "the teacher of Plato" (after all, (1) doesn't mention any English phrase), we could follow Russell's theory of descriptions and translate (1) into this:

(2)   It is false that that there is at least and at most one person who taught Plato.

Similarly, we could begin with the Fool's

(3)   God doesn't exist

and use Anselm's quasi-definition to get this:

(4)   Nothing fits the description, "something than which nothing greater can be conceived."

If, now, we wanted to get rid of the English phrase in (4), we might come up with this:

(5)   For any given thing, in the understanding or in reality, one greater than it can be conceived.

Someone might ask how the Fool could possibly know (5) to be true. But here it is well to keep in mind that the form of Anselm's argument is a *reductio*. Since the Fool is simply stating, in a dramatic way, the supposition Anselm wishes to show absurd, the Fool doesn't need to know that (5) is true, or even produce any evidence for thinking it is true. The Fool's role is simply to state that God does not exist so that Anselm can show that the Fool's statement leads to self-contradiction. If the Fool insists on having his statement of atheism understood as (5), he can avoid, it seems, Anselm's claim that the Fool has contradicted himself.

Interestingly, this Russell-type response to Anselm's argument *seems* to be anticipated in a comment St Thomas Aquinas makes in his *Summa contra gentiles*. This comment has gone largely unnoticed in the literature.[15] Instead, commentators have focused on objections to Anselm's argument that Aquinas makes in his other *summa*, the *Summa theologiae*. In that work Aquinas says that God's existence, though self-evident in itself, is not self-evident to us, since we do not know God's essence.[16] But Anselm can easily accommodate that objection, since he, too, thinks we do not know God's essence. As he argues in *Proslogion* 15, God is a something *greater than can be conceived*, that is, presumably, a being greater than can be comprehended, or fully understood. Thus we can know, Anselm thinks, that God is something than which nothing greater can be conceived without knowing fully what such a being is – that is, in Aquinas's way of putting the point, without knowing God's essence.

In his *Summa contra gentiles*, however, Aquinas makes this, more telling, objection:

> No difficulty befalls anyone who posits that God does not exist. For that, for any given thing, either in reality or in the understanding, something greater can be conceived, is a difficulty only to him who concedes that there is in reality something than which a greater cannot be conceived.[17]

In this passage Aquinas seems to be using Anselm's characterization of God to express the atheist's denial of God's existence. If to be God is, or would be, to be something than which nothing greater can be conceived, then for God to fail to exist is for (5) to be true. And, even if Anselm is right and the Fool who claims of something in the understanding that it is both something than which nothing greater can be conceived and something that fails to exist in reality contradicts himself, still, a more clever fool, one who insists on using (5) to express his atheism, would not contradict himself.

In my view, this "Thomistic/Russellian" response to Anselm's argument is a very serious objection to that argument. To say that it is a serious objection is not, however, to say that the Anselmian has no resources to respond to it. Perhaps the most effective response would be to argue for the reality of the intentional object, God-in-the-understanding. So far I have suggested arguing for the existence of this object as a way of allowing that a denial of God's existence might be meaningful, and even true. As we have seen from Aquinas and Russell, however, there is perhaps a better way to do that. A clever fool can succeed in denying the existence of something than which nothing greater can be conceived without appeal to an intermediate, mental or intentional object, in the understanding.

One could, however, take a different tack. One could argue that the history of Judaism, Christianity, and Islam provides evidence for supposing that there is a common object of worship in these traditions, a being than which nothing greater can be conceived. If we can provide evidence that there is indeed such a common object of worship, across various languages, and within different cultures, then we have good reason to say that God, not just as a formula or an idea, but as an object of worship, exists at least in the understanding. Having secured this referential peg, we could then follow Anselm's argument as before and prove, it seems, that God does not exist merely in the understanding, but in reality as well.

Proslogion 3

There is, of course, much more to Anselm's *Proslogion* than Chapter 2. In Chapter 3 Anselm argues that something than which nothing greater can be conceived not only exists in reality, it cannot be conceived *not to exist*. The proof of this conclusion, like the proof in later chapters that God is omnipotent, compassionate, supremely just, and so on, follows the pattern of proof established in *Proslogion* 2: Since x would be greater than y if x, but not y, could not be conceived *not* to exist, something than which nothing greater can be conceived is guaranteed to be such that it cannot be conceived not to exist.

The meaning of this surprising claim is not immediately obvious. Norman Malcolm, in the article of his referred to above, suggests that Anselm means by "God cannot be conceived not to exist" that God *necessarily exists*. He writes:

> What Anselm has proved is that the notion of contingent existence or of contingent nonexistence cannot have any application to God. His existence must either be logically necessary or logically impossible. The only intelligible way of rejecting Anselm's claim that God's existence is necessary is to maintain that the concept of God, as a being a greater than which cannot be conceived, is self-contradictory or nonsensical. Supposing that this is false, Anselm is right to deduce God's necessary existence from his characterization of Him as a being a greater than which cannot be conceived.[18]

Leibniz had made a somewhat similar claim. He chided Descartes for not bothering to establish that the existence of God is possible. He himself provided such a proof, with the assurance that if God's existence is possible, then it is necessary.[19]

It isn't, however, clear that Anselm understands "cannot be conceived not to exist" to mean "necessarily exists," let alone "exists by logical necessity." As I have already mentioned, Anselm argues in *Proslogion* 15 that God, i.e., something than which nothing greater can be conceived, is a being greater than can be conceived. By this claim he presumably means that God exceeds our powers of comprehension. In any case, he quite clearly does not mean that God is a being greater than is logically possible (and so, presumably, a logically impossible being).[20] Nevertheless, *Proslogion* 3 has inspired a tradition of developing ontological-style arguments, not just to prove that God exists, or exists in reality, but to prove that God has necessary existence.

Whether or not *Proslogion* 3 constitutes an independent argument for God's existence, it actually poses a threat to the cogency of Chapter 2. After all, as I have emphasized above, *Proslogion* 2 has the form of a *reductio*. In that reduction the Fool is made to state what is to be shown, by reduction, to lead to self-contradiction. But *Proslogion* 3 seems to conclude that, when the Fool says, "There is no God," he cannot even make sense of what he is saying. He cannot understand what he is saying precisely because, if the reasoning of *Proslogion* 3 is correct, God cannot be conceived not to exist.

Anselm addresses this new threat in Chapter 4, where he asks, appropriately, "How has the Fool said in his heart what he could not conceive?" Anselm replies that there are two ways of conceiving something in the heart, that is, two ways of having something in mind. In one way, he says, a thing is conceived when the word signifying it is thought, in another, when the object itself is understood. His idea seems to be that the Fool can conceive God according to the word and so state his atheism well enough for the *reductio* to work, even though his atheism rules out his being able to conceive God himself as not existing.

Does this move rescue the *reductio* of *Proslogion* 2? Or does it, perhaps, further cast the intelligibility of the reasoning there in doubt? After all, *Proslogion* 4 seems to allow the possibility that

(A1) "God" doesn't name anything

is a perfectly good way for the Fool to conceive God "according to the word" and thus to succeed in denying God's existence. But if the Fool insists on having his atheistic claim interpreted as (A1), it's hard to see how Anselm's style of argumentation can show atheism to be self-contradictory.

Again, Anselm does seem to have a plausible reply open to him. It is a pretty uninteresting atheism, he can say, that consists in making a claim about the English word, "God," or the Latin word, "deus," namely the claim that those particular words are empty. "You are something than which nothing greater can be conceived," Anselm says to God (or, as he supposes, to God), and then adds, "Or is there no such nature?" (*An ergo non est aliqua talis natura[?]*) For him the question of atheism should be the question of whether there exists, in reality, something than which nothing greater can be conceived. Can the Fool be coherently supposed to say these words, "either without any signification or with some extraneous signification" (*aut sine ulla aut com aliqua extranea significatione*) and manage, by these shabby means, to get God in his understanding?

Before we judge Anselm uncharitably on this question, it would be well to remember that, for a whole range of a priori truths, to attempt to prove them by *reductio* may land us in a similar puzzle. In a discussion of *reductio* arguments in mathematics, Alice Ambrose and Morris Lazerowitz have this to say:

> Still, there seems no escaping the question whether we are really making a *supposition* when we say "Suppose Goldbach's proposition is true" [that is, suppose there is an even number greater than 3 that is not the sum of two prime numbers], and whether we are really assuming anything when we start the proof of the irrationality

of √2 by saying "Suppose there is a rational number = √2". In the latter case the end result of the demonstration implies that we could not have conceived what we stated we were supposing. Are we merely going through the verbal motions of making an assumption or asking a question, without actually doing so? One can utter the words "I am in two different places simultaneously", but are we using the words to express something we are entertaining?[21]

Ambrose and Lazerowitz suggest in their article that "suppose" as it is used to introduce a statement in mathematics that is being reduced to absurdity has only an extended sense, since we can't really suppose the impossible. Similarly, Anselm suggests that "conceive" in our supposition that the Fool conceives God as not existing in reality must also be understood in an extended sense. The Fool can, so to speak, mumble inwardly the words, "Something than which nothing can be conceived." Even supposing that those words truly pick out God, when the Fool goes on to suppose that this something than which nothing greater can be conceived fails to exist in reality, he has failed to conceive God properly.

You might think that my efforts to defend Anselm have backfired. If I have succeeded in making plausible and appropriate Anselm's suggestion that the Fool mumbles the magic words and fails to appreciate their true signification, haven't I removed the peg *in intellectu* on which Anselm needs to hang the Fool's contradiction?

I don't think so. Whatever the Fool comes up with to associate with the words he mumbles in his heart ("something than which nothing greater can be conceived"), when he adds that it – that thing he has in mind, whatever it is – is both (a) something than which nothing greater can be conceived and (b) something that fails to exist in reality, the Fool has, Anselm can insist, contradicted himself. And that is the genius of Anselm's ontological argument, as he presents it in *Proslogion* 2.

Modal Arguments

I have already mentioned that Norman Malcolm claimed to find in *Proslogion* 3 a distinct ontological argument – one that would establish, not the mere existence of God, but God's necessary existence. Let's call any ontological argument meant to establish the *necessary* existence of God a "modal ontological argument." I have also suggested one reason for being skeptical about whether the argument Malcolm claims to find in Anselm is actually there. The reason for being skeptical is that "cannot be conceived not to exist" in *Proslogion* 3 does not mean "necessarily exists," let alone "exists by logical necessity."

There are, however, other passages in Anselm one might look to for an authentically modal argument. Robert Adams offers a very interesting reconstruction of an Anselmian text as a modal ontological argument.[22] But Adams looks for this proof, not to *Proslogion* 3, but rather to this rather turgid passage from the first chapter of *Liber apologeticus*, Anselm's reply to Gaunilo:

> For no one who denies or doubts that there exists something than which a greater cannot be conceived denies or doubts that if it did exist, its nonexistence, either in reality or in the understanding, would be impossible. For otherwise it would not be that than which a greater cannot be conceived. But as to whatever can be conceived and does not exist – if it did exist, its nonexistence, either in reality or in the understanding, would be possible. Therefore, if that than which a greater cannot be thought can even be conceived, it cannot be nonexistent.

From this passage Adams draws the following premise for his reconstruction of Anselm's argument (understanding "God" to be short for "something than which nothing greater can be conceived"):

(1)   Necessarily, if God exists then God necessarily exists.

To this premise Adams adds a second premise from the above passage, a premise which Adams identifies as an instantiation of Brouwer's axiom, a "somewhat controversial" axiom of modal logic:

(2)   If God does not exist, then necessarily it is not necessary that God exist.

One additional premise is needed, one which, Adams writes, "Anselm obviously meant his readers to supply," namely, the assumption "that the existence of a being than which nothing greater can be thought is at least possible," Thus:

(3)   It is not necessary that God does not exist.

With those three premises, plus some principles of modal logic, Adams produces a valid argument for the conclusion that, necessarily, God exists.

Robert Adams compares the argument he has reconstructed with a well-known modal argument proposed by Charles Hartshorne[23] and contrasts them both with the reasoning in *Proslogion* 2's "ontological" argument. He says that,

> unlike the argument of *Proslogion* 2, they need not depend on any assumptions at all about the relation of existence to predication. They do not presuppose that things which do not really exist can have predicates. They do not presuppose that existence, or existence in reality, is a predicate, nor even that necessary existence is a predicate. For their structure does not depend on predicate logic at all, but only on modal and nonmodal propositional logic.[24]

Adams thinks these differences mark an advantage for the modal argument he has reconstructed over the argument in *Proslogion* 2. But he takes a position quite like that of Leibniz in insisting that both arguments require the assumption that

God's existence is possible. "I think it is correct to say," he adds, "that although the modal argument for the existence of God helps us to see that the question of possibility is the crucial question about logically necessary divine existence, neither the modal nor the ontological argument [that is, the argument in *Proslogion* 2] provides us with grounds for answering it."[25]

David Lewis has offered a much-discussed modal ontological argument[26] that takes its initial inspiration from *Proslogion* 2 but moves quickly to translate it into possible-world semantics. Thus Lewis's first premise is "Whatever exists in the understanding can be conceived to exist in reality." Lewis understands this to mean "For any understandable being x, there is a world w such that x exists in w." Lewis, being a modal realist, supposes that things not in the actual world, but in other possible worlds, also exist. So he can make sense of Anselm's distinction between existing in the understanding alone and existing in reality as well. (Of course, only a limited number of things that exist in any possible world, including the actual one, have ever been thought about and so, in Anselm's way of putting matters, exist in the understanding.)

On the other hand, Lewis's modal realism leads him to deny that what we think of as the actual world has any special character, and so it leads him to reject this crucial premise of the ontological argument as he reconstructs it: "There is an understandable being x, such that for no world w and being y does the greatness of y in w exceed the greatness of x in the actual world." Here is part of Lewis's reasoning:

> Think of the ontological arguer in some dismally mediocre world – there are such ontological arguers – arguing that his world alone is actual, hence special, hence a fitting place of greatest greatness, hence a world wherein something exists than which no greater can be conceived to exist. He is wrong to argue thus. So are we.[27]

Alvin Plantinga, who has offered one of the recently most discussed modal arguments for God's existence, begins his chapter on "God and Necessity" in *The Nature of Necessity*[28] with a full quotation of *Proslogion* 2. Plantinga then turns what he considers to be the core of Anselm's reasoning into talk of logically possible worlds and, after a number of intermediate steps, finally ends up with the following, as we might say "stripped-down" version of the argument.

Where "unsurpassable greatness" is equivalent to "maximal excellence in every possible world:"

(42) There is a possible world in which unsurpassable greatness is exemplified.

(43) The proposition *a thing has unsurpassable greatness if and only if it has maximal excellence in every possible world* is necessarily true.

(44) The proposition *whatever has maximal excellence is omnipotent, omniscient, and morally perfect* is necessarily true.

[Therefore]

(45) *Possesses unsurpassable greatness* is instantiated in every world.[29]

The interested reader is invited to read Chapter 10 of Plantinga's classic work to see in detail how Plantinga motivates his movement from the text of *Proslogion* 2 to the "stripped-down" argument above. In the end Plantinga concedes, however, that this argument, for all its merits, "is not a successful piece of natural theology." The reason is, he says, that there are many properties, possibly instantiated, whose instantiation is incompatible with maximal greatness. So we need to know whether there is indeed a possible world in which maximal excellence in every possible world is exemplified, that is, whether it is possible that God, so understood, exists.

Peter van Inwagen has a somewhat different criticism of Plantinga's argument, and, indeed, of all ontological arguments for the existence of God. Even a minimal ontological argument, he insists, must presuppose that the property of existing at every possible world is compatible with the property of being a concrete entity, that is, something "we can see, hear, be cut or burned by, love, hate, worship, make, mend, trust in, fear, [or] covet."[30] Van Inwagen maintains, not only that we don't, in fact, know whether the property of necessary existence is compatible with the property of being a concrete entity, but that we *cannot* know whether they are compatible. If we cannot know whether the existence of God, as traditionally conceived, is thus even possible, then, it seems, any ontological argument will fail.

Graham Oppy has recently published a masterful summary and critical assessment[31] of the huge body of recent literature on Anselm's original argument, and the many related arguments it has inspired. Oppy's impressive work gives remarkable testimony to the high level of logical, philosophical, and scholarly understanding that has gone into recent discussion of Anselmian types of reasoning concerning knowledge of the existence of God. From his book we learn in rich detail that modern counterparts to Anselm's Fool, on whose behalf Gaunilo first wrote, have become, if not wise fools, certainly very sophisticated ones.

Notes

1 Bertrand Russell, "My Intellectual Development," in P. Schilpp, ed., *The Philosophy of Bertrand Russell*, second edn. (New York: Tudor, 1946), p. 10.
2 New York: Simon and Schuster, 1945, p. 417.
3 Ibid.
4 Mark 9:23–4.
5 Augustine, *Confessions*, 1.1.1.
6 More carefully, he thought, we couldn't meaningfully and truly say of anything that it *is not*. For him "is not" includes "doesn't exist," but also "is not F," for example, "is not wise." Thus he thought not only that we couldn't get away with saying truly and meaningfully, "Socrates does not exist," but equally that we couldn't truly and meaningfully say, "Socrates is not wise," on the grounds that the latter amounts to

"Wise Socrates doesn't exist." (See Montgomery Furth, "Elements of Eleatic Ontology," *Journal of the History of Philosophy*, 6 (1968), pp. 111–32.)

7   "The fool says in his heart, 'There is no God'" is the first verse of both Psalm 14 and Psalm 53.

8   Cf. Georges Dicker, "A Refutation of Rowe's Critique of Anselm's Argument," *Faith and Philosophy*, 5 (1988), pp. 193–202, esp. 200–1.

9   O. K. Bouwsma, "Anselm's Argument," in *Without Proof of Evidence: Essays of O. K. Bouwsma*, ed. J. L. Croft and Ronald E. Hustwit (Lincoln: University of Nebraska Press, 1984), p. 56. Bouwsma suggests that the Psalmist's fool might be someone who "stands grim at the door [of the temple], looking in upon those old men in their little black caps," but he does not go in.

10 Norman Malcolm, "Anselm's Ontological Arguments," *The Philosophical Review*, 69 (1960), p. 43.

11 Ibid., p. 44. This is a quote from Norman Kemp Smith (trans.), *Immanuel Kant's Critique of Pure Reason* (London, 1929), p. 505.

12 Kemp Smith, *Critique of Pure Reason*, p. 504.

13 *Pro insipiente* 6.

14 Cf. Alvin Plantinga, *God, Freedom, and Evil* (New York: Harper and Row, 1974), pp. 91ff.

15 But see my "Aquinas on Saying that God Doesn't Exist," *The Monist*, 47 (1963), pp. 472–7.

16 *Summa theologica* 1a.q2.

17 *Summa contra gentiles* 1.11.

18 Malcolm, "Anselm's Ontological Arguments," p. 49.

19 For a full discussion of Leibniz's attempts to show that the existence of God is possible see Robert Adams, *Leibniz: Determinist, Theist, Idealist* (New York: Oxford University Press, 1994) pp. 135–213.

20 Cf. Gareth B. Matthews, "On Conceivability in Anselm and Malcolm," *The Philosophical Review*, 70 (1961), pp. 110–11.

21 Alice Ambrose and Morris Lazerowitz, "Assuming the Logically Impossible," *Metaphilosophy*, 15 (1984), p. 93.

22 Robert Adams, "The Logical Structure of Anselm's Argument," *The Philosophical Review*, 80 (1971), pp. 41–8.

23 Charles Hartshorne, *The Logic of Perfection* (La Salle, Ill.: Open Court, 1962), pp. 50–1.

24 Adams, "Logical Structure," pp. 44–5.

25 Ibid., p. 48.

26 David Lewis, "Anselm and Actuality," *Noûs*, 4 (1970), pp. 175–88. Reprinted with a postscript in David Lewis, *Philosophical Papers* (New York: Oxford University Press, 1983), vol. 1, pp. 1–25.

27 Ibid., p. 20.

28 Alvin Plantinga, *The Nature of Necessity* (Oxford: Oxford University Press, 1974), pp. 197–221.

29 Ibid., p. 216.

30 Peter van Inwagen, "Ontological Arguments," *Noûs*, 11 (1977), p. 380.

31 Graham Oppy, *Ontological Arguments and Belief in God* (New York: Cambridge University Press, 1996).

Suggested Further Reading

Barnes, Jonathan (1972) *The Ontological Argument*. London: Macmillan.

Barth, Karl (1960) *Anselm: Fides quaerens intellectum*, trans. I. Robertson. London: Macmillan.

Berg, Jan (1961) An Examination of the Ontological Proof. *Theoria*, 27, 99–106.

Charlesworth, M. J. (1965) *St. Anselm's Proslogion*. Oxford: Oxford University Press.

Coburn, Robert (1963) Professor Malcolm on God. *Australasian Journal of Philosophy*, 41, 143–62.

Hick, John, and McGill, Arthur (eds.) (1967) *The Many-Faced Argument: Recent Studies on the Ontological Argument for the Existence of God*. New York: Macmillan.

Mann, William E. (1967) Definite Descriptions and the Ontological Argument. *Theoria*, 33, 211–29.

Mann, William E. (1972) The Ontological Presuppositions of the Ontological Argument. *The Review of Metaphysics*, 26, 260–77.

Plantinga, Alvin (ed.) (1965) *The Ontological Argument*. New York: Doubleday.

Rowe, William L. (1989) *The Ontological Argument*. In Joel Feinberg (ed.), *Reason and Responsibility*, seventh edn. (pp. 8–17). Belmont, Calif.: Wadsworth.

Chapter 5

Cosmological Arguments

William L. Rowe

Within philosophy of religion, a cosmological argument is understood to be an argument from the existence of the world to the existence of God. Typically, such arguments proceed in two steps. The first step argues from the existence of the world to the existence of a first cause or necessary being that accounts for the existence of the world. The second step argues that such a first cause or necessary being has, or would very likely have, the properties associated with the idea of God. Cosmological arguments appeared in Plato and Aristotle, played a prominent role in Jewish, Christian, and Islamic thought during the medieval period, and were forcefully presented in the eighteenth century by the German philosopher Leibniz and the English theologian Samuel Clarke. In the modern period these arguments, particularly as presented by Aquinas, Leibniz, and Clarke, have been severely criticized by Hume, Kant, and others. Since the second half of the twentieth century, however, there has been a revival of interest in cosmological arguments, and several challenges to the major criticisms of these arguments have appeared.

Cosmological arguments may be divided into two broad types: those that depend on a premise denying an infinite regress of causes and those that do not depend on such a premise. Among the former are contained the first "three ways" presented by Aquinas, as well as an interesting argument, developed by Islamic thinkers, that the world cannot be infinitely old and, therefore, must have come into existence by the creative will of God. An important difference between the arguments represented by Aquinas's first "three ways" and the Islamic argument is that while both reject an infinite regress of causes, only the latter bases the objection on the alleged impossibility of an infinite *temporal* regress. Unlike Bonaventure, who adopted the Islamic argument, Aquinas did not think that philosophy could show that the world had a temporal beginning. But whether the world had a temporal beginning or has always existed, he insisted that the world requires a cause. For, according to Aquinas, things that now exist require a presently existing cause that *sustains* them in existence, and the series of sustaining causes (an essentially ordered series of causes), he argued, does terminate in a first cause. He therefore rejected an infinite regress of essentially ordered causes (a *non-temporal* causal series), identifying God as the first cause in such a non-temporal series. Leibniz and Clarke, however, allowed an infinite regress of causes, arguing only that there must be a sufficient reason for the existence of such a series of causes. Thus, unlike the cosmological arguments of both Bonaventure and Aquinas, the eighteenth-century arguments of Leibniz and Clarke do not depend on rejecting an infinite regress of causes. Appealing to the principle of sufficient reason, Leibniz and Clarke insist only that such a series could not be self-explanatory and, therefore, would require an explanation in the causal activity of some being outside the series.

Cosmological arguments relying on philosophical objections to an infinite *temporal* series of causes typically proceed as follows.

(1)   Whatever begins to exist has a cause.
(2)   The world began to exist.
(3)   Therefore, the world has a cause of its existence.

The philosophical argument for premise (2) is based on the alleged impossibility of an infinite series of past events. Why is such a series thought to be impossible? If we begin with some present event and consider further events proceeding endlessly into the future, such a series is *potentially infinite*. For at any future event in the series there will have actually occurred only a finite number of events between that event and the present event. But if we think of events preceding endlessly into the past from the present, we would be thinking of an infinite series that has actually occurred, a series that is *actually infinite*. The claim is that while a series of events can be potentially infinite, it cannot be actually infinite. So, the world could not have always existed. Arguments in support of this view are presented in William Craig (1979).

It must be admitted that it is difficult to imagine an absolutely infinite number of temporally discrete events having already occurred. But just what is the philosophical objection to it? It is sometimes suggested that if the series of events prior to the present is actually infinite, then there must be events in the past that are separated from the present by an infinite number of events. But this suggestion seems mistaken. As Quentin Smith (1987) argues, no particular past event is separated from the present by an infinite number of events. It is sometimes suggested that if the past is actually infinite then new events cannot be *added* to the series, for the series thus added to would be the same size as the series before the addition was made. The response given to this objection is that one can add to an infinite collection even though the number of entities in the collection before the addition will be the same as the number of entities in the collection after the addition. The fact that this is so does not prevent the old collection from being a proper subset of the collection composed of the old collection and the new member. For reasons such as these, many philosophers who have studied these matters remain unconvinced that an actually infinite series of past events is impossible.

In addition to the philosophical argument against the possibility that the world has always existed, some proponents endeavor to support premise (2) by appealing to recent scientific theories that imply that the world had a beginning. For example, they appeal to the Big Bang theory, according to which the universe probably began to exist some 10 to 20 billion years ago. After considering the more strictly philosophical versions of the cosmological argument we will examine the Big Bang theory and the version of the cosmological argument based on that theory.

A good example of a cosmological argument based on a rejection of a *non-temporal* infinite regress of causes is Aquinas's second way. This argument may be summarized as follows:

(1) Some things exist and their existence is caused.
(2) Whatever is caused to exist is caused to exist by something else.
(3) An infinite regress of (non-temporal) causes resulting in the existence of anything is impossible.
(4) Therefore, there is a first cause of existence.

There are two major difficulties in assessing the third premise of this argument. First, there is the difficulty of understanding exactly what a non-temporal causal series is. Second, there is the difficulty of determining exactly why such a series cannot proceed to infinity. To resolve the first difficulty we must distinguish the *earlier* cause that brought some presently existing object into existence from whatever *presently existing* things are causally responsible for its existence at this very moment. The basic idea is that if A (a human being, say) now exists, A is right now being caused to exist by something else B, which may itself be simultaneously caused by C to be causing A to exist. Although A would not exist now had it not been brought into existence by something else that existed temporally prior to A (a temporal causal series), it is also true, so Aquinas thought, that A would not *now* exist were it not now being caused to exist by something else B (a non-temporal causal series). In such a non-temporal series of causes of A's present existence, Aquinas held that the cause of any member in the series either is the first cause in the series or is itself being caused to cause that member by some non-temporally prior cause in the series.

Although Aquinas allowed that it is theoretically possible for a temporal series of causes to proceed backwards to infinity, he thought it obvious that a non-temporal causal series must terminate in a first member, itself uncaused. But why is this supposed to be obvious? Presumably, the idea is that it is obvious that if B is right now causing A to exist, and C is right now causing B to be causing A to exist, then if C and every prior member in the series were to have the same status as B, no causing would be occurring at all. Or, to put it differently, if there were no first cause in this series it would be simply inexplicable that such a series of causings is actually occurring. But once the argument is put in this fashion it invites the skeptical challenge that the fact that such causing goes on may simply be inexplicable. Thus, understanding the third premise of this argument and determining exactly why it must be true has proved to be difficult. And, of course, it would be question-begging to simply *define* a non-temporal causal series as one that terminates in a first cause. As a result, many philosophers find the argument unconvincing.

As noted above, the cosmological arguments developed by Leibniz and Clarke do not depend on a premise that rejects an infinite regress of causes. What they do depend on is a rather strong explanatory principle according to which there must be a determining reason for the existence of any being whatever. If we think of a *dependent being* as a being whose determining reason lies in the causal activity of other beings, and think of a *self-existent being* as a being whose determining reason lies within its own nature, the first step of Clarke's cosmological argument can be put as follows.

(1) Every being (that exists or ever did exist) is either a dependent being or a self-existent being.
(2) Not every being can be a dependent being.
(3) Therefore, there exists a self-existent being.

While the principle that there must be a determining reason for the existence of any being whatever immediately yields premise (1), it is difficult to see how it establishes premise (2). For if we allow for an infinite regress of dependent beings, each having the reason for its existence in some preceding member of the series, it is difficult to see how any being exists that lacks a reason or explanation of its existence. Of course, if we view the infinite series of dependent beings as itself a dependent being, we might argue that unless there is a self-existent being there would be no determining reason for the existence of the series itself. But it does not seem right to view the succession or series of dependent beings as still another dependent being. So, as strong as the principle we are considering appears to be, it does not appear to be strong enough to do away with the supposition that every being that exists or ever did exist is a dependent being. To carry out this task the cosmological arguments of Leibniz and Clarke required a stronger principle, the principle of sufficient reason (PSR).

The explanatory principle we've been considering is restricted to requiring an explanation for the existence of individual beings. PSR is a principle concerning facts, including facts consisting in the existence of individual beings. But PSR also requires an explanation for facts about individual beings, for example, the fact that John is happy. In addition, PSR requires an explanation for general facts such as the fact that someone is happy or the fact that there are dependent beings. Leibniz expresses PSR as the principle "that no fact can be real or existent, no statement true, unless there be a sufficient reason why it is so and not otherwise" (Leibniz, 1951, paragraph 32). And Clarke asserts: "Undoubtedly nothing is, without a sufficient reason why it is, rather than not; and why it is thus, rather than otherwise" (Clarke, 1956, third reply).

If we understand a contingent fact to be a fact that possibly might not have been a fact at all, it is clear that Leibniz held that every contingent fact has a sufficient reason or explanation. And so long as we restrict ourselves to contingent facts concerning the existence of things, it is clear that Clarke held that all such facts must have a sufficient reason. If either view should be correct, it does seem that Clarke's premise (2) must be true. For if every being were dependent it does seem that there would be a contingent fact without any explanation – the fact that there are dependent beings. But if PSR is true, the fact that there are dependent beings must have an explanation or sufficient reason. So, given Clarke's convictions about PSR, it is understandable why he should hold that not every being can be a dependent being. For if every being that exists or ever did exist is a dependent being, what could possibly be the sufficient reason for the fact that there are dependent beings? It won't do to point to some particular dependent being and observe that it produced other dependent beings. The question why there are any dependent beings cannot be answered by appealing to the causal activity of some particular dependent being, any more than the question why there are any human beings can be answered by appealing to Adam and Eve and their causal activity in producing other human beings. Nor will it do to observe that there always have been dependent beings engaged in causing other dependent beings. The question why there are any dependent beings cannot be answered by noting that there always have been dependent beings any more than the question why there are any elephants can be answered simply by observing that there always have been elephants. To note that there always have been elephants may explain how long elephants have been in existence, but it won't explain why there are elephants at all.

Should we conclude that the premises in Clarke's cosmological argument are true? No. For at best all we have seen is that the premises are true *if* PSR is true. But what of PSR itself? Is it true? In its unrestricted form PSR holds that every fact has an explanation; in its restricted form it holds that every contingent fact has an explanation. Even if we take PSR in its restricted form, there are serious objections to it.

One objection to PSR is that it cannot avoid the dark night of Spinozism, a night in which all facts appear to be necessary. This difficulty was particularly acute for Leibniz. He explained God's creation of this world by this world's being the best and God's choosing to create the best. But what accounts for God's choosing to create the best, rather than some inferior world or none at all? God chooses the best because of his absolute perfection – being absolutely perfect he naturally chooses to create the best. The difficulty is that God's being perfect is, for Leibniz, a necessary fact. It seems, then, that God's choice to create the best must also be necessary and, consequently, the existence of this world is necessary. If we avoid this conclusion by saying that God's being perfect is not the sufficient reason of his choice to create the best we run into an infinite regress of explanations of his choice to create the best. For suppose we say that it is God's perfection in conjunction with his choice to exercise his goodness that constitutes the sufficient reason for his choice to create the best. What then of his choice to exercise his goodness? A similar problem would arise in providing a sufficient reason for it. And we seem to be off to the races, each reason determining a choice only by virtue of a prior choice to act in accordance with that reason.

The problem of God's creation being necessary can be avoided by denying that there is a best possible world. For, if for every possible world there is a better possible world, it would seem to suffice that God creates, perhaps freely, a very good world, even though for any such world there is a better he could have created instead. But there would still remain a problem for PSR. PSR requires that God have a sufficient reason to create the particular world he chooses to create. But it is doubtful on the no best world hypothesis that God would have a *sufficient* reason for creating the world he does, rather than some equally good or better world.

A second objection to PSR holds that it is impossible for every contingent fact to have an explanation. For consider the huge conjunctive fact whose conjuncts are all the other contingent facts that there are. This huge conjunctive fact must itself be a contingent fact, otherwise its conjuncts would not all be contingent. Now what can be the sufficient reason for this huge conjunctive fact? It cannot be some necessary fact. For the sufficient reason for a fact is another fact that entails it; and whatever is entailed by a necessary fact is itself necessary. The huge conjunctive fact cannot be its own sufficient reason since only a necessary fact could be self-explanatory. So, the sufficient reason for the huge conjunctive fact would have to be one of the contingent facts that is a conjunct of it. But then that conjunct would have to be a sufficient reason for itself, since whatever is a sufficient reason for a conjunctive fact must be a sufficient reason for each of its conjuncts. It follows, then, that the huge conjunctive fact cannot have an explanation. It thus appears that PSR is false. I am inclined to think this argument against the truth of PSR has merit. However, Vallicella (1997) has criticized it on the grounds that a simple list of truths – say, p, q, r, etc. – may suffice to explain the contingent, conjunctive fact that (p & q & r & etc.). And if this is so, then the fact that each conjunct in the infinite conjunction is true may explain the fact that the infinite conjunction is true. Whereas, it would be odd to suggest the reverse: that each conjunct's being true is explained by the fact that the infinite conjunction is itself true.

In the above argument it is important not to confuse the huge conjunctive fact constituted by every other contingent fact with the general fact that there are contingent facts. The latter fact – that there are contingent facts – is not itself a contingent fact. It is a necessary fact. For every possible world contains some contingent fact or other. Consider the contingent fact that there are elephants. That there are elephants is a fact in the actual world. But if some possible world in which there are no elephants were to be actual, it would be a fact that there are no elephants. So, no matter what possible world is actual, either that *there are elephants* will be a fact or that *there are no elephants* will be a fact. Thus, that there are contingent facts is itself a necessary fact. But the huge conjunctive fact described above is itself a contingent fact. Had some other possible world been actual, the huge conjunctive fact described above would not have been a fact.

A third, somewhat more complicated, argument against PSR has been advanced by Rowe (1975). Consider the idea of a positive, contingent state of affairs, where x is a positive contingent state of affairs if and only if from the fact that x obtains it follows that at least one contingent being exists. Given this account, it is clear, for example, that *there being elephants* is a positive contingent state of affairs. For, since elephants are contingent beings, from the fact that *there being elephants* obtains, it follows that at least one contingent being exists. *There being no unicorns,* however, is not a positive contingent state of affairs. Consider now the following state of affairs:

(T)   There being positive contingent states of affairs.

(T) itself also is a positive contingent state of affairs. For if (T) obtains then it must also be true that at least one contingent being exists. But could there be a sufficient reason for the fact that (T) obtains? No. That it is impossible for there to be a sufficient reason for the fact that (T) obtains follows from two considerations. First, any sufficient reason (full explanation) for the fact that (T) obtains would itself be a positive contingent state of affairs. For from the fact that (T) obtains it follows that at least one contingent being exists. Therefore, since any sufficient reason for (T) would entail (T), and therefore entail whatever is entailed by (T), any sufficient reason for (T) would entail that at least one contingent being exists, and thus would itself be a positive contingent state of affairs.

This first consideration establishes that any sufficient reason for (T) must itself be a positive contingent state of affairs. Now we come to the second consideration. Any sufficient reason for the fact that (T) (there being positive contingent states of affairs) must constitute a full explanation for why there are positive contingent states of affairs. But surely, nothing that itself is a positive contingent state of affairs can be an explanation for why there are positive contingent states of affairs. For such a proposed explanation is simply circular. Rowe suggests that we can see the circularity involved by considering the following example. Suppose we try to explain why there are positive contingent states of affairs by citing the fact, let us suppose, that God willed that positive contingent states of affairs be actual – just as, for example, we might explain why there are men by citing the (supposed) fact that God willed that men should exist. The fact, then, consisting of God's willing that positive contingent states of affairs be actual is what explains why there are positive contingent states of affairs. But now let us consider the fact of God's willing that positive contingent states of affairs be actual. If that fact does explain why there are positive contingent states of affairs it must entail that some positive contingent states of affairs are actual. And if this is so, then the fact that God willed that there be positive contingent states of affairs entails that at least one contingent being exists. We then ask whether the fact in question is contingent or necessary. It cannot be necessary, for then it would be necessary that at least one contingent being exists – and, as we have seen, it seems to be a contingent matter that contingent beings exists. What follows, then, is that the fact consisting of God's willing that positive contingent states of affairs be actual is *itself* a positive contingent state of affairs; for it is contingent and, from the fact that it obtains, it follows that at least one contingent being exists. But clearly, the fact that *accounts* for why there are positive contingent states of affairs *cannot* itself be a positive contingent state of affairs.

As with the previous two objections to PSR, this objection also has been criticized in the literature on the cosmological argument. Quentin Smith (1995) argues that it is a mistake to think that there can be no sufficient reason for the fact that there are positive contingent states of affairs.

> All that needs to be explained is that there obtain positive contingent states of affairs, which is logically equivalent to the state of affairs *that there are contingent concrete objects.* Now this state of affairs does appear to have an explanation, namely, by the state of affairs: (s) God wills that there are contingent concrete objects. (Smith, 1995, p. 240)

What Smith says here seems right. The fact (supposing it is a fact) that God wills that there be contingent concrete objects does explain the fact that there are contingent concrete objects. But the issue is whether God's willing that there be contingent concrete objects can explain the fact that there are positive contingent states of affairs. To arrive at this further point, Smith appeals to what he calls "the principle of explanatory equivalence." According to this principle if p explains q, and r is "relevantly equivalent" to q, p also explains r. To understand this principle it is important to distinguish "strict equivalence" from "relevance equivalence." The proposition

> An isosceles triangle has three angles.

is strictly equivalent to

> All red things are red.

since any possible world in which the one is true is a world in which the other is true. If the principle of explanatory equivalence were stated in terms of strict equivalence it would clearly fall prey to obvious counterexamples. For an explanation of why an isosceles triangle has three angles need not be an explanation of why all red things are red. For two propositions to be *relevantly* equivalent, each must relevantly imply the other. And one proposition relevantly implies another if and only if it strictly implies it by virtue of its meaning. Smith then points out that the proposition

There are positive contingent truths.

is relevantly equivalent to

There are contingent concrete objects.

and concludes that since

God wills that there are contingent concrete objects.

explains the fact that there are contingent concrete objects, it also explains the fact that there are positive contingent truths.

The difficulty with Smith's argument is that the principle of explanatory equivalence is false. And, as argued in Rowe (1997), it is not just false when equivalence is understood as *strict* equivalence, it is also false when equivalence is understood as *relevance* equivalence. Consider, for example, the propositions

John is angry at t.

and

John exists at t and John is angry at t.

These two propositions are relevantly equivalent in Smith's sense. But an explanation of the former need not be an explanation of the latter. It is one thing to explain why John is angry at t and another thing to explain why he exists at t.

Given the attacks on PSR and the debate over the cogency of those attacks, it's clear that PSR is subject to significant objections, even if these objections themselves are not conclusive. In light of this, perhaps the best option for the proponent of the version of the cosmological argument set forth by Samuel Clarke is to employ a principle that is weaker than PSR, not subject to the objections to PSR that we've discussed, but still strong enough to support the premises of Clarke's argument. A principle like the following may satisfy these conditions.

(A) For every kind of being such that beings of that kind can be caused to exist or can cause the existence of other beings, there must be a sufficient reason for the existence of each being of that kind and for the general fact that there exist beings of that kind.

This principle is at least as initially plausible as PSR. What distinguishes it from PSR is that it does not require that every fact, or even every contingent fact, has an explanation. Also, it does not imply that every positive contingent state of affairs has an explanation. But since it is a fact that there are dependent beings, principle (A) requires that there be a sufficient reason (full explanation) for the fact that there are dependent beings. So principle (A), rather than the much stronger PSR, is all we need in order to justify the second premise of Clarke's cosmological argument: Not every being can be a dependent being. For as we've seen, if every being were dependent any proposed explanation of why there are dependent beings would be viciously circular. Thus, if every being (that can be caused or can cause other things to exist) were dependent, there would be a kind of being (dependent) such that the fact that there are beings of that kind would have no explanation. Also, so long as the first premise of Clarke's argument is restricted to beings that either can be caused or can cause the existence of other beings, principle (A) will justify the first premise: Every being is either a dependent being or a self-existent being. We should also note that principle (A), unlike PSR, does not raise problems for free acts of will. While there may be a determining cause of an individual being free (in the incompatibilist's sense) to will or not will, there can be no determining cause of the agent's freely causing one volition rather than another. It was this issue that made Clarke hesitant to fully endorse Leibniz's statement of the principle of sufficient reason. Principle (A) does not conflict with the existence of free acts of will. God's freely choosing to create Adam may constitute a determining cause of the existence of Adam. And this may be true even though there is no determining cause of God's freely choosing to create Adam.

What we've seen is that there is a weaker principle than PSR that supports the two premises of Clarke's cosmological argument equally well but is not subject to the objections raised against PSR. Should we then declare victory for Clarke's argument and conclude that it does prove there exists a being whose existence is accounted for by its own nature (a self-existent being)? This would be premature unless we are in the position of knowing that principle (A) is true. And it is doubtful that we do know that principle (A) is true. Short of a proof of principle (A), perhaps the best that can be said is that when we reflect on our cognitive expectations of the world we discover ourselves operating with something like principle (A) as a presupposition of inquiry. And if we do conclude that this is so and we come to see that Clarke's premises are supported by principle (A), we would be inconsistent in rejecting the premises of Clarke's cosmological argument.

Earlier we noted that in addition to the *philosophical* argument against the possibility that the world has always existed, we may appeal to a *scientific* argument to support premise (2) of the following argument.

(1) Whatever begins to exist has a cause.
(2) The world began to exist.
(3) Therefore, the world has a cause of its existence.

The scientific argument involves the Big Bang theory according to which the world began to exist some 10 to 20 billion years ago. The standard Big Bang theory holds that the present universe, if continually traced backwards in time, would continually diminish both spatially and temporally until finally reaching

– between 10 and 20 billion years ago – what is called a *singularity*, which for practical purposes can be understood to be a point at which the universe came into existence in an explosion of such force that since then the universe has been continually expanding outwards. An important part of this scientific theory is that space and time also came to exist with the Big Bang, making it difficult to intelligibly ask "What, if anything, transpired *before* the Big Bang?", or "Just *where* in space did the Big Bang occur?" Nevertheless, since science tells us that the universe is finitely old, and since, according to our first premise the universe would then require a cause, it appears that we are only left to determine whether that cause would possess the properties of the theistic God. But before turning to that question, it should be noted that critical questions have been raised about the first premise of this argument. Since on the current scientific theory of the origin of the universe there is no time prior to the Big Bang, some philosophers have concluded that there cannot be a cause of the Big Bang since, on their view, a cause must be temporally prior to its effect. In addition, it is argued that since all we have evidence for concerning the coming into existence of physical things is evidence for things being produced out of *earlier existing things*, we have no reason to think that the universe was caused to come into existence – for that would be something being caused to come into existence out of nothing at all. And even if there is no impossibility in the idea of something being produced out of absolutely nothing, we have no evidence at all that it ever occurs. To these objections defenders of the first premise of the argument have argued that simultaneous causation is possible, and have contended that the first premise of the argument (Whatever begins to exist has a cause) is not grounded on our experience of how things come to exist from pre-existing things. Instead, they hold that the first premise, while not true by virtue of the meaning of its terms, is, nevertheless, metaphysically necessary in the way in which the proposition expressed by "An effect never precedes its cause" is thought to be metaphysically necessary, even though it is not necessary simply by virtue of the meanings of its terms. So they may admit that in our experience things that are caused to come into existence are produced out of earlier existing things, but argue that the first premise of the argument (Whatever begins to exist has a cause) is metaphysically necessary, and therefore not dependent for confirmation on the evidence derived from our experience of how things come to exist in the universe. And there is another possible basis for support to which the defender of the first premise may appeal. For it does seem that many, if not all, of us are so constituted that we cannot help but believe, or at least expect, that if something comes into existence then there is a cause or explanation of its coming into existence. It is as though we are hard-wired to view our world in this way. Perhaps we are mistaken in having this belief or expectation. After all, the world doesn't have to be the way we are bound to expect it to be. But if we are so constituted as to expect or believe that things can't just pop into existence without a cause or explanation, then we would be inconsistent to also believe that there is no cause or explanation for the coming to be of the universe in the Big Bang.

Supposing that it is reasonable to infer a cause of the Big Bang, is there any good reason to identify that cause with the God of traditional theism, an infinitely powerful, all-knowing, eternal, perfectly good being? Here the proponent of the cosmological argument is confronted with the rather difficult task of justifying the view that whatever caused the universe has the properties of the theistic God. And while it is clear that whatever caused the Big Bang would possess enormous power, it is quite difficult to see how a successful argument can be made for the cause of the universe being a perfectly good being. There is some reason, perhaps, to view the eternal cause of the universe as a person. Craig, for example, argues as follows.

> Moreover, the personhood of the cause of the universe is implied by its timelessness and immateriality, since the only entities we know of which can possess such properties are either minds or abstract objects, and abstract objects do not stand in causal relations. Therefore, the transcendent cause of the origin of the universe must be of the order of mind. (Craig, 1999, pp. 734–5)

Since space, time, and matter come to exist in the Big Bang, Craig reasons that on the premise that the universe has a cause of its coming to exist, its cause must be both timeless and immaterial. But how do we get from the timelessness and immateriality of the cause of the universe to the conclusion that the cause of the universe must be a person? Given that a mind is a person, Craig proposes the following argument.

(1) The cause of the universe is timeless and immaterial.
(2) The only entities we know of which can be timeless and immaterial are minds or abstract objects.
(3) Abstract objects cannot cause something to come into existence.
Therefore,
(4) The cause of the universe is a mind (i.e., a person).

As it stands, there are two difficulties in Craig's argument. First, the argument is invalid. Given its premises, for the argument to be valid the conclusion has to be

(4a) The only entity we know of which can be the cause of the universe is a mind.

But (4a), due to the limitations of our knowledge, leaves it open that the cause of the universe is not a mind at all. For it may be both that among the entities we know of only a mind could cause the Big Bang and that, owing to the paucity of our knowledge, the cause of the universe is not a mind. And if we render the argument valid by replacing premise (2) with

(2a) The only entities which can be timeless and immaterial are minds or abstract objects.

we face the formidable difficulty of establishing the truth of (2a). Why suppose that human knowledge has a grasp of all the possible kinds of timeless and immaterial entities there may be? Or, even supposing we do have such a grasp, why suppose we know them all well enough to know that among them only minds cause something to come into existence? So, when we render Craig's argument valid by replacing (4) with (4a), the conclusion doesn't give us what Craig wants to establish. And if we render his argument valid by replacing (2) with (2a), we will then have a valid argument for the conclusion Craig wants at the cost of introducing a premise that we don't know to be true.

Even granting that the cause of the Big Bang is a mind, is it clear that it is a single mind rather than a multiplicity of minds who collaborated on the project of producing the Big Bang? Or, supposing it is shown that it is likely that the cause of the Big Bang is a single, immensely powerful mind, why suppose that this immensely powerful mind is God, an eternal being of such immense goodness, knowledge, and power that it is not possible for there to have been a better, wiser, or more powerful being than it? And what of the eternal existence of this mind who caused the universe to come into existence? Is it just an accident that it eternally exists, as opposed to not existing at all? If so, it would not satisfy one standard conception of the theistic God. But why isn't it just an accident? What philosophical principle justifies us in taking its eternal existence to be metaphysically necessary? And what proof can we give of that principle? Perhaps, however, God need not be taken to be a metaphysically necessary being. Perhaps by virtue of the simplicity of his nature, God provides a more plausible explanation for the temporally finite existence of the world than we would have if there were no God. If so, then the cosmological argument might justify belief in God without our having to suppose that God's existence is metaphysically necessary. But until we have convincing answers to these and other skeptical questions, the version of the cosmological argument based on the Big Bang theory will fall short of a successful argument for the existence of the God of traditional theism. Nevertheless, it must be acknowledged that the emergence of the Big Bang theory of the origin of the universe has given new weight to an argument for the existence of some sort of creator.

References

Clarke, Samuel, and Leibniz, Gottfried (1956) *The Leibniz–Clarke Correspondence*, ed. H. G. Alexander. Manchester: Manchester University Press. Originally published in 1717.

Craig, William Lane (1979) *The Kalam Cosmological Argument*. London: Macmillan.

Craig, William Lane (1999) The Ultimate Question of Origins: God and the Beginning of the Universe. *Astrophysics and Space Science*, 269–70, 723–40.

Leibniz, Gottfried (1951) Monadology. In P. P. Wiener (ed.), *Leibniz Selections*. New York: Charles Scribner's Sons. Originally published in 1714.

Rowe, William L. (1975) *The Cosmological Argument*. Princeton: Princeton University Press. Reprinted with a new foreword by Fordham University Press, 1998.

Rowe, William L. (1997) Circular Explanations, Cosmological Arguments, and The Principle of Sufficient Reason. *Midwest Studies in Philosophy*, 21, 188–201.

Smith, Quentin (1987) Infinity and the Past. *Philosophy of Science*, 54, 63–75.

Smith, Quentin (1995) Explanatory Rationalism and Contingent Truths. *Religious Studies*, 31, 237–42.

Vallicella, William (1997) On an Insufficient Argument Against Sufficient Reason. *Ratio*, 11, 76–81.

Suggested Further Reading

Craig, William Lane (1980) *The Cosmological Argument from Plato to Lebiniz*. London: Macmillan.

Swinburne, Richard (1979) *The Existence of God*. Oxford: Oxford University Press.

Van Inwagen, Peter (1993) *Metaphysics*. San Francisco: Westview Press. Chapter 6.

The Design Argument

Elliott Sober

The design argument is one of three main arguments for the existence of God; the others are the ontological argument and the cosmological argument. Unlike the ontological argument, the design argument and the cosmological argument are a posteriori. And whereas the cosmological argument can focus on any present event to get the ball rolling (arguing that it must trace back to a first cause, namely God), design theorists are usually more selective.

Design arguments have typically been of two types – *organismic* and *cosmic*. Organismic design arguments start with the observation that organisms have features that adapt them to the environments in which they live and that exhibit a kind of *delicacy*. Consider, for example, the vertebrate eye. This organ helps organisms survive by permitting them to perceive objects in their environment. And were the parts of the eye even slightly different in their shape and assembly, the resulting organ would not allow us to see. Cosmic design arguments begin with an observation concerning features of the entire cosmos – the universe obeys simple laws, it has a kind of stability, its physical features permit life and intelligent life to exist. However, not all design arguments fit into these two neat compartments. Kepler, for example, thought that the face we see when we look at the moon requires explanation in terms of intelligent design. Still, the common thread is that design theorists describe some empirical feature of the world and argue that this feature points towards an explanation in terms of God's intentional planning and away from an explanation in terms of mindless natural processes.

The design argument raises epistemological questions that go beyond its traditional theological context. As William Paley (1802) observed, when we find a watch while walking across a heath, we unhesitatingly infer that it was produced by an intelligent designer. No such inference forces itself upon us when we observe a stone. Why is explanation in terms of intelligent design so compelling in the one case, but not in the other? Similarly, when we observe the behavior of our fellow human beings, we find it irresistible to think that they have minds that are filled with beliefs and desires. And when we observe non-human organisms, the impulse to invoke mentalistic explanations is often very strong, especially when they look a lot like us. When does the behavior of an organism – human or not – warrant this mentalistic interpretation? The same question can be posed about machines. Few of us feel tempted to attribute beliefs and desires to hand calculators. We use calculators to help us add, but they don't literally figure out sums; in this respect, calculators are like the pieces of paper on which we scribble calculations. There is an important difference between a device that *we* use to help us think and a device that *itself* thinks. However, when a computer plays a decent game of chess, we may find it useful to explain and predict its behavior by thinking of it as having goals and deploying strategies (Dennett, 1987b). Is this merely a useful fiction, or does the machine really have a mind? And if we think that present-day chess-playing computers are, strictly speaking, mindless, what would it take for a machine to pass the test? Surely, as Turing (1950) observed, it needn't look like us. In all these contexts, we face *the problem of other minds* (Sober, 2000a). If we understood the ground rules in this general epistemological problem, that would help us think about the design argument for the existence of God. And conversely – if we could get clear on the theological design argument, that might throw light on epistemological problems that are not theological in character.

What is the Design Argument?

The design argument, like the ontological argument, raises subtle questions concerning what the logical structure of the argument really is. My main concern here will not be to describe how various thinkers have presented the design argument, but to find the soundest formulation that the argument can be given.

The best version of the design argument, in my opinion, uses an inferential idea that probabilists call *the likelihood principle*. This can be illustrated by way of Paley's (1802) example of the watch on the heath. Paley describes an observation that he claims discriminates between two hypotheses:

(W) O1: the watch has features G1 ... Gn.
     W1: the watch was created by an intelligent designer.
     W2: the watch was produced by a mindless chance process.

Paley's idea is that O1 would be unsurprising if W1 were true, but would be very surprising if W2 were true. This is supposed to show that O1 *favors* W1 over W2; O1 supports W1 more than it supports W2. Surprise is a matter of degree; it can be captured by the concept of conditional probability. The probability of O given H – Pr(O | H) – represents how unsurprising O would be if H were true. The likelihood principle says that comparing such conditional probabilities is the way to decide what the direction is in which the evidence points:

(LP)   Observation O supports hypothesis H1 more than it supports hypothesis H2
       if and only if $\Pr(O \mid H1) > \Pr(O \mid H2)$.

There is a lot to say on the question of why the likelihood principle should be accepted (Hacking, 1965; Edwards, 1972; Royall, 1997; Forster and Sober, 2003; Sober, 2002); for the purposes of this essay, I will take it as a given.

We now can describe the likelihood version of the design argument for the existence of God, again taking our lead from one of Paley's favorite examples of a delicate adaptation. The basic format is to compare two hypotheses as possible explanations of a single observation:

(E)   O2:   the vertebrate eye has features F1 . . . Fn.
      E1:   the vertebrate eye was created by an intelligent designer.
      E2:   the vertebrate eye was produced by a mindless chance process.

We do not hesitate to conclude that the observations strongly favor design over chance in the case of argument (W); Paley claims that precisely the same conclusion should be drawn in the case of the propositions assembled in (E).[1]

Clarifications

Several points of clarification are needed here concerning likelihood in general and the likelihood version of the design argument in particular. First, I use the term "likelihood" in a technical sense. Likelihood is not the same as probability. To say that H has a high likelihood, given observation O, is to comment on the value of $\Pr(O \mid H)$, not on the value of $\Pr(H \mid O)$; the latter is H's *posterior probability*. It is perfectly possible for a hypothesis to have a high likelihood and a low posterior probability. When you hear noises in your attic, this confers a high likelihood on the hypothesis that there are gremlins up there bowling, but few of us would conclude that this hypothesis is probably true.

Although the likelihood of H (given O) and the probability of H (given O) are different quantities, they are related. The relationship is given by Bayes's theorem:

$$\Pr(H \mid O) = \Pr(O \mid H)\Pr(H)/\Pr(O).$$

$\Pr(H)$ is the *prior probability* of the hypothesis – the probability that H has before we take the observation O into account. From Bayes's theorem we can deduce the following:

$$\Pr(H1 \mid O) > \Pr(H2 \mid O) \text{ if and only if } \Pr(O \mid H1)\Pr(H1) > \Pr(O \mid H2)\Pr(H2).$$

Which hypothesis has the higher posterior probability depends on how their likelihoods are related, but also on how their prior probabilities are related. This explains why the likelihood version of the design argument does not show that design is more probable than chance. To draw this further conclusion, we'd have to say something about the prior probabilities of the two hypotheses. It is here that I wish to demur (and this is what separates me from card-carrying Bayesians). Each of us perhaps has some subjective degree of belief, before we consider the design argument, in each of the two hypotheses E1 and E2. However, I see no way to understand the idea that the two hypotheses have *objective* prior probabilities. Since I would like to restrict the design argument as much as possible to matters that are objective, I will not represent it as an argument concerning which hypothesis is more probable.[2] However, those who have prior degrees of belief in E1 and E2 should use the likelihood argument to update their subjective probabilities. The likelihood version of the design argument says that the observation O2 should lead you to increase your degree of belief in E1 and reduce your degree of belief in E2.

My restriction of the design argument to an assessment of likelihoods, not probabilities, reflects a more general point of view. Scientific theories often have implications about which observations are probable (and which are improbable), but it rarely makes sense to describe them as having objective probabilities. Newton's law of gravitation (along with suitable background assumptions) says that the return of Halley's comet was to be expected, but what is the probability that Newton's law is true? Hypotheses have objective probabilities when they describe possible outcomes of a chance process. But as far as anyone knows, the laws that govern our universe were not the result of a chance process. Bayesians think that *all* hypotheses have probabilities; the position I am advocating sees this as a special feature of *some* hypotheses.[3]

Just as likelihood considerations leave open what probabilities one should assign to the competing hypotheses, they also don't tell you which hypothesis you should *believe*. I take it that belief is a dichotomous concept – you either believe a proposition or you do not. Consistent with this is the idea that there are three attitudes one might take to a statement – you can believe it true, believe it false, or withhold judgment. However, there is no simple connection of the matter-of-degree concept of probability to the dichotomous (or trichotomous) concept of belief. This is the lesson I extract from the lottery paradox (Kyburg, 1961). Suppose 100,000 tickets are sold in a fair lottery; one ticket will win and each has the same chance of winning. It follows that each ticket has a very high probability of not winning. If you adopt the policy of believing a proposition when it has a high probability, you will believe of each ticket that it will not win. However, this conclusion contradicts the assumption that the lottery is fair. What this shows is that high probability does not suffice for belief (and low probability does not suffice for disbelief). It is for this reason that many Bayesians prefer to say that individuals have *degrees* of belief. The rules for the dichotomous concept are unclear; the matter-of-degree concept at least has the advantage of being anchored to the probability calculus.

In summary, likelihood arguments have rather modest pretensions. They don't tell you which hypotheses to believe; in fact, they don't even tell you which hypotheses are probably true. Rather, they evaluate how the observations at hand discriminate among the hypotheses under consideration.

I now turn to some details concerning the likelihood version of the design argument. The first concerns the meaning of the intelligent design hypothesis. This hypothesis occurs in W1 in connection with the watch and in E1 in connection with the vertebrate eye. In the case of the watch, Paley did not dream that he was offering an argument for the existence of *God*. However, in the case of the eye, Paley thought that the intelligent designer under discussion was God himself. Why are these cases different? The bare bones of the likelihood arguments (W) and (E) do not say. What Paley had in mind is that building the vertebrate eye and the other adaptive features that organisms exhibit requires an intelligence far greater than anything that human beings could muster. This is a point that we will revisit at the end of this essay.

It is also important to understand the nature of the hypothesis with which the intelligent design hypothesis competes. I have used the term "chance" to express this alternative hypothesis. In large measure, this is because design theorists often think of chance as the alternative to design. Paley is again exemplary. *Natural Theology* is filled with examples like that of the vertebrate eye. Paley was not content to describe a few cases of delicate adaptations; he wanted to make sure that even if he got a few details wrong, the weight of evidence would still be overwhelming. For example, in Chapter 15 he considers the fact that our eyes point in the same direction as our feet; this has the convenient consequence that we can see where we are going. The obvious explanation, Paley (1802, p. 179) says, is intelligent design. This is because the alternative is that the direction of our eyes and the direction of our gait were determined by chance, which would mean that there was only a $\frac{1}{4}$ probability that our eyes would be able to scan the quadrant into which we are about to step.

I construe the idea of chance in a particular way. To say that an outcome is the result of a *uniform chance process* means that it was one of a number of *equiprobable* outcomes. Examples in the real world that come close to being uniform chance processes may be found in gambling devices – spinning a roulette wheel, drawing from a deck of cards, tossing a coin. The term "random" becomes more and more appropriate as real-world systems approximate uniform chance processes. However, as R. A. Fisher once pointed out, it is not a "matter of chance" that casinos turn a profit each year, nor should this be regarded as a "random" event. The financial bottom line at a casino is the result of a large number of chance events, but the rules of the game make it enormously probable (though not certain) that casinos end each year in the black. All uniform chance processes are probabilistic, but not all probabilistic outcomes are "due to chance."

It follows that the two hypotheses considered in my likelihood rendition of the design argument are not exhaustive. Mindless uniform chance is one alternative to intelligent design, but it is not the only one. This point has an important bearing on the dramatic change in fortunes that the design argument experienced with the advent of Darwin's (1859) theory of evolution. The process of evolution by natural selection is *not* a uniform chance process. The process has two parts. Novel traits arise in individual organisms "by chance;" however, whether they then disappear from the population or increase in frequency and eventually reach 100 percent representation is anything but a "matter of chance." The central idea of natural selection is that traits that help organisms survive and reproduce have a better chance of becoming common than traits that hurt. The essence of natural selection is that evolutionary outcomes have *un*equal probabilities. Paley and other design theorists writing before Darwin did not and could not cover all possible mindless natural processes. Paley addressed the alternative of uniform chance, not the alternative of natural selection.[4]

Just to nail down this point, I want to describe a version of the design argument formulated by John Arbuthnot. Arbuthnot (1710) carefully tabulated birth records in London over 82 years and noticed that, in each year, slightly more sons than daughters were born. Realizing that boys die in greater numbers than girls, he saw that this slight bias in the sex ratio at birth gradually subsides until there are equal numbers of males and females at the age of marriage. Arbuthnot took this to be evidence of intelligent design; God, in his benevolence, wanted each man to have a wife and each woman to have a husband. To draw this conclusion, Arbuthnot considered what he took to be the relevant competing hypothesis – that the sex ratio at birth is determined by a uniform chance process. He was able to show that if the probability is $\frac{1}{2}$ that a baby will be a boy and $\frac{1}{2}$ that it will be a girl, then it is enormously improbable that the sex ratio should be skewed in favor of males in each and every of the years he surveyed (Stigler, 1986, pp. 225–6).

Arbuthnot could not have known that R. A. Fisher (1930) would bring sex ratio within the purview of the theory of natural selection. Fisher's insight was to see that a mother's mix of sons and daughters affects the number of *grand*offspring she will have. Fisher demonstrated that when there is random mating in a large population, the sex ratio strategy that evolves is one in which a mother invests equally in sons and daughters (Sober, 1993, p. 17). A mother will put half her reproductive resources into producing sons and half into producing daughters. This equal division means that she should have more sons than daughters, if sons tend to die sooner. Fisher's model therefore predicts the slightly uneven sex ratio at birth that Arbuthnot observed.[5]

My point in describing Fisher's idea is not to fault Arbuthnot for living in the eighteenth century. Rather, the thing to notice is that what Arbuthnot meant by "chance" was very different from what Fisher was talking about when he described how a selection process might shape the sex ratio found in a population. Arbuthnot was right that the probability of there being more males than females at birth in each of 82 years is extremely low, if each birth has the same chance of producing a male as it does of producing a female. However, a male-biased sex ratio in the population is extremely probable, if Fisher's hypothesized process is doing the work. Showing that design is more likely than chance leaves it open that some third, mindless, process might still have a higher likelihood than design. This is not a defect in the design argument, so long as the conclusion of that argument is not overstated. Here the modesty of the likelihood version of the design argument is a point in its favor. To draw a stronger conclusion – that the design hypothesis is more likely than *any* hypothesis involving mindless natural processes – one would have to attend to more alternatives than just design and (uniform) chance.[6]

I now want to draw the reader's attention to some features of the likelihood version of the design argument (E) concerning how the observation and the competing hypotheses are formulated. First, notice that I have kept the observation O2 conceptually separate from the two hypotheses E1 and E2. If the observation were simply that "the vertebrate eye exists," then since E1 and E2 both entail this proposition, each would have a likelihood of unity. According to the likelihood principle, this observation does not favor design over chance. Better to formulate the question in terms of explaining the properties of the vertebrate eye, not explaining why the eye exists. Notice also that I have not formulated the design hypothesis as the claim that God exists; this existence claim says nothing about the putative designer's involvement in the creation of the vertebrate eye. Finally, I should point out that it would do no harm to have the design hypothesis say that God created the vertebrate eye; this possible reformulation is something I'll return to later.

Other Formulations of the Design Argument, and Their Defects

Given the various provisos that govern probability arguments, it would be nice if the design argument could be formulated deductively. For example, if the hypothesis of mindless chance processes entailed that it is *impossible* that organisms exhibit delicate adaptations, then a quick application of *modus tollens* would sweep that hypothesis from the field. How ever much design theorists might yearn for an argument of this kind, there apparently are none to be had. As the story about monkeys and typewriters illustrates, it is *not* impossible that mindless chance processes should produce delicate adaptations; it is merely very *improbable* that they should do so.

If *modus tollens* cannot be pressed into service, perhaps there is a probabilistic version of *modus tollens* that can achieve the same result. Is there a law of improbability that begins with the premise that $Pr(O \mid H)$ is very low and concludes that H should be rejected? There is no such principle (Royall, 1997, chapter 3). The fact that you won the lottery does not, by itself, show that there is something wrong with the conjunctive hypothesis that the lottery was fair and a million tickets were sold and you bought just one ticket. And if we randomly drop a very sharp pin onto a line that is 1,000 miles long, the probability of its landing where it does is negligible; however, that outcome does not falsify the hypothesis that the pin was dropped at random.

The fact that there is no probabilistic *modus tollens* has great significance for understanding the design argument. The logic of this problem is essentially comparative. To evaluate the design hypothesis, we must know what it predicts and compare this with the predictions made by other hypotheses. The design hypothesis cannot win by default. The fact that an observation would be very improbable if it arose by chance is not enough to refute the chance hypothesis. One must show that the design hypothesis confers on the observation a higher probability, and even then the conclusion will merely be that the observation *favors* the design hypothesis, not that that hypothesis *must be true*.[7]

In the continuing conflict (in the United States) between evolutionary biology and creationism, creationists attack evolutionary theory, but never take even the first step in developing a positive theory of their own. The three-word slogan "God did it" seems to satisfy whatever craving for explanation they may have. Is the sterility of this intellectual tradition a mere accident? Could intelligent design theory be turned into a scientific research program? I am doubtful, but the present point concerns the logic of the design argument, not its future prospects. Creationists sometimes assert that evolutionary theory "cannot explain" this or that finding (e.g., Behe, 1996). What they mean is that certain outcomes are *very improbable* according to the evolutionary hypothesis. Even this more modest claim needs to be scrutinized. However, if it were true, what would follow about the plausibility of creationism? In a word – *nothing*.

It isn't just defenders of the design hypothesis who have fallen into the trap of supposing that there is a probabilistic version of *modus tollens*. For example, the biologist Richard Dawkins (1986, pp. 144–6) takes up the question of how one should evaluate hypotheses that attempt to explain the origin of life by appeal to strictly mindless natural processes. He says that an acceptable theory of this sort can say that the origin of life on earth was somewhat improbable, but it must not go too far. If there are n planets in the universe that are "suitable" locales for life to originate, then an acceptable theory of the origin of life on earth must say that that event had a probability of at least $\frac{1}{n}$. Theories that say that terrestrial life was less probable than this should be rejected. How does Dawkins obtain this lower bound? Why is the number of planets relevant? Perhaps he is thinking that if α is the actual frequency of life-bearing planets among "suitable" planets (i.e., planets on which it is possible for life to evolve), then the true probability of life's evolving on earth must also be α. There is a mistake here, which we can uncover by examining how actual frequency and probability are related. With small sample-size, it is perfectly possible for these quantities to have very different values (consider a fair coin that is tossed three times and then destroyed). However, Dawkins is obviously thinking that the sample size is very large, and here he is right that the actual frequency provides a good estimate of the true probability. It is interesting that Dawkins tells us to reject a theory if the probability it assigns is too *low*, but why doesn't he also say that it should be rejected if the probability it assigns is too *high*? The reason, presumably, is that we cannot rule out the possibility that the earth was not just *suitable* but was *highly conducive* to the evolution of life. However, this point cuts both ways. Although α is the *average* probability of a suitable planet's having life evolve, it is still possible that different suitable planets might have different probabilities – some may have values greater than α while others may have values that are lower. Dawkins's lower bound assumes that the earth was above average; this is a mistake that might be termed the "Lake Wobegon fallacy."

Some of Hume's ([1779] 1980) criticisms of the design argument in his *Dialogues Concerning Natural Religion* depend on formulating the argument as something other than a likelihood inference. For example, Hume at one point has Philo say that the design argument is an argument from analogy, and that the conclusion of the argument is supported only very weakly by its premises. His point can be formulated by thinking of the design argument as follows.

> Watches are produced by intelligent design.
> Organisms are similar to watches to degree p.
> p[===============================
> Organisms were produced by intelligent design.

Notice that the letter "p" appears twice in this argument. It represents the degree of similarity of organisms and watches, and it represents the probability that the premises confer on the conclusion. Think of similarity as the proportion of shared characteristics. Things that are 0 percent similar have no traits in common; things that are 100 percent similar have all traits in common. The analogy argument says that the more similar watches and organisms are, the more probable it is that organisms were produced by intelligent design.

Let us grant the Humean point that watches and organisms have relatively few characteristics in common (it is doubtful that there is a well-defined totality consisting of all the traits of each, but let that pass). After all, watches are made of metal and glass and go "tick tock"; organisms metabolize and reproduce and go "oink" and "bow wow." This is all true, but entirely irrelevant, if the design argument is a likelihood inference. It doesn't matter how overall-similar watches and organisms are. With respect to argument (W), what matters is how one should explain the fact that watches are well adapted for the task of telling time; with respect to (E), what matters is how one should explain the fact that organisms are well adapted to their environments. Paley's analogy between watches and organisms is merely heuristic. The likelihood argument about organisms stands on its own (Sober, 1993).

Hume also has Philo construe the design argument as an inductive argument, and then complain that the inductive evidence is weak. Philo suggests that for us to have good reason to think that our world was produced by an intelligent designer, we'd have to visit other worlds and observe that all or most of them were produced by intelligent design. But how many other worlds have we visited? The answer is – not even one. Apparently, the design argument is an inductive argument that could not be weaker; its sample size is zero. This objection dissolves once we move from the model of inductive sampling to that of likelihood. You don't have to observe the processes of intelligent design and chance at work in different worlds to maintain that the two hypotheses confer different probabilities on your observations.

Three Possible Objections to the Likelihood Argument

There is another objection that Hume makes to the design argument, one that apparently pertains to the likelihood version of the argument that I have formulated and that many philosophers think is devastating. Hume points out that the design argument does not establish the attributes of the designer. The argument does not show that the designer who made the universe, or who made organisms, is morally perfect, or all-knowing, or all-powerful, or that there is just one such being. Perhaps this undercuts some versions of the design argument, but it does not touch the likelihood argument we are considering. Paley, perhaps responding to this Humean point, makes it clear that his design argument aims to establish the *existence* of the designer, and that the question of the designer's *characteristics* must be addressed separately.[8] My own rendition of the argument follows Paley in this regard. Does this limitation of the argument render it trivial? Not at all – it is *not* trivial to claim that the adaptive contrivances of organisms are due to intelligent design, even when details about this designer are not supplied. This supposed "triviality" would be *big* news to evolutionary biologists.

The likelihood version of the design argument consists of two premisses – Pr(O | Chance) is very low and Pr(O | Design) is higher. Here O describes some observation of the features of organisms or some feature of the entire cosmos. The first of these claims is sometimes rejected by appeal to a theory that Hume describes under the heading of the Epicurean hypothesis. This is the monkeys-and-typewriters idea that if there are a finite number of particles that have a finite number of possible states, then, if they swarm about at random, they eventually will visit all possible configurations, including configurations of great order.[9] Thus, the order we see in our universe, and the delicate adaptations we observe in organisms, in fact had a high probability of eventually coming into being, according to the hypothesis of chance. Van Inwagen (1993, p. 144) gives voice to this objection and explains it by way of an analogy: Suppose you toss a coin 20 times and it lands heads every time. You should not be surprised at this outcome if you are one among millions of people who toss a fair coin 20 times. After all, with so many people tossing, it is all but inevitable that some people should get 20 heads. The outcome you obtained, therefore, was not improbable, according to the chance hypothesis.

There is a fallacy in this criticism of the design argument, which Hacking (1987) calls "the inverse gambler's fallacy." He illustrates his idea by describing a gambler who walks into a casino and immediately observes two dice being rolled that land double-six. The gambler considers whether this result favors the hypothesis that the dice had been rolled many times before the roll he just observed or the hypothesis that this was the first roll of the evening. The gambler reasons that the outcome of double-six would be more probable under the first hypothesis:

Pr(double-six on this roll | there were many rolls) >
Pr(double-six on this roll | there was just one roll).

In fact, the gambler's assessment of the likelihoods is erroneous. Rolls of dice have the *Markov property*; the probability of double-six on this roll is the same ($\frac{1}{36}$), regardless of what may have happened in the past. What is true is that the probability that a double-six will occur *at some time or other* increases as the number of trials is increased:

Pr(a double-six occurs sometime | there were many rolls) >
Pr(a double-six occurs sometime | there was just one roll).

However, the *principle of total evidence* says that we should assess hypotheses by considering *all* the evidence we have. This means that the relevant observation is that *this* roll landed double-six; we should not focus on the logically weaker proposition that a double-six occurred *sometime*. Relative to the stronger description of the observations, the hypotheses have identical likelihoods.

Applying this point to the criticism of the design argument that we are presently considering, we must conclude that the criticism is mistaken. It *is* highly probable (let us suppose), according to the chance hypothesis, that the universe will contain order and adaptation somewhere and at some time. However, the relevant observation is more specific – *our* corner of the universe is orderly and the organisms now on earth are well adapted. These events *do* have very low probability, according to the chance hypothesis, and the fact that a weaker description of the observations has high probability on the chance hypothesis is not relevant (see also White, 2000).[10]

If the first premise in the likelihood formulation of the design argument – that Pr(O | Chance) is very low – is correct, then the only question that remains is whether Pr(O | Design) is higher. This, I believe, is the Achilles heel of the design argument. The problem is to say how probable it is, for example, that the vertebrate eye would have features F1 ... Fn, if the eye were produced by an intelligent designer. What is required is not the specification of a single probability value, or even a precisely delimited range of values. All that is needed is an argument that shows that this probability is indeed higher than the probability that chance confers on the observation.

The problem is that the design hypothesis confers a probability on the observation only when it is supplemented with further assumptions about what the designer's goals and abilities would be if he existed. Perhaps the designer would never build the vertebrate eye with features F1 ... Fn, either because he would lack the goals or because he would lack the ability. If so, the likelihood of the design hypothesis is zero. On the other hand, perhaps the designer would want above all to build the eye with features F1 ... Fn and would be entirely competent to bring this plan to fruition. If so, the likelihood of the design hypothesis is unity. There are as many likelihoods as there are suppositions concerning the goals and abilities of the putative designer. Which of these, or which class of these, should we take seriously?

It is no good answering this question by assuming that the eye was built by an intelligent designer and then inferring that he must have wanted to give the eye features F1 ... Fn and that he must have had the ability to do so since, after all, these are the features we observe. For one thing, this pattern of argument is question begging. One needs *independent* evidence as to what the designer's plans and abilities would be if he existed; one can't obtain this evidence by *assuming* that the design hypothesis is true (Sober, 1999). Furthermore, even if we assume that the eye was built by an intelligent designer, we can't tell from this what the probability is that the eye would have the features we observe. Designers sometimes bring about outcomes that are not very probable given the plans they have in mind.

This objection to the design argument is an old one; it was presented by Keynes (1921) and before him by Venn (1866). In fact, the basic idea was formulated by Hume. When we behold the watch on the heath, we know that the watch's features are not particularly improbable on the hypothesis that the watch was produced by a designer who has the sorts of *human* goals and abilities with which we are familiar. This is the deep disanalogy between the watchmaker and the putative maker of organisms and universes. We are invited, in the latter case, to imagine a designer who is radically different from the human craftsmen with whom we are familiar. But if this designer is so different, why are we so sure that he would build the vertebrate eye in the form in which we find it?

This challenge is not turned back by pointing out that we often infer the existence of intelligent designers when we have no clue as to what they were trying to achieve. The biologist John Maynard Smith tells the story of a job he had during World War II inspecting a warehouse filled with German war material. He and his co-workers often came across machines whose functions were entirely opaque to them. Yet, they had no trouble seeing that these objects were built by intelligent designers. Similar stories can be told about archaeologists who work in museums; they often have objects in their collections that they know are artifacts, although they have no idea what the makers of these artifacts had in mind.

My claim is not that design theorists must have independent evidence that singles out a specification of the exact goals and abilities of the putative intelligent designer. They may be uncertain as to which of the goal-ability pairs GA-1, GA-2, . . . , GA-n is correct. However, since

Pr(the eye has F1 . . . Fn | Design) =
Σ_i Pr(the eye has F1 . . . Fn | Design & GA-i)Pr(GA-i|Design),

they do have to show that

Σ_i Pr(the eye has F1 . . . Fn | Design & GA-i)Pr(GA-i|Design) >
Pr(the eye has F1 . . . Fn | Chance).

I think that Maynard Smith in his warehouse and archaeologists in their museums are able to do this. They aren't sure exactly what the intelligent designer was trying to achieve (e.g., they aren't certain that GA-1 is true and that all the other GA pairs are false), but they are able to see that it is not terribly improbable that the object should have the features one observes if it were made by a human intelligent designer. After all, the items in Maynard Smith's warehouse were symmetrical and smooth metal containers that had what appeared to be switches, dials, and gauges on them. And the "artifacts of unknown function" in anthropology museums likewise bear signs of human handiwork.

It is interesting in this connection to consider the epistemological problem of how one would go about detecting intelligent life elsewhere in the universe (if it exists). The Search for Extraterrestrial Intelligence (SETI) project, funded until 1993 by the US National Aeronautics and Space Administration and now supported privately, dealt with this problem in two ways (Dick, 1996). First, the scientists wanted to send a message into deep space that would allow any intelligent extraterrestrials who received it to figure out that it was produced by intelligent designers (namely, us). Second, they scan the night sky hoping to detect signs of intelligent life elsewhere.

The message, transmitted in 1974 from the Arecibo Observatory, was a simple picture of our solar system, a representation of oxygen and carbon, a picture of a double helix representing DNA, a stick figure of a human being, and a picture of the Arecibo telescope. How sure are we that if intelligent aliens find these clues, they will realize that they were produced by intelligent designers? The hope is that this message will strike the aliens who receive it as evidence favoring the hypothesis of intelligent design over the hypothesis that some mindless physical process (not necessarily one involving uniform chance) was responsible. It is hard to see how the SETI engineers could have done any better, but still one cannot dismiss the possibility that they will fail. If extraterrestrial minds are very different from our own – either because they have different beliefs and desires or because they process information in different ways – it may turn out that their interpretation of the evidence will differ profoundly from the interpretation that human beings would arrive at, were they on the receiving end. To say anything more precise about this, we'd have to be able to provide specifics about the aliens' mental characteristics. If we are uncertain as to how the mind of an extraterrestrial will interpret this evidence, how can we be so sure that God, if he were to build the vertebrate eye, would endow it with the features we find it to have?

When SETI engineers search for signs of intelligent life elsewhere in the universe, what are they looking for? The answer is surprisingly simple. They look for narrow-band radio emissions. This is because human beings have built machines that produce these signals and, as far as we know, such emissions are not produced by mindless natural processes. The SETI engineers search for this signal, not because it is "complex" or fulfills some a priori criterion that would make it a "sign of intelligence," but simply because they think they know what sorts of mechanisms are needed to produce it.[11] This strategy may not work, but it is hard to see how the scientists could do any better. Our judgments about what counts as a sign of intelligent design must be based on empirical information about what designers often do and what they rarely do. As of now, these judgments are based on our knowledge of *human* intelligence. The more our hypotheses about intelligent designers depart from the human case, the more in the dark we are as to what the ground rules are for inferring intelligent design. It is imaginable that these limitations will subside as human beings learn more about the cosmos. But for now, we are rather limited.

I have been emphasizing the fallibility of two assumptions – that we know what counts as a sign of extraterrestrial intelligence and that we know how extraterrestrials will interpret the signals we send. My point has been to shake a complacent assumption that figures in the design argument. However, I suspect that SETI engineers are on much firmer ground than theologians. If extraterrestrials evolved by the same type of evolutionary process that produced human intelligence, that may provide useful constraints on conjectures about the minds they have. No theologian, to my knowledge, thinks that God is the result of biological processes. Indeed God is usually thought of as a *super*natural being who is radically different from the things we observe *in* nature. The problem of extraterrestrial intelligence is therefore an intermediate case; it lies between the watch found on the heath and the God who purportedly built the universe and shaped the vertebrate eye, but is much closer to the first. The upshot of this point for Paley's design argument is this: *design arguments for the existence of human (and human-like) watchmakers are often unproblematic; it is design arguments for the existence of God that leave us at sea.*

I began by formulating the design hypothesis in argument (E) as the claim that an intelligent designer made the vertebrate eye. Yet, I have sometimes discussed the hypothesis as if it asserted that *God* is the designer in question. I don't think this distinction makes a difference with respect to the objection I have described. To say that some designer or other made the eye is to state a disjunctive hypothesis. To figure out the likelihood of this disjunction, one needs to address the question of what each putative designer's goals and intentions would be.[12] The theological formulation shifts the problem from the evaluation of a disjunction to the evaluation of a disjunct, but the problem remains the same. Even supposing that God is omniscient, omnipotent, and perfectly benevolent, what is the probability that the eye would have features F1 . . . Fn, if God set his hand to making it? He *could* have produced those results if he had wanted. But why think that this is what he *would* have wanted to do? The assumption that God can do anything is part of the problem, not the solution. An engineer who is more limited would be more predictable.

There is another reply to my criticism of the design argument that should be considered. I have complained that we have no way to evaluate the likelihood of the design hypothesis, since we don't know which auxiliary assumptions about goal-ability pairs we should use. But why not change the subject? Instead of evaluating the likelihood of design, why not evaluate the likelihood of various conjunctions – (Design & GA-1), (Design & GA-2), etc.? Some of these will have high likelihoods, others will have low, but it will no longer be a mystery what likelihoods these hypotheses possess. There are two problems with this tactic. First, it is a game that two can play. Consider the hypothesis that the vertebrate eye was created by the mindless process of electricity. If I simply get to *invent* auxiliary hypotheses without having to *justify* them independently, I can just stipulate the following assumption: if electricity created the vertebrate eye, the eye must have features F1 . . . Fn. The electricity hypothesis now is a conjunct in a conjunction that has maximum likelihood, just like the design hypothesis. This is a dead end. My second objection is that it is an important part of scientific practice that conjunctions be broken apart (when possible), and their conjuncts scrutinized (Sober, 1999, 2000). If your doctor runs a test to see whether you have tuberculosis, you will not be satisfied if she reports that the likelihood of the conjunction "you have tuberculosis & auxiliary assumption 1" is high while the likelihood of the conjunction "you have tuberculosis & auxiliary assumption 2" is low. You want your doctor to address the first *conjunct*, not just the various *conjunctions*. And you want her to do this by using a test procedure that is *independently* known to have small error probabilities. Demand no less of your theologian.

My formulation of the design argument as a likelihood inference, and my criticism of it, have implications concerning the problem of evil. It is a mistake to try to *deduce* the non-existence of God from the fact that so much evil exists. Even supposing that God is all-powerful, all-knowing, and entirely benevolent, there is no contradiction in the hypothesis that God allows various evils to exist because they are necessary correlates of greater goods, where we don't understand in any detail what these correlations are or why they must obtain (Plantinga, 1974). The status of the problem changes, however, when we think of it as *non-deductive* in character (Madden and Hare, 1968; Rowe, 1979; Plantinga, 1979). Within the framework of likelihood inference, there are two quantities we must evaluate: What is the probability that there would be as much evil as there is, if the universe were produced by an all-powerful, all-knowing, and entirely benevolent God? And what is the probability of that much evil's existing, if the universe were produced by mindless natural processes? The logical observation that saves theism from the attempt to deduce the non-existence of God comes back to haunt the theistic hypothesis in this new context. If the ways of God are so mysterious, we have no way to evaluate the first of these likelihoods. The theistic hypothesis is saved from disconfirmation by the fact that it is untestable.

The Relationship of the Organismic Design Argument to Darwinism

Philosophers who criticize the organismic design argument often believe that the argument was dealt its death blow by Hume. True, Paley wrote after Hume, and the many Bridgewater treatises elaborating the design argument appeared after Hume's *Dialogues* were published posthumously. Nonetheless, for these philosophers, the design argument after Hume was merely a corpse that could be propped up and paraded. Hume had taken the life out of it.

Biologists often take a different view. Dawkins (1986, p. 4) puts the point provocatively by saying that it was not until Darwin that it was possible to be an intellectually fulfilled atheist. The thought here is that Hume's skeptical attack was not the decisive moment; rather, it was Darwin's development and confirmation of a substantive scientific explanation of the adaptive features of organisms that really undermined the design argument (at least in its organismic formulation). Philosophers who believe that theories can't be rejected until a better theory is developed to take its place often sympathize with this point of view.

My own interpretation coincides with neither of these. As indicated above, I think that Hume's criticisms largely derive from an empiricist epistemology that is too narrow. However, seeing the design argument's fatal flaw does not depend on seeing the merits of Darwinian theory. The likelihood principle, it is true, says that theories must be evaluated comparatively, not on their own. But for this to be possible, each theory must make predictions. It is at this fundamental level that I think the design argument is defective.

Biologists often present two criticisms of creationism. First, they argue that the design hypothesis is untestable. Second, they contend that there is plenty of evidence that the hypothesis is false. Obviously, these two lines of argument are in conflict.[13] I have already endorsed the first criticism, but I want to say a little about the second. A useful example is Stephen Jay Gould's (1980) widely read article about the panda's thumb. Pandas are vegetarian bears who have a spur of bone (a "thumb") protruding from their wrists. They use this device to strip bamboo, which is the main thing they eat. Gould says that the hypothesis of intelligent design predicts that pandas should *not* have this inefficient device. A benevolent, powerful, and intelligent engineer could and would have done a lot better. Evolutionary theory, on the other hand, says that the panda's thumb is what we should expect. The thumb is a modification of the wrist bones found in the common ancestor that pandas share with carnivorous bears. Evolution by natural selection is a tinkerer; it does not design adaptations from scratch, but modifies pre-existing features, with the result that adaptations are often imperfect.

Gould's argument, I hope it is clear, is a likelihood argument. I agree with what he says about evolutionary theory, but I think his discussion of the design hypothesis leads him into the same trap that ensnared Paley. Gould thinks he knows what God would do if he built pandas, just as Paley thought he knew what God would do if he built the vertebrate eye. But neither of them knows this. Both help themselves to *assumptions* about God's goals and abilities. However, it is not enough to make assumptions about these matters; one needs independent evidence that these auxiliary assumptions are true. Paley's problem is also Gould's.

Anthropic Reasoning and Cosmic Design Arguments

Evolutionary theory seeks to explain the adaptive features of organisms; it has nothing to say about the origin of the universe as a whole. For this reason, evolutionary theory conflicts with the organismic design hypothesis, but not with the cosmic design hypothesis. Still, the main criticism I presented of the first type of design argument also applies to the second. I now want to examine a further problem that cosmic design arguments sometimes encounter.[14]

Suppose I catch 50 fish from a lake, and you want to use my observations O to test two hypotheses:

O: All the fish I caught were more than 10 inches long.
F1: All the fish in the lake are more than 10 inches long.
F2: Only half the fish in the lake are more than 10 inches long.

You might think that the likelihood principle says that F1 is better supported, since

(1) $Pr(O \mid F1) > Pr(O \mid F2)$.

However, you then discover how I caught my fish:

(A1) I caught the fish by using a net that (because of the size of its holes) can't catch fish smaller than 10 inches, and I left the net in the lake until there were 50 fish in it.

This leads you to replace the analysis provided by (1) with the following:

(2) $Pr(O \mid F1 \,\&\, A1) = Pr(O \mid F2 \,\&\, A1) = 1.0$.

Furthermore, you now realize that your first assessment, (1), was based on the erroneous assumption that

(A0)   The fish I caught were a random sample from the fish in the lake.

Instead of (1), you should have written

Pr(O | F1 & A0) > Pr(O | F2 & A0).

This inequality is true; the problem, however, is that (A0) is false.

This example, from Eddington (1939), illustrates the idea of an *observational selection effect* (an OSE). When a hypothesis is said to render a set of observations probable (or improbable), ask yourself what assumptions allow the hypothesis to have this implication. The point illustrated here is that the procedure you use to obtain your observations can be relevant to assessing likelihoods.[15]

One version of the cosmic design argument begins with the observation that our universe is "fine-tuned." That is, the values of various physical constants are such as to permit life to exist, but if they had been even slightly different, life would have been impossible. McMullin (1993, p. 378) summarizes some of the relevant facts as follows:

> If the strong nuclear force were to have been as little as 2 percent stronger (relative to the other forces), all hydrogen would have been converted into helium. If it were 5 percent weaker, no helium at all would have formed and there would be nothing but hydrogen. If the weak nuclear force were a little stronger, supernovas could not occur, and heavy elements could not have formed. If it were slightly weaker, only helium might have formed. If the electromagnetic force were stronger, all stars would be red dwarfs, and there would be no planets. If it were a little weaker, all stars would be very hot and short-lived. If the electron charge were ever so slightly different, there would be no chemistry as we know it. Carbon (^{12}C) only just managed to form in the primal nucleosynthesis. And so on.

I'll abbreviate the fact that the values of these physical constants fall within the narrow limits specified by saying that "the constants are right." A design argument can now be constructed, one that claims that the constants' being right should be explained by postulating the existence of an intelligent designer, one who wanted life to exist and who arranged the universe so that this could occur (Swinburne, 1990a). As with Paley's organismic design argument, we can represent the reasoning in this cosmic design argument as the assertion of a likelihood inequality:

(3)   Pr(constants are right | Design) > Pr(constants are right | Chance).

However, there is a problem with (3) that resembles the problem with (1). Consider the fact that

(A3)   We exist, and if we exist the constants must be right.

We need to take (A3) into account; instead of (3), we should have said:

(4)   Pr(constants are right | Design & A3) = Pr(constants are right | Chance & A3)
       = 1.0.

That is, given (A3), the constants must be right, regardless of whether the universe was produced by intelligent design or by chance.

Proposition (4) reflects the fact that our observation that the constants are right is subject to an OSE. Recognizing this OSE is in accordance with a *weak anthropic principle* – "what we can expect to observe must be restricted by the conditions necessary for our presence as observers" (Carter, 1974). The argument involves no commitment to *strong anthropic principles*. For example, there is no assertion that the correct cosmology must entail that the existence of observers such as ourselves was inevitable, nor is it claimed that our existence *explains* why the physical constants are right (Barrow, 1988; Earman, 1987; McMullin, 1993).[16]

Although this point about OSEs undermines the version of the design argument that cites the fact that the physical constants are right, it does not touch other versions. For example, when Paley concludes that the vertebrate eye was produced by an intelligent designer, his argument cannot be refuted by claiming that:

(A4)   We exist, and if we exist vertebrates must have eyes with features F1 ... Fn.

If (A4) were true, the likelihood inequality that Paley asserted would have to be replaced with an equality, just as (1) had to be replaced by (2) and (3) had to be replaced by (4). But fortunately for Paley, (A4) is false. However, matters change if we think of Paley as seeking to explain the modest fact that organisms have at least one adaptive contrivance. If this were false, we would not be able to make observations; indeed, we would not exist. Paley was right to focus on the details; the more minimal description of what we observe does not sustain the argument he wanted to endorse.

The issue of OSEs can be raised in connection with other cosmic versions of the design argument. Swinburne (1990b, p. 191) writes that "the hypothesis of theism is that the universe exists because there is a God who keeps it in being and that laws of nature operate because there is a God who brings it about that they do." Let us separate the *explananda*. The fact that the universe exists does *not* favor design over chance; after all, if the universe did not exist, we would not exist and so would not be able to observe that it does.[17] The same point holds with respect to the fact that the universe is law-governed. Even supposing that lawlessness is possible, could we exist and make observations if there were no laws? If not, then the lawful character of the universe does not discriminate between design and chance. Finally, we may consider the fact that our universe is governed by one set of laws, rather than another. Swinburne (1968) argues that the fact that our universe obeys *simple* laws is better explained by the hypothesis of design than by the hypothesis of chance. Whether this observation also is subject to an OSE depends on whether we could exist in a universe obeying alternative laws.

Before taking up an objection to this analysis of the argument from fine-tuning, I want to summarize what it has in common with the fishing example. In the fishing example, the source of the OSE is obvious – it is located in a device outside of ourselves. The net with big holes insures that the observer will make a certain observation, regardless of which of two hypotheses is true. But where is the device that induces an OSE in the fine-tuning example? There is none; rather, it is the observer's own existence that does the work. Nonetheless, the effect is the same. Owing to the fact that we exist, we are bound to observe that the constants are right, regardless of whether our universe was produced by chance or by design.[18]

This structural similarity between fishing and fine-tuning may seem to be undermined by a disanalogy. In the latter case, we know that proposition (3) is correct – the probability that the constants will be right if the universe is created by a powerful deity bent on having life exist is greater than it would be if the values of the constants were set by a uniform chance process. This inequality seems to hold, regardless of how or whether we make our observations. The fishing example looks different; here we know that proposition (1) is false. There is no saying whether a likelihood inequality obtains until we specify the procedure used to obtain the observations; once we do this, there *is* no likelihood inequality. Thus, in fine-tuning, we have an inequality that is true because it reflects the metaphysical facts; in fishing, we have an inequality that is false for epistemic reasons. My response is that I agree that this point of difference exists, but that it does nothing to save the argument from fine-tuning. Although proposition (3) is true, we are bound to observe that the constants are right, regardless of whether our universe arose by chance or by design. My objection to proposition (3) is not that it is false, but that it should not be used to interpret the observations; (4) is the relevant proposition to which we should attend.

To visualize this point, imagine that a deity creates a million universes and that a chance process does the same for another million. Let's assume that the proportion of universes in which the constants are right is greater in the former case. Doesn't it follow that if we observe that the constants are right in our universe, this observation favors the hypothesis that our universe arose by design? In fact, this does not follow. It *would* follow if we had the same probability of observing any of the first million universes if the design hypothesis were true, and had the same probability of observing any of the second million universes if the chance hypothesis were true. But this is not the case – our probability of observing a universe in which the constants are right is unity in each case.

What this means is that a full understanding of the workings of OSEs must acknowledge that there are two stages at which a bias can be introduced. There is first the process by which the system described by the hypotheses under test generates some state of the world that we are able to observe. Second, there is the process by which we come to observe that state of the world. This two-step process occurs in fishing and fine-tuning as follows:

Composition of the lake → Contents of the net → We observe the contents of the net.

Origin of the universe → Constants are right → We observe that the constants are right.

The OSE in the fishing example arises in the first step; the OSE in fine-tuning crops up in the second step.

Leslie (1989, pp. 13–14, 107–8), Swinburne (1990a, p. 171), and van Inwagen (1993, pp. 135, 144) all defend the fine-tuning argument against the criticism I have just described. Each mounts his defense by describing an analogy with a mundane example. Here is Swinburne's rendition of an example that Leslie presents:

On a certain occasion the firing squad aim their rifles at the prisoner to be executed. There are twelve expert marksmen in the firing squad, and they fire twelve rounds each. However, on this occasion all 144 shots miss. The prisoner laughs and comments that the event is not something requiring any explanation because if the marksmen had not missed, he would not be here to observe them having done so. But of course, the prisoner's comment is absurd; the marksmen all having missed is indeed something requiring explanation; and so too is what goes with it – the prisoner's being alive to observe it. And the explanation will be either that it was an accident (a most unusual chance event) or that it was planned (e.g., all the marksmen had been bribed to miss). Any interpretation of the anthropic principle which suggests that the evolution of observers is something which requires no explanation in terms of boundary conditions and laws being a certain way (either inexplicably or through choice) is false.

First a preliminary clarification – the issue isn't whether the prisoner's survival "requires explanation" but whether this observation provides evidence as to whether the marksmen intended to spare the prisoner or shot at random.[19]

My response takes the form of a dilemma. I'll argue, first, that if the firing squad example is analyzed in terms of the likelihood principle, the prisoner is right and Swinburne is wrong – the prisoner's survival does not allow him to conclude that design is more likely than chance. However, there is a different analysis of the prisoner's situation, in terms of the *probabilities* of hypotheses, not their *likelihoods*. This second analysis says that the prisoner *is* mistaken; however, it has the consequence that the prisoner's inference differs fundamentally from the design argument that appeals to fine-tuning. Each horn of this dilemma supports the conclusion that the firing squad example does nothing to save this version of the design argument.

So let us begin. If we understand Swinburne's claim in terms of the likelihood principle, we should read him as saying that

(L1)   Pr(the prisoner survived | the marksmen intended to miss) >
        Pr(the prisoner survived | the marksmen fired at random).

He thinks that the anthropic principle requires us to replace this claim with the following irrelevancy:

(L2)   Pr(the prisoner survived | the marksmen intended to miss & the prisoner survived) = Pr(the prisoner survived | the marksmen fired at random & the prisoner survived) = 1.0.

This equality would lead us to conclude (Swinburne thinks mistakenly) that the prisoner's survival does not discriminate between the hypotheses of design and chance.

To assess the claim that the prisoner has made a mistake, it is useful to compare the prisoner's reasoning with that of a bystander who witnesses the prisoner survive the firing squad. The prisoner reasons as follows: "given that I now am able to make observations, I must be alive, whether my survival was due to intelligent design or chance." The bystander says the following: "given that I now am able to make observations, the fact that the prisoner is now alive is made more probable by the design hypothesis than it is by the chance hypothesis." The prisoner is claiming that he is subject to an OSE, while the bystander says that he, the bystander, is not. Both, I submit, are correct.[20]

I suggest that part of the intuitive attractiveness of the claim that the prisoner has made a mistake derives from a shift between the prisoner's point of view and the bystander's. The bystander is right to use (L1) to interpret his observations; however, the prisoner has no business using (L1) to interpret his observations since he, the prisoner, is subject to an OSE. The prisoner needs to replace (L1) with (L2). My hunch is that Swinburne thinks the prisoner errs in his assessment of likelihoods because we bystanders would be making a mistake if we reasoned as he does.[21]

The basic idea of an OSE is that we must take account of the procedures used to obtain the observations when we assess the likelihoods of hypotheses. This much was clear from the fishing example. What may seem strange about my reading of the firing squad story is my claim that the prisoner and the bystander are in different epistemic situations, even though their observation reports differ by a mere pronoun. After the marksmen fire, the prisoner thinks "I exist" while the bystander thinks "he exists;" the bystander, but not the prisoner, is able to use his observation to say that design is more likely than chance, or so I say. If this seems odd, it may be useful to reflect on Sorensen's (1988) concept of *blindspots*. A proposition p is a blindspot for an individual S just in case, if p were true, S would not be able to know that p is true. Although some propositions (e.g., "nothing exists," "the constants are wrong") are blindspots for everyone, other propositions are blindspots for some people but not for others. Blindspots give rise to OSEs; if p is a blindspot for S, then if S makes an observation to determine the truth value of p, the outcome must be that not-p is observed. The prisoner, but not the bystander, has "the prisoner does not exist" as a blindspot. This is why "the prisoner exists" has an evidential significance for the bystander that it cannot have for the prisoner.[22]

To bolster my claim that the prisoner is right to think that likelihood does not distinguish between chance and design, I want to describe a slightly different problem. Suppose that a firing squad always subjects its victims to the same probabilistic process, which has the result that the prisoner either survives or is killed. 1,000 prisoners who have one by one each survived the firing squad are assembled and are asked to pool their knowledge and estimate the value of an unknown probability. What is the probability that a prisoner will survive if the firing squad fires? The standard methodology here is *maximum likelihood estimation*; one finds the value of the parameter of interest that maximizes the probability of the observations. This is why, if a coin lands heads 512 out of 1,000 tosses, the "best" estimate of the probability that the coin will land heads when it is tossed is 0.512. Those who believe that the single prisoner has evidence about his firing squad's intentions are obliged to conclude that the best estimate in this new problem is that the probability is unity. However, those persuaded that the single prisoner is subject to an OSE will want to maintain that the 1,000 prisoners are in the same boat. These skeptics will deny that the observations provide a basis for estimation. Isn't it *obvious* that testimony limited to survivors provides no evidence on which to base an estimate of the probability that someone will survive the firing squad's shooting? And if this is true of a 1,000 survivors, how can a *single* survivor be said to know that design is more likely than chance?

I now turn to a different analysis of the prisoner's situation. The prisoner, like the rest of us, knows how firing squads work. They always or almost always follow the order they receive, which is almost always to execute someone. Occasionally, they produce fake executions. They almost never fire at random. What is more, firing squads have firm control over outcomes; if they want to kill (or spare) someone, they always or almost always succeed. This and related items of background knowledge support the following *probability* claim:

(Pf) Pr(the marksmen intended to spare the prisoner | the prisoner survived) > Pr(the marksmen intended to spare the prisoner).

Firing squads rarely intend to spare their victims, but the survival of the prisoner makes it very probable that his firing squad had precisely that intention. The likelihood analysis led to the conclusion that the prisoner and the bystander are in different epistemic situations; the bystander should evaluate the hypotheses by using (L1), but the prisoner is obliged to use (L2). However, from the point of view of probabilities, the prisoner and the bystander can say the same thing; both can cite (Pf).[23]

What does this tell us about the fine-tuning version of the design argument? I construed that argument as a claim about likelihoods. As such, it is subject to an

OSE; given that we exist, the constants must be right, regardless of whether our universe was produced by chance or by design. However, we now need to consider whether the fine-tuning argument can be formulated as a claim about probabilities. Can we assert that

(Pu) Pr(the universe was created by an intelligent designer | the constants are right)
    > Pr(the universe was created by an intelligent designer)?

I don't think so. In the case of firing squads, we have frequency data and our general knowledge of human behavior on which to ground the probability statement (Pf). But we have neither data nor theory to ground (Pu). And we cannot defend (Pu) by saying that an intelligent designer would ensure that the constants are right, because this takes us back to the likelihood considerations we have already discussed. The prisoner's conclusion that he can say nothing about chance and design *is* mistaken if he is making a claim about probabilities. But the argument from fine-tuning can't be defended as a claim about probabilities.

The rabbit/duck quality of this problem merits review. I have discussed three examples – fishing, fine-tuning, and the firing squad. If we compare fine-tuning with fishing, they seem similar. This makes it intuitive to conclude that the design argument based on fine-tuning is wrong. However, if we compare fine-tuning with the firing squad, *they* seem similar. Since the prisoner apparently has evidence that favors design over chance, we are led to the conclusion that the fine-tuning argument must be right. This shifting gestalt can be stabilized by imposing a formalism. The first point is that OSEs are to be understood by comparing the *likelihoods* of hypotheses, not their *probabilities*. The second is that it is perfectly true that the prisoner can assert the *probability* claim (Pf). The question, then, is whether the design argument from fine-tuning is a likelihood argument or a probability argument. If the former, it is flawed because it fails to take account of the fact that there is an OSE. If the latter, it is flawed, but for a different reason – it makes claims about probabilities that we have no reason to accept; indeed, we cannot even *understand* them as objective claims.[24]

A Prediction

It was obvious to Paley and to other purveyors of the organismic design argument that if an intelligent designer built organisms, that designer would have to be far more intelligent than any human being could ever be. This is why the organismic design argument was for them an argument for the existence of *God*. I predict that it will eventually become clear that the organismic design argument should never have been understood in this way. This is because I expect that human beings will eventually build organisms from non-living materials. This achievement will not close down the question of whether the organisms we observe were created by intelligent design or by mindless natural processes; on the contrary, it will give that question a practical meaning, since the organisms we will see around us will be of both kinds.[25] However, it will be abundantly clear that the fact of organismic adaptation has nothing to do with whether God exists. When the Spanish conquistadors arrived in the New World, several indigenous peoples thought these intruders were gods, so powerful was the technology that the intruders possessed. Alas, the locals were mistaken; they did not realize that these beings with guns and horses were merely *human* beings. The organismic design argument for the existence of God embodies the same mistake. Human beings in the future will be the conquistadors, and Paley will be our Montezuma.

Notes

I am grateful to Martin Barrett, Nick Bostrom, David Christensen, Ellery Eells, Branden Fitelson, Malcolm Forster, Alan Hajek, Daniel Hausman, Stephen Leeds, William Mann, Lydia McGrew, Derk Pereboom, Roy Sorensen, and Richard Swinburne for useful comments. I have used portions of this chapter in seminars and lectures that I have given at many colleges and universities, too numerous to list here. My thanks to participants for their stimulating and productive discussion.

1   Does this construal of the design argument conflict with the idea that the argument is an *inference to the best explanation*? Not if one's theory of inference to the best explanation says that observations influence the assessment of explanations in this instance via the vehicle of likelihoods.

2   Another reason to restrict the design argument to likelihood considerations is that it is supposed to be an *empirical* argument. To invoke prior probabilities is to bring in considerations *besides* the observations at hand.

3   In light of the fact that it is possible for a hypothesis to have an objective likelihood without also having an objective probability, one should understand Bayes's theorem as specifying how the quantities it mentions are related to each other, *if all are well defined*. And just as hypotheses can have likelihoods without having (objective) probabilities, it also is possible for the reverse situation to obtain. Suppose I draw a card from a deck of unknown composition. I observe (O) that the card is the four of diamonds. I now consider the hypothesis (H) that the card is a four. The value of $Pr(H \mid O)$ is well defined, but the value of $Pr(O \mid H)$ is not.

4   Actually, Paley (1802) *does* consider a "selective retention" process, but only very briefly. In Chapter 5 (pp. 49–51) he explores the hypothesis that a random process once generated a huge range of variation, and that this variation was then culled, with only stable configurations surviving. Paley argues against this hypothesis by saying that we should see unicorns and mermaids if it were true. He also says that it mistakenly predicts that organisms should fail to form a taxonomic hierarchy. It is ironic that Darwin claimed that his own theory *predicts* hierarchy. In fact, Paley and Darwin are both right. Darwin's theory includes the idea that all living things have common ancestors, while the selection hypothesis that Paley considers does not.

5   More precisely, Fisher said that a mother should have a son with probability p and a daughter with probability (1 − p), where the effect of this is that the expected

expenditures on the two sexes are the same; the argument is not undermined by the fact that some mothers have all sons while others have all daughters.

6   Dawkins (1986) makes the point that evolution by natural selection is not a uniform chance process by way of an analogy with a combination lock. This is discussed in Sober (1993, pp. 36–9).

7   Dembski (1998) construes design inference as allowing one to argue in favor of the design hypothesis, and "sweep from the field" all alternatives, without the design hypothesis ever having to make a prediction. For criticisms of Dembski's framework, see Fitelson, Stephens, and Sober (1999).

8   Paley (1802) argues in Chapter 16 that the benevolence of the deity is demonstrated by the fact that organisms experience more pleasure than they need to (p. 295). He also argues that pain is useful (p. 320) and that few diseases are fatal; he defends the latter conclusion by citing statistics on the cure rate at a London hospital (p. 321).

9   For it to be certain that all configurations will be visited, there must be infinite time. The shorter the time-frame, the lower the probability that a given configuration will occur. This means that the estimated age of the universe may entail that it is very *im*probable that a given configuration will occur. I set this objection aside in what follows.

10 It is a standard feature of likelihood comparisons that O_w sometimes fails to discriminate between a pair of hypotheses, even though O_s is able to do so, when O_s entails O_w. You are the cook in a restaurant. The waiter brings an order into the kitchen – someone ordered bacon and eggs. You wonder whether this information discriminates between the hypothesis that your friend Smith ordered the meal and the hypothesis that your friend Jones did. You know the eating habits of each. Here's the probability of the order's being for ±bacon and ±eggs, conditional on the order's coming from Smith and conditional on the order's coming from Jones:

Pr(– | Smith)   Pr(– | Jones)

	Eggs +	Eggs –			Eggs +	Eggs –
Bacon +	0.4	0.1		Bacon +	0.1	0.4
Bacon –	0.2	0.3		Bacon –	0.5	0

The fact that the customer ordered bacon does not discriminate between the two hypotheses (since 0.5 = 0.5). And the fact that the customer ordered eggs doesn't help either (since 0.6 = 0.6). However, the fact that the customer ordered bacon *and* eggs favors Smith over Jones (since 0.4 > 0.1).

11 The example of the SETI project throws light on Paley's question as to why we think that watches must be the result of intelligent design, but don't think this when we observe a stone. It is tempting to answer this question by saying that watches are "complicated" while stones are not. However, there are many complicated natural processes (like the turbulent flow of water coming from a faucet) that don't cry out for explanation in terms of intelligent design. Similarly, narrow-band radio emissions

may be physically "simple" but that doesn't mean that the SETI engineers were wrong to search for them.

12 Assessing the likelihood of a disjunction involves an additional problem. Even if the values of $\Pr(O \mid D1)$ and $\Pr(O \mid D2)$ are known, what is the value of $\Pr(O \mid D1$ or $D2)$? The answer is that it must be somewhere in between. But exactly where depends on further considerations, since $\Pr(O \mid D1$ or $D2) = \Pr(O \mid D1)\Pr(D1 \mid D1$ or $D2) + \Pr(O \mid D2)\Pr(D2 \mid D1$ or $D2)$. If either God or a superintelligent extraterrestrial built the vertebrate eye, what is the probability that it was God who did so?

13 The statement "p is both false and untestable" is logically consistent (assuming that the verificationist theory of meaning is mistaken). However, the *assertion* of this conjunction is paradoxical, akin to Moore's paradoxical statement "p is true but I don't believe it." Both conjunctions embody pragmatic, not semantic, paradoxes.

14 To isolate this new problem from the one already identified, I'll assume in what follows that the design hypothesis and the chance hypothesis with which it competes have built into them auxiliary assumptions that suffice for their likelihoods to be well defined.

15 This general point surfaces in simple inference problems like the ravens paradox (Hempel, 1965). Does the fact that the object before you is a black raven confirm the generalization that all ravens are black? That depends on how you gathered your data. Perhaps you sampled at random from the set of *ravens*; alternatively, you may have sampled at random from the set of *black ravens*. In the first case, your observation confirms the generalization, but in the second it does not. In the second case, notice that you were bound to observe that the object before you is a black raven, regardless of whether all ravens are black.

16 Although weak and strong anthropic principles differ, they have something in common. For example, the causal structure implicitly assumed in the weak anthropic principle is that of two effects of a common cause:

(WAP)   Origin of universe ⟨ We exist now. / Constants now are right.

In contrast, one of the strong anthropic principles assumes the following causal arrangement:

(SAP)   We exist now → Origin of the universe → Constants now are right.

Even though (WAP) is true and (SAP) is false, both entail a *correlation* between our existence and the constants now having the values they do. To deal with the resulting OSEs, we must decide how to take these correlations into account in assessing likelihoods.

17 Similarly, the fact that there is something rather than nothing does not discriminate between chance and design.

18 The fishing and fine-tuning examples involve *extreme* OSEs. More modest OSEs are possible. If C describes the circumstances in which we make our observational determination as to whether proposition O is true, and we use the outcome of this determination to decide whether H1 or H2 is more likely, then a *quantitative* OSE is present precisely when

$Pr(O \mid H1 \ \& \ C) \neq Pr(O \mid H1)$ or
$Pr(O \mid H2 \ \& \ C) \neq Pr(O \mid H2)$.

A *qualitative* OSE occurs when taking account of C alters the likelihood ordering:

$Pr(O \mid H1 \ \& \ C) > Pr(O \mid H2 \ \& \ C)$ and $Pr(O \mid H1) \ngtr Pr(O \mid H2)$ or
$Pr(O \mid H1 \ \& \ C) = Pr(O \mid H2 \ \& \ C)$ and $Pr(O \mid H1) \neq Pr(O \mid H2)$.

Understood in this way, an OSE is just an example of *sampling bias*.

19 There is a third possibility – that the marksmen intended to kill the prisoner. But for the sake of simplicity (and also to make the firing squad argument more parallel with the argument from fine-tuning), I'll ignore this possibility.

20 The issue, thus, is not whether (L1) or (L2) are true (both are), but which an agent should use in interpreting the bearing of observations on the likelihoods of hypotheses. In this respect the injunction of the weak anthropic principle is like the principle of total evidence – it is a pragmatic principle, concerning which statements should be used for which purposes.

21 In order to replicate in the fine-tuning argument the difference between the prisoner's and the bystander's points of view, imagine that we observe through a telescope another universe in which the constants are right. We bystanders can use this observation in a way that the inhabitants of that universe cannot.

22 Notice that "I exist" when thought by the prisoner, is a priori, whereas "the prisoner exists," when thought by the bystander, is a posteriori. Is it so surprising that an a priori statement should have a different evidential significance than an a posteriori statement?

I also should note that my claim is that the proposition "I am alive" does not permit the prisoner to conclude that design is more likely than chance. I do not say that there is no proposition he can cite after the marksmen fire that discriminates between the two hypotheses. Consider, for example, the observation that "no bullets hit me." This favors design over chance, even after the prisoner conditionalizes on the fact that he is alive. Notice also that if the prisoner were alive but riddled with bullets, it is not so clear that design would be more likely than chance.

23 I have argued that the prisoner should assign the same likelihoods to chance and design, but that he is entitled to think that his survival lowers the probability of chance and raises the probability of design. On its face, this contradicts the following consequence of Bayes's theorem:

$$\frac{Pr(\text{Chance} \mid \text{I survive})}{Pr(\text{Design} \mid \text{I survive})} = \frac{Pr(\text{I survive} \mid \text{Chance})}{Pr(\text{I survive} \mid \text{Design})} \times \frac{Pr(\text{Chance})}{Pr(\text{Design})}.$$

If the ratio of posterior probabilities is greater than the ratio of priors, this must be because the two likelihoods have different values.

The reason my argument implies no such contradiction is that I have argued, first, that the relevant likelihoods are *not* the ones displayed above, but are ones that take account of the presence of an OSE. I further imagined that the prisoner possesses knowledge (inferred from frequencies) that the two posterior probabilities displayed above are, respectively, low and high. This inference might be called "direct" since it proceeds without the prisoner's having to assign values to likelihoods. Bayes's theorem describes how various quantities are related when each is well defined; it does not entail that all of them are well defined in every situation (Sober, 2002). It is a familiar point made by critics of Bayesianism that likelihoods can be well defined even when prior and posterior probabilities are not. This severing of the connection between likelihoods and probabilities, or something like it, arises in the firing squad problem. The prisoner can know that chance is improbable and that design is highly probable, given his observation after the firing squad fires that he exists, even though his evaluation of likelihoods should focus on likelihoods that are identical in value.

24 The hypothesis that our universe is one among many has been introduced as a possible explanation of the fact that the constants (in our universe) are right. A universe is here understood to be a region of spacetime that is causally closed. See Leslie (1989) for discussion. If the point of the multiverse hypothesis is to challenge the design hypothesis, on the assumption that the design hypothesis has already vanquished the hypothesis of chance, then the multiverse hypothesis is not needed. Furthermore, in comparing the multiverse hypothesis and the design hypothesis, one needs to attend to the inverse gambler's fallacy discussed earlier. This is not to deny that there may be other evidence for the multiverse hypothesis; however, the mere fact that the constants are right in our universe does not favor that hypothesis.

25 As Dennett (1987a, pp. 284–5) observes, human beings have been modifying the characteristics of animals and plants by *artificial selection* for thousands of years. However, the organisms thus modified were not *created* by human beings. If the design argument endorses a hypothesis about how organisms were brought into being, then the work of plant and animal breeders, per se, does not show that the design argument should be stripped of its theological trappings.

References

Arbuthnot, John (1710) An Argument for Divine Providence, Taken from the Constant Regularity Observ'd in the Births of Both Sexes. *Philosophical Transactions of the Royal Society of London*, 27, 186–90.

Barrow, John (1988) *The World Within the World*. Oxford: Clarendon Press.

Behe, Michael J. (1996) *Darwin's Black Box*. New York: Free Press.

Carter, Brandon (1974) Large Number Coincidences and the Anthropic Principle in Cosmology. In M. S. Longair (ed.), *Confrontation of Cosmological Theories with Observational Data* (pp. 291–8). Dordrecht: Reidel.

Darwin, Charles (1859) *On the Origin of Species*. London: John Murray. Cambridge, Mass.: Harvard University Press, 1964.

Dawkins, Richard (1986) *The Blind Watchmaker*. New York: Norton.

Dembski, William A. (1998) *The Design Inference*. Cambridge: Cambridge University Press.

Dennett, Daniel C. (1987a) Intentional Systems in Cognitive Ethology – the "Panglossian Paradigm" defended. In *The Intentional Stance* (pp. 237–86). Cambridge, Mass.: MIT Press.

Dennett, Daniel C. (1987b) True Believers. In *The Intentional Stance* (pp. 13–42). Cambridge, Mass.: MIT Press.

Dick, Stephen J. (1996) *The Biological Universe – the Twentieth-Century Extraterrestrial Life Debate and the Limits of Science.* Cambridge: Cambridge University Press.

Earman, John (1987) The Sap Also Rises – a Critical Examination of the Anthropic Principle. *American Philosophical Quarterly*, 24, 307–17.

Eddington, Arthur (1939) *The Philosophy of Physical Science.* Cambridge: Cambridge University Press.

Edwards, A. W. F. (1972) *Likelihood.* Cambridge: Cambridge University Press.

Fisher, R. A. (1930) *The Genetical Theory of Natural Selection.* New York: Dover. Second edn. 1957.

Fitelson, Branden, Stephens, Christopher, and Sober, Elliott (1999) How Not to Detect Design – a Review of William Dembski's *The Design Inference. Philosophy of Science*, 66, 472–88. Also available at the following URL: http://philosophy.wisc.edu/sober.

Forster, Malcolm R. and Sober, Elliott (2003) Why likelihood? In M. Taper and S. Lee (eds.), *The Nature of Scientific Evidence.* Chicago: University of Chicago Press. Also available at the following URL: http://philosophy.wisc.edu/forster.

Gould, Stephen Jay (1980) *The Panda's Thumb.* New York: Norton.

Hacking, Ian (1965) *The Logic of Statistical Inference.* Cambridge: Cambridge University Press.

Hacking, Ian (1987) The Inverse Gambler's Fallacy: The Argument from Design. The Anthropic Principle Applied to Wheeler Universes. *Mind*, 96, 331–40.

Hempel, Carl G. (1965) Studies in the Logic of Confirmation. In *Aspects of Scientific Explanation and Other Essays in the Philosophy of Science.* New York: Free Press.

Hume, David ([1779] 1980) *Dialogues Concerning Natural Religion.* Indianapolis: Hackett Publishing.

Keynes, John Maynard (1921) *A Treatise on Probability.* London: Macmillan.

Kyburg, Henry (1961) *Probability and the Logic of Rational Belief.* Middletown, Conn.: Wesleyan University Press.

Leslie, John (1989) *Universes.* London: Routledge.

Madden, Edward and Hare, Peter (1968) *Evil and the Concept of God.* Springfield: Charles Thomas.

McMullin, Ernan (1993) Indifference principle and anthropic principle in cosmology. *Studies in the History and Philosophy of Science*, 24, 359–89.

Paley, William (1802) *Natural Theology, or, Evidences of the Existence and Attributes of the Deity, Collected from the Appearances of Nature.* London: Rivington.

Plantinga, Alvin (1974) *The Nature of Necessity.* New York: Oxford University Press.

Plantinga, Alvin (1979) The Probabilistic Argument from Evil. *Philosophical Studies*, 35, 1–53.

Rowe, William L. (1979) The Problem of Evil and Some Varieties of Atheism. *American Philosophical Quarterly*, 16, 335–41.

Royall, Richard M. (1997) *Statistical Evidence – a Likelihood Paradigm.* London: Chapman and Hall.

Sober, Elliott (1993) *Philosophy of Biology.* Boulder, Colo.: Westview Press.

Sober, Elliott (1999) Testability. *Proceedings and Addresses of the American Philosophical Association*, 73, 47–76. Also available at the following URL: http://philosophy.wisc.edu/sober.

Sober, Elliott (2000a) Evolution and the Problem of Other Minds. *Journal of Philosophy*, 97, 365–86.

Sober, Elliott (2000b) Quine's Two Dogmas. *Proceedings of the Aristotlean Society*, 74, 237–80.

Sober, Elliott (2002) Bayesianism – Its Scope and Limits. In R. Swinburne (ed.), *Bayesianism*. London: British Academy. Also available at the following URL: http://philosophy.wisc.edu/sober.

Sorensen, Roy (1988) *Blindspots*. Oxford: Oxford University Press.

Stigler, Stephen M. (1986) *The History of Statistics*. Cambridge, Mass.: Harvard University Press.

Swinburne, Richard (1968) The Argument from Design. *Philosophy*, 43, 199–212.

Swinburne, Richard (1990a) Argument from the Fine-Tuning of the Universe. In. J. Leslie (ed.), *Physical Cosmology and Philosophy* (pp. 160–179). New York: Macmillan.

Swinburne, Richard (1990b) The Limits of Explanation. In D. Knowles (ed.), *Explanation and its Limits* (pp. 177–93). Cambridge: Cambridge University Press.

Turing, Alan (1950) Computing Machinery and Intelligence. *Mind*, 59, 433–60.

van Inwagen, Peter (1993) *Metaphysics*. Boulder, Colo.: Westview Press.

Venn, John (1866) *The Logic of Chance*. New York: Chelsea.

White, Roger (2000) Fine-Tuning and Multiple Universes. *Noûs*, 34, 260–76.

Suggested Further Reading

Pennock, Robert T. (ed.) (2001) *Intelligent Design Creationism and its Critics*. Cambridge, Mass.: MIT Press.

Pennock, Robert T. (2002) *Tower of Babel: The Evidence Against the New Creationism*. Cambridge, Mass.: MIT Press.

Ruse, Michael (2003) *Darwin and Design: Does Evolution have a Purpose?* Cambridge, Mass.: Harvard University Press.

Chapter 7

The Problem of Evil

Derk Pereboom

Virtually all monotheistic religions profess that there is a divine being who is significantly good, knowledgeable, and powerful. The evils of this world present various challenges for such religions. The starkest challenge is directed towards views according to which there exists a being who is wholly good, omniscient, and omnipotent.[1] For it would seem that such a being would have the moral disposition, the knowledge, and the power to prevent any evil whatsoever, and from this one might readily conclude that if there were such a being, there would be no evil. On one version of this challenge, the coexistence of evil with a God defined in this way is logically or metaphysically impossible. This has come to be called *the logical* or *the modal problem of evil*. Another is that the existence of such a God is improbable given the evils of this world, or at least that the existence of these evils significantly lowers the probability that such a God exists. The concern expressed is that these evils provide good evidence against the existence of such a God. This version is known as *the evidential problem of evil*.

One traditional response to these problems for theistic belief is to provide reasons why God would produce or allow evil. This is the project of *theodicy* – the defense of God in the face of the problem of evil. Prominent among such attempts are the free will theodicy, according to which evils are not due to God but rather to the free choices of other agents; the soul-building theodicy, in which God allows or brings about evil in order to elicit virtue and to build character; and the punishment theodicy, by which God allows or brings about evil as punishment for sin. Part of the idea of a theodicy is that it is represented as true or at least highly probable given the existence of God. Potential difficulties for this project are reflected by the concern that various theodicies are inadequate, and by the worry that because theodicies are essentially attempts to account for evil in terms of some good, they threaten to misrepresent evil as a good of some sort, and to misrepresent the nature of God by way of ascribing the endorsement of that "good" to God. Accordingly, a second theistic response is to deny the value or appropriateness of the project of theodicy and to argue instead that the existence of evil does not undermine rationality of belief in God for the reason that human understanding is inadequate to discern God's reasons for allowing evil. This response has come to be known as *skeptical theism*. This position is inspired by the book of Job, in which his friends claim that Job's suffering is divine punishment for his sins, to which God responds by expressing his incomprehensibility and by rebuking them because they "have not spoken of me what is right."[2] Another response, intermediate between theodicy and a radical skeptical theism according to which we have no inkling as to why God might allow evil, is motivated by the problems for theodicy, but is nevertheless concerned to provide a positive answer to the problem of evil. In his reply to the modal version of the problem, Alvin Plantinga introduces the notion of a *defense*, which is not, like a theodicy, a claim to grasp the actual reasons why God allows evil, but is rather a fairly well-specified hypothesis according to which the existence of God is consistent with the existence of evil, but which is advanced not as true, nor even as plausible, but simply as possible, or at least for which there is no reason to believe that it is impossible. As we shall see, Peter van Inwagen has emended the notion of defense to range over hypotheses whose degree of credibility is somewhat more impressive.

The Logical Problem of Evil for Traditional Theism

Is the coexistence of evil with an omnipotent, omniscient, and wholly good God impossible, as J. L. Mackie argues?[3] The most discussed reply to the logical problem of evil is the free will defense, formulated by Plantinga.[4] One might consider two distinct problems under this rubric: one is the *abstract* logical problem of evil, which poses the challenge that the existence of God and the existence of *any evil at all* are not logically compossible; the other is the *concrete* logical problem of evil, which raises the issue that the existence of God and the existence of *the world's actual evils* are not logically compossible. Of these, Plantinga focuses on the abstract logical problem of evil. (More precisely, he takes on the abstract *modal* problem of evil – he wants not only to show that God and some evil are compossible in that there is no logical contradiction or inconsistency involved in claiming the existence of both, but also that they are compossible in the "broadly logical" or metaphysical sense of (com)possibility.) His strategy is to find a hypothesis whose possible truth is obvious, that is compossible with

(1)   God, a being who is omniscient, omnipotent, and wholly good, exists

and that entails

(2)   There is evil.

Plantinga calls his proposed hypothesis *the free will defense*.[5]

This hypothesis involves first of all the claim that God is justified in creating beings that are *significantly free*. If a being is *free* with respect to a decision to perform an action, then, holding fixed the entire history of the universe up to the time of the decision, it is causally possible both that he make this decision and that he refrain from making this decision. Plantinga has in mind a paradigmatic type of libertarian freedom. If a being is causally determined to make a choice, then by definition he is not free with respect to that decision. Further, an action is *morally significant* for a person at a time if it would be wrong for him to perform the action then and right to refrain, or vice versa. A person is *significantly free* at a time if he is then free with respect to an action that is morally significant for him.

Now Mackie asks why it would not be possible for God to create a world of significantly free beings all of whom always freely choose the good.[6] Plantinga agrees that there is a possible world that has this feature, but the core of the free will defense is that it is possible that God could not have actualized this world. In making his case, he first distinguishes between two senses of actualization, *strong* and *weak*.[7] God can *strongly actualize* only what he can cause to be actual, so given that he cannot, as a matter of logical fact, cause our free decisions, God cannot strongly actualize any of our free decisions. But if God knows that an agent would freely perform an action if God were to place her in circumstances in which she is significantly free with respect to that action, and if God then causes her to be in that situation, then he *weakly actualizes* her free decision. So then, Mackie's hypothesis might be recast as the claim that God could have weakly actualized a world of significantly free beings all of whom always do only what is right.

Plantinga argues that it is possible that this claim is false.[8] For in his view it is possible that (God knows that) every possible person – i.e. every person-essence – has *transworld depravity*. For such an essence to suffer from transworld depravity is for it to be such that if God had created the person, and had given her significant freedom, then no matter what circumstances God were to place her in, she would go wrong with respect to at least one action, so long as God left her significantly free. Consequently, if an essence suffers from transworld depravity, it is not within God's power to weakly actualize a possible world in which the corresponding person is significantly free and yet never makes a wrong free decision. But if it is possible that every relevant essence suffers from transworld depravity, then no matter what world featuring significantly free beings God weakly actualizes, there will be evil in that world. Consequently, there is indeed a possibly true proposition, viz.,

(3)   Every (relevant) essence suffers from transworld depravity

that is clearly consistent with

(1)   God, a being who is omniscient, omnipotent, and wholly good, exists

and that entails

(2)   There is evil,

and the free will defense is complete.

Many of those involved in this debate agree that Plantinga has provided a successful response to the abstract logical problem of evil. Michael Tooley contends, however, that this is only a small victory, for the genuinely pressing issue is raised instead by the concrete version of the problem.[9] Tooley believes that the more significant concern is that the existence of God and the existence of the world's actual evils – their kinds, amounts, and distributions – might not be compossible. But others have expressed misgivings about the plausibility of the free will defense itself. David Lewis points out that even if (3) is possible, God could nevertheless have avoided evil by allowing creatures to have significant freedom only when he foresees that they will make right choices.[10] So if God foresees that a creature would make the wrong choice if left alone, God might then causally determine her to make the right one instead. One answer to this "selective freedom" response is John Bishop's, that if God pursued this policy for every wrong free choice he foresees, much of the value of giving creatures significant freedom would be lost.[11] But this claim can obviously be contested.

Keith De Rose contends that we should be at least somewhat dubious about whether

(3)   Every (relevant) essence suffers from transworld depravity

is possibly true – he for one, has no clear intuition that it is.[12] Our reason, he thinks, for believing that (3) is possibly true is that there doesn't seem to be anything that threatens its possible truth. Perhaps this is the only reason – Plantinga himself offers no argument in favor of its possibility. But as De Rose points out, Plantinga would then seem to be relying on the *presumption of the possibility of a proposition* – which one might formulate as follows:

(PPP)   If nothing threatens the possibility of a proposition, then one can justifiably regard it as possible.

But Plantinga himself contends that (PPP) is dubious. For, in general, suppose that I want to enlist (PPP) to justify my claim that some proposition p is possible. Someone could just as well use (PPP) to assert the possibility of *necessarily not-p* or *impossibly p*, and, by standard modal logic, the possible truth of each of these claims entails that p is impossible. It would seem, then, that if (PPP) has any legitimacy at all, there must be some restriction on the propositions to which it can be applied. Jonathan Bennett argues that (PPP) be restricted to propositions that do not themselves have modal concepts nested within them.[13] But given this limitation, (PPP) does not legitimately apply to (3), for the reason that it has nested within it certain complex modal relationships. In effect (3) asserts that every possible person is such that, were God to actualize that being in some world, there is no possible world accessible to it in which that creature is significantly free and always does what is right.

Marilyn Adams agrees with Tooley that the concrete version of the logical problem of evil is the more pressing one, and she endeavors to explain the compossibility of God and the world's actual evils. Adams points out that especially intractable have been the horrendous evils which she defines as "evils the participation in which constitutes prima facie reason to doubt whether the participant's life could be a great good to him/her on the whole."[14] As examples, she cites "the rape of a woman and axing off her arms, psycho-physical torture whose ultimate goal is the disintegration of personality, betrayal of one's deepest loyalties, child abuse of the sort described by Ivan Karamazov, child pornography, parental incest, slow death by starvation." Her strategy is to specify a possible scenario in which God is good to all persons by insuring each a life that is a great good to the person on the whole, not merely by *balancing off* but also by *defeating* her participation in horrendous evils within the context of the world as a whole and of that individual's life.[15] Roderick Chisholm distinguishes the defeat from the balancing off of an evil: an evil is balanced off within a larger whole if that whole features goods that equal or outweigh it; while an evil is defeated within a larger whole when it actually contributes to a greater good within that whole. Adams doubts that the required scenario can be delineated without recourse to values that are specifically religious, such as the good of intimacy with the divine, but she acknowledges that this move would render its possibility less credible to atheists. She in fact claims that any successful defense will make sense only within the framework of controversial philosophical and theological assumptions.[16]

In Adams's account, balancing off of horrendous evil could be guaranteed by an afterlife in wholesome environments in which persons live in beatific intimacy with God. But, in addition, actual defeat of such evil is also possible. For it is possible that God defeat human suffering by empathetically identifying with it, since this would allow human beings to re-envision their suffering as a point of identification with God. And so, "by virtue of endowing horrors with a good aspect, Divine identification makes the victim's experience of horrors so meaningful that she would not retrospectively wish it away."[17] At the same time Adams denies that participation in horrors is necessary for an individual's incommensurate good, for "a horror-free life that ended in beatific intimacy with God would also be one in which the individual enjoyed incommensurate good."[18] Accordingly, one might question why God would then allow anyone at all to suffer horrendous evil. Adams claims not to have any more than partial reasons in response to this question.[19]

Theodicies

Theodicies are more ambitious than defenses, for theodicies aim to provide explanations for God's allowing or bringing about evil that we can know to be true or that are at least highly probable given God's existence. Theodicies might be divided into two categories. *Traditional theodicies* retain the notion of God as omnipotent, omniscient, and wholly good, while *non-traditional theodicies* dispense with this notion. Of the traditional theodicies the most influential today are the free will, the soul-building, and the punishment theodicies. Both currently and historically the most prominent non-traditional theodicies dispense with divine omnipotence.

It is fairly often granted that the various traditional theodicies provide reasonable explanations for the existence of some evils. For example, most would agree that some evils, such as certain pains, would be balanced off by making possible higher-order goods such as free choice between right and wrong and courage in the face of adversity. It is generally agreed that theodicies encounter severe difficulties in accounting for cases of especially horrible evils.

The free will theodicy

The free will theodicy in systematized form dates back at least to St Augustine, and remains the most prominent of all theodicies. On the most common version, God had the option of creating or refraining from creating significantly free beings. A risk incurred by creating such beings is that they might freely choose evil and the choice be unpreventable by God. Benefits include creatures having moral responsibility for their actions and being creators in their own right. Since the benefits outweigh the risks, God is morally justified in creating significantly free beings, and he is not culpable when they choose wrongly. An obvious concern for this theodicy is that there is considerable controversy about whether we have the libertarian free will entailed by significant freedom. Part of the task of this theodicy, then, is to make it plausible that we are free in the required libertarian sense.

Another issue for the free will theodicy is that many of the more horrible evils would not seem to be or result from freely willed decisions.[20] People being injured and dying as a result of earthquake, volcanic eruptions, diseases – including mental illnesses that give rise to unfree evil choices – would not seem to result from freely willed decisions, and for this reason are standardly classified as *natural* as opposed to *moral* evils. In response, Plantinga suggests the hypothesis that evils of this sort result from the free choices of beings such as demons, and they would then count as moral evils after all.

A further objection, raised by Lewis, is that even if we have free will of the libertarian sort, and many of our choices are freely willed in this libertarian sense,

God could still have acted so as to prevent the consequences of those decisions.[21] Given the nature of libertarian free will, God might not have been able to prevent the Nazi leaders from making their decisions to perpetrate genocide, supposing the circumstances of these decisions are held fixed. Nevertheless, God could still have prevented the genocide, by, say, having key leaders die of illnesses before being able to act on their decisions, or arranging circumstances differently so that prior to leaders acting on their decisions would-be assassins had succeeded rather than failed, or by a dramatic manifestation of the divine at an appropriate moment, or by miraculously causing the means of genocide to fail. One reply is that if God were regularly to prevent evils in such ways, we free agents would not adequately grasp the sorts of consequences our choices could have, and this would have considerable disvalue. But it would seem that much greater overall value would be secured if God so intervened in at least some of the more horrible cases.

A response developed by Swinburne is that not only free decisions, but complete freely willed actions successfully executed have a high degree of intrinsic value, and this value is high enough for God to be justified in not preventing such evil consequences.[22] Freely willed actions successfully executed exhibit freedom that is much more intrinsically valuable than free decisions whose consequences are prevented. Moreover, the sharper the moral contrast between the options, the more valuable the free choice for the good. An example of especially horrible evil that would result from free choices concerns the slave trade from Africa in the seventeenth and eighteenth centuries. About this practice Swinburne writes:

> But God allowing this to occur made possible innumerable opportunities for very large numbers of people to contribute or not to contribute to the development of this culture; for slavers to choose to enslave or not; for plantation-owners to choose to buy slaves or not and to treat them well or ill; for ordinary white people and politicians to campaign for its abolition or not to bother, and to campaign for compensation for the victims or not to bother; and so on.[23]

A first problem for this line of thought is that it conflicts with deeply ingrained intuitions about moral practice when horrible evil is at issue. First, as Lewis points out, for us the evildoer's freedom is a weightless consideration, not merely an outweighed consideration; that is, when one is deliberating about whether to prevent or allow evil, an evildoer's free will has no value that we take into consideration.[24] For example, when during World War II the inhabitants of a village in the Soviet Union decided to resist the SS unit threatening them with annihilation, we would not have expected these villagers to consider at all the value of their attackers' freely willed actions successfully executed. But this value would be immense if value of this sort were sufficient to justify God in not preventing the slave trade. In addition, if Swinburne were right, then when a thousand SS soldiers are attempting to perpetrate genocide, potentially a thousand times as much value is at stake as when there is only one. Furthermore, all else being equal, there would be significantly less reason to harm in self-defense an attacker who appears to have free will than someone who is understood to be mentally ill and not capable of free choice.[25] Genuinely endorsing Swinburne's view would seem to require a radical change in the way we deliberate morally, a change that would not clearly be salutary.

Another problem for the free will theodicy is occasioned by Swinburne's plausible view that to choose freely to do what is right in a serious and valuable way one must have an appreciably strong countervailing desire to do what is wrong, strong enough that it might actually motivate a free choice.[26] Swinburne thinks that this point supports the free will theodicy, since it can explain why God allows us to have desires to do evil, and, by extension, why he allows choices in accord with those desires. But this point rather serves to undermine the force of the free will theodicy as an explanation for many horrible evils. For we do not generally believe that the value of a free choice outweighs the disvalue of having desires to perform horribly evil actions that are strong enough that they may result in choice. For example, the notion that it is more valuable than not for people to have serious desires to rape and kill young children for the reason that this gives them the opportunity to choose freely not to do so has no purchase on us. Our practice for people with desires of this sort is to have them undergo therapy to diminish or eradicate such desires. We have no tendency to believe that the value of a free decision not to rape and kill made in struggle against a desire to do so carries any weight against the proposal to provide this sort of therapy. Furthermore, were we to encounter someone with a strong desire to reinstate slavery but who nevertheless resisted actively seeking to do so, we would not think that his condition has more value overall than one in which he never had the desire to reinstate slavery in the first place. Moreover, I daresay that a significant proportion of people alive today – well over 90 percent – has neither intentionally chosen a horrendous evil nor had a genuine struggle with a desire to do so – they have never, for instance, tortured, maimed, or murdered, nor seriously struggled with desires to do so. But we do not think that their lives would have been more valuable had they possessed such desires even if every struggle against them was successful. Thus it is dubious that God would allow such desires in order to realize the value of certain free choices for the good. This aspect of Swinburne's theodicy may have some credibility with respect to evils that are not especially terrifying, but has at best little when it comes to horrendous evils.

The punishment theodicy

Another traditional theodicy is that God brings about or allows evil as punishment for sin. One problem with this theodicy is that much suffering that occurs cannot reasonably be justified as punishment. On no account that can be taken seriously does a five-year-old deserve to be punished by being raped and beaten.

Does an average 65-year-old man who has committed no serious crime, and is not an extraordinary sinner, deserve the lingering, excruciating pain of a disease and then death as punishment for his wrongdoing? Our judicial system would regard punishment of this sort *for crimes* as monstrous. Imagine if we were to punish murderers by inducing such suffering – very few would find that conscionable. Someone might reply that since each of us deserves an eternity of torture, a fortiori each of us also deserves suffering of this sort. But since it is doubtful that anyone genuinely understands why we all might merit punishment of this sort, this line of thought does not suggest a theodicy, but at best a defense or a version of skeptical theism.

It is useful to keep in mind the various theories for justifying punishment – retribution, deterrence, and moral education. The horrible evils just discussed would constitute punishments far too harsh to be justified retributively, and even if these evils have the potential of deterring similar wrongdoing or morally educating wrongdoers, a limitation on the severity of punishment is understood to be a constraint on punishment justified in these ways. Moreover, clearly communicating the reason for punishment to the wrongdoer or to others is required for deterrence and moral education, and such horrible evils are at least typically not accompanied by any such communication. It might nevertheless be suggested that these horrible evils could somehow be a means to improvement or development of moral character, but this would not be by virtue of their counting as just punishment.

The soul-building theodicy

John Hick has in recent times advocated a theodicy according to which evil is required for the best sort of human intellectual, technological, moral, and spiritual development.[27] Sin and suffering is valuable, on his account, because it occasions freely chosen efforts whereby it might be overcome, and because improvement of character – both within an individual and throughout human history – results from such efforts. Without evil there would be no stimulus to the development of economic, technological, and social structures, which lie at the core of human civilization. And without evil there would be no occasion for care for others, devotion to the public good, courage, self-sacrifice – for the kind of love that involves bearing one another's burdens, or for the kind of character that is built through these qualities.

Eleonore Stump advocates a version of the soul-building theodicy that adduces an explicitly theological good. She argues that moral and natural evil contribute to a humbling recognition of oneself as having a defective will, which in turn can motivate one to turn to God to fix the defect in the will.[28] The defect in the will is that one has a bent towards evil, so that one has a diminished capacity to will what one ought to will. In Stump's account, both the turning towards God and God's fixing the will have considerable value for a person.

The main problem for this sort of theodicy, which Hick is indeed concerned to address, is that evils often do not give rise to the specified goods, and in fact sometimes destroy a person rather than contributing to his salutary development. Here Hick cites massive disasters like earthquakes and famines, but also particular sorts of individual illnesses:

> when a child dies of cerebral meningitis, his little personality undeveloped and his life unfulfilled; or when a charming, lively, and intelligent woman suffers from a shrinking of the brain which destroys her personality and leaves her in an asylum, barely able to recognize her nearest relatives, until death comes in middle life as a baneful blessing; or when a child is born so deformed and defective that he can never live a properly human life, but must always be an object of pity to some and revulsion to others ... when such things happen we can see no gain to the soul, whether of the victim or of others, but on the contrary only a ruthlessly destructive process which is utterly inimical to human values.[29]

Hick's main response is that such evils are only apparently without purpose. For in a world without such evils

> human misery would not evoke deep personal sympathy or call forth organized relief and sacrificial help and service. For it is presupposed in these compassionate reactions both that the suffering is not deserved and that it is bad for the sufferer ... in a world that is to be the scene of compassionate love and self-giving for others, suffering must fall upon mankind with something of the haphazardness and inequity that we now experience. It must be apparently unmerited, pointless, and incapable of being morally rationalized.[30]

However, evils on the order of World War II or the bubonic plague are clearly not required to occasion virtuous responses of these kinds or the attendant personal development. But still, it might be argued that these and similar calamities did provide unusually challenging opportunities for virtuous responses, and that they did in fact result in especially valuable instances of such responses. Yet one might well doubt whether refraining from preventing these calamities could be justified by the expected or foreseen gain. Similarly, for more localized evils such as a child suffering and dying of cerebral meningitis, one might also doubt whether the good effects, such as sympathy and efforts to aid, could justify a failure to prevent those evils. It is telling that we would not consider the loss of occasion for virtue and character development as even a mild countervailing reason to the development of a vaccine for this disease. More generally, the pressing doubt about the soul-building theodicy is that virtuous responses and admirable character development would be possible even if human life featured much, much, less apparently pointless suffering than it does; and even if allowing this suffering would result in some gain, the gain seems insufficient to justify it.

Non-traditional theodicies

Throughout history, people have been willing to deny divine omnipotence as a component of an answer to the problem of evil. Zoroastrianism and its successors, such as the Manichaean position, countenance two very powerful but non-omnipotent supernatural beings, one good, the other evil. The history of the universe is a great struggle between these two forces. Evil is explained by the activity of the evil being and allied forces, and by the limited power of the good being and its cohort to prevent it. This view at the same time accommodates the force of several of the key reasons for belief in the existence of a good God, such as those displayed by the argument from design and by arguments from religious experience. Purely as a solution to the problem of evil, this position is impressive, but most Christians, Jews, and Muslims have been unwilling to give up the omnipotence of God, perhaps mainly due to the degree to which divine providence would be compromised. Nevertheless, certain elements of this view have always been found in Christianity in particular. The New Testament affirms the existence of Satan, demons, "principalities and powers," against whom God actually struggles for victory. In fact, as we have seen, Plantinga suggests that such beings may indeed be responsible for some of the evils that we find in the world.

More recently, theistic views have emerged that deny divine omnipotence without positing a powerful supernatural evil being. Process theologians, influenced by A. N. Whitehead, provide a prominent example.[31] Charles Hartshorne, for instance, contends that each created being has a power of self-determination of some degree or other, and that divine power is restricted to the power of persuasion, and that thus God cannot prevent creatures from going wrong when they determine themselves to do so and resist the persuasive power to do what is right.[32] From the point of view of traditional theism, such a position faces several problems. One is that if God's lack of power alone (and not in addition some countervailing evil force) explains why he did not in the past prevent diseases such as smallpox, then since we can prevent smallpox now, we are in some respects now more powerful than God, at least than he was in the past. And since we are not worthy of worship, God's worthiness to be worshiped is thus rendered doubtful. Another problem is that if God's lack of power explains why he did not prevent smallpox, or the people in the Lisbon earthquake of 1754 from being crushed by the rubble of the churches they were attending that Easter Sunday morning, then how could he be powerful enough to create bacteria and viruses or wood and stones, let alone the entire universe? Furthermore, if God is not powerful enough to be the creator, the reasons for believing in God expressed by the argument from design will have to be relinquished.

Baruch Spinoza retained omnipotence but rejected instead divine goodness.[33] In his view, any conception of the good is essentially interest-relative, and indeed the human conception of the good is tied to the kinds of concerns we have. But Spinoza's God has no interests, and indeed no desires or plans or wishes, and thus there could be no such thing as divine goodness per se. Spinoza's position has not won large numbers of adherents among those predisposed towards theism, undoubtedly in part because it rejects divine providence, a cornerstone of traditional theism, and also because it too must dispense with the reasons for belief in God expressed by the argument from design. Nevertheless, the existence of evil does not raise a problem for the existence of Spinoza's God.

Skeptical Theism

The skeptical theist position avoids theodicy, and claims instead that the nature of the good is or at least might be beyond our understanding to such a degree that we should not expect to understand how it is that God's governance of the universe accords with his goodness.[34] In recent times, Stephen Wykstra has developed an influential version of this view. One expression of the challenge to God's existence from evil is this:

> It appears that there is no moral purpose God could have that would justify his bringing about or allowing certain horrendous evils to occur.

In response, Wykstra proposes the following general "condition of reasonable epistemic access:"

> On the basis of cognized situation s, human H is entitled to claim 'It appears that p' only if it is reasonable to believe that, given her cognitive faculties and the use she has made of them, if p were not the case, s would likely be different than it is in some way discernible by her.[35]

For example, in a situation in which Joey is standing next to Billy, and Billy is crying with an apparently fresh bite-mark on his arm, and Joey is triumphantly holding Billy's toy car, and no one else is nearby, a parent is entitled to claim "It appears that Joey bit his brother" only if given how the parent has gathered evidence and given the evidence she has, if Joey did not bite his brother, the situation would likely be different than it is in some way discernible by her. Normally, a parent would be entitled to a claim of this sort in this kind of situation. But if the situation includes the parent's cognition of frequent and elaborate deception of the relevant sort on Billy's part, the parent may not be entitled to the claim. Wykstra employs this condition of reasonable epistemic access to argue that our cognitive situation does not entitle us to claim that it appears that there are evils that serve no God-justifying purpose – it does not justify us in affirming that it appears that there are states whose occurrence God would not allow. The reason for this is that if God existed, our understanding of the good would be so minimal by comparison to the divine understanding that we would have no reason to hold that the evils we are inclined to think serve no

God-justifying aim in fact do have such a purpose. We might not understand the full nature of goods of which we have some understanding, or there might be goods of which we have no understanding whatsoever, or there might be connections that we fail to grasp completely between goods (and evils) and certain types of states of affairs. An apt analogy is provided by William Alston.[36] When, I, a chess-novice, while watching a Karpov–Kasparov match have no inkling of the point of one of Karpov's moves, I am not entitled to claim "It appears that Karpov's move was pointless," for given my poor understanding of chess, if that move did have a point, I would not likely discern this fact.

An advantageous way of casting the issue is in terms of the extent to which the world's evils reduce the probability of God's existence. Let (E) be a proposition that details the kinds and amount of evil that the world features, and (G) be the hypothesis that God exists. What is the probability of (G) on (E)? According to skeptical theism generally, given the limited nature of our cognitive capacity to understand the nature of the good, (E) does not reduce the probability of (G) so as to make it less likely than not. In fact most skeptical theists will not concede that (E) significantly reduces the probability of (G) – whatever probability the existence of God has independently of (E) is substantially retained given (E). A reason for taking this stance is that once the theist admits that (E) can significantly reduce the probability of (G), she is in the position of having to haggle over the precise extent of the reduction. According to an importantly distinct strategy, developed by van Inwagen, the limitations of our cognitive capacities and of our actual knowledge and understanding render it true that we are in no position to assess the probability of (G) on (E). Van Inwagen's version is of a piece with his more general – but limited – skepticism about probability assessments. In his view, our capacity for assessing probabilities is scant in domains removed from the ordinary concerns of everyday life.

Different versions of skeptical theism concur that we do or might well have only limited cognitive capacities for understanding the nature of the good. But significantly, they diverge in their formulation of the result this limitation has for our attitude towards the existence of the requisite God-justifying purposes. In one version, because our cognitive capacities for understanding the nature of the good are limited, *we are in no position to deny* (or, equivalently, *we are in no position to rule out*) that there are moral reasons for God's allowing the world's evils to occur, even if we have no inkling as to what these reasons might be, and hence we have no good reason to believe that not-(G) is more likely on (E) than (G) is. But this statement of the position is vulnerable, for, by close analogy, a skeptic about quantum mechanics would then have an easy argument against his quarry. Is the claim that quantum mechanics is approximately true, (Q), well supported by the evidence physicists have currently amassed for it, (V)? Well, because our cognitive capacities for understanding physics are limited, we are in no position to deny that there is a currently unspecified theory distinct from quantum mechanics that is metaphysically more plausible and that explains (V) as well, and hence we have no reason to believe that (Q) is more likely on (V) than not. Skepticism about historical claims can also be easily generated along these lines. Our cognitive capacity to discern historical truths is indeed limited, but there are many cases in which we reasonably judge some historical claim to be more likely than not on the evidence, while at the same time we are in no position actually to deny or rule out the existence of some as yet unspecified alternative hypothesis. The general problem is that one's rationally assigning a high probability to p is compatible with one's not being in a position to deny the existence of some unspecified alternative hypothesis. Thus one's being in no position to deny that there is some unspecified God-justifying purpose for some evil to occur is compatible with one's rationally assigning a high probability to there being no such purpose.

A possible remedy is to supplement skeptical theism with more developed skeptical hypotheses, a role naturally played by defense hypotheses. A crucial question is whether the extent to which skeptical theism is plausible depends on the plausibility of such hypotheses. In the quantum mechanics case an analogous claim would clearly hold – the plausibility of skepticism about quantum mechanics would be dependent on the plausibility of the skeptic's hypothesis. But furthermore, here it also seems clear that the lowering effect of a skeptical hypothesis on the probability of the claim that the skeptic targets is merely a function of the probability of the skeptical hypothesis. So the lower the probability of a skeptical hypothesis about quantum mechanics, the smaller its lowering effect on the probability of the received theory. The analogous claim would seem to hold for skeptical theism. The lower the probability of a defense hypothesis, the smaller its lowering effect on not-(G) given (E). So it would appear that a plausible skeptical theism requires a defense hypothesis or a set of such hypotheses whose probability is significantly high.

Furthermore, William Rowe points out that skeptical theists of the sort we are now discussing – those who affirm that we are in no position to rule out that there are moral reasons for God's allowing the world's evils to occur – have typically not conceded that the unavailability of a reason for God's permitting some evil significantly lowers the probability of God's existence given this evil, no matter how horrendous the evil and no matter how little reason we have for believing the proposed defense:

> What their view comes to is this. Because we cannot rule out God's knowing goods we do not know, we cannot rule out there being goods that justify God in permitting *any amount of evil whatever* that might occur in our world. If human and animal life on earth were nothing more than a series of agonizing moments from birth to death, the position of my friends would still require them to say that we cannot reasonably infer that it is even likely that God does not exist. For, since we don't know that the goods we know of are representative of the goods there are, we can't know that it is likely that there are no goods that justify God in permitting human and animal life on earth to be nothing more than a series of agonizing moments from birth to death. But such a view is unreasonable, if not absurd.[37]

But one's not being in a position to deny or rule out a skeptical theist's defense hypothesis does not undermine the rationality of believing that not-(G) is more likely on (E) than (G) is, nor, a fortiori, the rationality of believing that (G) is significantly lowered by (E). Rowe is clearly right here. Moreover, the problem Rowe points out here is threatening for skeptical theism generally. For if a skeptical theist strategy works equally well no matter what the degree of evil in a world, one is thereby given reason to doubt its value.

Matters are not improved if the skeptical theist's claim is not simply that we are in no position to deny or rule out that there are God-justifying goods of which we have no inkling, but rather, as Alston suggests, if the claim is that there are goods of which we have some inkling such that we are in no position to deny that they are God-justifying.[38] But even if we are not in a position to deny some partially specified hypothesis, we may still be in a position to assign it a low probability. For example, Alston argues that as a result of our cognitive limitations for grasping the nature of the good we are in no position to deny that Sam's horrible suffering from a long-term, painful disease can be accounted for as his punishment for sin.[39] For we are in no position to deny that retributive punishment, meted out in proportion to sin, is a good, and that Sam has sinned inwardly to the degree that merits his suffering. Indeed, we are in no position to deny that there are sins that many don't countenance, such as rejection of God, that contribute to his meriting this suffering. And thus the probability of God's existence is not lowered by the fact of Sam's suffering.

But it is doubtful that the kind of strategy that Alston advocates here constitutes an advance. For given his view, why shouldn't the cognitive limitations hypothesis together with the punishment defense then also justify no such concession in the case of a child who is brutally beaten and raped? After all, given our cognitive limitations, we are in no position to deny that punishment, justified on retributivist grounds, and meted out in proportion to sin, is a good. Furthermore, given our cognitive limitations, we are in no position to deny that the retributive good can be realized by punishment that precedes the crime. For all we know the reason we find it just to punish only after the crime is epistemic, but God, who foresees sin, is not bound by this epistemically grounded limitation. In addition, given our cognitive limitations, we are in no position to deny that the child may in the future commit sins that merit being brutally beaten and raped. Suppose the child is killed, and it is not plausible that she has committed any sin meriting judicial beating, rape, and murder. But then, given our cognitive limitations, we are in no position to deny that she will be given a second chance in an afterlife in which she performs actions that merit being brutally beaten, raped, and murdered. Imagine that this is the best defense we can devise for the evil at issue. This defense is seriously implausible, and it does not significantly affect the probability of (G) on (E) – or of not-(G) on (E). Consequently, even if it is true that due to our cognitive limitations we are in no position to deny that a good of which we have some inkling is God-justifying with respect to some horrible evil, this might do little to advance the cause of skeptical theism.

An obvious remedy is to find a defense hypothesis with higher probability. But the heart of skeptical theism is that such hypotheses will be difficult if not impossible to come by. So the skeptical theist seems to face a dilemma: at best minimally specified hypotheses, or fairly well-specified defense hypotheses with low probability, are inadequate to counter the claim that (E) significantly reduces the probability of (G), and she maintains that defense hypotheses with a higher probability are unavailable. A promising way out has been suggested by van Inwagen – his aim is to devise a defense hypothesis that would show that *we are in no position to judge* that the sufferings of this world are improbable on the existence of God. In his conception, a defense of the right sort must first of all be a reasonably well-specified hypothesis that is true for all anyone knows (and not simply one that we are in no position to deny). Then, if a defense of this sort, (D), can be found such that (S) – a proposition that details the actual degree of the world's suffering – is highly probable on (G) and (D), and, crucially, is such that we are in no position to make a judgment about the probability of (D) on (G), then it will have been established that we are in no position to judge that (S) is improbable on the existence of God.[40]

Suppose that van Inwagen's schema is valid (as it seems to me to be). Then the challenge is to find a defense that meets these specifications – one worry is that in the last analysis, any candidate will turn out to have a fairly well circumscribed probability on (G). Van Inwagen proposes a defense, and it consists of these three claims:

(1) Every possible world that contains higher-level sentient creatures either contains patterns of suffering morally equivalent to those recorded by (S), or else is massively irregular.

(2) Some important intrinsic or extrinsic good depends on the existence of higher-level sentient creatures; this good is of sufficient magnitude that it outweighs the patterns of suffering recorded by (S).

(3) Being massively irregular is a defect in a world, a defect at least as great as the defect of containing patterns of suffering morally equivalent to those recorded by (S).

But are we really in no position to assess the probability of this defense on the existence of God? A misgiving about this claim arises from the fact that through fairly recent advances in technology and medicine we have prevented a significant amount of suffering, and, obviously, we have by these means prevented this suffering without introducing massive irregularity. But if we are now able in this way to prevent suffering, it would seem that God could have done so long ago without introducing massive irregularity. For instance, a significant component of human suffering results from clinical depression, but we have produced drugs that relieve many forms of this illness, and we are on a trajectory for finding more. It is far from unlikely that within a century we will be able to insert mechanisms in the body that dispense such drugs automatically – and this would be accomplished without introducing massive irregularity. But if it is possible for us to produce and implant such mechanisms, it is far from unlikely that, supposing God exists, God could have designed us with similar mechanisms without introducing massive irregularity. And if this is so, then we are in a position to judge that the probability of (1) on (G) is low. Nevertheless, even if this proposed defense does not meet van Inwagen's specifications, there might be one that does.

Another challenge to the skeptical theistic position further explores the claim that the degree of skepticism to which the skeptical theist is committed generalizes to skeptical claims that are unacceptable, or at any rate, skeptical claims that actual skeptical theists would not accept. One important version of this challenge has been advanced by Bruce Russell, and it claims that this view will have skeptical consequences for our moral practice.[41] If the theist claims that there are goods not fully understood by us that could not have been realized had God prevented various horrible evils, and that God might well be justified in allowing these evils in order to realize those goods, then there might well be situations in which we fail to prevent evils of these kinds where we do no wrong. In fact, we may on some such occasions be obligated not to prevent these evils. Or at the very least, on certain occasions we might have to give serious consideration to reasons not to prevent those evils when ordinary moral practice does not feature giving serious consideration to such reasons. Let us call this *the challenge from skeptical consequences for morality.*

Now Alston, Daniel Howard-Snyder, and Michael Bergmann have replied to this objection by claiming in effect that in morally justifying our actions, we are limited to goods that we understand, while the possible goods the skeptical theist is adducing are at least to some degree beyond our understanding.[42] But this does not seem right; our moral justifications should not be limited to goods we understand – as Russell in fact argues. One might amplify Russell's contention in the following way.[43] Consider first an analogy to the skeptical theist's situation that features only human agents. Jack, a nurse, assists doctors in a clinic that specializes, among other things, in a painful bone disease. He has excellent reason to trust the doctors as thoroughly competent. The clinic stocks morphine as a painkiller, and Jack knows that if morphine were administered to the bone disease patients, their acute pain would be relieved. But the bone specialists have never, in his experience, given morphine to patients suffering from this disease, even though they have, in his experience, given it to other patients in the clinic. Jack has no inkling why the doctors do not administer the morphine to the bone disease patients. However, for all he knows, they might have given it to such patients in certain circumstances in the past, although he has no reasonable guess as to frequency, and he has no idea of what these circumstances might be. One day, as a result of bad weather, all the doctors are away from the clinic, but Jack is there. A patient is suffering from the bone disease, and Jack has the opportunity to administer morphine. It would seem that he has some significant moral reason not to do so.

Now consider the analogous situation. Sue, a doctor, knows that there have been thousands of cases of people suffering horribly from disease x. Suppose at a certain time she becomes a skeptical theist who believes that God is justified for the sake of goods beyond her ken in not preventing these thousands of cases of suffering (she trusts God in a way analogous to the way in which Jack trusts the bone specialists). Suppose that her belief in God is rational, and also that her belief regarding the God-justifying goods is rational. In addition, for all she knows, God in the past might have prevented people from suffering from this disease under certain circumstances, although she has no reasonable guess as to how often God might have done this, and she has no idea of what these circumstances might be. Around the same time a drug that cures disease x is developed and is made available to Sue, and she is now deciding whether to administer it. Sue's situation seems similar to Jack's: it would seem that insofar as Sue is rational in believing that God has significant moral reason to allow thousands of people to suffer from disease x, she has significant moral reason not to administer the drug that cures disease x.[44] Consequently, this problem for skeptical theism is not as easily resolved as some of the advocates of this view have claimed.

Swinburne points out a further important difficulty for the skeptical theist's position, one that entertains the possibility that due to our cognitive limitations we might also fail to understand that apparent goods really serve greater evils:

> . . . while our moral beliefs (and factual beliefs, we may add) may indeed be in error in some relevant respects, we need some further argument to show that they are more likely to be biased in the direction of failing to understand that some apparent bad states really serve greater goods, rather than in the direction of failing to understand that some apparent good states really serve greater bad states.[45]

Swinburne's idea is that independent of other evidence relevant to the existence of God, and given the skeptical theist's claim about our cognitive limitations, it is equiprobable that apparently bad states serve greater goods and that apparently good states serve greater evils. So given our cognitive limitations, it may be just as likely that apparent goods have consequences that render allowing these goods illegitimate. So if on the face of it, independent of considerations regarding our cognitive limitations, (E) significantly lowers the probability of (G), then even counting these considerations, (E) will still significantly lower the probability of (G). Note that even if Swinburne's claim is true, it still may be that once the other evidence relevant to God's existence is counted in, (E) will not significantly lower the probability of (G). For if this evidence weighs heavily in favor of (G), then it will be much more likely that apparent bad states serve greater goods than that apparent good states serve greater evils.

Finally, part of the skeptical theist's position is that the possible goods we know of need not be representative of the possible goods there are. This claim all by itself should be uncontroversial. Within the past century human beings, or at least many of them, arguably became aware of the good realized by professional psychological counseling and equal treatment across gender and race. It would be rash to deny that there are further goods of which many are not aware. For our appreciation of the goods that there are develops over time. But the skeptical theist needs much more than this – he needs there to be unrecognized goods the realization of which can justify inaction in the face of the most horrendous kinds of evil the world has ever seen.

Conclusions

Even if there is a successful response to the logical problem of evil, it does seem that consideration of the world's evils reduces the probability of the existence of God – conceived of as omnipotent, omniscient, and wholly good, at least considered independently of the other evidence. The traditional theodicies do not seem to provide a credible explanation for the coexistence of God with horrendous evils, and the skeptical theist approach faces a series of problems that have yet to be adequately addressed.

Nevertheless, it is true that all of this is compatible with the claim that when one considers all of the evidence, the horrendous evils do not lower the probability of God's existence at all. Here one should keep in mind a point urged by Plantinga, that even if the probability of p on q is very low, so that q significantly reduces the probability of p, that fact all by itself does not render the probability of p low.[46] Under these circumstances q may not reduce the probability of p at all, and q need not render epistemically irrational a high degree of belief in p. To use Plantinga's example, consider:

(P) Feike can swim.
(Q) Feike is Frisian and nine out of ten Frisians can't swim.

The probability of (P) on (Q) is 0.1. But if I am now swimming with Feike, the probability of (P) for me in my epistemic situation may be close to 1.0, and my epistemically rational degree of belief would conform to this assessment. Plantinga points out that in fact each of many propositions that I rationally believe is such that its probability is low on some other proposition I rationally believe. Hence, even if the probability on (G) on (E) is low, that all by itself does not preclude my having a high rational degree of belief in (G).

Plantinga argues that many have non-propositional evidence for God's existence – he adduces the testimony of the Holy Spirit, and Calvin's *sensus divinitatis*, an innate sense of the divine. Others might add other types of religious experience, mystical religious experience for example. If it turns out that for some individual the testimony of the Holy Spirit provides evidence for the existence of God analogous to that which swimming with Feike yields for the claim that Feike can swim, then it may well be that the fact of horrendous evil does not significantly reduce the probability of God's existence all things considered. So perhaps our verdict should be that there may be individuals who have a high rational degree of belief that God exists, for whom the fact of horrendous evil should not have a lowering effect on this degree of belief. This is compatible with there also being those who have a low rational degree of belief that God exists, perhaps individuals who have seriously considered the problem of evil, but do not have the *sensus divinitatis*, the testimony of the Holy Spirit, or any religious experience.

A problem with this line of reasoning is that the fact of horrendous evil may well provide a much deeper challenge to the claim that God exists than the fact that nine out of ten Frisians can't swim does to the claim that Feike can't swim. For if I swim with Feike every day, my being apprised of the fact that nine out of ten Frisians can't swim clearly should have no effect on the extremely high degree to which I believe that Feike can swim. It should not, for example, indicate that I should seriously consider the possibility that my experiences of Feike swimming are non-veridical. However, many people, even those strongly inclined toward theism, have never had experiences of God relevantly analogous to experiences of Feike swimming (or at least do not believe they have had such experiences). But furthermore, suppose that I do regularly have experiences as of the presence of an extremely powerful and good being, but then find that I lack any theodicy or even a remotely plausible defense for horrendous evil. Perhaps this is more like a case in which a longtime friend, whom I've always experienced to be a very good person, is accused of a crime, and there is impressive evidence that he is guilty. In this case, this evidence might well yield a much stronger challenge to my belief in my friend's innocence than the statistical evidence about Frisians provides for my belief that Feike can swim.

The problem of evil remains a very difficult issue for theists. Although the last 30 years have produced very careful, imaginative, and important work on the issue, this problem still constitutes the greatest challenge to rational theistic belief.

Notes

1   See for example, David Hume, *Dialogues Concerning Natural Religion* (Indianapolis: Hackett Publishing, 1980), part 10, p. 63.
2   Job 42:7.
3   J. L. Mackie, "Evil and Omnipotence," in *The Problem of Evil*, ed. Marilyn McCord Adams and Robert Adams (Oxford: Oxford University Press), pp. 25–37. First published in *Mind*, 64 (1955), pp. 200–12.
4   Alvin Plantinga, *The Nature of Necessity* (Oxford: Oxford University Press, 1974), pp. 164–90.
5   Ibid., pp. 165–7.
6   Mackie, "Evil and Omnipotence," p. 33.
7   Plantinga, *The Nature of Necessity*, p. 173.
8   Ibid., pp. 184–90.

9 Michael Tooley, "The Argument from Evil," *Philosophical Perspectives*, 5 (1991), pp. 89–134, at pp. 91–3.

10 David Lewis, "Evil for Freedom's Sake," *Philosophical Papers*, 22 (1993), pp. 149–72, at p. 162.

11 See Lewis, "Evil for Freedom's Sake," pp. 161–8, for a thorough discussion of selective freedom.

12 Keith De Rose, "Plantinga, Presumption, Possibility, and the Problem of Evil," *Canadian Journal of Philosophy*, 21 (1991), pp. 497–512.

13 Jonathan Bennett, *A Study of Spinoza's Ethics* (Indianapolis: Hackett Publishing, 1984), p. 72.

14 Marilyn McCord Adams, *Horrendous Evil and the Goodness of God* (Ithaca: Cornell University Press, 1999), p. 26.

15 Ibid., p. 55.

16 Ibid., p. 179.

17 Ibid., p. 167.

18 Ibid., p. 167.

19 Ibid., pp. 165–6.

20 I discuss these problems for the free will theodicy in "Free Will, Evil, and Divine Providence," in *God and the Ethics of Belief: New Essays in Philosophy of Religion*, ed. Andrew Chignell and Andrew Dole (Cambridge: Cambridge University Press, forthcoming).

21 Lewis, "Evil for Freedom's Sake," p. 154. On a related note, Mackie remarks that "Why should [God] not leave men free to will rightly, but intervene when he sees them beginning to will wrongly?," "Evil and Omnipotence," p. 34.

22 Richard Swinburne, *Providence and the Problem of Evil* (Oxford: Oxford University Press, 1998), pp. 82–107.

23 Ibid., p. 245.

24 Lewis "Evil for Freedom's Sake," p. 155.

25 Mark Moyer made this point in conversation.

26 Swinburne, *Providence and the Problem of Evil*, pp. 86–9.

27 John Hick, *Evil and the God of Love*, Revised edition (New York: Harper and Row, 1978).

28 Eleonore Stump, "The Problem of Evil," *Faith and Philosophy*, 2 (1985), pp. 392–418.

29 Hick, *Evil and the God of Love*, p. 330.

30 Ibid., p. 334.

31 A. N. Whitehead, *Process and Reality* (New York: Free Press, 1978).

32 Charles Hartshorne, *Omnipotence and Other Theological Mistakes* (Albany: State University of New York Press, 1984).

33 Baruch Spinoza, Ethics, in *The Collected Works of Spinoza*, ed. E. Curley (Princeton, Princeton University Press, 1985), pp. 408–617, esp. part 1.

34 Kant advocates a position of this sort in "On the Miscarriage of all Philosophical Trials in Theodicy," in Immanuel Kant, *Religion Within the Bounds of Mere Reason and Other Writings*, ed. Allen Wood and George di Giovanni (Cambridge: Cambridge University Press, 1998), pp. 17–30. For contemporary developments of this position see Stephen J. Wykstra, "The Humean Obstacle to Evidential Arguments from Suffering: On Avoiding the Evils of 'Appearance,'" in Adams and Adams, *The Problem of*

Evil, pp. 138–60 (first published in the *International Journal for Philosophy of Religion*, 16 (1984), pp. 73–93); Stephen J. Wykstra, "Rowe's Noseeum Arguments from Evil," in *The Evidential Argument from Evil*, ed. Daniel Howard-Snyder (Bloomington, Ind.: Indiana University Press, 1996), pp. 126–74; William P. Alston, "The Inductive Argument from Evil and the Human Cognitive Condition," in *The Evidential Argument from Evil*, pp. 97–125 (first published in *Philosophical Perspectives*, 5 (1991), pp. 29–67); Daniel Howard-Snyder, "The Argument from Inscrutable Evil," in *The Evidential Argument from Evil*, pp. 286–310. All of these contemporary developments respond to Rowe's work on the evidence against theism.

35 Wykstra "The Humean Obstacle to Evidential Arguments from Suffering," p. 152.

36 William Alston "Some (Temporary) Final Thoughts on Evidential Arguments from Evil," in Howard-Snyder, *The Evidential Argument from Evil*, pp. 311–32, at p. 317.

37 Daniel Howard-Snyder, Michael Bergmann, and William Rowe, "An Exchange on the Problem of Evil," in *God and the Problem of Evil*, ed. William Rowe (Oxford: Blackwell, 2001), pp. 124–58, at pp. 156–7.

38 Alston, "The Inductive Argument from Evil and the Human Cognitive Condition," p. 103.

39 Ibid., pp. 103–4.

40 Peter van Inwagen, "The Problem of Evil, the Problem of Air, and the Problem of Silence," in Howard-Snyder, *The Evidential Argument from Evil*, pp. 151–74 (originally published in *Philosophical Perspectives*, 5 (1991), pp. 135–65); "Reflections of the Chapters by Russell, Draper, and Gale," in Howard-Snyder, *The Evidential Argument from Evil*, pp. 219–43. Van Inwagen argues that judgments of epistemic probability are judgments about possible world proportions. In accordance with that conception, he expresses the (valid) general principle at work here as follows:

> We are not in a position to judge that only a small proportion of the p-worlds are q-worlds if there is a proposition h that has the following two features:
> - a large proportion of the p & h worlds are q-worlds;
> - we are not in a position to make a judgment about the proportion of the p-worlds that are h-worlds. ("Reflections of the Chapters by Russell, Draper, and Gale," p. 228)

41 Bruce Russell, "Defenseless," in Howard-Snyder, *The Evidential Argument from Evil*, pp. 193–205, at pp. 197–8.

42 Alston "Some (Temporary) Final Thoughts on Evidential Arguments from Evil," p. 321; Michael Bergmann, "Skeptical Theism and Rowe's New Evidential Argument from Evil," *Noûs*, 35 (2001), pp. 278–96; Daniel Howard-Snyder, "The Argument From Inscrutable Evil," in Howard-Snyder, *The Evidential Argument from Evil*, pp. 286–310, at pp. 292–3.

43 I present this pair of cases in "Free Will, Evil, and Divine Providence."

44 Thanks to David Christensen, Michael Bergmann, and Daniel Howard-Snyder for discussions that helped formulate this case.

45 Swinburne, *Providence and the Problem of Evil*, p. 27.

46 Alvin Plantinga, "Epistemic Probability and Evil," in Howard-Snyder, *The Evidential Argument from Evil*, pp. 69–96, at pp. 87–9.

Suggested Further Reading

Howard-Snyder, Daniel, and Moser, Paul K. (eds.) (2002) *Divine Hiddenness.* Cambridge: Cambridge University Press.

van Inwagen, Peter (1995) *God, Knowledge and Mystery.* Ithaca: Cornell University Press.

Part III

Religious Belief

Chapter 8

Christian Faith
as a Way of Life

Alfred J. Freddoso

Introduction

The New Testament authors emphasize unremittingly that the key to genuine human flourishing is faith in Jesus Christ as the revealed and revealing Word of God, "the Way, the Truth, and the Life" (John 14:6). In the Gospels Jesus speaks and acts with a hitherto unknown authority that confounds his enemies but induces many others to seek him out and put him at the center of their lives. The latter he praises for their faith; the former he reproaches in the strongest terms, threatening that on the day of reckoning they will fare even worse than the inhabitants of Sodom and Gomorrah. Similarly, in his Epistles St Paul insists that it is faith in Jesus Christ, rather than observance of the moral, judicial, and ritual precepts of the Mosaic law, that effects our liberation from the slavery of sin and the dawn of a new life as the adopted sons and daughters of our father God. And even though Paul cautions that faith in Christ is worthless without the filial love of God and concomitant fraternal love of neighbor that Christ has made possible for us, it is clear that faith is prior to charity at least insofar as it gives us our initial cognitive and affective access to the object of our supernatural love.

Faith in Christ, then, lies at the heart of the Christian way of life. But what exactly is this faith and how exactly does it function within the Christian life? What vision of ultimate truth does it set before us? What ideal way of life does it propose for us? And how does one imbued with that vision and that ideal, along with the wisdom they promise, look upon the main alternatives proposed by philosophers who have sought wisdom outside the framework of faith in Jesus Christ? These are some of the questions I wish to broach here.

My purpose thus differs at least formally from that of the many contemporary Christian philosophers who have been trying to show that faith in Christ is reasonable by standards of rationality that have some purchase even on non-believers. This is an important project for Christian philosophers to undertake, especially in our present philosophical culture, which by and large rejects, oftentimes aggressively, Jesus Christ and faith in him.[1] What's more, much good fruit has come of this project. Not only have currently fashionable accounts of rationality been subjected to rigorous scrutiny, but comprehensive and philosophically interesting alternatives have been proposed in their stead.[2]

Still, this is not the project I am engaged in here, even if some of what I say will be pertinent to it. Instead, my main purpose is to explore faith in Christ from the inside, so to speak.[3] In particular, my goal is to investigate faith as a virtue that (a) flows from God's communication of his very life to us, (b) gives shape to a distinctive vision of the truth about God, the world, and ourselves, and (c) is embedded within a set of cognitive, affective, and behavioral practices that promise the way to genuine human fulfillment.

In carrying out this investigation, I will be guided by St Thomas Aquinas's "exceptionally fine example of a philosophical discussion concerning the nature of faith,"[4] as well as his teaching on grace and virtue. With St Thomas I will assume that the beginning of the Christian life consists not just in God's forgiving our sins, but also in his effecting within us an interior transformation that needs to be spelled out in straightforward metaphysical terms. Accordingly, I will begin with a general characterization of divine grace and the infused habits that flow from this grace: the three "theological" virtues of faith, hope, and charity; the infused moral virtues; and the so-called "gifts of the Holy Spirit," which, though frequently neglected in theoretical treatments of Christian ethics, lie at the heart of the Christian way of life. I will then go on to describe faith in Christ more precisely as an intellectual act (and associated habit) that involves both cognitive and affective elements and has its own peculiar brand of certitude. Along the way, I will lay out in seminal form some of the most important elements of the ideal Christian way of life by examining the four gifts of the Holy Spirit associated with cognition. Finally, I will briefly examine what the various classical philosophical alternatives to Christianity look like from the perspective of the devout Christian.

The Life: Grace and Inner Transformation

In the Gospels Jesus repeatedly promises "new life" to his disciples, a life he identifies with himself ("I am . . . the Life") as well as with the indwelling of Father, Son, and Holy Spirit in the believer.[5] Notice here that the believer's relationship with God is characterized as qualitatively distinct from, and inexpressibly more intimate than, the more basic relationship of a creature, even a rational creature, to the creator who makes it and sustains it in being. St Thomas calls this new relationship a type of friendship – more specifically, filial friendship, in keeping with John 1:5: "To all who received him, who believed in his name, he gave the power to become children of God." And it is precisely this sort of intimacy with God – possessed inchoatively now, but perfectly hereafter – that according to Christians constitutes the only genuine fulfillment of our natural desire for happiness or, as the rich young man of the Gospel puts it, for "eternal life."[6]

St Thomas is quick to point out, however, that original sin renders us unfit not only for filial friendship with God but even for rightly ordered creaturehood.[7] So although we desire happiness, we begin with a willful ignorance of the fact that it is only by intimate union with God that this desire can be satisfied. Worse yet, our affective condition is such that intimate union with God would not appear attractive to us even if we could envision it. To the contrary, we have a (postlapsarian) natural inclination to try to satisfy the desire for eternal life with other lesser goods which are inherently incapable of satisfying this desire and which at some level of reflection we can sense to be incapable of satisfying it.[8] So our postlapsarian condition is this: we cannot fulfill our deepest desire, we have no very clear idea of what object could possibly fulfill it, and we would spurn the object that can in fact fulfill it even if it were presented to us. This is the hopeless starting point of a people that has turned its back on God and stubbornly set off on its own.

The well-nigh incredible Christian message – the "Good News" – is precisely that God himself has taken the initiative to liberate us from our desperate plight. We stand in need of an interior transformation that renders us both desirous of and fit for friendship with the Father as his adopted sons and daughters.[9] And it is precisely the possibility of such a transformation that, according to Christians, has been won for us by Jesus Christ, the God-man, who through his sacrificial suffering and death has reconciled us with his Father.

But how is this transformation to be characterized in metaphysical terms? According to St Thomas, it consists in God's affecting the very core of our being, the "essence of the soul",[10] by imparting to it – or, in technical terms, "infusing" into it – a quality that constitutes spiritual health and at the same time initiates us into the intimate "family life" of the triune God.[11] This quality, which elevates us to the status of sons and daughters of the Father, is called "habitual" or "sanctifying" grace. In insisting that the immediate ontological subject of this grace is the very essence of the soul, and not just the cognitive and appetitive powers that flow from the soul and serve as the immediate subjects of the various virtues, St Thomas is underscoring the radical nature of the transformation. It is, literally, an alteration – more specifically, an enhancement – of our very nature as human beings. In speaking of the infused virtues that emanate or flow from habitual grace, St Thomas puts it this way:

In *Physics* 7 the Philosopher says, "A virtue is a disposition of what is perfect, where by 'perfect' I mean that which is disposed in accord with its nature." From this it is clear that a thing is said to have a virtue with reference to a preexisting nature, so that it has a virtue when it is disposed in a way that befits its nature. Now it is obvious that the virtues acquired through human acts . . . are dispositions by which a man is fittingly disposed with reference to the nature by which he is a man.

In contrast, the infused virtues dispose a man in a higher way and with respect to a higher end; hence, it must also be the case that they dispose him with reference to a higher nature. But this means with reference to a participated divine nature, in keeping with 2 Peter 1:4: "He has given us the greatest and most precious promises, in order that through these promises you might be made participants in the divine nature." And it is because of the reception of this nature that we are said to be re-generated as children of God.[12]

Echoing sacred scripture and the fathers of the Church, St Thomas here employs the startling language of divinization. By the infused quality of habitual grace, we are literally given a participation or share in the very nature and life of God, so that grace establishes within the believer a sort of replication (or, as St Thomas puts it, a similitude) of the union within Jesus Christ himself of a human nature and a divine nature.[13] What the son of God is by his own proper being, believers can become by "adoption." But, as should be clear by now, this divine "adoption" has an interior depth that goes far beyond anything found in its human analogue:

> God is said to adopt men insofar as, out of his goodness, he admits them into the inheritance of [divine] happiness. But this divine adoption involves more than human adoption does. For through the gift of grace God renders the one whom he adopts fit to receive a heavenly inheritance, whereas a man does not render the one whom he adopts fit [to receive an inheritance], but chooses one who is already fit by adopting him.[14]

> A creature is assimilated to the eternal Word in the third [and final] way according to the unity which the Word has with the Father – a unity that is effected in the creature through grace and charity. Hence, in John 17 the Lord prays that "they may be one in us, even as we are one." It is this sort of assimilation that satisfies the concept of adoption, since an eternal inheritance is due to those who are assimilated in this way. Thus, it is obvious that to be adopted belongs only to the rational creature – and not to every rational creature, but only to one who has charity. This charity is diffused in our hearts by the Holy Spirit (Romans 5). And that is why, in Romans 8, the Holy Spirit is called the spirit of the adoption of children.[15]

The believer's interior participation in the very life and unity of the three divine persons outstrips our common notion of participation in the lives of others to such an extent that it boggles the imagination: "Eye has not seen, nor ear heard, neither has it entered into the heart of man, what things God has prepared for those who love him" (1 Cor. 2:9). Perhaps the closest analogue we have is the combination of physical, spiritual, emotional, and social unity exemplified by the friendship between husband and wife in the ideal of Christian marriage – and even this unity pales in comparison to the intimacy with God that St Thomas is pointing to in the passages just quoted.

This, then, is the context within which any discussion of faith or the other infused virtues must be set. For these virtues "flow from" habitual grace into the powers or faculties of the soul and constitute, as it were, the specifications that define more precisely what active participation in God's life and happiness amounts to. The powers (or faculties) in question are those that serve as the immediate subjects of the moral and intellectual virtues – namely, the power of intellection (the "intellect"), the power of intellective appetite or desire (the "will"), and the power of sentient appetite or desire, which is the seat of the concupiscible and irascible passions.[16] By grace these very powers are themselves enhanced and thus become capable of acts that would otherwise be impossible for a human being. In one of his arguments for the claim that habitual grace affects the very essence of the soul, St Thomas gives us in passing a succinct portrait of how the infused virtues elevate the powers of the soul to a participation in the cognitive and affective aspects of the life of the triune God:

> Since grace is prior to virtue, it has a subject prior to the powers of the soul. Thus, it exists in the essence of the soul. For just as by means of his intellective power a man participates in the divine knowledge through the virtue of faith, and just as by means of the power of the will he participates in the divine love through the virtue of charity, so too by means of the nature of the soul he participates, according to a certain similitude, in the divine nature through a kind of re-generation or re-creation.[17]

So the infused virtues are the instruments by which the main powers of the soul take part in the divine life. To describe the effects of the believer's participation in the very life of God, St Thomas draws upon an analogy between the natural "light of reason," to which the virtues acquired through repeated action are ordered, and the "light of grace," from which all the infused virtues flow and to which they are ordered: "Just as the acquired virtues perfect man for living in a way consonant with the natural light of reason, so the infused virtues perfect man for living in a way consonant with the light of grace."[18] The acquired virtues, each of which falls under one or another of the four cardinal virtues – namely, (a) prudence, which perfects our intellect insofar as it engages in practical reasoning, (b) justice, which perfects our will with respect to other-regarding actions, (c) fortitude, which harmonizes our irascible passions with well-ordered practical reason, and (d) temperance or self-control, which harmonizes our concupiscible passions with well-ordered practical reason – make us fit for friendship with others and hence for a life of interdependence within one or another human community.[19] In like manner, the theological virtues that flow from habitual grace make us intrinsically fit for eternal life in the divine community. In particular, faith gives us cognitive access to God's inner life and to his designs for our salvation, hope leads us to put our complete trust in God's ability and God's resolve to help us overcome the obstacles to attaining the perfection of everlasting life, and charity is just the special friendship with God which constitutes even now the beginning of eternal life and toward which both faith and hope are ordered. In the same way, the infused moral virtues enable us to exercise self-control, fortitude, and justice in a way that is motivated and ordered by the theological virtues.

Here, though, we must note a difference between those virtues that are directly infused by God and those that are acquired naturally. The latter are generated by repeated action and in this way become "firmly rooted" in the human agent. Since every virtuous action is voluntary, it involves a free act of the will. But the disposition or inclination toward eliciting this act of will can vary in intensity, so that when contrary desires or fears are themselves intense, they can carry the will along with them, as it were, and in this way impede the operation of the virtue. Virtues acquired through repeated actions are better able to withstand and overcome these contrary desires and fears because the very manner in which they are acquired is intrinsically connected with their intensity. In short, the voluntary self-control and performance of good works necessary for acquiring such virtues make it easier for us to exercise them consistently.

However, things are not the same with the virtues that flow from habitual grace, since they are not acquired habits, but are instead given directly by God through a gratuitous infusion or "in-pouring." So, at least at the beginning, these habits are relatively weak dispositions not firmly rooted in the agent. As a result, one who has them still needs to be encouraged and cajoled from the outside, as it were, in order to exercise them in the face of various obstacles, including a general tendency toward forgetfulness of our divine calling – in much the same way that children need to be reminded and encouraged by their parents to exercise, say, the self-control or courage they are struggling to attain. This is why the gifts of the Holy Spirit are necessary for the consistent exercise of the theological virtues and infused moral virtues. These gifts are supplementary dispositions directly aimed not at the exercise of the infused virtues, but rather at rendering believers attentive to the cognitive and affective promptings of the Holy Spirit and at making them ready to be moved by those promptings to exercise the relevant virtues. Just as in the case of children, this sort of attentiveness must be cultivated, and in the Christian life it is the practice of prayer that fosters it, leading to an intensification of the gifts themselves.[20] Thus, prayer – both communal liturgical prayer and private meditative prayer – is, in addition to self-denial and good works, crucial for living a devout Christian life. For it is prayer that cultivates a lively sense of God's presence and heightens the believer's sensitivity to the thoughts and affections that constitute the promptings of the Holy Spirit.

The central role played by the gifts of the Holy Spirit helps account for the pronounced element of passivity – more specifically, trusting abandonment to God's will – that characterizes a devout Christian life. The practice of being open to advice, persuasion, prompting, and coaxing from outside sources is important in every morally upright life, even though some moral theories underplay this fact because of their commitment to a strong (I would say excessively strong) notion of autonomy or self-rule as a moral ideal for human beings. From a Christian perspective believers are always in need of guidance and firm direction, since they are the "little ones" to whom God has revealed what "he has hidden from the wise and the learned" (Matt. 11:25) and who want to be led by the Father to a peace and joy that would otherwise be impossible in the travails of the present life. In fact, since it is God who is the "source of all holiness" (*fons omnis sanctitatis*),[21] the believer's conception of the ideal moral life is primarily one in which no obstacles obstruct the action of the Holy Spirit. That is, to the extent that believers simply allow themselves to be led by the action of the Holy Spirit and resist putting up obstacles to that action, their lives will participate more fully in the "divine adventure."

Some will find this notion of "spiritual childhood" repugnant because of the humility and docility it requires.[22] Yet from a Christian perspective it is precisely filial subservience to the Holy Spirit that reflects the plain truth about the human condition and that frees believers from a slavish subservience to the power of their own passions and, just as significantly, from a similarly slavish subservience to worldly powers such as political, social, economic, and intellectual elites.

In the next section I will examine in more detail the four gifts of the Holy Spirit that affect cognition: understanding, knowledge, counsel, and wisdom.

The Truth: Faith and Its Role in the Life of Believers

By faith, then, believers participate in God's cognitive life – coming more and more to understand him intimately in himself, to see themselves and the world as he does, and to recognize his providence at work in their own lives.

St Thomas identifies the principal object of the act (or habit) of faith as that which has been revealed as true by God precisely insofar as it has been revealed by him and made public through sacred scripture and the teachings of the Church.[23] While this general object of faith can be divided into the particular statements contained in the creed, the essential point is that anything one assents to through the theological virtue of faith is assented to under the rubric or "formality" of its having been revealed as true by God and made public through sacred scripture and the teachings of the Church.

In several places St Thomas draws a distinction among the particular objects of faith. Some of the truths God has revealed – the so-called "preambles" of the faith – are such that in principle human reason can come to an evident or clear cognition of them through philosophical inquiry without the aid of special divine revelation, while others – the so-called "articles" or "mysteries" of the faith – are such that without recourse to divine revelation human reason cannot even in principle come to any well-grounded cognition of them at all. St Thomas himself counts among the preambles a large number of propositions concerning God's existence, nature, and activity that can be gleaned, he believes, from treating various features of the world as effects and reasoning back to God as their cause.[24] In this regard he is more optimistic about the prospects for philosophical inquiry than are other medieval and modern thinkers, who are decidedly less sanguine about the power and range of "natural reason," that is, of reason unaided by special divine revelation.[25] Still, everyone agrees that the central Christian doctrines, those having to do with the nature and history of human salvation, are all mysteries that must in this life be accepted on faith if they are accepted at all. These include doctrines about the inner life of the triune God; about the creation of the world in time; about original sin along with its transmission and its consequences; about the establishment of the people of Israel as the carrier of the promise of salvation; about the incarnation of the Word; about his life, death, and resurrection; and about the Church, under the guidance of the Holy Spirit, as the extension in time of Christ's salvific mission. Moreover, even though the distinction between the preambles and the mysteries is an important one for certain apologetic reasons, it does not play a central role in the lives of the overwhelming majority of Christian believers.[26] Rather, it is by the infused virtue of faith that they assent to *all* revealed doctrines – whether preambles or mysteries – as non-evident truths revealed by God.[27]

But what exactly is it to have faith in these objects? In general, accepting something on faith is just voluntarily assenting to it as true on the word of someone we consider trustworthy – even though we cannot clearly "see" it to be true – and to do this with some good in mind. Reflection on the relationship between teachers and their students is helpful here, and St Thomas often invokes it. Trust lies at the center of this relationship, especially when the students are just beginning their study of a particular discipline.[28] As a means to attaining some good – perhaps a high-minded good such as the acquisition of truth or expertise in the discipline, or perhaps only some less noble good such as passing a course needed for graduation – students voluntarily assent to many propositions basic to the discipline in question, even though they are barely able to understand those propositions, let alone see their truth clearly. They simply put their trust in their teachers or the authors of the books they are reading, with the expectation that if they put the propositions in question to good use and come to see their connections with other important propositions, then their understanding of the basic propositions themselves will gradually increase. Indeed, if they are among the few who pursue the study of the discipline long enough and intensely enough, they may ultimately become experts themselves and be in a position to see those basic propositions as evident in themselves.

This analogy takes us part way. In the case of revealed truths, St Thomas designates God and the blessed in heaven as the relevant "experts" who see clearly what the faithful now see only darkly. And like students, devout believers have a goal in mind in freely putting their trust in the word of God – namely, the attainment of eternal life, that is, genuine human flourishing.

However, the analogy falls short once we notice that in the case of Christian faith, the believer's love for the one who reveals the truth is itself a factor that contributes to an increase in understanding.[29] This suggests another analogy that is closer to the mark – that of filial friendship, especially when the children in

question are young. Their love for their parents, along with an implicit acknow-
ledgment of their own dependence and lack of experience, prompts a desire –
defeasible, to be sure, in the face of conflicting desires and fears – to see the world
as their parents see it out of love for them. This love helps them not just to
understand better what their parents have taught them and demanded of them, but
also, as they participate more fully in the way of life that accompanies the teaching
and the demands, to develop insights that they would not otherwise have had. In
like manner, when faith is motivated (or, to use St Thomas's term, "formed") by
charity, and when the way of life proposed by the object of faith is lived with
intensity, believers come to insights that might otherwise have failed to material-
ize. In short, believers with the right affections who strive to live in accord with
the theoretical object proposed by divine revelation will undergo a profound
cognitive transformation as they become more and more adept at seeing their
lives and the world in general from the perspective of their heavenly Father.

The manner and extent of this transformation become clear from an examination
of the gifts of the Holy Spirit that pertain to cognition. Each of these gifts plays
a role in the acquisition and transmission of divine cognition, in the meditative
study of revealed truths, and in the believer's perseverance in the faith.

The first is the gift of understanding (*intellectus*), which is a fixed disposition to
receive from the Holy Spirit intellectual illumination with respect to the central
truths of the faith, that is, the first principles of divine revelation.[30] In its most
obvious function, which has to do with the initial grasp of these truths, the gift of
understanding is analogous to (and, in Latin, bears the same name as) our natural
intellectual power to grasp substances initially with enough insight to categorize
them and distinguish them from one another, thus setting the stage for further
inquiry into their natures. Of course, this natural power does not of itself provide
deep comprehension of the relevant substances – and so, too, it is with the
believer's understanding of central revealed principles. Still, even though believers
cannot have perfect comprehension of the mysteries of the faith, they can at least
grasp them well enough to identify them, distinguish them intuitively from their
contraries, and persevere in their assent to them. Furthermore, in its second
function the gift of understanding provides further illumination when, moved
by love for and gratitude to their heavenly Father, believers make the effort to
deepen their comprehension of the mysteries and of their interrelations with
one another. In the normal course of events, this deeper understanding comes
through participation in the liturgy of the Church and through the sort of study
and prayerful reflection on revealed truths that almost all believers are capable
of, especially when they have a good teacher – for instance, a writer who can
present the relevant material in a way consonant with their level of intellectual
maturation.

Even though the gift of understanding, which is available to all the faithful,
does not of itself guarantee the ability to engage in sophisticated intellectual
inquiry into the truths of the faith, it does carry with it a defeasible intuitive
ability to sense what is and what is not consonant with divine revelation. And

it is precisely this sort of ability that is presupposed in the more sophisticated assessment of theories and arguments that marks formal theological inquiry of the sort that is undertaken by only a few of the faithful. The very fact that the gift of understanding is open to all the faithful helps keep in check the gnostic tendency – a characteristic temptation for intellectuals – to split the faith into two faiths, one for the vulgar and one for the learned, to use Berkeley's terms. For the community served by the more sophisticated intellectual inquirers is just as securely guided by the Holy Spirit as the intellectuals themselves. To be sure, members of either group can succumb to what St Thomas dubs "blindness of mind" and "dullness of sense," which lead to sins directly opposed to the virtue of faith.[31] But God's intention in bestowing the gift of understanding is to bring about unity of belief and a consequent unity among believers.

Given that believers have a grasp of the basic principles of the faith, the next cognitive step is to make judgments in light of those principles.[32] This brings us to the other three gifts of the Holy Spirit pertaining to cognition.

Through the gift of knowledge (*scientia*), believers are disposed to make sound judgments, in light of the principles of the faith, about the created world in general and human affairs in particular. To put it more simply, by means of this gift they come to see various aspects of the created world as God sees them. Many philosophers, beginning with the ancients, have held that it is only by reference to unseen realities that we make our most reliable judgments about the world we see. (In fact, this is almost a truism in contemporary natural science.) Likewise, according to Christians, the most penetrating view of creatures is hidden from us in the absence of divine revelation, and it is only to the extent that the judgments we make about created things participate in God's knowledge that we see the world aright – even when, perhaps *especially* when, our judgments run counter to what St Paul calls the "wisdom of this world" (1 Cor. 3:19). The gift of knowledge is especially important for the moral progress of believers toward holiness and genuine human fulfillment. For, once again, the most accurate and reliable perspective we have on our own character, intentions, and actions is God's perspective, and this is precisely the perspective that the gift of knowledge is meant to provide us with. Needless to say, the attainment of accurate self-knowledge is often a painful experience, but it is absolutely crucial if we are to see ourselves truthfully. And the truth, according to Christian revelation, is that we are deeply flawed and yet deeply loved by the Lord of the world. Human fulfillment demands that both poles of this opposition be vigorously asserted, internally appropriated, and held in creative tension in all of our theoretical and practical reasoning.[33]

The gift of knowledge is also crucial for one of the key aspects of the Christian way of life, namely, the believer's identification with the crucified Christ. From a Christian perspective, suffering is neither a surd nor an evil merely to be endured for the sake of strengthening one's character.[34] Rather, Christian doctrine views suffering of all kinds as redemptive when the believer joins it to the sacrifice of Christ on the cross. More specifically, when suffering is embraced out of love for

God and neighbor, it takes on a positive value and can be supernaturally effi-cacious not only for oneself but also for all the others to whom one is joined (or, in the case of non-believers, potentially joined) in the "communion of saints." This helps explain the distinctive character of the practice of self-denial or "mortifica-tion" in the Christian way of life – where such mortification is not limited only to great sufferings or to those that are actively self-inflicted, but extends as well to all the little joyful sacrifices (so-called "passive mortifications") that one is called upon to make by the unpredictable circumstances of ordinary everyday life in community with others. Such mortification is not so much a test of one's will-power as it is an act of supernatural charity.[35]

To be sure, the Christian account of suffering and the practice of mortification will strike some people, especially those in comfortable circumstances, as strange and even perverse. Yet, according to Christians, it is part of the "paradox of the cross" that our greatest joy lies in sacrificing ourselves out of love for God and neighbor, and that we find our lives only by losing them for the sake of Christ (Matt. 10:39).[36] And we have the age-old and ever-new witness of the saints to confirm that this is the way to genuine peace and joy.

Whereas the gift of knowledge helps believers to make sound theoretical judg-ments about themselves and their circumstances, the gift of counsel (*consilium*) disposes them to make sound practical judgments in concrete situations and to follow through on those judgments. In other words, the gift of counsel helps believers to bring their theoretical judgments to bear on day-to-day situations of all sorts. More specifically, it makes them amenable to the promptings of the Holy Spirit as they carry out the various cognitive operations associated with the virtue of prudence.[37] Thus with the gift of counsel they receive direction from God in a way analogous to that in which someone receives the advice of other people in reaching the determinations of practical reason.

There are two things to note here. First, in a given case the upshot of the gift of counsel might be to single out a piece of advice the believer has been getting from another person as the embodiment of God's will in that particular situation. So in this sense the Holy Spirit's promptings may sometimes be indirect. In fact, the Christian life has traditionally incorporated built-in safeguards against idio-syncratic interpretations of these promptings. This is in part what lies behind the practice of spiritual direction in the various forms it takes in the life of the Church. Second, while believers will try to be particularly attentive to the Holy Spirit when they find themselves faced with important vocational decisions or morally ambiguous situations, the promptings associated with the gift of counsel are meant to guide them in *all* their actions and decisions. So, for instance, one finds devout Christians praying for counsel about how to spend their money, or about how to divide their time among the different demands made on them, or about how to best handle a tense situation with their spouses or children at home or their colleagues at work, or about how to arrange their daily schedule so as to make time for various acts of piety or evangelization, etc. This reinforces the claim made above that Christianity proposes a comprehensive way of life, one that includes not only an expansive theoretical framework, but also practical guidance in day-to-day situations.

Finally, there is the gift of wisdom (*sapientia*), an intellectual disposition that St Thomas directly associates with the theological virtue of charity, even though it has an obvious connection with the virtue of faith as well. For while this gift pertains directly to the believer's knowledge of divine realities in themselves, the knowledge in question springs primarily from filial love and bespeaks an intimacy of the sort that Christian doctrine encourages believers to cultivate with the persons of the Trinity through prayer and through the prayerful "pondering" of revealed truth, taking as their model Mary the mother of Christ, who "pondered all these things in her heart" (Luke 2:19) The lives of the saints, those particularly close friends of God, are replete with evidence of such knowledge born of intimacy. Especially striking is the familiarity with which they address God, even to the point of seeming irreverence – as when, after a particularly trying experience, St Teresa of Avila is said to have exclaimed, only partly in jest, "Dear Lord, if this is how you treat your friends, it's no wonder you have so few!"

By the gift of wisdom, then, believers are disposed to seek and delight in intimacy with God in such a way that they order all their other loves by reference to their desire for union with God. This is why the theological virtues are said to give believers even in this life a foretaste of heavenly peace and joy. In short, it is through the gift of wisdom that all created things are accurately judged to be infinitely less desirable than intellectual and affective union with the persons of the Trinity. And it is through this judgment that believers become wise in the classical sense of having a firm certitude about the "highest causes" that allows them to "order things rightly and govern them well."[38]

According to Christians, this is genuine wisdom – a wisdom that fulfills the promise of the classical philosophical schools. In the next section of the paper I will examine how Christians view the sapiential claims of those schools. But first I want to dwell briefly on the certitude of the wisdom of the faithful. Upon reading the lives of the saints, one is struck by their utter confidence in the deliverances of Christian revelation and in the God who stands behind those delieverances. How can this be, given that they all acknowledge the central articles of the faith to be mysteries that cannot even in principle become intellectually evident to us in this life? Isn't it the height of foolishness, not to mention a blatant sin against reason, for them to put their full trust in what they themselves cannot clearly see to be true?

Several points are in order here. First of all, under normal circumstances devout believers do not worry themselves about such epistemic questions. To be sure, they typically study and reflect on their faith and engage in acts of piety meant to keep that faith at the forefront of their minds. Still, they do so not primarily in order to build a reasoned case for the epistemic credentials of their belief, but rather in order to better understand their own central convictions and to better conform their lives to those convictions. Beyond that, they are mainly concerned with performing the works of charity and justice demanded by the various social roles they play in their homes, at work, and in the wider community. If they were to spend time reflecting on sophisticated epistemic questions instead, they would not be able to fulfill their responsibilities. In this, of course, they do not differ from the vast majority of non-believers. What's more, most believers lack either the ability or the training or the inclination to engage in serious intellectual inquiry. Typically, they study the deliverances of the faith formally in their youth and may take a few philosophy or theology courses as undergraduates. But their level of philosophical sophistication falls far short of what is required for independent formal inquiry into Christian doctrine. In fact, if they were to attempt serious intellectual inquiry on their own, it might well prove harmful to them, since inexperience and lack of sophistication could cause the sort of needless confusion that would paralyze them and keep them from living the Christian life to the full – a deplorable condition for "soldiers of Christ," who must keep their minds firmly focused on immediate battles with their own faults and weaknesses and with the "principalities and powers" (Rom. 8:38) that threaten to obstruct the spread of the good news.

From the perspective of certain accounts of epistemic rationality, devout believers will thus appear irrational and foolish. For example, John Locke and John Stuart Mill hold in effect that, at least within liberal democracies, each normal adult has an obligation to become his or her own philosophical expert.[39] However, as adumbrated above, such accounts of epistemic rationality, with their excessive demands for intellectual effort on the part of everyone, seem hopelessly out of touch with the reality of ordinary people's abilities, inclinations, and expertise – not to mention their busy lives and their many familial and social responsibilities. (Neither Locke nor Mill had children.) A much more sane view, it seems to me, is expressed by St Thomas in Chapter 4 of *Summa contra gentiles* 1, where he explains why it was fitting for God to reveal to us, for acceptance on faith, even those truths about himself that human reason could in principle have come to know in the absence of divine revelation:

> There are three reasons that keep most people from enjoying intense inquiry, that is, the discovery of truth. First of all, because of a lack of natural ability, and this is the reason why many people are ill-suited for pursuing knowledge ... Second, the necessities imposed by ordinary affairs prevent some people from pursuing knowledge. For they are charged with taking care of temporal affairs, and so they cannot spend enough time in the leisure of contemplative inquiry to reach the pinnacle of human inquiry, which is the cognition of God. Third, there are some who are impeded by indolence ... For one cannot arrive at the investigation of [divine] truth without a expending a great deal of effort in study. But there are few who wish to submit themselves to such an effort out of a love for knowledge – even though God has instilled a natural desire for such knowledge in the human mind.

Still, to make this point is not to claim that the Church *as a community* should not be concerned with epistemic questions. That is an entirely different matter, and I will return to it in a moment.

A second point to be made on behalf of devout believers is that the type of certitude they have with respect to the articles of faith is arguably superior – even on ostensibly epistemic grounds – to the type of certitude that would ideally emerge from intellectual inquiry. St Thomas himself draws a distinction between two types of certitude, one associated with the virtue of faith and the gifts of the Holy Spirit treated above, and the other associated with the natural intellectual virtues of *intellectus* (evident grasp of first principles), *scientia* (evident knowledge of conclusions derived from those principles), and *sapientia* (wisdom that combines *intellectus* and *scientia* so defined). The first type of certitude involves putting one's complete trust in God as a trustworthy revealer of truth, whereas the second is based on the evidentness to the knowing subject of the objects of assent:

> Certitude can be thought of in two ways. First, in terms of the *cause* of certitude and, accordingly, that which has a surer cause is said to be more certain. And in this sense faith is more certain than the three intellectual virtues mentioned above, since faith is founded on divine truth, whereas those three virtues are founded on human reason. In the second way, certitude is thought of in terms of the *subject* and, accordingly, that which the human intellect preceives more fully is said to be more certain; and because the things that belong to faith, but not the things that belong to the three virtues in question, lie beyond human understanding, faith is less certain in this sense. Yet since each thing is judged absolutely according to its cause ... it follows that faith is more certain absolutely speaking.[40]

Thus, even though the natural intellectual virtues in their perfected states exceed faith in the degree of evidentness with which one who has them grasps their objects, Christian faith in its perfected state exceeds the natural intellectual virtues in the degree of firmness and confidence with which the believer can responsibly adhere to divinely revealed truth – even to the point of voluntarily undergoing martyrdom in order to give witness to that truth.[41] This makes perfectly good sense once we come to see ourselves in our present condition as neophyte students of Christ the teacher. Just as beginning students reasonably put their faith in their teachers and the authors of their textbooks and wisely trust the judgment of those authorities more than their own untutored judgments, so too believers trust that God, who is perfectly truthful, is epistemically better situated than they are when he reveals mysteries about himself that they could not ascertain on their own. Needless to say, this docility to Christ the teacher, as well as other aspects of the Christian ideal of "spiritual childhood," flies in the face of the ideal of democratic enlightenment promoted by the likes of Locke and Mill.[42] But from a Christian perspective, docility to Christ is an altogether appropriate response to our true epistemic condition with regard to ultimate metaphysical and moral truth.

To be sure, certain contemporary philosophers have claimed that no comprehensive metaphysical and moral world-view of the sort that Christian faith proposes can be shown to have more rational warrant than any other.[43] The mere proliferation of such world-views and their proponents' inability to convince their opponents are themselves taken as reasons for this type of skepticism. The philosophers in question concede that we are free as private individuals to adopt one or another such world-view (as long as it is politically tolerable), but the affective commitment and level of confidence involved in such a choice is, if not irrational, then at least arational.

In reply, we should note, first of all, that St Thomas – like all mainstream Catholic thinkers and many reformed thinkers as well – takes the role of intellectual inquirer to be an important one within the ecclesiastical community, and that he considers both gullibility and intellectual arrogance to be serious faults. For even though he agrees with the skeptical philosophers that reason on its own is incapable of attaining true wisdom in this life, he is nonetheless much more optimistic about the power of reason than they are.

Second, and more to the point, St Thomas holds that Christian faith can be shown to be reasonable by any plausible standard of epistemic warrant – and, indeed, more reasonable than any alternative. I cannot develop his line of thought fully here, but in outline it goes like this:[44] given that our goal is to attain true wisdom and that, as even the great classical philosophers admitted, we are incapable of doing this on our own, the key question becomes not *whether* we should entrust our lives to some putatively authoritative teacher, but rather *which* such teacher we should trust. To this question St Thomas answers unabashedly: Jesus Christ and the church he founded. And against the charge that it is foolish for us to assent to the mysteries of the faith, he replies not by trying to prove the mysteries or even by trying to give plausible arguments for them, but rather by pointing to the marks of trustworthiness that characterize the Christian claim to revelation: the character, teaching, and miracles of Jesus Christ; the rapid spread of the early Church despite its being led by a band of generally uneducated and deeply flawed apostles; the witness of thousands of saints down through the centuries and especially of the martyrs; the nature of the way of life it proposes, which appeals to our most noble aspirations and does not pander to our weaknesses, etc. His claim in the end is that the credentials of Christian revelation are superior to those of any alternative.

There is obviously much more to be said here – for instance, concerning the reliability of sacred scripture.[45] But devout Christians will find themselves identifying with St Peter's sentiments at John 6:68–9. After many of Jesus' followers have walked away from him in the wake of his Eucharistic teaching, he turns to the apostles and asks whether they, too, wish to leave. Peter replies poignantly: "Master, to whom shall we go? You have the words of eternal life. We have come to believe and are convinced that you are the Holy One of God." In the end, the question is: just what are the alternatives? To these I now turn.

The Way: Christian Life and Its Competitors

To this point I have been describing in broad outline what the ideal life of Christian faith looks like from the inside. I now want to consider the way in which devout Christians have tended to view the alternatives to Christianity. I will limit my discussion to the classical alternatives, given that their contemporary counterparts are arguably just variations on themes that were already present in the ancient world.

A bit of history is in order here. As is evident from the Acts of the Apostles, at the very beginning of Church history, the Gospel was preached mainly as the fulfillment of the aspirations of the people of Israel. But as Pope John Paul II points out in his encyclical *Fides et ratio*, the search for the way, the truth, and the life has been common to all times and cultures.[46] So once the apostles and early fathers of the Church began to come into contact with intellectually sophisticated gentiles, it was not long before the Gospel was being presented to the pagan world as the fulfillment of the aspirations of the many philosophical movements which had sprung up around the Mediterranean Sea and beyond. Jesus Christ himself was now being portrayed as the true philosopher, the one who teaches and guides us to genuine wisdom.

Within the world of the Roman empire, for earnest seekers after wisdom to embrace a philosophy or philosophical school was for them to adopt not only an expansive theoretical account of the world's origins and destiny and of the human condition, but also a set of practices meant to bring them to human fulfillment as understood by that theoretical account.[47] These practices were in intent both positive, including especially the cultivation of good habits, and negative, aimed at rooting out bad habits and preparing the aspirant to avoid typical pitfalls and to withstand typical temptations. The ideal was that there should be a perfect complementarity between theory and practice. The theoretical framework was meant to validate and sustain the practices, and the cultivation of the practices was meant in part to deepen the aspirant's intellectual grasp of the theoretical framework. In short, the philosophy of a serious-minded lover of wisdom constituted a comprehensive way of life and required extensive doctrinal and moral training.

So, for instance, when St Augustine became inflamed with the love for wisdom by his reading of Cicero's *Hortensius*, he did not react by simply taking a few philosophy courses at his local college. Instead, after a hasty rejection of Christianity, he joined the Manicheans as a catechumen, submitting himself to the discipline of the Manichean way of life, replete with its demanding doctrinal and moral formation.[48] Afterwards, when he grew closer to Christianity, he did not go off on his own, but joined together with other like-minded men in a communal life of study and prayer.

In the preface to *Beyond Good and Evil* Nietzsche writes that Christianity is "Platonism for the masses." Without giving a blanket endorsement to Nietzsche's sometimes insightful and sometimes outlandish ruminations about Christianity, and keeping in mind that Stoicism claims a similarly universal appeal, we can at least acknowledge that the Christian faith makes available to people of all stripes what, according to many of the classical philosophical schools, would otherwise have been available only to those with a very rare combination of intellectual prowess, moral excellence, and good fortune – namely, the pinnacle of human fulfillment. More specifically, the Christian ideal of the life of the saint, which supplants the classical ideal of the philosophical life, is a possibility for the simple as well as for the intellectually gifted, for the poor as well as for the leisured elite, for the unfortunate (in the world's eyes) as well as for the fortunate.[49] In fact, according to Christian revelation, even the best of the pagan ideals of excellence were never really possible for human beings left to their own resources. It was only through the inner transformation of grace, elevating us from the status of mere creatures to that of sons and daughters of our father God, that the pagan dream could be both rectified and realized. For only this transformation – made available through the merits of Jesus Christ, effected by the sacraments of the Church, and nurtured through prayer, mortification, and good works – could heal and elevate their minds and hearts in such a way as to make genuine human fulfillment possible.

So in the primitive Church the Christian way was already being presented as a full-fledged alternative to, and the fulfillment of the most noble aspects of, the culturally indigenous sapiential ways of the philosophers – be they Platonists, neo-Platonists, Aristotelians, Stoics, Epicureans, Pyrrhonian skeptics, Cynics, Manicheans, etc.

What I have said so far is, of course, an oversimplification, because the Church is a big place, so to speak, and its early history witnessed the development of a wide variety of so-called "spiritualities," all of them centered around sound doctrine, the sacraments, and prayer, but each with its own distinctive emphases and customs tailored to the particular style of life characteristic of its adherents. In essence, these "spiritualities" were providing their adherents with a precise analogue of the detailed ways of life proposed by the pagan schools of wisdom, but now within the framework of revealed Christian faith and morals.

Given this background, we can now ask how Christians have tended to view the main alternative ways of life proposed by classical non-Christian philosophers. I will not pretend that my treatment here is thorough; rather, I wish simply to indicate in broad strokes the general types of reasons Christians have for judging these alternatives to be defective and unsatisfactory.[50]

Christianity shares in common with most of these alternatives the imperative to live a life that has the single-minded desire for, and pursuit of, wisdom at its center. So Christians concur with Socrates that normal adult human beings should be constantly reflecting on the nature of the best sort of life and on how their own lives compare with that ideal.[51] A life lived unreflectively in accord with prevailing cultural customs (or fads) is deemed unworthy of a human being.

Christians likewise agree with most of the classical schools in holding that our souls are initially disordered in such a way that some form of ascetic practice aimed at self-control is essential to a genuinely happy life. Hence, they are especially wary of the insidious temptation to make goods such as wealth, honor, fame, sexual pleasure, and power – whether political or social or economic – the dominant ends of their lives.

Beyond this, Christians agree with Socrates, Plato, Aristotle, and the Stoics – against the Epicureans – that the best sort of human life must not be ordered toward the pleasant and the comfortable. From a Christian perspective, this is an alluring road to perdition that caters to our weakness and is born of a deep despair about the human condition – a point confirmed by Epicurean metaphysics, which posits a materialistic universe wholly indifferent to human aspirations and invites us, in the manner of Simonides the ancient poet, to keep our gaze fixed on things here below and thus to avoid irrevocable self-transcending life-commitments.[52] (In this respect Epicureanism is strikingly similar to what is sometimes called "pragmatism" in contemporary parlance, as well as to a certain type of scientific-minded naturalism that is nowadays popular in some intellectual circles.[53]) From a Christian perspective, to live in this way is not unlike extending to the whole of one's own life the otherwise praiseworthy practice of making terminal patients comfortable in their last hours.

The alternative is to live a life unified by a dominant noble end, passionately desired, that makes possible permanent life-commitments consonant with that end. To be sure, such a life presupposes certitude – if not that of Christian faith, then at least that of a Socratic faith in the superiority of the philosophical life to all competitors. This is one reason why permanent self-transcending commitments are terrifying (I can think of no better word for it) to those – especially within pluralistic liberal democracies – who are skeptical of sapiential claims. However, I noted that the dominant end in question should be noble, and one mark of a noble end is (or should be) that the pursuit of it makes one more fit for and desirous of genuine friendship with others. This is certainly the case with the goal of knowing and loving the triune God that lies at the core of the Christian way of life, but it was equally true of the ideals set forth by Aristotle in his *Ethics* and *Politics*, by Plato in his *Republic*, and, it seems, by the Stoics as well.[54] So the skeptics have less to worry about than they seem to think.

So Christians are similar to the Platonists, Aristotelians, and Stoics in a number of important respects.[55] But there are significant differences as well. I will end by briefly mentioning two of them, one having to do with the primary motivation for living a morally upright life and the other having to do with the nature of the end sought. On both these counts Christians take themselves to have a great advantage over their classical counterparts.

Even though these classical philosophies are meant in some way or other to make human beings fit for friendship, the primary motivation for an aspirant's living in accord with one of these classical ways seems to be impersonal at its base. By this I mean that what motivates individuals to lead a morally upright life is the desire to make themselves measure up to a certain impersonal standard of human flourishing – in something like the way that, say, my daughter Katie might want to make herself into the sort of basketball player who makes 90 percent of her free throws. The desire for happiness is thus accompanied by what, from a Christian perspective, is a prideful desire for self-sufficiency. Because of this, failures in the moral life are regretted not primarily because they are offenses against another whom we love, but rather because they make manifest our own weakness. So, from this perspective, just insofar as we have acted badly, we feel embarrassment rather than guilt or contrition, and our failure is a failure in our resolve to make ourselves better rather than a failure of love.

St Augustine noticed this very point when he lamented in his *Confessions* about what he had found lacking in the works of the Platonists: "the writings of the Platonists contain nothing of all this. Their pages show nothing of the face of that love, the tears of confession, Your sacrifice, an afflicted spirit, a contrite and humbled heart . . ."[56] For devout Christians, by contrast, the deepest motivation for living well is love for another, and, more specifically, loving gratitude for God's gift of salvation and grace. Failures to respond to God's gracious initiative are thus failures of love – that is, failures in conforming one's will to the will of God. For from a Christian perspective, the desire to be lovingly obedient to God's will is extensionally equivalent to the desire for happiness.[57] This is because God has made us in such a way that to conform ourselves to his will satisfies our desire for genuine human flourishing as defined by our very natures.

The second difference concerns the nature of the end we hope to attain by living in a morally upright way. From a Christian perspective, the main problem with the classical philosophical schools is that, in the absence of divine revelation, they set their sights too low. In the *Phaedo* Socrates hopes for an afterlife in which he will possess philosophical wisdom and enjoy the company of other philosophers. Interestingly, this is exactly what Dante gives him, placing him in the first circle of the inferno along with other noble philosophers, including Plato, Aristotle, Zeno, Cicero, Seneca, Avicenna, and Averroës. In commenting on this scene from the *Inferno* Dorothy L. Sayers expresses the Christian perspective perhaps as well as anyone could:

> [These souls] enjoy that kind of after-life which they themselves imagined for the virtuous dead; their failure lay in not imagining better. They are lost (as Virgil says later) because "they had not faith" – primarily the Christian Faith, but also, more generally, faith in the nature of things. The allegory is clear: it is the weakness of Humanism to fall short in the imagination of ecstasy; at its best it is noble, reasonable, and cold, and however optimistic about a balanced happiness in this world, pessimistic about a rapturous eternity. Sometimes wistfully aware that others claim the experience of this positive bliss, the Humanist can neither accept it by faith, embrace it by hope, nor abandon himself to it in charity.[58]

The upshot is that the Aristotelians, Platonists, and Stoics suffered from a despair which, even if not as pronounced as the despair of the Epicureans, was nonetheless in the end debilitating. Indeed, when one reads the Gospel account of the rich and virtuous young man who walks away in sadness when Jesus asks him to leave everything in order to gain eternal life (Matt. 19), it is hard not to think of, say, Aristotle's good man or the ideal Stoic or even perhaps Socrates himself. The rich young man suspects that there is something more he must do to gain eternal life – that is, something more than the Mosaic law demands (or the philosophers demand). He also suspects, it seems, that there is something more to eternal life itself than he has understood up to this point. But he lacks the will to commit himself passionately and without reserve to Jesus Christ. He mistrusts Jesus' suggestion that there is a happiness for which it is worth sacrificing everything he has – an everlasting life of ecstasy to be gained if only he will "lose" the way of life he has now.

And so there is, according to the Christian faith: we can live forever as sons and daughters in intimacy with Father, Son, and Holy Spirit. That is the promise of Christian faith as a way of life.

Notes

1 This rejection is noted with concern by Pope John Paul II in his encyclical *Fides et ratio* (1998), even though the Holy Father goes out of his way to praise the many positive contributions to human self-understanding made by philosophers who presuppose a split between faith and reason. For more on *Fides et ratio*, see my "*Fides et ratio*: A 'Radical' Vision of Intellectual Inquiry," in *Faith, Scholarship and Culture in the 21st Century (American Maritain Association, 2000)*, ed. Alice Ramos and Marie George (Washington, D.C.: Catholic University of America Press, 2002), pp. 13–31.

2 Here I have in mind especially Alvin Plantinga's trilogy of *Warrant: The Current Debate* (New York: Oxford University Press, 1993), *Warrant and Proper Function* (New York: Oxford University Press, 1993), and *Warranted Christian Belief* (New York: Oxford University Press, 2000).

3 For a defense of the idea that believing philosophers should not limit their agenda to engaging non-believing philosophers, see my "Two Roles for Catholic Philosophers," in *Recovering Nature: Essays in Natural Philosophy, Ethics, and Metaphysics in Honor of Ralph McInerny*, ed. John P. O'Callaghan and Thomas S. Hibbs (Notre Dame, Ind.: University of Notre Dame Press, 1999), pp. 229–53.

4 Nicholas Wolterstorff, "Faith," in *Routledge Encyclopedia of Philosophy*, ed. Edward Craig (London and New York: Routledge, 1998).

5 See especially John 14. In John 15 Jesus uses the striking image of the vine and the branches to convey in more concrete terms that his followers will share in his very life and, by implication, in the very life of God. St Thomas follows St Paul and the fathers of the Church in taking these words to express a sober (and stunning) metaphysical reality.

6 See Matthew 19.

7 See especially *Summa theologiae* (hereafter: *ST*) 1–2, 109, 3–4, on the necessity we have for God's grace to fulfill even the precepts of the natural law, including the precept to love our creator God above all things.

8 It is true, of course, that many people seem, at least at certain times of their lives and at least on the surface, to be oblivious to what Christians claim is their desperate plight. This sort of indifference is a feature of our culture that some have taken note of. See, e.g., Walker Percy, "A 'Cranky Novelist' Reflects on the Church," in Walker

Percy, *Signposts in a Strange Land*, ed. Patrick Samway (New York: Ferrar, Straus and Giroux, 1991), pp. 316–25.

9 See *ST* 3, 23.

10 Throughout this paper I am assuming the truth of a philosophical anthropology which is a form of neither dualism nor materialism, but instead holds that the human organism includes both a material and an immaterial component. For more on this, see my "Good News, Your Soul Hasn't Died Quite Yet," *Proceedings of the American Catholic Philosophical Association*, 75 (2001), pp. 99–120.

11 For a popular and yet profound treatment of the "family life" of the Trinity and our share in it, see Scott Hahn, *First Comes Love: Finding Your Family in the Church and the Trinity* (New York: Doubleday, 2002).

12 *ST* 1–2, 110, 3, resp.

13 The language of divinization is also reflected in liturgical practice. In the Mass of the Roman Rite, for example, the following prayer is said as a small quantity of water is added to the wine that is soon to be consecrated: "By the mystery of this water and wine may we come to share in the divinity of Christ, who humbled himself to share in our humanity."

14 *ST* 3, 23, 1, resp.

15 *ST* 3, 23, 3, resp. The first two modes of assimilation to the Word of God are (a) the assimilation of each actualized creature to the Word insofar as the Word is the locus of the divine idea corresponding to that creature and (b) the assimilation of all intelligent creatures to the intellectual nature of the Word by virtue of the higher intellectual powers they possess by their natures.

16 The division of the basic passions into the *concupiscible* and the *irascible* is based on the objects toward which the passions are directed. The concupiscible passions have as their object a good or evil taken simply in itself. St Thomas identifies six basic concupiscible passions arranged in two ordered triplets: (a) *love* (inclination toward a good), *desire* (motion toward an object of love), and *pleasure* or *enjoyment* (possession of what is loved); and (b) *hate* (inclination away from an evil), *aversion* (motion away from an object of hate) and *pain* or *sadness* (possession of what is hated). The irascible passions kick in when the good loved is difficult to attain or when the evil hated is difficult to avoid or overcome. The five basic irascible passions are *fear* (movement away from an evil that is difficult to overcome), *daring* (movement toward an evil that is difficult to overcome), *hope* (movement toward a good that is difficult to attain), *despair* (movement away from a good that is difficult to attain), and *anger* (reaction to an evil as something to be avenged). See *ST* 1–2, 22–3 for St Thomas's general treatment of the passions; the subsequent questions are devoted to the particular passions. According to St Thomas, the cardinal virtues of fortitude and temperance, along with the virtues related to them, have the sentient appetite itself as their immediate subject.

17 *ST* 1–2, 110, 4, resp.

18 *ST* 1–2, 110, 3, resp. Why is grace said to give off light? It is not just intellectual light that is in question here. Rather, St Thomas is taking his cue from John 1:4 ("In him was life, and the life was the light of men") and Eph. 5:8 ("For you were heretofore darkness, but now light in the Lord; walk then as children of the light"). This in turn accords with the idea, articulated in *ST* 1–2, 86, that one of the main effects of sin is the *macula peccati*, the stain or pollution or defilement caused by sin, a sort of

darkness of the soul that permeates all its powers, resulting in effects such as ignorance in the intellect, malice in the will, and weakness and disordered desire (or concupiscence) in the sentient appetite. By contrast, a soul in God's good graces is radiant and unblemished – immaculate, if you will.

19 For an excellent treatment of St Thomas's view of the acquired virtues, see Brian Shanley, OP, "Aquinas on Pagan Virtue," *The Thomist*, 63 (1999), pp. 553–77. St Thomas, unlike some other scholastics – most notably, Duns Scotus, holds that there must be infused moral virtues in addition to the acquired virtues. See *ST* 1–2, 63, 3–4. I will not pursue this issue here.

20 Strictly speaking, the intensification of the gifts of the Holy Spirit is God's doing alone. But he has promised to give an increase of his grace – and, a fortiori, of the gifts – to anyone who follows him faithfully. This phenomenon falls under the notion of *merit*, whereby God establishes a framework within which he promises to bestow an abundance of grace on those who persevere in their love of him. See *ST* 1–2, 114.

21 Eucharist Prayer II in the Roman Missal.

22 A cautionary note is in order here. In the early history of the Church, as recorded in the Acts of the Apostles, it is clear that believers were encouraged to take counsel from the wise among them who were assumed to have a special "grace of state" for this role. This practice was meant to prevent believers from adopting idiosyncratic and even spiritually and morally dangerous interpretations of the promptings of the Holy Spirit. This practice survives today under the rubric of "spiritual direction." I will say a bit more about this below.

23 *ST* 2–2, 1, 1.

24 One can consult the table of contents of the first three books of the *Summa contra gentiles* to see which truths about God St Thomas counts as preambles.

25 For a discussion of the relevant differences among some medieval Christian thinkers, see my "Ockham on Faith and Reason," in *The Cambridge Companion to Ockham*, ed. Paul V. Spade (Cambridge: Cambridge University Press, 1999), pp. 326–49.

26 For a discussion of the significance of the distinction between the preambles and the mysteries, see my "Two Roles for Catholic Philosophers."

27 For confirmation of this point in St Thomas, see *Summa contra gentiles* 1, chapters 1–9, esp. chapter 4. I will elaborate later on in this section.

28 This analogy works best for the scientific and mathematical disciplines, in which at any given time there are fundamental propositions and first principles that all practitioners of the discipline take for granted. One must grasp and accept them for the time being even in order to be in a position to criticize them at some later time.

29 This does not in general seem to be a feature of the teacher–student relationship, though perhaps ideally it should be. But I will not pause to pursue this issue here.

30 St Thomas treats this gift in *ST* 2–2, 8.

31 See *ST* 2–2, 15, 1–2. St Thomas defines blindness of the mind (*caecitas mentis*) as the complete privation of the light of grace (or light of faith) and dullness of sense (*hebetudo sensus*) as "a certain weakness of mind in the consideration of spiritual goods," a lack of insight. Insofar as they pertain to matters of faith, both these defects are consequences of sin – especially, says St Thomas, of carnal sins.

32 While it is true that understanding precedes judgment, it is also the case that correct judgments can deepen understanding. However, I will not pursue this point directly here.

33 For a brilliant description of the way in which Christianity holds opposites in tension with one another, see G. K. Chesterton, "The Paradoxes of Christianity," chapter 6 of *Orthodoxy* (San Francisco, Calif.: Ignatius Press, 1908, 1995).

34 For a profound meditation on the Christian understanding of suffering, see Pope John Paul II's Apostolic Letter *Salvifici doloris* (1984).

35 This point is consonant with what I will say in the final section of this chapter about the devout Christian's motivation for leading a morally upright life.

36 See *Fides et ratio*, no. 23.

37 See *ST* 2–2, qq. 47–52. The cognitive operations associated with the virtue of prudence are (a) deliberating well about means and ends, (b) making sound judgments about means and ends, and, especially, (c) formulating and following through on appropriate precepts (or maxims) for action. According to St Thomas, each exercise of prudence involves the following elements: grasping basic moral principles; reasoning validly from those principles; remembering the past accurately and without self-deception; being receptive to the advice of others; having moral insight into concrete situations; accurately assessing the prospects for successfully realizing our intended ends; taking into account all the relevant circumstances of the action; and exercising caution with respect to possible harmful consequences of the action.

38 This is the characterization of wisdom that St Thomas gives in *Summa contra gentiles* 1, chapter 1.

39 In his *Essay Concerning Human Understanding*, esp. chapters 16–20, Locke insists that all normal adults have the ability and the obligation to apply an epistemic methodology that will ensure that their assent to any proposition is proportioned strictly to the evidentness of that proposition's claim to truth. And in *On Liberty*, chapter 2, Mill brings this enlightenment ideal into the public forum by arguing that the best way for the citizen of a democracy to attain truth on important metaphysical, moral, and political questions is to participate in the ongoing free discussion of these questions among intellectually autonomous citizen-philosophers.

40 *ST* 2–2, 4, 8.

41 We should note here the difference between being willing to die for something – a trait exemplified by the Christian martyrs – and being willing to kill for something.

42 A Christian need not deny that the ideal of inquiry proposed by Locke or Mill might have some legitimate role with respect to conflicting political opinions that fall within the limits of Christian orthodoxy – though to the extent that such ideals entail that every citizen of a democracy must become a "political junkie," they are implausible on other grounds.

43 For an astute exposition, emendation, and defense of a position built on this sort of skepticism, see Gary Gutting, *Pragmatic Liberalism and the Critique of Modernity* (Cambridge: Cambridge University Press, 1999).

44 See especially *Summa contra gentiles* 1, chapters 5–6.

45 On this matter, I have little to add to the contributions of Michael Dummett ("The Impact on Scriptural Studies on the Content of Belief," pp. 3–21) and Peter van Inwagen ("Critical Studies of the New Testament and the User of the New Testament," pp. 159–90) in *Hermes and Athena: Biblical Exegesis and Philosophical Theology*, ed. Thomas Flint and Eleonore Stump (Notre Dame, Ind.: University of Notre Dame Press, 1993).

46 See the introduction to *Fides et ratio*.

47 For a thorough defense of this claim, see Pierre Hadot, *Philosophy As a Way of Life: Spiritual Exercises from Socrates to Foucault* (Oxford: Blackwell, 1995). Hadot acknowledges that the tradition of conceiving of philosophy as a way of life was continued in the monastic movements of the early Church, but claims that it was lost when philosophy and theology became the object of study in the universities in the high middle ages. However, this claim hardly does justice to St Bonaventure or St Thomas, to name just two stellar figures. In fact, the simple truth is that St Thomas's *Summa theologiae* cannot be deeply understood except as both expressing and directing the practice of the Christian life. As I see it, this flaw in Hadot's otherwise compelling work is in part caused by the inordinate opposition he posits between theory and practice and by his excessive disdain for theory.

48 See St Augustine of Hippo, *The Confessions*, 3, chapters 4–6.

49 It must be confessed that at times in the history of the Church the fact that the vocation to holiness or sanctity is universal – that is, meant for all baptized Christians – has been muted, so that striving for perfection was thought, in practice, if not in theory, to be limited to the clergy or those who professed the evangelical vows of poverty, chastity, and obedience.

50 To my mind, the best modern defense of Christianity against contemporary alternatives is still G. K. Chesterton's *Orthodoxy*. Anything I say here is little more than a footnote to Chesterton's argument.

51 I specify normal adults (or, better, those who have the use of reason) because, unlike Socrates, Christians deem those who for pathological reasons are incapable of rational reflection – for example, the mentally handicapped, the insane, the terminally comatose, etc. – as fully human nonetheless and capable of ultimate human flourishing. This is because Christians understand such happiness to be in the first place a divine gift rather than an achievement. To be sure, this gift demands a response, but one that is appropriate to one's circumstances.

52 Aristotle quotes this line from Simonides in *Nicomachean Ethics* 10, chapter 7 (1177b31), and St Thomas cites Aristotle's allusion to Simonides in *Summa contra gentiles* 1, chapter 5.

53 The *locus classicus* for the modern version of scientific-minded naturalism is Bertrand Russell's essay *A Free Man's Worship*, in which Russell famously claims that given what modern science tells us about the purposelessness of the universe, it is "only on the firm foundation of unyielding despair [that] the soul's habitation [can] henceforth be safely built." See *The Collected Papers of Bertrand Russell*, ed. Kenneth Blackwell et al., vol. 12, *Contemplation and Action, 1902–14* (London: Routledge, 1985). For an exposition of pragmatism, see Gutting, *Pragmatic Liberalism and the Critique of Modernity*.

54 I say this even while acknowledging the limitations Aristotle and Plato put on just who counts as someone worthy of the philosopher's friendship.

55 This similarity extends as well to other monotheists such as Jews and Muslims and to Buddhists and many Hindus as well. However, my purpose here is to concentrate on the world-views of prominent Western philosophers.

56 St Augustine of Hippo, *The Confessions* 7, chapter 21.

57 Not all Christian authors agree with this sentiment. For a compelling argument that they *should* agree, see Servais Pinckaers, OP, *The Sources of Christian Ethics* (Washington, D.C.: Catholic University of America Press, 1995), esp. chapters 1 and 2.

58 *The Comedy of Dante Alighieri the Florentine, Cantica 1: Hell*, trans. Dorothy L. Sayers (Baltimore, Md.: Penguin Books, 1949), pp. 95–6.

Suggested Further Reading

Flint, Thomas P. (ed.) (1990) *Christian Philosophy*. Notre Dame, Ind.: University of Notre Dame Press.

Morris, Thomas V. (ed.) (1988) *Philosophy and the Christian Faith*. Notre Dame, Ind.: University of Notre Dame Press.

Penelhum, Terence (ed.) (1989) *Faith*. New York: Macmillan Publishing Company.

Plantinga, Alvin, and Wolterstorff, Nicholas (eds.) (1983) *Faith and Rationality: Reason and Belief in God*. Notre Dame, Ind.: University of Notre Dame Press.

Chapter 9

Mysticism and Perceptual Awareness of God

William P. Alston

Introduction

Many people, especially in industrial societies in these pluralistic and scientistic times, suppose that we can know (reasonably believe) that God exists and what God is like only if we have sufficient reasons for that, reasons that are drawn from what we know about the world in other spheres of our experience and thought. The classical arguments for the existence of God, such as the cosmological argument and the argument from design, (see chapters 5–6), are designed to provide such reasons. This approach to the matter treats God, in effect, as a theoretical "posit," invoked to explain various features of the world. It is thought that since God is not observable by the five senses, we will have sufficient reason to believe in God's existence and nature only if this is required for an adequate explanation of what we can sensorily observe. But this way of thinking of the matter is foreign to the religious commitments of most people in most societies throughout human history. The overwhelming preponderant attitude has been that God (or whatever is taken as ultimate reality) makes himself known by impinging on our lives in various ways. God is as much an experienced part of what confronts us in the world as mountains, oceans, buildings, and other people, though, no doubt, in a very different way. If God has been *present* to one's experience, there is no need to postulate him as a part of an explanatory theory in order to be assured of his existence, any more than I have any such need with respect to my wife.

This essay will be an exposition and defense of that approach – of the thesis that for many people God is known through their experiential awareness of God. After exploring the variety in such experience, I will consider reasons for affirming and denying that such experience is what it seems to be, viz., a veridical experience of an objectively existing deity.

Some Basic Terms

The first order of business is to examine and clarify the terms in my title. And, perversely enough, I will begin with the last word of that title, "God." The great monotheistic religions – Judaism, Christianity, and Islam – recognize only one object of worship, in the strict sense, and this being is thought of as personal, as an agent who acts on the basis of knowledge, purposes, evaluations, and so on. Orthodox Christianity thinks of God as one God in "three persons," but it does not take that to amount to polytheism. But most religions in human history have been polytheistic, recognizing many personal objects of worship, even though some are of higher status than others. Buddhism exists in many forms, some of which recognize no personal deity at all. Popular Hinduism is also polytheistic, and the more philosophical and mystical varieties of Hinduism consider personal objects of worship to be mere manifestations of a completely unified and undifferentiated ultimate reality that is, indeed, the only true reality. And so it goes. We might use the term "ultimate reality" as a maximally generic term for an object of religious worship. And a completely inclusive treatment of perceptual awareness of religious objects of worship would have to consider all the ways in which ultimate reality is construed. But such a treatment would far outrun the space available for this essay. To avoid that fate, and for the sake of greater concreteness, I will limit myself here to God, as a unique personal object of worship. The choice is further motivated by the fact that this volume is designed as a guide to philosophy of religion as it has developed in Western thought, where the focus has been on monotheistic religion, and more specifically on the Juadeo-Christian form.

Now for "mysticism." Although the term is used in popular speech for a wide variety of experiences that are unusual and completely absorbing, scholars tend to restrict it to experiences in which all distinctions are transcended in an undifferentiated unity. Here there is no possibility of even distinguishing the experience, or the subject of the experience, from the object experienced. I will term this "extreme mystical experience." Here are two formulations from widely different traditions. "As pure water poured into pure water remains the same, thus, O Gautama, is the Self of a thinker who knows. Water in water, fire in fire, ether in ether, no one can distinguish them: likewise a man whose mind has entered into the Self" (*The Upanishads*, Max Müller, 1884, vol. 2, p. 334). "What he sees . . . is not seen, not distinguished, not represented as a thing apart. The man who obtains the vision becomes, as it were, another being. He ceases to be himself, retains nothing of himself. Absorbed in the beyond he is one with it, like a center coincident with another center" (Plotinus, 1964, 6, p. 9).

I will use "mystical experience" (hereinafter "ME") in a much more inclusive sense to range over any experience that is taken by the subject to be an experience of God, either at the moment of the experience or in retrospect. It is this last clause that enables me to include extreme ME as one type, perhaps the highest type, of my general category. Even if one who has an extreme ME is not aware during the experience of any distinction between oneself and what one is aware of, that distinction can be, and usually is, made after the fact. But it also includes many other less extreme types, as I will illustrate abundantly in the next section.

As for "perceptual awareness of God," rather than present a preliminary presentation of that idea, I will develop the thesis that (many) experiences of God constitute a kind of *perception*, as I proceed with the subject.

Features of Mystical Experience

As an initial basis for an exploration of the varieties of ME consider the following examples.

(1) ... all at once I ... felt the presence of God – I tell of the thing just as I was conscious of it – as if his goodness and his power were penetrating me altogether ... I thanked God that in the course of my life he had taught me to know him, that he sustained my life and took pity both on the insignificant creature and on the sinner that I was. I begged him ardently that my life might be consecrated to the doing of his will. I felt his reply, which was that I should do his will from day to day, in humility and poverty, leaving him, The Almighty God, to judge of whether I should some time be called to bear witness more conspicuously. Then, slowly, the ecstasy left my heart; that is, I felt that God had withdrawn the communion which he had granted ... I asked myself if it were possible that Moses on Sinai could have had a more intimate communication with God. I think it well to add that in this ecstasy of mine God had neither form, color, odor, nor taste; moreover, that the feeling of his presence was accompanied by no determinate localization ... But the more I seek words to express this intimate intercourse, the more I feel the impossibility of describing the thing by any of our usual images. At bottom the expression most apt to render what I felt is this: God was present, though invisible; he fell under no one of my senses, yet my consciousness perceived him. (James, 1902, pp. 67–8)

(2) Now it fares in like manner with the soul who is in rest and quiet before God: for she sucks in a manner insensibly the delights of *His presence*, without any discourse ... She sees her spouse *present* with so sweet a view that reasonings would be to her unprofitable and superfluous ... Nor does the soul in this repose stand in need of the *memory*, for she has her lover *present*. Nor has she need of imagination, for why should we represent in an exterior or interior image Him whose *presence* we are possessed of? (St Frances de Sales, *Treatise of the Love of God*. Quoted in Poulain, 1950, 75–6)

(3) That which the Servitor saw had no form, neither any manner of being; yet he had of it a joy such as he might have known in the seeing of the shapes and substances of all joyful things. His heart was hungry, yet satisfied, his soul was

full of contentment and joy: his prayers and hopes were all fulfilled. And the Friar could do naught but contemplate this Shining Brightness; and he altogether forgot himself and all other things. Was it day or night? He knew not. It was, as it were, a manifestation of the sweetness of Eternal Life in the sensations of silence and of rest. (Henry Suso, *Life*. Quoted in Underhill, 1955, p. 187)

These cases are typical of many others, but also differ from still others, in the following respects.

They are experiential, as contrasted with thinking of God or reasoning about God. Like sense experience, it seems to involve a *presentation* of the object. This feature is the main basis for construing mystical experience as a kind of perception – "mystical perception" (hereinafter "MP"). The most fundamental fact about sense perception (hereinafter "SP"), with respect to its intrinsic character as a mode of conscious cognition, is the way in which, for example, *seeing* my house differs from thinking about it, remembering it, forming mental images of it, and reasoning about it. It is the difference between *presence* (to consciousness) and *absence*. If I stand before the house with my eyes shut and then open them, I am suddenly presented with the object itself; it *appears* to me as blue and steep roofed. People who report being experientially aware of God often take this to contrast with thinking about God or reasoning about God in just the same way, as is especially made explicit in (2).

We must be careful with perceptual verbs like "see," "hear," and "perceive" itself. They are ordinarily used with a strong "success" implication. If it seemed to be a car in the distance, but what I saw was really a cow or a shadow, then I didn't really see a car. It wasn't a car that was presented or given to my awareness; it wasn't a car that looked a certain way to me. Similarly if I take myself to "see" God, or, more cautiously, to "perceive" God in a certain way, but what I am aware of is just some subjective image or feeling or mind, then I didn't really see God after all. But there is also a purely phenomenological use of perceptual verbs, in which we say of the sufferer from delirium tremens that he "sees" rats, even though there are no rats in his vicinity to be seen. When, at this stage of the exposition, I make the claim that experience that is taken to be an experience of God is a form of perception (of God), I am not begging the question against the atheist, who denies that there is any God to be seen. I am using "see" or "perceive" in a purely phenomenological sense to specify the kind of cognitive consciousness involved. The subject's experience is distinctively of the *presentational* sort. To the subject it is just as if a divine being is presented to his consciousness, whether or not it is really a divine being of which he is aware. Later in this essay, I will be much concerned with the question of whether such experiences are ever veridical perceptions of God, perceptions of God in the strong "success" sense of the term.

The (putative) perception is direct. But how can any perception not be direct, if it always involves a *presentation* of the object, the object's being present to one? Well, we have to distinguish between direct and indirect, immediate and mediated presentations. Think of the difference between seeing Bill Clinton face to face and seeing him on television. In both cases there is a visual presentation of Clinton; but in the second case, but not the first, one sees Clinton *through* seeing something else, the television screen. In a similar fashion we can contrast cases of direct perception of God, like the above, with the following cases of indirect perception.

(4) There was a mysterious presence in nature and sometimes met within the communion and in praying by oneself, which was my greatest delight, especially when, as happened from time to time, *nature became lit up from inside with something that came from beyond itself* (or seemed to do so to me). (Beardsworth, 1977, p. 19)

(5) I feel him [God] in the sunshine or rain . . . (James, 1902, p. 70)

There are those who hold that all experience of God is indirect. (Baillie, 1962, p. 39; Hick, 1966, pp. 98–113.) But though indirect perception undoubtedly occurs, and not infrequently, I deny that it exhausts the field. In addition to (1)–(3), which are most naturally read as involving direct perception of God, here is a general theoretical statement.

(6) . . . in the mystic union, which is a *direct apprehension* of God, God acts immediately upon the soul in order to communicate Himself to her; and it is God, *not an image of God*, not the illusion of God, that the soul perceives and attains to. (Fr. Roure, in *Les Études*, August 5, 1908, p. 371. Quoted in Poulain, 1950, p. 83)

The perception is non-sensory. This is made fully explicit in (1), and it is strongly suggested in (2) and (3). Here is another example from an "amateur" mystic, taken from Beardsworth's collection.

(7) Then, in a very gentle and gradual way, not with a shock at all, it began to dawn on me that I was not alone in the room. Someone else was there, located fairly precisely about two yards to my right front. Yet there was no sort of sensory hallucination. I neither saw him nor heard him in any sense of the word "see" and "hear," but there he was; I had no doubt about it. He seemed to be very good and very wise, full of sympathetic understanding, and most kindly disposed towards me. (Beardsworth, 1977, p. 122)

Many people find it incredible, unintelligible, or incoherent to suppose that there could be something that counts as *presentation*, that contrasts with abstract thought in the way sense perception does, but is devoid of sensory content. However, so far as I see, this simply evinces lack of speculative imagination. Why should we suppose that the possibilities of experiential givenness, for human beings or other cognitive subjects, are exhausted by the powers of *our* five senses? Surely it is possible, to start with the most obvious point, that other creatures should possess a sensitivity to other physical stimuli that plays a role in their functioning analogous to that played by our five sense in our lives. And, to push the matter a bit further, why can't we also envisage presentations that do not stem from the activity of any physical sense organs, as is apparently the case with MP?

But not all MP is devoid of sensory content. Here is an example from Beardsworth.

(8)   During the night of September 9th, 1954, I awoke and looking out of my window saw what I took to be a luminous star which gradually came nearer, and appeared as a soft slightly blurred white light. I was seized with violent trembling, but had no fear. I knew that what I felt was great awe. This was followed by a sense of overwhelming love coming to me, and going out from me, then of great compassion from the Outer Presence. After that I had a sense of overpowering peace, and indescribable happiness. (Beardsworth, 1977, p. 30)

It is a focal experience, one in which the awareness of God attracts one's attention so strongly as to blot out everything else. But there are also milder experiences that persist over long periods of time as a *background* to everyday experiences.

(9)   God surrounds me like the physical atmosphere. He is closer to me than my own breath. In him literally I live and move and have my being. (James, 1902, p. 71)

In terms of these distinctions I will focus in this essay on *direct, non-sensory,* and *focal* experiences, since I consider the case for their veridicality to be the strongest.

There is another distinction worth mentioning, that between (a) experiences that occur spontaneously without the subject's having done anything that is directed to inducing them, and (b) experiences that are deliberately sought. Most of the examples above are of the first sort. The most important examples of the second sort are those that involve systematic spiritual disciplines that aim at achieving a more intimate communion with God, and the consequences of that for one's life generally. These practices are found mostly, though not exclusively, in monastic orders of the contemplative sort. Items (2) and (3) are of that sort.

(a) and (b) have complementary strengths and weaknesses. It might seem that (a) carries a stronger presumption of veridicality, since it is, so to say, forced on the subject, rather than something the subject produces because motivated to have it. Experiences we deliberately seek carry, in general, a weak presumption of providing objectively accurate information. But we must be careful not to caricature the Christian contemplative tradition and other such traditions. It is not as if the contemplative figures out in advance the kind of experience she or he would like to have and then looks around for a technique for producing it. That would be a no-no. The discipline involves opening oneself up to the presence and activity of God within, and letting God work within one as he will. The contemplative's only "activity" is what is involved in doing what one can to remove blocks and obstacles to the conscious realization of what God is doing and to the more intimate communion with God. But, having said all that, it remains true that spontaneously occurring experiences of God are likely to carry more conviction to the skeptically minded, and perhaps it is right that they should. A notable strength of (b) is that it carries the promise of developing a more stable and a closer communion with God than a momentary encounter like (a) does in itself. (b) involves a practice that has developed over the centuries and has been continually tested and refined with the aim of attaining such communion and effecting appropriate transformations in the life of the individual.

The Case for Mystical Perception

So much for a brief sketch of the phenomenology of mystical experience – its generic character and its varieties. This was a prologue to the central issue of this essay – whether ME is a source of knowledge of God. Though this is the most intuitively natural way of formulating the issue, we might also put it as the question of whether ME is a source of justification or rationality for beliefs that stem from it. The claim that it is, is more modest than the claim that it is a source of knowledge, for knowledge has more stringent conditions than rational belief. I will be thinking here primarily of the more modest version. Though I will sometimes speak in terms of knowledge, that should be understood as a stylistic variation of the formulation in terms of justified (rational) belief.

Even though ME is, phenomenologically, a perception of God, that does not in itself guarantee that it is a source of knowledge of God. Reflection on sense perception shows us that an experience can be phenomenologically a perception of a certain (kind of) object without yielding knowledge concerning any such objects. The rats of the deluded sufferer from delirium tremens, and other hallucinations, are enough to establish that. And there are many milder examples of misleading sensory experiences (hereinafter "SE"). We do not, unless we are extreme philosophical skeptics, raise doubts about the epistemic credentials of SP generally. We take it for granted that SE is generally a source of justified belief about what seems to be perceived in a given experience. Beliefs about what seems to be sensorily perceived are subject to doubt and critical scrutiny only when there is special reason to doubt them. But the epistemic credentials of ME by no means enjoy such near-universal acceptance. Many persons, especially in these times and in certain societies, doubt or deny that ME reveals anything about objective reality. To be sure, we should not overestimate the acceptance of this position. A number of sociological surveys in recent decades have uncovered a large proportion of the population in American society that believe themselves to have enjoyed an awareness of the presence of God. See Stark and Glock (1968) for a good example. Nevertheless, the view that ME is a source of knowledge of any ultimate, transcendent reality is controversial enough to require extended critical examination, an examination to which I now proceed.

First, let us be clear that not all beliefs based on ME can be true. The not infrequent contradictions between such beliefs are enough to establish this. Such contradictions are found not only between such beliefs in radically different religious traditions, but even within the same tradition, broadly conceived. The bizarre alleged messages from God that are central to certain cults that claim continuity with the Christian tradition are testimony enough to that. For such alleged messages often conflict with the picture of God built up in mainstream Christianity, at least partly on the basis of ME. Here too there are parallels in SE, even if not to the same extent. Divergent reports of the same automobile accident are salient examples. The serious issue is not whether mystical perceptual reports are always true or rational, but whether they ever are, or, better, whether they are in a significant proportion of cases.

In discussing the question I will first consider reasons for a positive answer and then proceed to reasons for a negative answer together with responses to those reasons.

So far as I can see, the only impressive reason for giving credence to beliefs based on ME is a particular application of a more general epistemic principle that can be stated as follows.

> (PF)   The fact that a subject, S, has an experience that seems to be a case of x's appearing to S as so-and-so renders a belief that x (exists and) is so-and-so prima facie justified.

To say that a belief is prima facie justified is to say that it is (unqualifiedly) justified provided there is no sufficient reason to deny it or the epistemic efficacy of its grounds. (I will term such reasons *overriders* of the prima facie justification in question.) In other words, the belief is "initially credible," worthy of belief in the absence of sufficient reasons to the contrary, "innocent until proven guilty." Beliefs based on experience are rationally acceptable until or unless they are shown to be otherwise. They don't need any further *positive* support to be acceptable. They only need an absence of sufficient *negative* considerations. (Note that by crediting experience with conferring only prima facie justification on the beliefs that stem from it, we have abandoned any supposition that experience by itself renders beliefs absolutely certain in the sense of infallible, impossible to be mistaken.) Our principle is essentially the same as what in Swinburne 1979 is called the "principle of credulity." It is widely accepted, at least in application to SP. (See, e.g., Chisholm, 1977, pp. 76–8 and Price, 1932, p. 185.)

Before launching into a discussion of the principle in application to MP, it is necessary to be explicit as to what it is reasonable to expect, at most, in the way of justified belief about God, from ME. Our sights can be set higher or lower. The highest expectation would be an unqualified one, taking any case of x's seeming to appear to experience as so-and-so to ground a prima facie justification of the belief that x is so-and-so. Lower expectations would involve such a commitment only for some subset of such cases. One might think that in view of the extent of incompatibilities between beliefs based on mystical experience, both interreligiously and intrareligiously, the unqualified expectation would be thoroughly unreasonable. But the elasticity of the notion of prima facie justification enables one to adopt the unqualified principle, while handling even a torrent of incompatible beliefs. For each such incompatibility all but one of the incompatible contenders might be eliminated at a second stage by overriders. So we have a choice between admitting any experientially based beliefs as prima facie justified, realizing that many will be subsequently eliminated by overriders, or being more selective in what sorts of beliefs we admit to that prima facie justified status. This is analogous to the choice between admitting all applicants to a university with the expectation that a large proportion will flunk out early on, and being more selective with admissions. For that analogue it is clear that the former, more lenient alternative, is much more wasteful, financially and in terms of well-being of the persons involved, than the latter, more discriminating alternative. I am inclined to make a similar point with respect to the epistemological choice before us. We will get a cleaner and more defensible version of the position favoring the epistemic efficacy of MP if we restrict the claims of prima facie justification to those areas in which we are not so inundated with incompatibilities as we are with, e.g., messages from God and any experiential reports that support distinctive beliefs of some particular religion.

We have a wide choice, of course, between ways of being selective. What strikes me as a natural choice is a restriction to experientially based beliefs concerning the existence and basic nature of God (henceforth "G-beliefs"), leaving aside more specific beliefs about God's plans, purposes, requirements, and actions in history, and particular messages for particular people. Using the terminology already introduced, I will now identify the principle that applies (PF) to G-beliefs generated by ME.

> (PFG) The fact that a subject, S, has a mystical experience that seems to be a case of God's appearing to S as so-and-so renders a G-belief that God (exists and) is so-and-so prima facie justified.

The central issue of this article is whether to a accept (PFG). I will be defending the principle, but I will give careful consideration to arguments on the other side.

What is to be said in favor of (PFG)? As I said earlier, (PF) is widely accepted for SP. The chief reason for this is that it provides the only escape from an extreme scepticism that denies that we get any knowledge from SP. One might think that we have abundant evidence for the epistemic efficacy, the reliability, of SP as a source of (mostly) true beliefs about the environment. But when we scrutinize arguments for this conclusion, as I do in detail in Alston (1993), we find that those that are not otherwise defective suffer from "epistemic circularity," taking premises from the very source under examination. Here I will have time only to give a simple illustration of this. It is often said that we can be sure that SP gives us genuine knowledge of what we perceive because by relying on it and reasoning from its products we have been able to make great strides in the prediction and control of natural phenomena, and on that basis to achieve astounding technological advances. That sounds like an impressive argument. And so it is, until we ask how we know that we have made great strides in prediction and control and technological invention. To narrow down to one part of this, how do we know that a particular prediction has turned out to be correct? Why, by taking a look (listen . . .) to see whether things have turned out as predicted. It is not as if an angel tells us this, or that it is a rationally self-evident truth. Thus we have confidence in the reasons offered for the reliability of SP only because we take SP to be reliable. If, as I argue in Alston (1993), we cannot find any otherwise effective argument for the reliability of SP that does not presuppose the conclusion, it is clear that the only way to save our conviction that SP is generally reliable – something that no one doubts in practice – is to take all perceptually generated beliefs as prima facie justified, to be taken as true in the absence of sufficient overriders.

Clearly, we cannot use exactly this same rationale for (PFG). For the supposition that ME is a source of rational belief does not command the universal assent that attaches to the analogue for SP. But we can build on the results for SP to construct what might be called an "undue partiality" or "anti-parochialism" argument. How can we justify according initial credibility to sense perceptual beliefs and not to mystical perceptual beliefs when it seems to the subject in both cases that they are simply reporting what is directly presented to their consciousness? If we had an independent argument for the credibility of the former and not the latter, that would justify the discrimination. But, as I have just suggested, and argued elsewhere, there are no otherwise-sound arguments for attributing reliability to SP that do not presuppose that reliability. And if we allow "epistemic circularity," we can give arguments for the (general) reliability of beliefs (at least beliefs of certain sorts, as specified above) based on MP. For the doctrinal systems of monotheistic religions, based in part on MP, contain excellent reasons for supposing that God would make himself available to the experience of his human creatures. For example, such religious belief systems generally hold that God is concerned to establish intimate personal relations with human beings, and this is not possible unless the latter are experientially aware of the presence of God. Hence since in both areas beliefs arise with the strong conviction that they are warranted by just reporting what is directly presented to the subject, and since in neither area is there any strong independent reason for supposing that the mode of experience in question is a veridical awareness of what seems to be presented, it would be an arbitrary double standard to accord prima facie justification to experientially grounded beliefs in one area and not in the other.

But even though SP and MP are on the same footing so far as the availability of non-circular ways of validating their epistemic credentials are concerned, they do obviously differ in several important respects. And it is not infrequently thought that one or another of these differences justifies us in taking the outputs of SP to be prima facie justified but not the outputs of MP. I will consider several of these differences. Although I am currently involved in dealing with reasons for supposing MP to be a source of knowledge, and the considerations I am about to examine could properly be construed as reasons for denying this, I will deal with them now because they are best regarded as reasons against my positive case for (PFG).

Criticisms of the Positive Case

First, let's consider some obvious differences between SE and ME.

(1) SE is a common possession of mankind, while ME is not. To be sure, as I pointed out above, a number of recent surveys have shown that ME is more widely distributed than many of our contemporaries suppose, but still by no means all human beings enjoy mystical experiences. But none of us are without SE, and almost all of us have a rich variety thereof.
(2) SE is continuously and unavoidably present during all our waking hours. But for most of those not wholly deprived of ME it is, at best, enjoyed only rarely. It is very unusual for someone, like the famous Brother Lawrence, the author of *The Practice of the Presence of God*, to enjoy a constant experiential awareness of God.
(3) SE, especially visual experience, is vivid and richly detailed, while ME is typically meagre and obscure. Though one's experience of God is often deeply meaningful to one, and one often takes it to reveal something important about God, still it could not begin to compare in richness and complexity of detail with a single glance out my study window at my front yard, displaying details of flowers, trees, passing cars, houses, and so on.

Obvious differences like these make it difficult for many people to believe that MP can involve a genuine experience of objective reality. But on reflection we can see that this reaction lacks any significant basis.

We can usefully treat (1) and (2) together. The question is: what does the extent of distribution in a given individual's life, or in the population, have to do with whether or not the experience contains important information? Why suppose that what happens only occasionally cannot have cognitive value? No one would apply such a principle to scientific or philosophical insight. Those come only rarely and only to a few people, but they are not denigrated for that reason. Would anyone suggest that the kind of insight that led Einstein to the development of his general theory of relativity is inferior in cognitive value to everyday visual awareness of one's surroundings, on the grounds that the latter is more widely shared and occurs more frequently? We can safely neglect frequency as an index to the extent to which an experience can be a source of knowledge.

I can't see that (3) fares any better. Within SE itself there are important differences of this sort between the sense modalities. Vision is far ahead of the others in richness and detail, with hearing and touch a distant second, followed at a more considerable distance by taste and smell. One glance at what is before me gives a much greater variety of information than one taste or one sniff. And the latter are severely restricted in the kinds of information they contain. One glance tells me that I am looking across a valley at a hillside on which there are beautiful forests, meadows, barns, farmhouses, and sheep. How much more I learn from this than from a taste that tells me that the item tasted has a sour and pungent flavor. And yet this is no reason for denying that taste and smell can be veridical perception of external realities, giving us genuine information about them. Is less information no information at all? That would be like maintaining that since the crude map I draw to show you the route to my house gives much less geographical information than the Rand-McNally atlas, it gives no information.

A more serious reason for denying that ME is a source of prima facie justification of beliefs is the incidence of incompatibility between beliefs based on ME, a much greater incidence than is found in SE. I think there can be no doubt of this difference. Most normal observers will agree, at least roughly, in the beliefs they form about a scene at which they are looking. The incompatibilities come mostly in situations that are not favorable for accurate observation – being too far away, or what is perceived happening too rapidly. But even after the area of ME-grounded beliefs under consideration is restricted in the way suggested above, the incompatibilities appear to be much more serious. Here we run into the problem of "religious diversity." Although I have ruled that the MP I will be defending is confined to the monotheistic religions, when it comes to considering the bearing on the epistemic status of MP of incompatibilities among its outputs, I cannot, in good conscience, exclude non-theistic religions from consideration. It is often made a reproach to the claim of MP to be a source of knowledge, that if it were it would not yield such radically incompatible beliefs in different world religions. If ME involves a direct presentation of ultimate reality as so-and-so, how does it happen that the "so-and-so" differs so widely across the landscape? Of course, ME need not be infallible in order to constitute a source of genuine knowledge of its objects; infallibility is too much to expect of any human cognitive faculties. And yet when the beliefs about ultimate reality that issue from experience in various branches of Buddhism, Hinduism, Islam, and Christianity differ so sharply and widely, it would seem that the more reasonable hypothesis is that the experience is primarily molded by the antecedent expectations the subject brings to it from his tradition, rather than from the impact of any experienced objective reality on this consciousness. And this is a criticism that cannot be dismissed out of hand, whatever rulings I might have made.

In agreeing to take this objection seriously I have, in effect, broadened out the conception of MP by taking it to range over any experience that the subject takes to be an awareness of ultimate reality, however the latter is construed. And, of course, the question of how we develop a taxonomy of what is often termed "religious experience" is itself a serious and difficult question, one I cannot enter into in this essay. But even if I were to deny that theistic ME is the same sort of experience as the Buddhist's experience of Nirvana or the monistic Hindu's experience of the absolute undifferentiated one, I would still be faced with the fact that experiences of these different sorts, which obviously have important features in common, give rise to apparently incompatible views as to the nature of ultimate reality. And that in itself could well be taken as a reason for doubting or denying the epistemic credentials of theistic MP. So what are we to say about these incompatibilities, which go far beyond any that we find in SE? People in radically different cultures sensorily perceive their physical and social environment in roughly compatible ways, but the same cannot be said for the perception of what they take to be ultimate reality.

Again I must plead that this is too vast and complex a subject to be treated adequately in a short section of the present essay. I will confine myself to pointing to two considerations that are relevant to a resolution of the problem.

1   We should not be too quick to assume that apparent incompatibilities are the genuine article. Consider what seems to be the most serious conflict, whether ultimate reality is personal or impersonal. A commitment to one of these options is in genuine conflict with the other only if it is so construed as to exclude the other, and that is by no means the only way to construe it. The key point here is that one and the same being can have both personal and impersonal aspects. All of us do. We are all persons – endowed with consciousness, cognitive capacities, emotions, feelings, desires, aversions, etc. But each of us also shares aspects with non-personal realities – weight, size, shape, chemical constitution, physical energy, etc. Hence, the fact that Teresa of Avila perceives the ultimate as personal, while Sankara perceives it as impersonal, does not necessarily imply that they are perceiving different beings, or that though perceiving the same being, at least one is mistaken as to what that being is like. They could well be aware of different genuine aspects of the same being. To be sure, the theologies of each tradition are often crafted in such a way as to exclude the claims of the other. In Hinayana Buddhism one not only experiences the ultimate as impersonal; it is a fundamental article of faith that ultimate reality is non-personal and that any supposition to the contrary is mere illusion. And similarly, in theistic religions the dominant view is that the deepest truth about ultimate reality is that it is personal, that God has knowledge, purposes, plans, that he loves his creation, works for the salvation of mankind, and so on. But the concern here is not with the overall theologies, but with ME as a source of knowledge. And my present suggestion is that if we stick to what seems to mystical experiencers to be strictly presented to them experientially, even widely different apparent features of what is experienced could

often be compatible. I do not suggest that there are no such incompatibilities, but it may well be that they are not so numerous and varied as to rob ME of all epistemic worth.

2   The second point has to do with what is minimally required for an experiential source of belief to qualify as a source of prima facie justification. I have already made it explicit that it need not be infallible. That is the point of the prima facie qualification; it signals that the positive epistemic status is vulnerable to cancellation by overriders. But so far I have been, deliberately, giving the impression that a large proportion of true beliefs in the set is required. But now I want to show that that is not required. Here a comparison with SE is useful. When we perceive the environment, its denizens appear to us as bearing what since the seventeenth century have been termed "secondary qualities" – colors, the various qualitative dimensions of sounds like volume and timbre, qualitative dimensions of touch like rough, smooth, hot and cold, the various qualitatively different tastes and smells – and bearing them as objective features of the things in themselves. That is how they were regarded in most ancient and medieval science. But modern physical science has been able to make tremendous advances at the price of a mathematicized description of physical reality that recognizes as objective properties of physical things only "primary qualities," such as size, shape, motion, mass, electrical charge, and the many esoteric additions to that list of the last hundred years. The secondary qualities that bulk so large in our experience are construed as the result of the interaction of physical objects with our sensory receptors. They are simply how things appear to us, rather than properties physical things have in themselves apart from our ways of experiencing them.

Thus a large proportion of the beliefs about perceived objects that issue most directly from SE are tainted with falsehood. They are not strictly true. When I look at a shirt and take it to be red, when I feel a fabric and recognize it as very smooth, when I hear a bell ringing and recognize it as giving out a typical bell-like sound, I attribute to the perceived objects qualities that they do not, in strictness, bear. No doubt, I could, in principle, restrict myself to beliefs that do not suffer from falsity in this respect. I could, instead of taking the shirt to be red, take it to have primary qualities of such a sort that when it is seen under these conditions by a human being with normal vision, it will appear to have the color I call red. But that requires considerable reflection of the sort we do not typically engage in when perceiving things. And so it remains, as I said, that many of the beliefs that most directly issue from SE are false. Not all, because perceived objects also appear to me as bearing primary qualities like size and shape as well. We must also remember that the naive attribution of secondary qualities to physical objects is of practical usefulness, for those qualities are, in Leibniz's words in another connection, "phenomena well founded." They serve as reliable indications of genuine objective differences between objects. One shirt would not appear red to me and another blue (in normal circumstances and given normal operation of my visual apparatus) unless there were significant and relatively stable differences between them in their intrinsic primary qualities. But that does not alter the fact that what we take to be the case as the most direct result of SP is often not strictly the case.

It would seem that ME and MP are strongly analogous to SE and SP in this respect. A great deal of the reports of ME are given over to descriptions of the affective reactions of the subject – ecstasy, delight, sweetness, joy, contentment, peace, calm, awe. These terms, taken from the citations given earlier, are clearly ways in which the subject reacts to the presence of the perceived being, rather than ways that being is in itself. They are "secondary properties" of ME. There is a clear distinction between these and the features of God the subject takes to be presented to her – goodness, power, love, plenitude, wisdom, sympathy, compassion. But this doesn't give us a situation parallel to the one I sketched for SP above. For there the naive subject attributes secondary qualities to the object, whereas what I have just picked out as secondary qualities of SE are more plausibly taken as ascribed by the subject to her own reactions.

To see a strict parallel to the SP situation we would have to go much deeper into the problem of which of our concepts, if any, can be truly applied to God. Here the Christian tradition and other monotheistic traditions are mixed. On the one hand, many people, as in most of our quotations, take it to be unproblematically true that God is loving, powerful, wise, good, and so on, not to mention active in various ways. And theology is filled with such characterizations. On the other hand, there are strains in the traditions that emphasize the mystery, ineffability, incomprehensibility of God to such an extent that none of our concepts can be strictly true of him. Mystical movements in Christianity, a basic source of which is Dionysius the pseudo-Areopagite, constitute an extreme example of this. And no less a pillar of the church than St Thomas Aquinas says in his *Summa theologiae* that we can say of God only what he is not, not what he is, and in the *Summa contra gentiles* that as for the mode of signification every name is defective in application to God. Giving this tendency of the tradition full rein could well result in treating most of what is attributed to God on the basis of experience as secondary properties. This would imply that when someone reports experiencing God as wise or sympathetic or loving, he is reporting a result of God's interaction with his experiential receptivity, rather than what God is like in himself, even though here too what is experienced is a valid practical guide to one's relations with God. If we add that the secondary properties experienced in radically different traditions can themselves differ importantly without God himself (ultimate reality itself) being any different, we have available to us another way of revealing apparent incompatibilities as only apparent. (This would be to approach the well-known position of John Hick. See Hick, 1989.) There is no incompatibility in the same being appearing in different ways in different situations. I cannot go further into these issues here and now. Suffice it to say that the differences and apparent conflicts between beliefs about God that stem from ME might well be markedly reduced by a proper sense of the inadequacy of human faculties to attain an adequate conceptual grasp of God as he is in himself. If this can be done without dissipating all the epistemic efficacy of ME, it will significantly reduce the force of the objection from incompatible characterizations of ultimate reality stemming from ME.

But even if the suggestions I have been making can be successfully developed, the fact remains that the full range of MP presents much less unanimity than does the full range of SP. And so we will have to judge that the support ME gives to beliefs formed on its basis is significantly less than the support SE gives to beliefs formed on its basis (not that we have any way of measuring this). But just as with the obvious differences between SE and ME discussed earlier in this section, less support is a far cry from no support at all. It can still be maintained that when someone believes on the basis of a being's appearing to one as so-and-so that the being is so-and-so, that belief is thereby prima facie justified. And this means that (PFG) can be retained. G-beliefs formed on the basis of ME are to be judged as justified unless and until they run into strong enough overriders.

Does Mystical Perception Satisfy the Causal Requirement?

Having considered what can be said in favor of the claim that ME can be a source of knowledge (or justified belief), and having discussed objections to that positive case, we can turn to more directly negative reactions to the claim. A reason often given for a general dismissal of epistemological claims for MP is based on the general principle that one perceives an object x in having a certain experience only if x is among the causes of that experience. At best, having x among the causes of the experience is a necessary but not a sufficient condition for perceiving x. A visual experience, for example, depends on a variety of causes, by no means all of which are perceived in that experience. Most obviously, it depends on a complex concatenation of neural processes, none of which is perceived when, for example, one is looking at a tree. To come as close as we can to a sufficient casual condition for perceiving x in having a certain experience, we would have to specify the particular causal contribution x makes to that experience. And this differs for different sense modalities. With vision, for example, one sees a dog only if light reflected from the dog produces the retinal stimulation that sets off the neural chain reaction that eventually leads to the excitations in the brain that are responsible for the visual experience in question. We get analogous stories for other modes of SP. Extrapolating this line of thought to ME, such an experience can be a perception of God only if God plays a certain kind of causal role in the production of that experience. But it has frequently been claimed that mystical experience can be fully explained (its causes can be fully set out) in terms of processes within the natural world, without mentioning God at all. If so, God does not figure anywhere among its causes and therefore has no claim to be perceived in a mystical experience. And if one was not perceiving God, then the experience has nothing to tell one about God, at least directly.

Even if ME can be adequately explained in terms of purely this-worldly factors (and I will raise doubts about this later), it would be much too fast to conclude that God does not figure among its causes. Think of the analogy with SP. Even though SE can be adequately explained by what goes on in the brain, we all take it that objects outside the brain are perceived in those experiences. How can this be? Just because though brain processes are the *direct* cause of sensory experience, those processes themselves have causes, which in turn have causes . . . , and if we trace that causal chain back far enough we come to the external objects that are perceived. Analogously, even if the direct causes of a mystical experience are all within nature, God could figure further back in the causal chain that leads to that experience. And, indeed, that is the case according to theistic religions, which hold that God is the ultimate cause of the existence and functioning of the natural world.

But, it may be contended, that doesn't show that God figures in the causal chain in such a way as to be the object of perception. I have just pointed out that not every causal contributor to an experience is perceived in that experience. So to figure as a perceived object it is not enough that an item figure in some way among the causes of the experience. It must figure in a way that enables it to be perceived. And why should we suppose that God figures in *that sort of* way in the causal chain leading to ME?

When we reflect on this issue, we come to a startling result. Remember that in SP *how* a perceived object figures in the causal chain leading to the sensory experience differs for different sense modalities. In vision it is something like reflecting or generating light that then reaches the retina without certain kinds of additional reflection; for audition it is something like generating or reflecting sound waves that strike the eardrum; and so on. For MP it would be something different, the exact nature of which is obscure to us. Further note that the causal contribution required for objecthood in each case is something we can learn only from experience. We must have identified a number of genuine perceptions of x in a given modality before we are able to discover what kind of causal contribution is required for being perceived in that modality. There is no a priori way of determining this. But notice where this leaves us. Since we are in no position to say what kind of causal contribution is required for objecthood until we have some genuine cases of perception to work from, one can't even embark on the project of specifying the necessary causal contribution until one recognizes authentic cases of perception in that modality. Hence one who denies that people ever perceive God in ME has no basis for any view as to how God would have to be involved in the causal chain leading to ME if God is to be perceived in such an experience. Hence the critic can have no basis for maintaining that God's causal involvement is not of that sort. She could, of course, point out that the advocate of divine perception has no idea of what sort of causal contribution is required either. But that still leaves her without this *objection* to her opponent's position.

Hence we are left with the conclusion that even if there is an adequate naturalistic account of the proximate causes of ME, that does not rule out the possibility that God plays a role in eliciting such experience that renders him perceived therein. But there are also reasons for questioning the claim that there is such an account. If we consider the most prominent candidates (and this is not a popular research field for social and behavioral scientists), we must judge them to be highly speculative and, at best, sketchily supported by the evidence. ME poses severe problems for empirical research. It is something that cannot be induced at the will of the researcher and so is not amenable to experiment. Attempts to get around this by substituting drug-induced analogues are of little value, since it has not been shown that findings concerning them can be extrapolated to spontaneous cases. Since the states are usually short-lived, we must rely on autobiographical reports; a researcher can hardly be expected to hang around a person on the off chance that he might happen to have a mystical experience! Hence the data are subject to all the problems that attach to first-person reports. Moreover, the most prominent theories in the field invoke causal mechanisms that themselves pose unsolved problems of identification and measurement: unconscious psychological processes like repression and mechanisms of defense; social influences on belief and attitude formation. It is not surprising that theories like those of Freud, Marx, and Durkheim rest on a slender thread of evidential support and generalize irresponsibly from such evidence as they can muster. Nor have more recent attempts of this sort fared any better. (See, e.g., Lewis, 1989; Batson and Ventis, 1982.)

Can Reports of Mystical Perception Be Checked?

I will conclude this survey of criticisms of (PFG) with one that is based on the impossibility of effective public tests of the accuracy of G-beliefs formed on the basis of ME. The contention is that this prevents ME from being an awareness of any objective reality. Here are two representative formulations.

> But why can't we have an argument based upon religious experiences for the existence of the apparent object of a given religious experience and its bearing the right sort of causal relation to the experience? There can be such an argument only if religious experiences count as cognitive. But they can count as cognitive only if they are subject to similar tests to those which sense experiences are. (Gale, 1991, p. 316)

> But whereas questions about the existence of people can be answered by straightforward observational and other tests, not even those who claim to have enjoyed personal encounters with God would admit such tests to be appropriate here ... (Flew, 1966, pp. 138–9)

The first thing to be said in reply is that there *are* tests for the accuracy of particular reports of mystical perception. Contemplative communities that "specialize" in the perception of God have compiled systematic manuals of such tests; and many of them are used more informally by the laity. These include such things as (a) conformity with what would be expected by basic doctrines concerning the nature of God, (b) such "fruits" of the experience as a stable inner peace and growth in spirituality, (c) a content of the experience that the person would not have developed on his or her own. The satisfaction of such conditions counts in favor of the veridicality of the experience and their absence counts against it. Obviously these tests do not conclusively establish veridicality or the reverse, but that does not render them without value. Tests of the accuracy of sense perceptions don't always definitively settle the matter either.

But even taking that into account, it remains that reports of SP can be checked in ways that reports of MP cannot. Consider some of these ways. The most obvious ones appeal to the experiences of other persons. Suppose I claim to have seen a Russian plane flying over my house at a certain time. If we can find other people who were in the area at that time and looking up into the sky, we can determine whether they saw a Russian plane overhead. To be sure, if one or a few such people failed to notice a Russian plane, that would not decisively disconfirm my report. Perhaps they were inattentive, blinded by the sun, or preoccupied with other matters. But if a large number of people were in the area, had normal visual powers, were not especially preoccupied, and were disposed to look up to determine the source of any loud noise, and none of them saw any such plane, my report would have been decisively disconfirmed. The general principle involved here is that if a visible object were present at a certain place and time, then any competent observer who was at that place and time and was looking in the right direction would (probably) have seen it. If a large number of such observers did not see any such thing, we must conclude that the object wasn't there at that time. If, on the other hand, all or most such observers saw it, that confirms the original report.

There are other kinds of public tests as well. The credentials of the reporter could be examined. Is his visual apparatus in order? Does he know how to distinguish a Russian plane from others? Was he in a drugged or intoxicated condition? Did he have his wits about him at the time? And so on. To change the example, suppose the report is that baking soda is on top of my serving of rice. In addition to taste tests by others, the substance can be subjected to chemical analysis.

There is nothing comparable to this with MP. God is always present everywhere, if present anywhere, and so the whereabouts of a subject has no bearing. If a mystical report were to be given a test by other observers in the SP way, we would have to say that S really perceived God at time t only if every competent subject perceives God all the time. But no one would take this to be an appropriate test. To put the point more generally, there is no set of conditions we can specify such that if God is present to me at time t, then any other person satisfying those conditions would also perceive God at t. To be sure, we can say something about what is *conducive* to perceiving God. One must be sufficiently "receptive," sufficiently "spiritually attuned," and so on. It is only if one who possesses those characteristics fails to perceive God that this counts against the original report. But how can we tell whether a given subject qualifies? Again, something can be said. Contemplatives typically lay down such characteristics as the possession of certain virtues (humility, compassion) and a loving, obedient attitude toward God as productive of openness to the presence of God. "Blessed are the pure in heart, for they shall see God." But there are two reasons why we still lack the kinds of test we have for reports of SP. First, we are far from having reliable intersubjective tests for humility and a loving attitude toward God. And second, we can't seriously suppose that any set of conditions we can list is such that one will perceive God *if and only if* those conditions are satisfied. The situation with MP is much more obscure and mysterious, much looser than this. God can, presumably, reveal himself to someone whenever he chooses to do so, whatever worldly conditions are satisfied. Hence we are still a long way from being able to carry out the kind of *other observers* tests we have for SP. What I have just said about God's not being bound by any worldly necessary and sufficient conditions for perceiving him implies that we have no effective *state of observers* test to rely on here either. And obviously nothing like chemical analysis is relevant.

But what epistemic relevance do these differences have? Why should we suppose that they prevent mystical reports from enjoying prima facie justification? Those who take this line make an unjustifiable assumption that reports of MP are properly treated by the same standards as reports of SP, so that if the former cannot be tested in the same way as the latter they cannot be a cognitive access to objective reality. But this assumption is no more than a kind of epistemic imperialism, subjecting the outputs of one belief-forming practice to the requirements of another. It can easily be seen that not all our standard belief-forming practices work like those based on SP. Consider introspection. If I report feeling excited, there are no conditions under which my report is correct *if and only if* someone who satisfies those conditions also feels excited. Introspective reports can be publicly checked to a certain extent, but not in that way. Again, the fact that we can't use perceptual checks on mathematical reports has no tendency to show that rational intuition cannot yield objective truths. Different belief-forming practices work differently.

Thinkers like Gale and Flew will undoubtedly respond to this last example by saying that the availability of tests like those for SP are at least required for the epistemic efficacy of *experiential* sources of belief. But that has no stronger credibility than the claim for belief sources generally. What basis do we have for supposing that the features of SP constitute *necessary* conditions for any effective experiential cognitive access to objective reality? I take it as uncontroversial that

SP is *a* way of acquiring reliable beliefs of certain sorts about the world. SP satisfies sufficient conditions for epistemic efficacy. But why suppose that this is the only set of sufficient conditions for such a status? Experience amply attests that, in cognitive as well as in other matters, sharply different maneuvers can achieve a certain goal. Excellent dishes can be prepared by meticulously following well-tested recipes or, with experienced cooks, by inspired improvisation. Mathematical problems can be solved by following established algorithms or, in some cases, by flashes of intuition. The picture of an ancient civilization can be built up from archaeological remains or from extant documents or from some combination thereof. And so it goes. It would be the reverse of surprising if the purchase on objective reality attained by SP is only one of many experiential ways of achieving such a result. And the fact that the aspects of reality that MP claims to put us in contact with are very different from those that are explored by SP tells against the idea that only what conforms to the latter can reveal anything about reality.

References

Alston, William P. (1993) *The Reliability of Sense Perception*. Ithaca: Cornell University Press.

Baillie, John (1962) *The Sense of the Presence of God*. New York: Scribner's.

Batson, Daniel, and Ventis, W. (1982) *The Religious Experience: A Sociological-Psychological Perspective*. New York: Oxford University Press.

Beardsworth, Timothy (1977) *A Sense of Presence*. Oxford: Religious Experience Research Unit.

Chisholm, Roderick M. (1977) *Theory of Knowledge*, second edn. Englewood Cliffs, N.J.: Prentice-Hall, Inc.

Flew, Antony (1966) *God and Philosophy*. London: Hutchinson.

Gale, Richard M. (1991) *On the Nature and Existence of God*. Cambridge: Cambridge University Press.

Hick, John (1966) *Faith and Knowledge*, second edn. Ithaca: Cornell University Press.

Hick, John (1989) *An Interpretation of Religion*. New Haven, Conn.: Yale University Press.

James, William (1902) *The Varieties of Religious Experience*. New York: The Modern Library.

Lewis, I. M. (1989) *Ecstatic Religion*, second edn. London: Routledge.

Müller, Friedrich Max, trans. (1884) *The Upanishads*. Oxford: Clarendon Press.

Plotinus (1964) *Enneads*, trans. S. J. Elmer O'Brien. In *Varieties of Mystical Experience*. New York: Holt, Rinehart, and Winston.

Poulain, Anton (1950) *The Graces of Interior Prayer*, trans. Leonora Yorke Smith and Jean Vincent Bainvel. London: Routledge & Kegan Paul.

Price, H. H. (1950) *Perception*, second edn. London: Methuen & Co. Ltd.

Stark, Rodney, and Glock, Charles Y. (1968) *American Piety: The Nature of Religious Commitment*. Berkeley and Los Angeles: University of California Press.

Swinburne, Richard (1979) *The Existence of God*. Oxford: Clarendon Press.

Underhill, Evelyn (1955) *Mysticism*. New York: World Publishing Co.

Suggested Further Reading

Alston, William P. (1991) *Perceiving God.* Ithaca: Cornell University Press.

Edwards, Jonathan (1959) *A Treatise Concerning Religious Affections.* New Haven, Conn.: Yale University Press.

Flew, Antony, and MacIntyre, Alasdair (eds.) (1955) *New Essays in Philosophical Theology.* London: SCM Press.

Gellman, Jerome I. (1997) *Experience of God and the Rationality of Theistic Belief.* Ithaca: Cornell University Press.

Gutting, Gary (1982) *Religious Belief and Religious Skepticism.* Notre Dame, Ind.: University of Notre Dame Press.

Katz, Steven T. (ed.) (1978) *Mysticism and Philosophical Analysis.* New York: Oxford University Press.

Mavrodes, George I. (1970) *Belief in God: A Study in the Epistemology of Religion.* Washington: University Press of America.

O'Hear, Anthony (1984) *Experience, Explanation, and Faith.* London: Routledge & Kegan Paul.

Pike, Nelson (1992) *Mystic Union: An Essay in the Phenomenology of Mysticism.* Ithaca: Cornell University Press.

Proudfoot, Wayne (1985) *Religious Experience.* Berkeley and Los Angeles: University of California Press.

Saudreau, Auguste (1924) *The Mystical State, its Nature and Phases.* London: Burns, Oates, & Washbourne.

Stace, Walter T. (1960) *Mysticism and Philosophy.* Los Angeles: Jeremy P. Tarcher.

Wainwright, William J. (1981) *Mysticism.* Brighton, UK: Harvester Press.

Wall, George (1995) *Religious Experience and Religious Belief.* Lanham, Md.: University Press of America.

Zaehner, R. C. (1961) *Mysticism: Sacred and Profane.* New York: Oxford University Press.

Chapter 10

Competing Religious Claims

William J. Wainwright

Awareness of human religious diversity isn't new. What is new is a more accurate knowledge of other religious traditions together with a deeper appreciation of their spiritual depth and intellectual sophistication. As a result it has become difficult for sensitive and knowledgeable religious believers to dismiss other religions out of hand. Yet, on the face of it, the traditions conflict. For example, if union with God is the ultimate goal, then entry into Nirvana is not. If reality is pure unlimited consciousness, then the theistic metaphysics of Judaism, Christianity, or Islam is fundamentally mistaken. How should we respond to this diversity?

Grading Religious World-Views

One popular response is to deny that the conflicts are real. Paul Griffiths calls attention to a prima facie objection to this, however. "Representative intellectuals" of the major traditions have thought of the doctrinal claims they are defending as "possessing universal truth, and as being comprehensible to, applicable to, and desirable for" all human beings. They have also believed that their claims conflicted with some of those made in other traditions. Muslim intellectuals, for instance, thought that if their doctrine of God's absolute unity was true, Christian doctrines of the Trinity were false. Advaitin intellectuals believed that their doctrines were incompatible with those advocated by Buddhist intellectuals. If we add Griffiths's "principle of hermeneutical charity," namely, that "other things being equal, one should take representative intellectuals of a religious community to be engaged in the kind of intellectual discipline in which they think they are engaged when constructing" and defending doctrinal statements, then the burden of proof is on those who deny that apparent conflicts between the doctrinal statements of competing traditions are real (Griffiths, 1991, p. 20). How might this burden be discharged?

One way of doing so is by arguing that competing doctrinal claims are incommensurable. The meaning of a religious claim, and hence the standards for assessing it, are fixed by its role in a way of life and in the vision of reality that shapes it. Ways of life conflict in the sense that one can't simultaneously live as a Christian, say, and as a Buddhist. Nor can one simultaneously view the world through both Christian and Buddhist eyes. The doctrinal claims these ways of life incorporate, however, are incommensurable and so can't conflict.

This view founders on the fact that representative intellectuals of the major traditions implicitly acknowledge the existence of *universal* standards for assessing disputed doctrinal claims.

These standards include requirements of factual fidelity. For example, the data the doctrinal scheme purportedly explains must actually exist and the existence of the relevant data is sometimes contentious. Both Christianity and Islam contain doctrines about Jesus. But for Christians, the data these doctrines illuminate includes Jesus' crucifixion and death and for Muslims it doesn't. Doctrinal systems should also be compatible with well-established facts and theories although the facts and theories that are regarded as established depend upon the context. Vedantin and Mimansaka controversialists take the authority of the Vedas for granted. Buddhists do not but both Hindu and Buddhist disputants assume the truth of the doctrine of reincarnation.

Doctrinal schemes must also meet formal requirements. They should avoid logical inconsistencey and self-stultification. (A statement is self-stultifying if its assertion implies that it is either false or can't be expressed, or that it can't be known to be true.) Other things being equal, one doctrinal scheme is preferable to another if it is simpler or more coherent. (Coherent theories exhibit a certain amount of internal interconnectedness or systematic articulation; their parts "hang together.")

Finally, doctrinal schemes should meet two substantive requirements. As with any good theory, they must possess explanatory power. Explanatory power is measured by such things as scope (that is, comprehensiveness), precision, and fruitfulness. ("Fruitfulness" refers to a theory's ability to generate interesting new problems and solutions, predict new facts, or explain facts which were not envisaged when the theory was constructed.) The most important measure of explanatory power, however, is a theory's ability to "illuminate" the facts that it is designed to explain by producing appropriate feelings of grasp or comprehension in the intended audience. Phenomena are illuminated by showing that they follow from the theory's postulates and theorems, for example, or by drawing analogies with better-understood phenomena, or by placing a puzzling phenomenon in a framework that coherently integrates a set of apparently unrelated phenomena. There are also negative measures. Other things being equal, the use of ad hoc hypotheses reduces a theory's explanatory power.

The other substantive test is pragmatic. Comprehensive world-views must enable those who use them to act successfully and enter into satisfactory relations with "the cosmos in its totality." Doctrinal schemes meet the pragmatic criterion when they lead to human flourishing.

These standards are vague and their judicious application calls for judgment. What is important for our purposes, however, is that they are appealed to in interreligious disputes.

In defending his theistic version of Vedanta, Ramanuja argues that Samkara's Advaita Vedanta is logically inconsistent and self-stultifying, and that it implicitly undercuts the data on which it rests. Samkara claims that the Brahman is *nirguna* – without attributes. According to Ramanuja, however, the concept of a substance without attributes is logically inconsistent since, by definition, substances just are what have or underlie properties. Ramanuja also argues that one can't know something without properties. For cognitively grasping x involves identifying x, classifying it as a thing of a certain kind, and things are classified on the basis of their attributes. Hence, if the *nirguna* Brahman lacks properties, it can't be known. Finally, all Vedantin views are based on the authority of the Vedas. The Vedas are articulated in language, however, and language involves distinctions. If all distinctions are unreal, then the Vedas don't mirror reality and their authority is called into question.

St Augustine provides a second example. The immediate occasion for *The City of God* was the shock occasioned by the sack of Rome in 410. Many citizens of the empire blamed Rome's fall on its adoption of Christianity. Augustine's book is an extended attempt to show that Christianity provides a more illuminating explanation of Rome's rise and fall than paganism does.

Finally, consider some Confucian charges against Buddhism. Buddhists are regarded as life denying and selfish. Rather than cultivating the self, Buddhists renounce it. Instead of discharging their obligations to their families, teachers, and rulers by subordinating their selfish desires to them, they reject society in their egocentric desire to escape suffering. And because the Buddhist's strivings are unnatural they are also futile. As Chu Hsi points out, they can't escape from the social relationships they would destroy. For example, Buddhists repudiate the relationships between father and son, and elder and younger brother. Nevertheless, they pay respect to their preceptors as if they were their fathers while their preceptors treat them as sons, and the relationship between older and younger monks reproduces that between elder and younger brothers. In short, Confucians think that the Buddhist way of life is not only selfish but inherently self-defeating. It fails to respect the nature of human life and hence can't lead to human flourishing. Confucians thus implicitly argue that Confucianism meets the pragmatic criterion more successfully than Buddhism.

It is clear, then, that there *are* intercommunity standards for settling doctrinal disputes. There is, at present, however, no consensus that one doctrinal system comes off better than another when assessed by these standards. What accounts for this lack of agreement? The relevant standards aren't algorithms. Their judicious application calls for judgment, and one's judgment is affected not only by one's education, experience, and so on, but also by what William James called our "passional nature" (our yearnings and emotions, desires and hopes, values and intimations). Since our passional natures are shaped by our temperaments and personal histories, and these vary, it is unrealistic to expect a consensus among even the seemingly rational (those whose irrationality isn't apparent to all fair-minded observers). Agreement isn't to be looked for this side of the eschaton. (More on this later.)

Responses to Intractable Diversity

Faced with pervasive and apparently intractable disagreements, it is tempting to downplay their importance. There are three popular ways of doing so.

The devaluation of propositional truth and belief

The first is Wilfred Cantwell Smith's. Smith argues that propositional truth isn't the only or most important kind of truth. Truth is also personal authenticity. Ultimately, God or the transcendent is the truth. One's propositional beliefs about the transcendent are comparatively unimportant. What matters is one's relation to it – whether one responds to it or not and, if one does, whether or not one's response is characterized by love, truth, fidelity, peace, and the like. As Smith says, religion is not itself true or false but "becomes less or more true in the case of particular persons as it informs their lives . . . and shapes and nurtures their faith" (Smith, 1981, p. 187). A person's religion is not to be evaluated by his beliefs, but by the quality of his life, the degree to which it is "an immediate embodiment of his faith" (Smith, 1964, p. 161). Differences in belief obscure what is truly important – that in all of the major traditions, men and women faithfully respond to the transcendent.

William Christian points out that, in spite of its intentions, this approach doesn't really defuse conflicts. For the major traditions recommend and embody *different* ways of responding to ultimate reality, and while recommendations like "the Dharma [the Buddha's teaching] is the path to attainment of Nirvana" and "the Torah teaches us how to respond rightly to God" aren't *formally* incompatible, one can't consistently accept both (partly because one can't consistently live both as a Buddhist and an orthodox Jew, and partly because the competing recommendations are based on other doctrines about "how things are" and things can't both be the way Buddhists say they are and the way Jews say they are). Course-of-action recommendations also presuppose evaluations and these too may be opposed. Thus, the Buddhist recommendation presupposes "Nirvana is the supreme goal of life" while the orthodox Jewish recommendation presupposes "God is holy," and each of these evaluations rests on claims which imply that the referent of the other evaluation doesn't exist. For example, the Buddhist evaluation rests on the claim that "*all* beings are subject to becoming and perishing" (my emphasis). If this claim is true, God doesn't exist. In addition, each evaluation implicitly ascribes unrestricted primacy to its subject. Yet if "Nirvana" and "God" have different referents (and they seem to), Nirvana and God can't both rank first in all categories. (Christian, 1972, pp. 67–73.) The upshot is that we can't elide doctrinal conflicts by shifting attention from religious belief to religious life and practice.

The denial of real differences

Another way of minimizing the importance of doctrinal conflicts is by arguing that the major traditions teach the same thing. Taken literally, this is patently mistaken. One might maintain, however, that their *essential* doctrines either mean the same or are logically equivalent, or that the virtuosi within each tradition have the same experiences and teach the same things. Aldous Huxley's "perennial philosophy" is an example of this position. Walter Stace's *Mysticism and Philosophy* is another. The problem with views like these is that they too are pretty clearly false. "Nirvana is ultimate" and "Yahweh, the God of Abraham, Isaac, and Jacob, is ultimate" are essential to Buddhism and Judaism respectively, yet, on the face of it, neither mean the same (since they incorporate descriptions whose meanings differ) nor are logically equivalent. It is also false that the virtuosi of the major traditions have the same experiences and teach the same doctrines. The theistic mystical experiences of such figures as Ramanuja or Julian of Norwich or John of the Cross are clearly distinct from the experiences cultivated by Advaitins or Zen Buddhists. Nor do the teachings of these mystics radically depart from those of the larger communities to which they belong. If the teachings of the latter neither mean the same nor are logically equivalent, then neither are those of the former.

One might insist that the essential doctrines of the major traditions nevertheless *symbolize* or *hint at* the same thing. But this implies that the doctrines in question (a) *are* symbols and (b) *do* "point to" the same thing, and (as Christian points out) both may be doubted. The first claim is plausible if the traditions being compared contain hermeneutical principles which claim that the doctrines in question are (only) symbols. If they do not (and many don't), one needs arguments to show that the relevant doctrines really are symbols even though the tradition which includes them doesn't understand them as such. As for the second, "ordinarily, it is not put forward as just a generalization arrived at by studying the histories and the literatures and the ways of life of the major religions." Rather, "the speaker is himself proposing and advocating the one destination, experience and path, which he claims is being hinted at in" the traditions that he is examining. (Christian, 1972, p. 114.) That is, he isn't making an empirical or logical claim about the actual use of religious language but proposing that we reinterpret it so that it comports with his own favored religious views. Claims like these deserve to be taken neither more nor less seriously than other substantive religious proposals.

Pluralism: John Hick

The most intellectually sophisticated way of downplaying the significance of doctrinal disagreements is pluralism.

John Hick's version is rooted in three allegedly incontrovertible facts and in a profession of faith. The facts are these. First, no major religious tradition satisfies our criteria better than any other. Second, we have no grounds for epistemically privileging the experiences of one tradition over those of another. Jews report experiences of Yahweh and Buddhists experiences of emptiness. But Jews are neither more nor less intelligent, informed, or religiously and morally sensitive than Buddhists. Hence either none of the experiences of the major traditions should be accepted as veridical or *all* should. Third, all the major traditions seem equally productive of "saints," men and women who embody "the ethical ideal, common to all the great traditions, of *agape/karuna* (love/compassion)" (Hick, 1989, p. 14). The profession of faith is that religion is not a "purely human projection" but involves "a response to a transcendent reality" (Hick, 1995, p. 28).

Hick's "pluralistic hypothesis" is designed to accommodate these facts and this profession. His view is this. Human religious experience is a joint product of culture and the "Real." Jews, for instance, or Buddhists, or Christians experience the same transcendent reality but do so through various cultural filters. Thus Jews experience the Real as Yahweh, Buddhists as nirvana or *sunyata* (emptiness), Sri Vaisnavas as Visnu, and so on. Human experience of the Real takes two principal forms. Jews, Muslims, Christians, and Hindu theists structure their experience by the concept of "deity" (God). The experiences of non-theistic Hindus, Buddhists, Taoists, and the like are structured by the concept of a non-personal "absolute." These in turn take concrete shape as the "divine personae" and "metaphysical impersonae," respectively, of the major traditions. Yahweh, Allah, Visnu, and the triune God of Christianity are "concretizations" of deity. The Tao, Nirvana, the *nirguna* Brahman, and *sunyata* are concretizations of the absolute.

The Real as such, however, is neither deity nor absolute. It is a thing in itself that stands behind religious phenomena and accounts for the fact that they aren't mere projections. While we experience its manifestations, the Real in itself is inaccessible. Only formal concepts apply to it ("being a referent of a term" – namely, "the Real" – for example, or "being such that our substantial concepts do not apply to it"). "Substantial properties" such as benevolence, power, mindlessness (Buddhism), or even goodness can be appropriately ascribed to one or more of the divine personae and metaphysical impersonae. They cannot be appropriately applied to the Real. For our substantive concepts apply only to phenomena. They do not apply to the transcategorical noumenal reality that underlies them and ensures that they aren't mere projections. (Hick, 1989, p. 239.)

Is Hick's view tenable? Its most problematic feature may be its account of the Real. For one thing, it isn't clear that Hick is fully consistent. Hick thinks that human religion isn't merely projection because the divine personae and metaphysical impersonae are "manifestations" of the Real. There are two ways of understanding this. Hick may think that while the various "concretizations" of deity and the absolute are the *direct* objects of human religious experiences, the Real is their *indirect* object (as when I see the moon in a mirror, or experience one thing – my wife's anger, for example – in experiencing another – her angry tone or gestures). Alternatively, Hick may think that the Real isn't experienced at all but is, rather, an *inferred* entity or theoretical construct. In this view, the divine personae and metaphysical impersonae are something like Descartes' or Locke's ideas of shape, say, or color, from which we infer the presence of independently real physical objects which cause them. On either interpretation, though, "The Real manifests itself in the various concretizations of deity and the absolute" seems to say something substantive about *it*. For, on either interpretation, the Real is the cause or ground of religious experience, and "causality" isn't a purely formal category.

Hick's reluctance to ascribe goodness to the Real may also get him in trouble. His grounds for not doing so differ from his reasons for denying other substantive properties of the Real. Consider omniscience, for example, or omnibenevolence. Christians ascribe these attributes to the object of their devotion and Advaitins do not. Now Hick thinks that Christian religious experiences and Advaitin experiences are on an epistemic par. Hence, both must be discounted or both must be accepted as equally veridical. Since Hick believes that the major traditions aren't mere projections, he opts for the second. Hick also thinks that the major traditions are directed toward the same object, namely, the Real. But the Real can't (literally) be both omniscient and non-omniscient, benevolent and non-benevolent. He concludes that properties like these apply to concretizations of deity and the absolute, not to the Real in itself.

Goodness, however, isn't in the same boat, for *all* the major traditions think of the Real as good. So why can't we say that the Real is good? The variety of veridical but conflicting religious experiences have led us to postulate a Real in itself that transcends human thought and experience. Having made this postulate, we must accept its consequences. If the Real transcends *all* of our substantive conceptualizations of it, it transcends our conceptualization of it as good. The Real isn't good in itself. It is good only in the sense that it "causes" or "grounds" goodness (including the transformation from self-centeredness to Reality-centeredness).

Aside from the fact that "causes (is the ground of) goodness" is a substantive property, it is unclear why the fact that human beings experience the Real as good doesn't tell us something about it. Hick has suggested in correspondence that "there could conceivably be creatures (devils, perhaps) such that the impact of the Real upon them is rightly described in their thought-world as evil." The fact remains that no *saint* of the various traditions experiences the Real as evil or indifferent. On the contrary, the devout uniformly experience it as overwhelmingly good. Why doesn't this tell us something about the Real and not merely about how good people experience it? After all, morally and spiritually good people don't experience *everything* as good, and the explanation of *why* they don't appeals to facts about the *objects* of their experience as well as to facts about the way they view things. So if the saints invariably experience the Real as good, and not evil or indifferent, shouldn't we postulate something like goodness *in* the Real to explain it?

The issue is not purely theoretical since the thinness of Hick's concept of the Real raises the question of how he (or anyone) could know that a Reality-centeredness that displays itself in the active practice of *agapē/karuna* is a more appropriate response to the transcategorical reality than selfishness or violence or cruelty.

The problem is not that the Real might be evil or morally indifferent. If the Real transcends *all* substantive categories, it transcends the categories of evil and of moral indifference as well as the category of goodness. The problem is rather that, given the Real's transcategoricality, there appears to be no basis for asserting that one response to it is more appropriate than another.

In *An Interpretation of Religion*, Hick argues that, given that the diverse divine personae and metaphysical impersonae "are indeed manifestations of the ultimately Real, an appropriate human response to any one of them will also be an appropriate response to the Real" (Hick, 1989, p. 350). Responses that would be appropriate to Allah, for instance, or to the *nirguna* Brahman if there literally were such things, will also be appropriate to the Real. It is difficult to see how this claim could be justified, however.

An appropriate response to x is an appropriate response to y if and only if x is y or stands in a appropriate relation to y. Thus, the affection, trust, and fidelity which are appropriate responses to my wife are appropriate responses to Mimi because Mimi *is* my wife. Responses of gratitude appropriate to my parents and teachers are also appropriate to other benefactors who exhibit similar character-istics and stand in similar relations to me. Responses to a nation's ambassador are responses to the ambassador's nation because the former represents the latter. By parity of reasoning, then, responses appropriate to the diverse divine personae and metaphysical impersonae are appropriate to the Real if and only if the divine personae and metaphysical impersonae either are the Real or stand in an appropri-ate relation to it. Now, concretizations of deity and the absolute are *not* the Real, in Hick's view. Do they stand in the right relation to it?

It is difficult to see what could justify an affirmative answer. Since we have no knowledge of the Real's substantive properties, we have no reason to think that the divine personae and metaphysical impersonae are like the Real. Nor is the (alleged) fact that the Real is the cause or ground of our experiences of it sufficient. In the first place, if Hick is right, the Real is the cause or ground of the "devils'," experience of it as evil. In Hick's view, both the saints' experience of the Real as good and its expression in a life characterized by *agapē/karuna* are a joint product of the Real and their psychologically and culturally conditioned mindset. But the same is presumably true of the devils Hick alludes to. The devils' experiences of the Real as evil and the expression of their experiences in pride, cruelty, and the like are a joint product of the pressure of the Real and their psychologically and culturally conditioned "thought-world." So why are the saints' responses appropriate while the devils' responses aren't? In the second place, that x is a cause or ground of an experience of y isn't sufficient to show that an appropriate response to y is an appropriate response to x. A straight stick immersed in water can be a cause of my experience of a bent stick but responses appropriate to the latter aren't appropriate to the former.

Perhaps because of these difficulties Hick has recently shifted to another position – that we know that the change from self-centeredness to Reality-centeredness is appropriate because "all the great traditions teach" that it is, and we are "taking them to be authentic responses to the Real." In doing so, Hick says, we are "speaking from within the circle of religious faith [although not 'a tradition-specific faith'], not professing to establish the validity of that faith" (Hick, 1995, pp. 77–8). Whatever merits this answer has, it abandons the attempt to provide an independent *justification* of the claim that the saints' response to the Real is appropriate whereas the responses of the spiritually and morally stunted are not. Given the thinness of Hick's conception of the Real, however, this may be the only answer available to him.

Pluralism: Peter Byrne

Other versions of pluralism may be immune to these objections. Peter Byrne's is an example.

Byrne's pluralistic hypothesis has three parts: (a) "All major religious traditions are equal in making common reference to a single transcendent, sacred reality." (b) They "are likewise equal in offering some means or other to human salvation." (c) "All traditions are to be seen as containing revisable, limited accounts of the nature of the sacred" but "none is certain enough in its particular dogmatic formulations to provide the norm for interpreting the others" (Byrne, 1995, p. 12).

Byrne's hypothesis is thus broadly similar to Hick's. Furthermore, Byrne, too, thinks that the universality of religious experience together with the fact that apparent cognitions should initially be taken on trust gives reports based on religious experience some prima facie credibility. And, like Hick, he believes that the diversity of these reports is a reason for doubting elements in them which conflict with other reports. But Byrne also thinks that Hick's interpretation of the object of religious experiences is too thin. It leaves "too much (that is, all!) of the specific content of religious experience to the conceptual inheritance brought to experience by the religious subject – so much as to give the transcendent no work to do." "A realist view of religious experience should leave the real with *some* influence on the *content* of experience" (Byrne, 1995, pp. 171–2, my emphases).

Reports based on religious experience should be treated as we treat conflicting accident reports. Although we may have no reason to prefer one report to the others, we do have reason to trust what they have in common (that an accident occurred, for example, or that the driver of the Ford ran a red light). Similarly here; even if we have no reason to prefer reports which identify the transcendent with the *nirguna* Brahman to reports which identify it with the triune God of Christianity, it is reasonable to accept what the reports have in common (that the transcendent is good, for instance, or the ground of mundane reality). (Byrne, 1995, pp. 127–34.)

Byrne denies that we should predicate only formal properties of the Real or that (as Hick thinks) doctrinal schemes should be regarded as "myths" – true if (and only if) they evoke appropriate dispositional attitudes towards the Real. For this implies that religious doctrines have too little cognitive content; their meaning is almost entirely practical.

In Byrne's opinion, a religion's doctrinal claims should be interpreted as metaphors or models with a real referent. Whether he thinks that true positive literal statements can be made about the transcendent is less clear. On the one hand, Byrne appears to entertain the possibility that all true literal statements about the Real are relational or negative. He says, for example, that speaking of the Real as "absolute perfection . . . is largely negative and relational," saying only that the transcendent "possesses none of those defects and limitations which characterize the mundane" (Byrne, 1995, p. 142). But Byrne also raises the possibility that by either reflecting on the great traditions, or practicing natural theology, we might discover some positive non-relational analogical truths about the transcendent. For example, we might discover that "good" or "wise" refer to real properties of the transcendent although we would not be in a position to know *how* they refer to them, that is, what it is for the transcendent to be good or wise. (Byrne, 1995, pp. 140–54.)

Problems with pluralism

Byrne's version of pluralism avoids certain problems of Hick's. But does *either* version satisfactorily resolve the problems created by religious diversity?

In Hick's view, pluralism isn't a religious claim but a *meta*-religious hypothesis, namely, that the great traditions "are different [and more or less equally authentic] human responses to the Real" (Hick, 1995, p. 42). Its acceptance leaves the traditions more or less intact and, indeed, *must* do so. Participation in a tradition is needed to make effective contact with the Real, and if the traditions were to lose "their particularity [their distinctive scriptures, symbols, devotional practices, and the like], they would lose their life and their power to nourish." The "different traditions . . . with their associated forms of worship and life-styles" should therefore be retained. (Hick, 1982, p. 21.) Byrne too rejects the notion that the traditions are "contingent, ultimately dispensable means of expressing something which the philosopher . . . finally states," and he too thinks that one can only be salvifically related to the transcendent *through* a tradition. (Byrne, 1995, pp. 196–7.)

But Hick implicitly admits that embracing the pluralistic hypothesis *would* have a major effect on a tradition's *beliefs* since any member of the tradition who did so would be forced to eliminate beliefs which imply that his or her religion is truer or salvifically more effective than others. Christian pluralists, for example, would be forced to abandon their belief in the incarnation, and Advaitins their belief that non-dualism's insight into the nature of reality is only approximated by other systems. Since these beliefs are arguably *central* to the traditions in question, however, their elimination will require a radical reinterpretation of its scriptures, symbols, and practices. The traditions are thus *not* left as they are, and whether they can retain "their life and power to nourish" once beliefs historically regarded as essential to them have been abandoned is a moot point. If they can't, pluralism undercuts the very conditions needed for authentic responses to the Real.

Byrne's version of pluralism may be slightly better off here. He admits that there is a tension between pluralism's agnosticism towards particular doctrinal claims and the traditions' insistence on their own uniqueness and superiority. He suggests, however, that the pluralist's admission of the traditions' "referential success" and "metaphorical truth" together with their *agnosticism* towards, rather than *rejection* of, specific doctrinal claims may enable pluralists to participate in a tradition without undermining either "its identity and authenticity" or their own integrity. (Byrne, 1995, pp. 201–3.) By contrast, while Hick too insists upon the traditions' referential success, he thinks that doctrines such as the incarnation are false (and not merely not known to be true) and offers a non-cognitive interpretation of religious myth and metaphor. There is more tension, then, between Hick's version of pluralism and participation in the traditions than between Byrne's version and participation. Whether Byrne has retained enough of the traditions' cognitive substance to permit a pluralist's engaging in a tradition without undermining either it or her own integrity is a moot point. Still, it isn't immediately clear that he hasn't.

Another problematic feature of pluralism is its erasure of apparently important differences. Hick, for example, thinks that the transformations effected by the great traditions are fundamentally the same. Committing oneself in faith to Christ, serving Allah, extinguishing the ego by following the noble eightfold path, and the like "are variations within different conceptual schemes" on a common theme, namely, "the transformation of human existence from self-centredness to Reality-centredness." The traditions' success in achieving this goal is measured by the degree to which their members embody "the ethical ideal, common to all the great traditions, of *agape/karuna* (love/compassion)." In Hick's opinion, "no one tradition" succeeds in doing this more effectively than others; all are equally "productive of sainthood" (Hick, 1989, pp. 36, 14, 307). Hick does not deny the existence of qualitative differences between the lives of (for example) Christian and Taoist saints, for these lives are shaped by specifically Christian and Taoist beliefs, symbols, and practices, respectively. He does deny that the differences ultimately matter.

How can he justify this claim? It isn't enough to say that the differences are unimportant because Christian and Taoist responses to the Real are equally appropriate, for it is precisely the latter which his critics deny. Yet I doubt that a non-circular justification is possible. That all the great traditions are equally authentic responses to the Real seems less a consequence of Hick's arguments than their foundation. It is because Hick is *antecedently convinced* that these responses are more or less equally appropriate that he develops hypotheses to account for it. And that conviction rests less on argument, I think, than on Hick's personal experiences, first "in Birmingham, England, with its large Muslim, Sikh and Hindu communities, as well as its older Jewish communities," and later in India. Being

> drawn into the work which is variously called "race relations" and "community relations" [I] soon had friends and colleagues in all these non-Christian communities . . . And occasionally attending worship in mosque and synagogue, temple, and gurdwara, it was evident to me that the same kind of thing is taking place in them as in a Christian church – namely, human beings opening their minds to a higher divine Reality, known as personal and good and as demanding righteousness and love between man and man . . . Visits to India and Sri Lanka . . . further revealed something of the immense spiritual depth and power of these two oriental religions . . . I could see that within these ancient traditions [too] men and women are savingly related to the eternal Reality from which we all live. (Hick, 1982, pp. 17–18)

Hick's pluralism rests on a conviction shaped by his own experience of interreligious dialogue. It appears to be epistemically prior to the pluralistic hypothesis and depends less on argument than personal history. It is not surprising, then, that those whose personal histories and temperaments differ find both the conviction and the hypothesis it supports less compelling than Hick does. An examination of Byrne leads to similar conclusions.

Byrne denies that his pluralism erases differences since "it needs to assimilate the traditions of the world . . . *only in certain respects.*" It need only assert that "differences between the traditions do not matter when it comes to considering whether such traditions make reference to a common sacred reality and offer means of orienting human beings' lives toward that reality" (Byrne, 1995, p. 26).

This is misleading, however. Consider Byrne's claim that the pluralist thesis is not that divergent descriptions of the ultimate "don't exist or matter, but that *they do not count decisively when reference is judged*" (Byrne, 1995, p. 33). Yet even exclusivists can say this much. For example, a Christian exclusivist who thinks that her own creed is true while doctrines of other traditions that conflict with it are false may agree that "Allah," "Visnu," "the Tao," and the "*nirguna* Brahman" refer to the same sacred reality. She will quickly add, though, that that reality is the triune God of Christianity. The common-referent thesis becomes distinctively pluralistic only when we add Byrne's further contention – that we must be agnostic about the traditions' more specific descriptions of the sacred reality. When we do we are left with the distinct impression that what the traditions have in common is more important (more likely to be true, more central to human life) than the respects in which they differ.

Byrne's de facto erasure of differences, and its dependence upon his agnosticism, also emerges from his discussion of his second thesis – that "differences between the traditions do not matter when it comes to considering whether such traditions . . . offer means of orienting human beings' lives toward" the common sacred, transcendent reality. Important differences aren't erased because pluralism insists merely on a common concern for salvation, and thus a common goal or orientation.

The objection to this, as Byrne knows, is that one's concept of salvation is *defined* or *articulated* by one's beliefs about it, experiences of it, and methods for achieving it, and these differ from tradition to tradition. Orthodox Jews, for instance, are convinced that salvation is constituted by a proper relation to Yahweh and is achieved by observing the Torah. Yoga believes that it consists in the isolation of one's true self (*purusa*) from the entanglements of "matter" (*prakriti*), and is achieved by yogic practices. The relevant experiences also differ. It is thus misleading, at best, to speak of a *common* goal or orientation.

Byrne responds that the pluralist needn't deny that "accounts of salvation are importantly different in detail." He need only assert that "when we consider the worthwhileness or success of these accounts *these differences do not matter*" (Byrne, 1995, p. 96). "What makes" the various salvific practices "successful in this area is what unites them rather than what divides them" (Byrne, 1995, p. 97).

But, of course, from an *internal* perspective, these differences *do* matter in the relevant respect since the traditions believe that the worthwhileness or success of the paths they recommend is a *function* of them. For example, traditional Christians believe that it is *because* the ultimate is personal and not impersonal, *because* God gave his son for us, and so on, that the Christian path to salvation is more worthwhile and successful than the Muslim path, say, or the Advaitin. If the Christian account is no truer than that of the Muslim or Advaitin, then the Christian path doesn't have the kind of value and success he attributes to it. What is at stake, in other words, is what *constitutes* worthwhileness or success. Traditional Christians or Buddhists or Advaitins, on the one hand, and pluralists, on the other, appear to employ different standards of worthwhileness and success, and it isn't clear why the latter's should be preferred to the former's.

Byrne's response to this sort of objection is to admit the diversity but insist on a *substantive* commonality in the traditions' approaches to salvation. That the traditions are engaged in a *common* quest is supported by the existence of "overlaps and the like between concrete conceptions of the good [and of the virtues related to it] in the various traditions" (Byrne, 1995, p. 103). Yet why think that the common features are *what make for success*? Doesn't the claim that they do so implicitly presuppose that what the diverse accounts of salvation have in common is more important for effecting a proper relationship to the transcendent than the respects in which they differ? And doesn't this, too, depend upon Byrne's agnosticism toward the specific claims of the diverse traditions? For if Christianity, say, or Buddhism is true, the *specific* features of the Christian or Buddhist path are precisely what make for (the most) salvific success.

So Byrne's agnosticism towards specific doctrinal claims seems essential to his response to the charge that pluralism erases important differences. What lies behind it? At least two things. The first is pluralism's commitment "to the raising of critical questions about the faiths and" its reliance "on the results of critical, historical scholarship applied to human religious life." This commitment "is linked to the Enlightenment and its intellectual inheritance" and results in an acute consciousness of the culturally conditioned character of specific or thick religious concepts. (Byrne, 1995, p. 27.) The second (and more revealing) emerges in Byrne's admission that the rejection of exclusivist confessionalism depends upon something else

> inherited from the Enlightenment – the dislike of claims to epistemic privilege . . . [S]ince we all live in the same world, the experience of all of us should count in determining its character. We should be suspicious of anyone or any group who claims to have access to certainty about this common world which others cannot have. It is this [epistemic] universalism and egalitarianism which leads to the conclusion that conflicts which cannot be resolved by publicly assessable arguments are good indicators of the need to be agnostic about the subject matter in question. (Byrne, 1995, p. 193)

Why, though, accept Byrne's Enlightenment commitments? Wouldn't a Calvinist who appeals to the inner illumination of the Holy Spirit, for example, or a Vedantin who appeals to the intrinsic luminosity of the Vedas, dismiss Byrne's commitments as mere ideology? Byrne realizes that they would and concedes that "the kind of critical thinking" that is associated with the Enlightenment "is not without its presuppositions." He insists, however, that "to acknowledge the presupposition-based and limited nature of philosophical inquiry is not yet to concede that it must be ideological in form, while such inquiry is prepared to support its questions and conclusions by reasons" (Byrne, 1995, p. 28). The "fallibilism" on which pluralism depends is itself fallible. The pluralist will therefore "be alive to the possibility that convincing arguments for the detailed, dogmatic scheme of" some "one tradition will be forthcoming" (Byrne, 1995, p. 116).

The deck is still stacked, however, for "convincing" in this context means convincing to all or most informed, intelligent, and fair-minded inquirers. "The normativity of a particular revelation or tradition should be capable of being supported by reasons which are universally available [i.e., in principle convincing] to all peoples . . . It should be a problem then that such reasons are not generally forthcoming," and that those that Buddhists, say, or Christians advance in practice "seem to have little neutral weight and tend to be convincing only after conversion" (Byrne, 1995, p. 20). And, indeed, if the epistemologies of the particular traditions correctly represent their epistemic practices, arguments of the sort Byrne is looking for *aren't possible*. Aquinas, for example, thinks that while there is good evidence for the special authority of scripture, it isn't sufficient to compel assent unless God moves a person "inwardly" to accept it. If this is correct, then the sort of arguments Byrne asks for can't be provided.

Pluralists, exclusivists, and the situatedness of reason

The problem is this. Pluralism (or at least Byrne's, and in part Hick's, versions of it) rests on a loaded concept of reason – an Enlightenment conception which has no place for the notion (common to the traditions) that information, intelligence, and fair-mindedness often aren't enough. The state of one's heart, or appropriate spiritual dispositions, may also be epistemically necessary. Byrne's requirement is also self-referentially incoherent since the claim that good reasons must be convincing to all or most informed, intelligent, and fair-minded inquirers cannot itself be supported by universally compelling arguments. Ultimately, one suspects that Byrne's not unadmirable commitment to Enlightenment ideals of reason is merely a reflection of his own "passional nature."

As William James noted, we approach issues with different personal histories, commitments, and passions. As a consequence, equally educated, intelligent, and fair-minded inquirers may evaluate the same body of evidence in radically different ways. James thought that, ultimately, our pictures of the world are "accidents more or less of personal vision" since they express our "temperament" – "our individual way of just seeing and feeling the total push and pressure of the cosmos." Our metaphysical hypotheses and world-views, our standards and deepest convictions, are expressions of our "willing" or "passional" natures – our temperament, needs, concerns, fears, hopes, passions, and "divinations." (James, 1909, p. 10; 1907, p. 18.) John Henry Newman, too, thought that there is no "common measure" between mind and mind which can be employed to conclusively settle fundamental disputes since reason is "personal" and reflects the history and cast of mind of the person who employs it. When "the question" is raised "What is to become of the evidence, being what it is," each person must ultimately decide "according to (what is called) the state of his heart" (Newman, 1843, p. 227).

James and Newman are not denying that we should try to view the evidence as clearly as we can. Neither are they denying that we should be open to objections and new evidence. Nor are they denying that we should pay especial attention to negative evidence, or try to be as fair-minded as possible, or subject our views to continuous criticism. What they *are* denying is both the possibility and the desirability of eliminating all passional factors from the process of reasoning. When we have done all we can to avoid error and eliminate prejudice, the ultimate test of the accuracy of our inferences must still be our own best judgment, a judgment which is unavoidably personal. Our varying assessments of the force of a body of evidence depend on our views of prior probabilities, of the evidence's relevance, of its overall weight, and so on. But these "have no definite ascertained value, and are reducible to no scientific standard." Rather, "what are such to each individual depends on his moral temperament," his personal history, and the like. (Newman, 1843, p. 191.)

What is true of reasoning in general is also true of the pluralist's reasoning. Hick and Byrne, too, ultimately rely on their sense of the overall weight of the evidence, of what epistemic standards are appropriate or relevant, of what is or is not important or illuminating, and so on – assessments which are neither more nor less obviously "objective" than the conflicting assessments of reflective and self-critical exclusivists. While there are, indeed, some "common measures" (coherence, explanatory power, and the like), their interpretation and application, and one's sense of their comparative importance, reflects values, temperament, and experience. There is no neutral standpoint from which one could judge that the pluralist's judgments and assessments are more objective or better grounded than the exclusivist's – or vice versa.

Why, then, should the exclusivist be bothered by the pluralist's strictures? Alvin Plantinga argues that she shouldn't.

For and Against Exclusivism

Plantinga considers three principles that pluralists frequently employ in arguing against exclusivism:

(1) If p is a doctrinal proposition to which S is committed and "S knows that others don't believe p and that he is in condition C with respect to p, then S should not believe p" (where C includes "being rather fully aware of other religions, . . . knowing that there is much that at the least looks like genuine piety and devoutness in them, and . . . believing you know of no arguments that would necessarily convince all or most honest and intelligent dissenters of your own religious allegiances").

(2) Where p is a doctrinal proposition to which one is committed, that opposed beliefs have similar "internal markers," "evidence, phenomenology, and the like," is a sufficient reason for withholding assent from p.

(3) "If S's religious or philosophical [or moral] beliefs are such that if S had been born elsewhere or elsewhen [or had been acculturated differently], she wouldn't have held them, then those beliefs are [probably?] produced by unreliable belief-producing mechanisms and hence have no warrant." (Plantinga, 1995, pp. 196, 200, 204, 212)

Byrne employs a version of the first principle, and Hick versions of the second and third.

Their application is obvious. Many Christian and Buddhist exclusivists who are aware that others dissent from their doctrinal claims are in condition C. Many would also concede that their conflicting beliefs have the same or relevantly similar internal markers. Finally, it is patently obvious that "in some ninety-nine percent of cases the religion which an individual professes and to which he or she adheres depends upon the accidents of birth" (Hick, 1989, p. 2).

As Plantinga points out, however, these principles can just as easily be turned against pluralists. The first is an instance of a more general principle from which it derives whatever plausibility it has: Where p is any proposition to which S is committed and S knows that others don't believe p and S is in condition C' with respect to p, then S should not believe p (where C' includes being rather fully aware of intellectual traditions or viewpoints which reject p, fully appreciating the fact that many of those who don't accept p are as informed, intelligent, and morally sensitive as those who do, and believing that one knows of no arguments that would convince all or most honest and intelligent dissenters of the truth of p). But this general principle obviously applies to the pluralist's assertions as well as to the doctrinal claims of Christian or Buddhist exclusivists. To make matters worse, pluralists can't assert the general principle without self-referential incoherence since they know that reflective exclusivists reject it and they are in condition C' with respect to it.

The second principle is also problematic. If apparent epistemic parity were a sufficient reason for withholding or withdrawing assent, I would have a sufficient reason for withholding assent from many moral and philosophical beliefs to which I remain deeply committed after careful reflection, and I don't. If the principle were true, for example, then both the libertarian who is convinced that contra-causal freedom is essential to moral responsibility and the compatibilist who denies that it is should abandon their positions once they become aware of the fact that their opponents are often as informed, intelligent, and well-trained as they are, and find their arguments as persuasive as they find their own. Indeed, one can't consistently accept the second principle and endorse *any* genuinely controversial philosophical, political, or moral belief since disagreement among apparent epistemic peers is precisely what *makes* these beliefs controversial. But, of course, pluralism too is a controversial philosophical thesis. So if the principle were true, one should withdraw one's assent from it. Finally, since the second principle is itself a controversial philosophical thesis, its assertion is self-referentially incoherent.

Neither am I necessarily being "intellectually *arbitrary*" in assenting to a controversial proposition under conditions of apparent epistemic parity since I may not believe that the competing beliefs really "*are* on a relevant epistemic par." I may think "that somehow the other person *has made a mistake* or *has a blind spot*, or hasn't been wholly attentive, or hasn't received some grace [I] have, or is in someway epistemically less fortunate" (Plantinga, 1995, pp. 202, 204–5). The Christian, for example, may think that the operation of the Holy Spirit enables her to see the force of evidence for Christian theism to which others are blind.

Nor are claims like these peculiar to religious exclusivists. Don't pluralists, when confronted with the fact that many religious exclusivists are their epistemic peers, typically appeal to the latter's alleged insensitivity to the force of certain kinds of evidence, to a lack of attention (to other traditions, for example), self-deception, or other epistemic infelicities? In continuing to hold their beliefs in the face of apparent epistemic parity, pluralists are thus neither more nor less "intellectually arbitrary" than reflective exclusivists.

The third principle, too, can be turned against the pluralist since it is surely not an accident that most pluralists are highly educated and comparatively affluent members of modern Western democracies. Those born elsewhere or elsewhen are more likely to be exclusivists than to hold views like Hick's or Byrne's. If the third principle is sound, pluralism is tarred with the same brush as exclusivism.

Plantinga has shown that the religious exclusivist needn't be irrational in adhering to her beliefs in the face of religious diversity. He has also shown that the epistemic position of the pluralist isn't clearly better than that of the exclusivist. His arguments have limitations, however.

They may show that a person who appreciates the sophistication and richness of other religions, knows that genuine piety and sanctity aren't confined to her own tradition, and the like, can continue to rationally adhere to her own doctrinal beliefs. They don't address the situation of persons who are trying to decide between traditions, or of those whose grip on their religious beliefs has been seriously weakened by their awareness of religious diversity and who are thus now in a position relevantly similar to that of people who have not yet committed themselves.

Suppose that there aren't any neutral grounds for asserting that one of the great religious traditions is closer to the truth than the others. From its own perspective, Christianity appears to be more illuminating and salvific than Buddhism. But the converse is true as well. There *are* criteria for assessing world-views but, from a neutral perspective that abstracts from the situated and passional character of our individual reasons, there are no compelling reasons for thinking that one religious world-view meets the criteria better than another. Furthermore, *each* of the great traditions appears to be self-confirming in the sense that the spiritual fruits which it promises its adherents are forthcoming. Now William Alston may be right in thinking that the existence of the Christian epistemic practice, its internal consistency, its coherence with other well-established epistemic practices, and the fact that those most deeply committed to it appear to flourish is a good reason for the uncommitted to embrace it. In the absence of religious diversity it might even be sufficient. But the introduction of other traditions with similar credentials alters the uncommitted's epistemic situation. For he or she now has similar reasons for accepting Buddhism, say, or Advaita Vedanta. Yet (assuming that Christianity and Buddhism and Advaita Vedanta are mutually incompatible) any reason for accepting one of them is a reason for rejecting the others. The reasons for accepting Christianity and Buddhism and Advaita Vedanta cancel each other out, leaving the uncommitted with *no* reason for preferring one to the others. (Whether this limitation in Plantinga's arguments is of any help to the pluralist, however, is doubtful. For similar considerations appear to apply to disputes between reflective religious exclusivists and pluralists. Each may be rational in maintaining their beliefs in the face of arguments to the contrary, a recognition that they have no evidence which would compel the assent of their adversaries, and an awareness that their adversaries are as informed, intelligent, and morally sensitive as they are. This very fact, though, provides the uncommitted with a reason for remaining agnostic with respect to the competing claims of exclusivists and pluralists.)

These limitations notwithstanding, religious exclusivism hasn't been shown to be *less* rational, further from the truth, or in some other way epistemically worse off than pluralism. Of course appeals to the inner testimony of the Holy Spirit, to the intrinsic luminosity of the Vedas, or to the proper basicality of peculiarly Christian or Buddhist beliefs are apologetically useless unless accompanied by tradition-neutral arguments for the epistemically privileged character of one's own claims and those of one's coreligionists, and it is doubtful that such arguments will be forthcoming. It may nonetheless be true that one of these appeals *is* correct, and that Christians, say, or Buddhists really *are* in an epistemically privileged position with respect to their claims. It is also important to note that exclusivists *need* internal explanations (in terms of the operation of the Holy Spirit, the inward working of the Buddha nature, and the like) for their failure to convince rational and fair-minded adherents of other traditions of the truth and importance of their doctrinal claims. Without it their second-order belief that their first-order religious beliefs are justified lacks justification and may consequently be psychologically insecure.

The exclusivists' position is not irrational, then, and it may be right. But isn't it egregiously arrogant? In discussing Karl Barth's claim that all religions except Christianity are products of human pride and self-interest, Keith Ward comments that

> the belief that everyone else's revelation is incorrect and only one's own is true, is [itself] a particularly clear example of human pride and self-interest . . . [O]ne has an interest in thinking one's religion is the only true one [since] it enables one to dismiss the others as of no account and so bask in the superiority of one's own possession of the truth. One may claim that [one possesses the truth] by the grace of God alone – but this only makes the element of human pride more pronounced, since one is now asserting that grace is only truly possessed by oneself. One can hardly get more proud, more self-righteous, and more short-sighted than that. (Ward, 1994, p. 17)

Exclusivists like Barth are like the self-righteous Pharisee who thanks God that he is not as other people are (Luke 18:9–14).

The exclusivist should not dismiss these charges too quickly. While Christian or Buddhist exclusivists come off well when judged by their own epistemic and evaluative standards, they come off less well when judged by those of their rivals. Of course Christian exclusivists reject the Buddhist's standards and Buddhist exclusivists reject the Christian's standards. Each also has explanations of the other's alleged blindness. Is the Christian or Buddhist exclusivist therefore entitled to dismiss her rival's standards and go about business as usual? Many exclusivists do so. Notice, however, that cases in which we dismiss others' standards out of hand are typically ones in which we are convinced that those who reject our standards hold absurd beliefs or employ patently irrational epistemic procedures. (Think of our attitude toward astrology or palmistry, for example.) It isn't surprising, then, that pluralists suspect that exclusivists regard the beliefs or epistemic procedures of their rivals as absurd or patently irrational, or that this suspicion leads to charges of arrogance.

Now reflective exclusivists *needn't* regard their rivals' beliefs and epistemic procedures as absurd or patently irrational. But I think that they *must* regard them as expressions of moral or spiritual failure. Confronted with religious diversity, and the fact that each tradition appears to be making similar epistemic moves, a reflective exclusivist will wonder why members of her own tradition have gotten things right while adherents of other traditions have gotten them wrong. Since information and intelligence are more or less equally distributed, the most natural explanation is that her rivals suffer from moral or spiritual blindness, and this charge can't help but seem benighted to outsiders.

Should the exclusivist be worried by this? I am not sure. On the one hand, "faults" of this kind are endemic. *Any* clear-headed person who adopts a position on a controversial topic is subject to it. Philosophers, for example, or historians who think they have good arguments on a disputed issue, must implicitly assume that their assessments of the evidence's force are more reliable than those of their opponents. They must therefore assume that the judgments of others who typically assess evidence as they do so are more reliable than the judgments of those who don't. But this implies that those who assess evidence of that kind as they do so are in a superior epistemic position with respect to it. And isn't this, indeed, tacitly presupposed in practice? Complicated assessments of historical or philosophical hypotheses not only reflect a person's intelligence, education, and information. They also reflect her experience in dealing with comparable issues, her imagination or lack of it, sensitivity to certain kinds of evidence, temperament, values, and a host of other tacit factors. If a good philosopher or textual scholar is challenged to justify a controversial assessment of the evidence's overall force, she may ultimately have to appeal to her critics' alleged blindness to the importance of certain kinds of evidence, their failures of imagination, deficiencies in their experience, or something else of the sort. If her critics deny that things like these are distorting their judgment, she will probably also conclude that their blindness to their deficiencies is *itself* partly caused by them. Now suppose that the issue in dispute is not only controversial but existentially important. Isn't the blindness that she attributes to her rivals likely to be at least partly moral or spiritual?

It is important to note that pluralists are as committed to making accusations of this type as anyone. Doesn't Hick, for example, find exclusivists morally and spiritually obtuse or insensitive? Or consider David Krieger, who accuses exclusivists of arrogance and "violence," and insists that they are religiously blind – not genuinely open to the transcendent that appears only when we step outside our closed systems and into the space where being discloses itself.

The fact that this "fault" is unavoidable, however, doesn't imply that it isn't a *real* fault. Robert Adams has argued that people can sometimes be blamed for involuntary sins. That the attitudes of members of the Hitler Jugend towards non-Aryans was unavoidable, for example, doesn't imply that they weren't at fault or shouldn't be blamed for them.

Yet why *should* one be blamed for accusing others of moral or spiritual blindness if one's religious views are *true*? I think that one shouldn't if the spiritual and moral defects of other traditions are as obvious as those of the Thugee, the Jonestown cult, or the Aztecs. The situation is different, however, when the alleged defects are comparatively hidden. Many of the saints of other traditions (a Ghandi, say, or a Rabi'a) are morally and spiritually impressive. Nor (on the face of it) are the devout of the other high traditions morally or spiritually inferior to one's coreligionists. Furthermore, if we are salvific inclusivists as well as doctrinal exclusivists, the problem is even graver. For we must recognize the possibility that their responses to the lesser light made manifest to them are more faithful than our responses to the greater light revealed to us.

Puritan divines argued that we should not question the profession of fellow Christians unless their behavior notoriously belied it. To do so was to sin against charity. Exclusivists who accuse others of moral and spiritual blindness should at least wonder whether their accusations, too, are rooted in a lack of love as well as in the force of their arguments and their superior insight, and whether their own blindness (while different) is any less egregious. The charge of moral and spiritual blindness may sometimes be in order. Exclusivists who make it, however, should do so in fear and trembling, and with considerable spiritual discomfort.

References

Alston, William P. (1991) *Perceiving God: The Epistemology of Religious Experience*. Ithaca and London: Cornell University Press. Chapter 7.

Byrne, Peter (1995) *Prolegomena to Religious Pluralism: Reference and Realism in Religion*. London: Macmillan; New York: St Martin's Press.

Christian, William A., Sr. (1972) *Oppositions of Religious Doctrines: A Study in the Logic of Dialogue*. New York: Herder and Herder.

Griffiths, Paul J. (1991) *An Apology for Apologetics: A Study in the Logic of Interreligious Dialogue*. Maryknoll, N.Y.: Orbis Books.

Hick, John (1982) *God Has Many Names*. Philadelphia: The Westminster Press.

Hick, John (1989) *An Interpretation of Religion: Human Responses to the Transcendent*. New Haven and London: Yale University Press.

Hick, John (1995) *A Christian Theology of Religions: The Rainbow of Faiths*. Louisville, Ky.: Westminster John Knox Press.

Huxley, Aldous (1945) *The Perennial Philosophy*. New York and London: Harper & Bros.

James, William (1907) *Pragmatism*. New York: Longmans, Green. Cited from Meridian edition, 1955.

James, William (1909) *A Pluralistic Universe*. New York: Longmans, Green. Cited from Longmans, Green edition, 1947.

Krieger, David (1991) *The New Universalism: Foundations for a Global Theology*. Maryknoll, N.Y.: Orbis Books.

Newman, John Henry (1843) *Fifteen Sermons Preached Before the University of Oxford*. Oxford: Rivingtons. Cited from the Christian Classics edition, SCM Press, 1966.

Plantinga, Alvin (1995) Pluralism: A Defense of Religious Exclusivism. In Thomas D. Senor (ed.), *The Rationality of Belief and the Plurality of Faith* (pp. 191–215). Ithaca and London: Cornell University Press.

Smith, Wilfred Cantwell (1964) *The Meaning and End of Religion: A New Approach to the Religious Traditions of Mankind*. New York: The New American Library.

Smith, Wilfred Cantwell (1981) *Towards a World Theology: Faith and the Comparative History of Religion*. Philadelphia: The Westminster Press.

Stace, Walter (1960) *Mysticism and Philosophy*. Philadelphia and New York: J. B. Lippincott.

Ward, Keith (1994) *Religion and Revelation: A Theology of Revelation in the World's Religions*. Oxford: Clarendon Press.

Suggested Further Reading

Christian, William A., Sr. (1987) *Doctrines of Religious Communities: A Philosophical Study*. New Haven and London: Yale University Press.

Cobb, John B., Jr. (1982) *Beyond Dialogue: Toward a Mutual Transformation of Christianity and Buddhism*. Philadelphia: Fortress Press.

D'Costa, Gavin (1996) The Impossibility of a Pluralist View of Religions. *Religious Studies*, 32, 223–32.

Griffiths, Paul J. (2001) *Problems of Religious Diversity*. Oxford: Blackwell.

Hick, John (1997) The Epistemological Challenge of Religious Pluralism. *Faith and Philosophy*, 14, 277–302. With replies by William Alston, George Mavrodes, and Peter van Inwagen.

Hick, John (2000) Ineffability. *Religious Studies*, 36, 35–46. Replies to Insole and Rowe.

Insole, Christopher J. (2000) Why John Hick Cannot, and Should Not, Stay Out of the Jam Pot. *Religious Studies*, 36, 25–33.

Quinn, Philip L., and Meeker, Kevin (eds.) (2000) *The Philosophical Challenge of Religious Diversity*. New York: Oxford University Press.

Rowe, William L. (1999) Religious pluralism. *Religious Studies*, 35, 139–50.

Senor, Thomas D. (ed.) (1995) *The Rationality of Belief and the Plurality of Faith*. Ithaca: Cornell University Press.

Wainwright, William J. (1984) Wilfred Cantwell Smith on Faith and Belief. *Religious Studies*, 20, 353–66.

Wainwright, William J. (1998) *Philosophy of Religion*, second edn. Belmont, Calif.: Wadsworth. Chapters 7 and 8.

Part IV

Religion and Life

Chapter 11

Human Destiny

Peter van Inwagen

What is to become of us?

The question is ambiguous. It might be understood to mean, What is to become of us *collectively*: what is to become of the human species? Alternatively, it might be understood to mean, What is to become of us *individually*: what is to become of you and what is to become of me and what is to become of Jack and what is to become of Joan and . . . ? In this essay I shall address only the first of these questions.

The essay has two parts. The first comprises general remarks about the question, What is to become of the human species? These remarks are something of a miscellany, united only by their common theme. The second part is devoted to the "Doomsday Argument" of Brandon Carter and John Leslie. It is my hope that some of the general remarks will justify the proportion of an essay on "human destiny" I have chosen to devote to the Doomsday Argument.

General Remarks

Whether there is an answer to the question, What is to become of the human species? depends upon whether any important aspects of the human future are determined or at least have determinate objective probabilities. That is: consider the set of "possible futures" consistent with both the present state of things and the laws of nature.[1] If all these futures share some feature – the imminent extinction of humanity; a 10,000-year Utopia; the second coming of Christ – there is at least a partial answer to the question, What is to become of the human species? If various subsets of these futures have non-trivial measures that satisfy the usual formal constraints – so that we can meaningfully say things like "In 57 percent of the futures that are consistent with the present and the laws of nature, the human species will become extinct before the year 2200" – then there is an answer to the question, What is to become of the human species? But this answer may be very complicated and may essentially involve probabilities. It might take the form of a set of functions that assign objective probabilities to dates and important "eventualities;" for example, one of these functions might assign to the eventuality "human extinction" and the date "January 1, 2220" the probability 0.57, meaning that there is an objective probability of 0.57 that our species will have become extinct by this date.[2] If no eventuality/date pairs, or none involving eventualities relevant to our hopes and fears concerning the future of humanity, have objective probabilities – if strict determinism is true, then every eventuality/date pair has an objective probability of either 0 or 1 – then there is simply nothing to be said about what is to become of the human species.

If there is an answer to the question, What is to become of the human species? it might nevertheless be idle to ask this question, owing simply to the fact that it is not humanly possible to discover its answer, or even to find any cogent reason to regard any of its possible answers as in any way epistemically preferable to any other (equally specific) answer. Suppose there is an urn in which someone has placed a certain number of black balls and a certain number of white balls, and that we have no way of knowing what these numbers are or of knowing anything non-tautological about the ratio of either to the other. If we know that one ball will be selected at random from the urn – by an ontologically indeterministic mechanism – we know that there is an answer, an informative response, to the question, Will the ball that is drawn be black or white? The answer is "black" if the number of white balls is 0 and the number of black balls is not 0; it is "There is a probability of 0.57 that it will be white and a probability of 0.43 that it will be black" if the number of white balls is 57 and the number of black balls is 43 . . . and so on. But we also know that the question is an idle one, since we can have no reason to accept any of the possible answers.

Some have thought the question answerable, and have given answers to it.

Aristotle and the Hindu religion agree that the world and the human species are eternal. For Aristotle, the past and the future will be pretty much the same as the present: the sun will always shine (and has always shone), there will continue to be the same climatic conditions and the same biological kinds there have always been, and cities and empires and languages will pass away and others will come to be. For the Hindus, although world-history is cyclical, in the long run things will always be pretty much the same: the same cycles are ordained to recur eternally in their given order, just as, in our experience, the same four seasons continually recur in their given order. The Pythagoreans and the ancient atomists allowed that the human race would someday become extinct and that the physical universe itself would dissolve into chaos; but, they held, the physical universe and the human species will be reborn: owing to nothing more than the chance recombination of the basic units of matter, the future of the universe comprises an infinity of deaths and rebirths. Nietzsche, who adopted this thesis, called it "the most scientific of hypotheses,"[3] although he never attempted any careful argument for the scientific necessity of this "eternal return."[4] (The necessity of the eternal return does not follow from the premises he seems to have thought entailed it: a universe that consists of two particles that draw ever nearer for the "first half" of eternity, pass each other like ships in the night, and then draw ever farther apart for the "second half" of eternity, is consistent with those premises. There is, however, an interesting theorem of Poincaré that says roughly this: in a bounded ideal mechanical system in which the elements of the system do not lose energy when they "bounce off the walls" – for example, an ensemble of ideal gas molecules confined forever to an unchanging, ideal container; our "two-particle universe" is not bounded – for all but a set of initial states of the system of 0 measure, the system will return to a state arbitrarily close to its initial state, given enough time.)

The Abrahamic religions[5] – Judaism, Christianity, and Islam – disagree with Aristotle, the Hindus, the Greek atomists, and Nietzsche. These religions maintain, first, that the physical universe came into existence at a certain moment in the past,[6] and, secondly, that at some moment in the future, the physical universe, the earth, and the human species – the theater, the stage, and the actors – will undergo a radical and irreversible transformation. And they hold that human beings (if not the physical universe or the earth) will thereafter always exist in the new state that this transformation will effect. (Each human being will exist eternally and there will be no reproduction.)[7]

Another sort of disagreement with Aristotle et al. can be found in the writings of "historicist" philosophers like Hegel and Marx. Ontologically speaking, historicism is a secular rewriting of Christian eschatology. (Historicism, like Gothic architecture, is an epiphenomenon of Latin Christianity.) The human species (but not the universe or the earth) is to undergo a radical and irreversible transformation. (A spiritual – *geistlich* – or economic transformation, not a biological transformation.) But this transformation will not be brought about by God – as, of course, the Abrahamic religions maintain with respect to the transformation they look forward to – but by the operation of impersonal historical principles. Epistemologically speaking, the coming "historicist eschaton" is said by historicists to be predictable by the exercise of human reason – as opposed to its being revealed by God, divine revelation being, of course, the source of our supposed knowledge of the eschaton according to Jews, Christians, and Muslims. According to historicists, the historical development of reason has reached a level – the "historical moment," which occurred at some point in the nineteenth century – at which reason became able to understand the laws of its own development.

I have given a sketch of three positions according to which important features of the human future are determined by the present state of things (according to the Abrahamic religions, "the present state of things" includes God's intentions as regards the human future), and, according to which, it is possible to know what some of these features will be. These seem to me to be the most important positions of this type that have actually been taken. What can be said for and against them?

The first or "Aristotelian" position may be rejected, for physics and cosmology have shown that the universe does not have an infinite past. (Or have they shown this? The currently "standard" cosmological theory implies that time had a beginning. According to that theory, "Alice lived 20 billion years ago" cannot be true – for a reason analogous to the reason "Alice lives 20,000 miles to the south" cannot be true: the phrase "20 billion years ago," although it is semantically suited for being the name of a time, is not the name of a time, just as "20,000 miles to the south" is not the name of a place although it is semantically suited for being the name of a place. But there are other cosmological theories than the standard theory, theories consistent with the cosmological evidence, according to which the universe does not have a beginning in time. What can be said for certain is this. One cannot properly regard it as having been established, or even as having been shown to be probable, that the age of the universe is infinite; the most one can say is that this is a possibility that hasn't been definitively ruled out.) As of this date the consensus among cosmologists is that the universe has an infinite future, but that only an initial segment of this future (finite, of course: all initial segments are finite) will be at all interesting. Following this initial segment, the physical universe will forever consist entirely of radiation, black-body radiation at a temperature that only respect for the law of the conservation of energy can lead us to distinguish from absolute zero. (There will come a time when the temperature of the radiation-universe in degrees Kelvin will differ from zero only in the seventy-second decimal place; later it will differ only in the eighty-ninth decimal place; later still only in the hundred-and-sixth decimal place, and so on. The radiation-universe of the future has nothing to look forward to but the eternal growth of the initial segment of zeros in the number that measures its temperature.) The heavens will indeed, in the words of Ps. 102, wear out like a garment. This is what cosmology tells us. Geology, paleontology, anthropology, archaeology, and historical scholarship tell us that the history of the earth, the biosphere, the human species, and human culture has been neither static nor cyclical.

As to the possibility of the eschaton expected by Jews, Christians, and Muslims, there is little to be said. I am a Christian and thus "look for the resurrection of the dead, and the life of the world [that is, age] to come." But this is a matter of faith (and it is a part of my faith that it is a matter of faith). If you do not share my faith, I have a great deal to say to you, but you (justifiably) are not reading this essay with the expectation of being evangelized, and neither I nor the editor nor Blackwell wishes to be accused of false advertising.

Historicism, at any rate in its "strong" Hegelian-Marxist form, cannot be taken seriously. Hegel and Marx (or at least Hegel and Marx the prophets) seem merely comic today. But various more modest forms of the thesis that important aspects of the human future are predetermined and knowable by human reason (or have determinate objective probabilities that are knowable by human reason) are worthy of serious consideration. It follows, obviously, from what we have said above about what cosmology tells us that the human species does not have an infinite future. (What we know about what the sun is going to do over the next 5 billion years is also relevant to the question, How long will the human species exist? But it is possible that we shall be able to migrate to other planetary systems. No one, however, is going to organize a migration to another cosmos. At least I don't *think* so.) But little else follows. For all cosmology (or stellar astronomy) can tell us, the human species might have a future that is "imaginatively infinite" – a future that is large in comparison with the human past as intergalactic distances are large in comparison with the walk from the parish church to the post office. (And even the modest conclusion that the human species has only a finite future depends on a premise that, uncontroversial though it may be in some circles, is not accepted by everyone – not, for example, by me and my house. This premise is naturalism, the thesis that the physical universe is "all there is or was or ever will be." If human beings are not, in the words of J. R. R. Tolkien, "confined for ever to the circles of the world," the heat-death of the physical universe does not imply the end of humanity.)

It is possible, then, that, although humanity does not have an infinite future, it has a very long future indeed, a future during which . . . what?

Philosophers of the classical world could suppose, consistently with the astronomical, biological, and historical knowledge of their times (if not with the creation stories they had heard at their mothers' knees), that the universe and the earth had always been much as they were then and always would be much as they were then. A fortiori, they could easily enough have believed in a terrestrial history and future that spanned thousands of millions of years, a history and future of a world at every time much like their own, a world of cities and agriculture, wars and empires. But (as regards the past) they did not know that biological life had a beginning and has a history; their cultural memory did not reach back to the last glaciation or even to the revolutions in agriculture and metallurgy that had created their world of city-states and empires. And (as regards the future) they could not foresee the technological revolution of the second Christian millennium and the population explosion of the nineteenth and twentieth centuries. *We* do not think of history (either cosmic, terrestrial, or human; but I am now thinking primarily of human history) or of the future, including the human future, as they did. We know that there had never in all history been a human world at all like the one we lived in during the second half of the twentieth century, and we are certain that the twenty-second century will be no more like the twentieth century than the twentieth century was like the eighteenth. It seems, therefore, that at least one feature of the human future is now predictable: it will not be like the human present or the human past. So we believe, and I have a hard time seeing how this belief could be wrong. The shape of our lives (to the extent that our biology allows this shape to vary) is to a very large degree a consequence of technology. Technological development has become a self-sustaining, impersonal thing, like a forest fire or a pandemic. (I mean these images to suggest things that are growing and impossible to control and have taken on "a life of their own," not things that are bad; I consider it still an open question whether the Luddites or the technophiles or the proponents of some intermediate view will turn out to be right. I suppose the fact that all the similes that serve my literary purpose are bad things should be a cause for *some* unease in the technophile camp.) Continuing technological innovation is inevitable – unless it should be curtailed by some global disaster (whether a consequence of unbridled technological growth or of some wholly unrelated cause, as in the recently popular spate of "big rock hits the earth" movies). And if such a global disaster were to happen, that, too, would have the result that the future will be very different from the present.

Detailed (and even rather general) predictions of the future of *homo technologicus*, insofar as they have been predictions of futures that have had time to become the present, have almost always been wrong. Indeed, it seems that the only way for a prediction of the future of a technological civilization to be right is for two people to make predictions that are logical contradictories. (And if two propositions are logical contradictories, one of them, at least, must be very general and abstract.)

Two sorts of people have offered such predictions in print: imaginative writers like Jules Verne and H. G. Wells and George Orwell and Aldous Huxley and Robert Heinlein, on the one hand, and self-described "futurologists" on the other. The former, claiming to be no more than tellers of tales, cannot, perhaps, in the strictest sense, be said have been engaged in the business of "predicting the future." Still, many of them did the best they could to predict the future (if they had thought some other future more likely than the one presented in their stories, they would have written stories set in that more likely future). Predictions of the future from either source tend to be (but are not invariably) of two types: utopian or dystopian. Wells's *The Time Machine* cleverly combines both: it "predicts" a utopia of vast duration to be followed, finally, by dystopia and human extinction. Orwell's *1984* and Huxley's *Brave New World* are the classic examples of dystopian literary predictions. (Huxley's forgotten *Ape and Essence*, should, I think, be in the list of classics.) Whether a detailed prediction of the human future is the result of a novelist's imagination or a futurologist's computer modeling (garbage in, garbage out, as they say), one thing is certain: it will be wrong. Predictions made in the 1940s or 1950s are now amusing. Those made in the 1920s and 1930s are hilarious. Those made in the nineteenth century are charming. And that is really all there is to be said about predicting the future in detail. There are a vast number of epistemologically possible futures, and any proposal of one of them as the actual future (any prediction) will be based on the author's hopes and fears, unconstrained speculations, and extrapolations from a minuscule proportion of even the available data: that is, it will be an essentially random choice from among a vast array of possibilities, most of which the chooser will not even have thought of. (Most of which *no one* will have thought of. Most of which no one *could have* thought of. There has been no "historical moment.")

There is, however, one prediction of an important aspect of the human future that is based not on speculation and the predictor's prejudices, but on philosophical argument; on one argument, an argument which, although it may be mistaken, is a good deal more worthy of the honorable name "argument" than anything that can be found in the writings of Hegel, Marx, or the twentieth-century futurologists. I refer to the notorious Doomsday Argument.[8] The prediction this argument makes is not specific in the way the predictions of the Club of Rome were specific, but it does not lack interest on that account. The conclusion of the Doomsday Argument is that there is a significant probability that the human species is going to become extinct: and not in a million or even in 10,000 years, but within the next few centuries.

The Doomsday Argument

Imagine that (contrary to your expectations when you went to bed) you awaken one morning in a hotel room. You are informed that you have been drugged and kidnapped and are being held on the island of Antiqua, an island of which you have never heard. (You are very ignorant of geography.) You look out the window – your room appears to be on something like the tenth floor of the hotel – and, a few hundred yards away, you observe the sea (or at least a body of water large enough that its farther shore cannot be seen from your window). Can you infer anything much from this fact about the island of Antiqua? Not obviously, for it is in the nature of an island to be bounded by water. But suppose you discover the following facts about the way hotels are distributed in Antiqua (perhaps you have found a page ripped from a brochure about the Antiqua hotel industry in the wastebasket in your room).

> Antiqua is topographically pretty uniform, and every place in Antiqua is suitable for the construction of a hotel. Partly in consequence of this fact, Antiqua is densely and uniformly populated with hotels: every square mile of Antiqua contains a largish number of hotels and the number of hotels in each square mile is about the same as the number in any other square mile (about 10 or 12, in fact).

And suppose you know (you have overheard one of your captors say this) that, for security reasons, the hotel you are in was chosen at random from among the hotels of Antiqua. That is, the names of every hotel in Antiqua were written on slips of paper, which were put into a hat, and one of the slips was drawn by a blindfolded member of the gang that kidnapped you. You were then taken to the hotel whose name was drawn.

Now suppose that, having this information at your disposal, you reason as follows:

> Suppose Antiqua were a large island, an island the size of Ireland, say, or even larger. [The depths of your geographical ignorance are such that, for all you know, there *is* an island the size of Ireland called "Antiqua."] If Antiqua were of that size, and

hotels on Antiqua were as numerous and as uniformly distributed as I know them to be, only a very small proportion of the hotels in Antiqua would be this close to the sea. (And the body of water I observe must be the sea or at any rate the body of water that surrounds Antiqua: if there were a huge lake or bay in Antiqua, then Antiqua wouldn't be "topographically uniform," which I know it is.) And I know that this hotel was chosen at random from among all the hotels of Antiqua. If Antiqua were the size of Ireland, therefore, it would be very improbable on what I know that I should be able to observe the sea from my window. I conclude that it is probable that Antiqua is much smaller than Ireland. I can even conclude that Antiqua is probably considerably smaller than, say, Long Island, although the probability I can assign to this conclusion is smaller than the "Ireland" probability. I therefore conclude that Antiqua is a small island.

This reasoning can seem very plausible. It can seem that you'd be justified in using its conclusion ("Antiqua is a small island") in some context in which something of great practical importance hung on its conclusion. Suppose, for example, you had formulated two promising escape plans that differed in only one important respect: plan A would be more likely to succeed on a small island and plan B would be more likely to succeed on a large island. One might suppose that you would be rationally justified in proceeding according to plan A, that it would, in fact, be positively irrational – all other things being equal – for you to prefer plan B to plan A.

But not so fast. There is a lacuna in your reasoning. You have forgotten to take into account the "prior" or "antecedent" or "posterior" probability of Antiqua's being a small island. You, the fictional "you" of the example, are, as I say, very ignorant of geography. Suppose you were to learn the following facts (facts in the fictional world of our example): there are exactly 100 islands in the world, and all but one are about the size of Ireland (and the other is very small); just as your captors chose the hotel in which they would hold you captive at random from among the hotels of Antiqua, so they chose Antiqua as the island of your captivity at random from among the 100 islands of the world. In that case, the prior or antecedent probability of the conclusion of the above reasoning (that this island you are on is a small island) – antecedent, that is, to your observing the sea from your window – is low: it is, in fact, 0.01 or 1 percent. Can you validly conclude that it is highly probable that you are on a small island if you know that the antecedent probability of this hypothesis is low? Can you validly conclude this if you have *no idea* what the antecedent probability of your being on a small island (given that you're on *some* island) is? The answer to the first question is, That depends. The answer to the second is, No. There is, nevertheless, something about your reasoning that is on the right track. It does lead validly to an interesting conclusion, but this conclusion is not that you are probably on a small island; it is that you should now assign to the hypothesis that you are on a small island a *higher*, perhaps a significantly higher, probability than you did before you looked out the window and saw the sea. The new piece of evidence you have acquired, as some people say, "raises the antecedent probability" of the hypothesis that this island you are on, Antiqua, is a small island. (A strictly meaningless phrase, since antecedent probabilities do not and cannot change, but it seems to convey to most people what it is intended to convey.) There is a theorem of the probability calculus, Bayes's theorem, that governs the degree to which antecedent probabilities are raised by new evidence. I will not undertake a technical, or even a non-technical, discussion of this theorem,[9] but I well mention some numbers, just to give a sense of orders of magnitude.

In the case we have imagined (the "100 islands" case), the antecedent probability that you are on a large (Ireland-sized) island is 99 percent and the antecedent probability that you are on a small island is 1 percent. Suppose that if one were placed on a large island at a place chosen at random, the chance of one's finding oneself near enough to the sea for it to be visible to one (under the conditions we have imagined) would be 0.0002 or $\frac{2}{100}$ of 1 percent. Suppose being placed at a randomly chosen spot on the sole small island would give one a 50/50 chance of being able to observe the sea.[10] This information, given Bayes's theorem, is sufficient for you to be able to calculate the probability you should assign to the hypothesis that you are on a small island, given the new piece of information that has just come your way, to wit, that you can observe the sea. It is over 96 percent.[11]

Let us now move from problems about one's location in space to problems about one's location in time. ("Size" – in this context, area – is a concept involving two dimensions, and time has only one dimension. At the cost of what little realism our "island" example had, however, we could as easily have considered "thin" islands, islands one of whose geographical dimensions could be ignored. We could have considered the effect that finding yourself near one "end" of an island should have on the probability you assigned to the hypothesis that it was a *short* island.)

Let us consider a temporal analogue of our "island" example. Some moment between the present and 1 million AP ("after present") is chosen at random. Call this moment B. Then a moment, A, is chosen at random from the moments between the present and B. I am taken by time machine to the moment A. On arrival, I discover that the year is "only" 2097. Can I conclude anything about how far in the future B is? The question is rather vague. Let us ask a more precise question. Let us call the next 100 years the "very near future," the next 1000 years the "near future," and the period from 1000 AP to 1 million AP the "distant future." Here is a precise question: what is the probability that B lies in the "near future," given that I have found myself in the "very near future"?

To calculate the probability that B lies in the near future (given that I have found myself in the very near future) using Bayes's theorem, we need three numbers: the antecedent probability of B's lying in the near future, the probability of my finding myself in the very near future if B lies somewhere in the near future, and the probability of my finding myself in the very near future if B is somewhere in either the near or the distant future. (The probability we are trying to determine will be the first probability multiplied by the ratio of the second to the third.)

The antecedent probability that B lies in the near future is 0.001, since the near and the distant future are together 1000 times as long as the near future. We can approximate the probability of my finding myself in the very near future given that B is in the near future by noting the following facts: if B were 100 years from now, the probability of my finding myself in the near future would be unity; if B were 200 years from now, this probability would be 1/2; if B were 300 years from now, the probability would be 1/3; ... ; if B were 1000 years from now, the probability would be 1/10. Intuitively, the probability of my finding myself in the very near future, given that B is *somewhere* in the near future, should be close to the *average* of these 10 probabilities – about 0.3. So we may say that if B is in the near future, the probability of my finding myself in the very near future is approximately 30 percent.[12] An exact calculation (one that substitutes integration for summation) shows that this approximation is pretty good; the actual probability is equal to $\frac{1}{10}$ the sum of 1 and the natural logarithm of 10, or about 0.3302. (The number 10 occurs where it does in this calculation because the near future is 10 times as long as the very near future; natural logarithms come into the picture when one integrates the function $1/x$; and where does the function $1/x$ come from? – well, remember the series of probabilities, 1/2, 1/3, ... , 1/10.) The probability of my finding myself in the very near future if B is in the near future is thus almost exactly 33 percent. A similar calculation shows that the probability of my finding myself in the very near future if B is randomly chosen from the next million years is $\frac{1}{10,000}$ the sum of 1 and the natural logarithm of 10,000. (A million years is 10,000 times as long as the very near future.) This number is about 0.00102. The probability that B lies in the near future given that I have found myself in the very near future is thus (by Bayes's theorem)

$$0.001 \times (0.3302 \,/\, 0.00102) = 0.3234.$$

The bottom line is: if I find myself in the very near future (in the circumstances imagined), I can conclude that the probability that B lies within the next 1000 years is just over 32 percent. (A considerable multiple of the antecedent probability of this hypothesis, which was $\frac{1}{10}$ of 1 percent.)

Now let us map this example on to another example. Suppose that God, as in the book of Genesis, created the human race on a particular day and at a particular hour: at 11 o'clock on that day there were no human beings and at noon there were (fully formed adult language-users). Let us call this event the Creation. But suppose that, departing from the Genesis story, God created several hundred human beings, and that (by his will) the human species was destined to number in the low hundreds and to live clustered together in a single community for the duration of its existence. (Every generation of human beings, moreover, had lifespans of the three-score-and-ten order: there were no Methuselahs.) God told his human creations the following fact immediately after the Creation: they were not (that is, their species was not) to exist forever. At some point (the Omega Point), humanity would come to an end in a natural disaster (always a real possibility for a population confined to a small geographical area). God revealed only this about the time-frame of the extinction of humanity: the Omega Point was *at most* 1 million years after the Creation. The Omega Point in due course arrived and the human species came to an end, like a tale that is told. Many millions of years later, the earth was inhabited by another intelligent species. This race invented time machines and, using these marvelous devices, had covertly observed human history, from the Creation to the Omega Point (the dates of both of which some of them of course knew). For a crime unintelligible to us, a member of this species was sent into temporal exile, to live among the long-extinct human beings. He did not himself know the date of the Omega Point or how long after the Creation it was, but he understood the concept, and he was told this by the authorities: "We are going to place you at a point in human history that we shall choose at random; in effect, we will put all the dates between the Creation and the Omega Point in a hat and draw one of them. (If your 'arrival time' turns out to be only a year or two before the Omega Point – well, that's just too bad.)" After the exile had been placed among the human beings and had learned their language, he was rather surprised to learn that he had "arrived" only 96 years after the Creation.

Could he conclude anything about how long it was till the Omega Point? (We assume the human beings have told him what *they* know: that the Omega Point would occur at most 1 million years after the Creation.) If our reasoning in the previous example is correct, one thing he was in a position to conclude is this: the probability that the Omega Point was within 1000 years of the Creation on the proposition that he has found himself within 100 years of the Creation was about 32 percent. And, of course, any human being to whom he told his story would have been able validly to infer the same conclusion.

Now: remove the "temporal exile" from the story. Or turn him into a fiction within the story: a science-fiction writer among the human beings of the First Century tells the story of the appearance in their century of an alien temporal exile from the far future, and of the unsettling piece of reasoning that his appearance in the First Century occasions. A reader of this tale smiles at its cleverness – and then a disquieting line of argument occurs to him:

Am *I* not in a position very like that of the Temporal Exile? True, I "arrived" in the First Century not by being brought from another era in a time machine to a point in human history that was chosen at random, but by being born in it. Nevertheless, I simply *find myself* in the First Century – just as the exile in the story did. Now maybe the metaphysical theory of the essentiality of origins is correct, and *I* couldn't have been born at any other point in human history. Maybe the probability of my being born in any other century is precisely 0 – whereas the Temporal Exile was as likely to find himself at any point in human history as any other. Still, this consideration, if true, seems somehow irrelevant to my worries. Suppose God were to reveal to us human beings that we don't come into existence in our mothers' wombs. Suppose he told us that we had some sort of pre-existence in a Platonic heaven, and that the year of each person's physical birth was selected by angels throwing celestial dice.

Would that revelation change the way I should regard the logical force of the unpleasant argument that has occurred to me? I am imagining that I have learned that it is literally true that for any two calendar years in human history there was an equal and non-zero probability of my being born in either year. Having learned this, should I say, "*Now* I see that the argument that troubles me is a good one – but if I hadn't learned the strange truth about my pre-existence and how the year of my birth was selected, I ought to have said that the argument had no force"? (There can be no doubt that if the imaginary revelation were true, my epistemic position would be exactly that of the Temporal Exile.) For the life of me, I can't see that the imaginary revelation would make a difference to the force of the argument. Whatever I should conclude on the assumption of pre-existence-and-random-selection-of-year-of-birth, I should conclude the same thing on the assumption that I came into existence in my mother's womb and could not possibly have come into existence at any other point in history. I very much fear that my reasoning is right: I must conclude that there is a probability of 32 percent that the human species will come to an end by the thousandth year after Creation. If I were a bookmaker (an ideally rational bookmaker), and if someone came to me and wanted to bet that the Omega Point would come by the thousandth year after Creation, then (assuming there was some way to settle the bet) I shouldn't be able to offer him very attractive odds. I should have to offer to pay him some amount less than $2.12 on the dollar if he won.[13]

This reasoning seems to me (me, the author of this paper, not me, the fictional reasoner) to be pretty good. If it has a weak point, that weak point has, I believe, nothing to do with the applications of Bayes's theorem it contains or with the determination of this or that probability. It is, rather, a premise of this reasoning that could be put a little more explicitly in these words:

> Let n be the number of years humanity exists – from beginning to end. If a human being (who does not know what number n is) knows he was born m years after the beginning of humanity, he may, for the purposes of probabilistic reasoning like that illustrated in our examples, treat m as a number chosen at random from among the numbers 1, 2, 3, . . . , n–1, n.

I am really not too sure how plausible this premise is. I had my fictional reasoner defend it by a clever mixture of rhetoric and picture-thinking. But how plausible is it – really? Again: I'm not sure. I'll leave it to the reader to decide. In aid of this task, I leave the reader with two more imaginary cases, cases that are intended to serve as "intuition pumps." The first (these are my own subjective reactions; the reader's may differ) works against the principle and the second works in its favor. (I am at a loss to explain my differing reactions to these two cases.)

In the first case, suppose you are a passenger on a fully automated "generation ship," which is crossing some vast intersidereal or even intergalactic gulf at a very small fraction of the speed of light. As generally happens in science-fiction stories about generation ships, the passengers have, after a generation or two, somehow forgotten all the essential information about their voyage, including its destination and length (except this one fact: they know that the voyage will not be longer than 1 million years). You have no reason to regard any hypothesis about the length of the voyage as preferable to any other equally specific hypothesis, provided both hypotheses respect the 1-million-year upper bound and the lower bound established by the currently elapsed time-in-voyage. And you know that there will be passengers on the ship for the whole voyage – the automated systems that care for the passengers will see to it that the generations do not fail. At a certain moment, as you stare at the Great Chronometer (which registers elapsed time-in-voyage), it strikes you that it has been 96 years since the voyage began. You reason as follows: "Since human beings will inhabit the ship for the whole voyage, I may treat the number 96 (which corresponds to the point in the voyage at which the population of the ship currently 'finds itself') as a number chosen at random from among the numbers 1, 2, 3, . . . , n–1, n, where n is the length of the voyage in years. I can therefore calculate that there is a 32 percent chance that the length of the voyage is 1000 years or less."

In the second case, suppose you are a member of a tribe that lives on the banks of the Great River – and your tribe has always lived there, since the beginning of time. The ancient stories of your tribe (which cannot be doubted) tell you that the gods who made the Great River were constrained to make it 1 million miles long or less. Casting the sacred knuckle-bones, the gods chose at random a number n between 1 and 1,000,000 and made the River n miles long. (What the number n is, only the gods know.) Owing to the bounty of the gods, the River is densely populated by tribes much like your own along its entire length. The rules forbid members of your tribe ever to venture downstream, but great heros of the old days have explored the River upstream and have found (as expected) other tribes every few miles – *and* they have found that your tribal village lies 96 miles from the source of the River. You reason as follows: "Since the River is densely and uniformly populated along its entire length, I may treat the number 96 (which corresponds to the location at which *my* tribe 'finds itself') as a number chosen at random from among the numbers 1, 2, 3, . . . , n–1, n, where n is the length of the River in miles. I can therefore calculate that there is a 32 percent chance that the length of the River is 1000 miles or less."

As I say, I am not sure how plausible the premise I have called attention to is. There are, however, many objections to the kind of reasoning exemplified by the foregoing arguments, that are unrelated to the question of the plausibility of this premise. None of them seems very convincing to me. I will mention only one, the first to occur to almost everyone (including me) on his or her first encounter with the Doomsday Argument. Applied to our last example, this objection could be put as follows. "Look, given that the banks of the Great River are populated in the way you have imagined, *some* tribes have to find themselves within 100 miles of the source of the River. To simplify the picture, assume that the River is divided into 100-mile 'segments,' and that exactly one tribe lives in each segment. Your imaginary reasoner's tribe just happens to be the one that does 'find itself' in segment 1. They can't *infer* anything from this fact. Suppose there were 10,000 rivers, one of them one segment long, one two segments long, and so on ... up to the one that is 10,000 segments or 1 million miles long, all of them having one tribe living in each of its constituent segments. On each of these rivers, there will be a tribe that lives in its first segment. But only 10 of these tribes, $\frac{1}{10}$ of 1 percent of them, will live on the banks of a river 1000 miles long or less. A member of one of the first-segment tribes should therefore believe that there's only one chance in 1000 that 'his' river is 1000 miles long or less."

Answer. Well, yes – so he should, if he knows he is on the bank of one of 10,000 rivers having the lengths and population-distributions you have imagined. But the situation is different for a tribal reasoner who knows that there's just one river and, antecedently to his observation that his tribe lives in its first segment, has no reason to prefer any of the hypotheses "The River is 1 segment long," ..., "The River is 10,000 segments long" to any other. Both these "states of knowledge," and the reasoning each authorizes, can be represented by "pre-existence and random placement" analogies, but the appropriate analogies are different.

Here's the appropriate pre-existence-and-random-placement analogy for the case in which the tribal reasoner knows there are 10,000 rivers. There *are* 10,000 rivers, and they have the lengths you have imagined. Simple arithmetic shows that these rivers together contain a total of 50,005,000 segments.[14] Suppose that these segments have been numbered in the obvious way, and that each of 50,005,000 people (myself among them) is assigned a number from 1 to 50,005,000 at random and is then placed in the segment whose number he has been assigned. When all this has been accomplished, I am surprised to find myself in the initial segment of one of the rivers. (Surprised because there was only about one chance in 5000 that I'd find myself so placed. Still, I might reflect, it had to happen to someone; in fact it had to happen to 10,000 people.) Now what is the probability that the river on which I have been placed is at most 10 segments (1000 miles) long? Why, just the proportion of the rivers that are at most 10 segments long: $\frac{1}{10}$ of 1 percent. Note that the antecedent unlikelihood of my finding myself in the initial segment of one of the rivers does not figure in this calculation. I'd make the same calculation if I knew that I had been set down in a segment randomly chosen from the initial segments.

Here's the appropriate pre-existence-and-random-placement analogy for the case in which the reasoner knows there is one river. Again, there are 10,000 rivers of the different lengths you have imagined. One of the rivers is chosen at random. Then one of that river's segments is chosen at random, and I am placed in it. I find myself in its first segment. Now what is the probability that the river on which I have been placed is 10 segments long or less? As our earlier calculations show, it is about 30 percent.[15] In this analogy, it is the initial choice of one river that corresponds to there *being* one river; once that choice has been made, the other rivers might as well not exist. The chance that this one, chosen river will be 10 segments long or less is of course only $\frac{1}{10}$ of 1 percent. This is the antecedent probability of the river I find myself on being 10 segments long or less. But this antecedent probability is raised by the fact that I have found myself in its first segment, for the probability of this outcome is about 0.3 on the hypothesis that the river is 10 segments long or less, and only about 0.001 on the hypothesis that the river is 10,000 segments long or less.

I conclude that the reasoning that led our First Century human being to assign a probability of 32 percent to the hypothesis that the Omega Point would occur within 1000 years of the Creation is at the least very plausible.

Now what is the application of this reasoning to *our* situation, the actual human situation? Someone might protest that it has none, because (even if it contains no mistake) we *don't* "find ourselves" at a point in time that is at all close to the origin of our species. After all, however we define "human being," there have been human beings for a least 100,000 years. If there have been human beings for 100,000 years, it seems, reasoning in the style of the Doomsday Argument may convince us that it is likely that the human species will come to an end in the next million years, but not that it is likely that it will come to an end in the next 1000 years.

But note. Suppose humanity lasts another 10,000 years and that population levels remain at least what they are now for the remainder of our existence. (The assumption that the human population will be at least as large as it is now for the remainder of our existence as a species is very plausible. It is not, of course, certain: it is possible that some natural or man-made disaster – or some revolution in human reproductive ethics – will reduce the human population to a few millions, and that human beings will thereafter gradually decrease in numbers till the species finally flickers out of existence 10,000 years from now.) In that case, we present-day human beings do not find ourselves close to the point of human origin if we measure "closeness" in terms of simple duration: we find ourselves perhaps 90 percent of the way along the road from the origin to the extinction of our species. But suppose we measure "closeness to origin" another way: in terms of the number of human beings who have preceded us and the number of human beings who will follow us. By that measure, we are very close to the point of human origin indeed, since only a very small proportion of the whole set of human beings – past, present, and future – precedes us; almost every member of this set is yet to be born. This is, of course, because of the extraordinary population explosion of the last 200 years: for most of human history, the number of human beings has been only a very small fraction of what it is now and (given our assumption about the future) of what it will be at any time in the next 10,000 years.

If the human population were always about the same (or so the Doomsday Argument attempts to convince us), one would not expect to find oneself in the first $\frac{1}{100}$ of its span of existence; that is to say, one would not expect to find oneself among the first 1 percent of the human beings who ever live. But is it not reasonable to suppose that this second way of describing what human beings would not expect would apply no matter what a graph plotting the human population against time looked like? If the human species ends a few hundred years from now (and if its numbers remain high till shortly before their final, precipitous drop to 0), you and I shall be "average" human beings in this sense: the number of human beings who lived before us and the number of human beings who will live after us are roughly comparable. But if humanity lasts another 10,000 years at current or higher population levels, the number of human beings who will live after us is vastly greater than the number who lived before us. It seems that reasoning similar to the "doomsday" reasoning we have considered – but without the "constant population" assumption – suggests that there is a significant probability that the human species will come to an end soon. Again, the reader is invited to consider spatial analogies. Suppose one is an inhabitant of an island (its size is unknown: it may be anywhere from 200 miles across to the size of Australia) that is very sparsely populated near its coasts but becomes increasingly densely populated along any line drawn from a point on its coast to its center – or at least this increase displays itself on the first 100 miles of any such line. You find yourself at a point 100 miles from the coast. The interior of the island is somehow hidden from you: you are able to look only "outward," toward the coast. A powerful telescope shows you that the island is very sparsely populated within 90 miles of the coast (at the coast, the population density is about one person per 1000 square miles, a figure that gradually increases to about one person per 700 square miles 90 miles inland). Between 90 and 98 miles inland, the population density increases rapidly and between 98 and 100 miles inland, it increases explosively: at 98 miles inland there are four people per square mile, and, at 100 miles inland (where you live) there are 40 people per square mile. Would it be more reasonable for you to believe that the island's center is just a few miles inland from you or that it is hundreds of miles inland from you? If you had always unreflectively believed that your island was a huge island, an island the size of Australia, should the discovery of the facts about the increase in population density between the coast and the point at which you find yourself lead you to revise the probability of the "huge island" hypothesis downward? Significantly downward? In considering these questions, it might be useful to ask yourself whether someone in your situation can properly think of himself as living very close to the shores of a "population island," an island that is, as it were, made of people, and to ask yourself whether you can properly phrase the "huge island" question this way: Do I live near the shores of a large or of a small population island? (If so, the question seems closely analogous to the question, "Am I on a large or a small island?" as it presents itself to the central character in the "hotel room" case.)

Here I leave and commend study of the Doomsday Argument to you.

I close with two observations.

First, as we have seen, the cogency of the Doomsday Argument depends partly on the antecedent probability of the hypothesis that the human species will come to an end soon. Bayesian reasoning can suggest to us that we ought to revise our antecedent estimate of this probability upward, perhaps significantly upward, perhaps to multiply it by, say, 100. But an insignificant probability multiplied by 100 may still be an insignificant probability. Is there any good reason, any good reason independent of the considerations put forward in the Doomsday Argument, for thinking that the human species may come to an end soon? Well, there are all sorts of perfectly respectable scenarios (scenarios put forward by recognized authorities as representing real possibilities) according to which humanity will come an end within a few hundred years.[16] There are various all-too-real possibilities that any thinking person must recognize: thermonuclear or ecological or epidemiological catastrophe. And there are a large number of scenarios that are (at a reasonable guess) individually of small probability but which must each be added into the aggregate reckoning: a comet or asteroid may hit the earth in the near future; a nearby (astronomically speaking) supernova may irradiate us; an ill-advised experiment in high-energy physics may tip us catastrophically out of the metastable false vacuum in which, for all we know, we exist into the yawning abyss of the true vacuum; our computers and automated systems may eventually achieve intelligence, or a reasonable facsimile thereof, and decide to dispense with us. About 30 or 40 such "small probability" extinction scenarios have been suggested by respectable scientists; no doubt even their aggregate probability is not very large, but we can't be sure that a few of them don't have a much greater objective probability than we suppose. And, of course, there is always the unknown: our species may soon enough face dangers that we can no more conceive of than Jules Verne could have conceived of hydrogen bombs.[17] In sum, we are not in a position to say that the antecedent probability (antecedent to our consideration of the Doomsday Argument) of humanity's coming to an end in the next few hundred years is negligible. Any argument, therefore, that tells us that this probability is significantly greater than we could have guessed simply by contemplating "doomsday scenarios" and trying to estimate their aggregate probability is of real interest. (For all sorts of reasons: for one thing, if it were generally accepted, it might lead us to be more cautious in our military and political and scientific undertakings. The conclusion of the Doomsday Argument is not, and has never been presented as, a *sentence* of doom; the argument concerns probabilities, not certainties.)

Secondly, there is a theological point to be made. Let us return to the eschaton expected by the Abrahamic religions. Suppose one believes, as I do, that there will someday be such an eschaton. If so, there will be no doomsday – not in the sense of the extinction of the human species,[18] for humanity has, we believers suppose, an eternal future. Is the Doomsday Argument therefore an argument that should lead us believers to revise downward the probability we assign to the expected eschaton (and therefore to the whole set of our religious beliefs, for the eschaton is an essential and inseparable component of those beliefs)? By no means. Doomsday, in both the popular sense and the strict theological sense (the eschaton) implies the end of human life as it has always been: the end of the cycle of reproduction and death, the end of the addition of new members to the human species. Proponents of metaphysical naturalism naturally take "the end of human life as it has always been" to be just exactly the end of human life. Those who believe in a coming eschaton, I would suggest, should regard the Doomsday

Argument this way: whatever probability they assign to the eschaton's coming in the next few centuries, they should regard the Doomsday Argument, or Bayesian reasoning in the doomsday style, as significantly raising this probability. If naturalists who find the Doomsday Argument cogent doubt whether Jews, Christians, and Muslims can so comfortably accommodate doomsday reasoning to their belief in an eschaton, I suggest they consider the following story. Suppose the search for extraterrestrial intelligence is finally successful, and we receive a message from an ancient species elsewhere in the galaxy. This information is contained in the message: there are many intelligent and technologically able species in the universe, hundreds of which the originators of the message have been in contact with, and *every* such species sooner or later achieves physical immortality, and thereafter ceases to reproduce, continuing in existence for geologically vast periods of time simply in virtue of the immortality of its individual members – those fortunate enough (or in my view unfortunate enough; but that's beside the point) to have been alive when their species achieved immortality. Let us call a species' transition to this state its secular eschaton. After this information has been given us, it is reasonable to for us to believe that the human species will one day experience a secular eschaton. Should not anyone who, before this information was made known to us, regarded the Doomsday Argument as significantly raising the probability that humanity would become extinct soon, now regard the argument, or the style of reasoning it embodies, as significantly raising the probability that humanity will achieve its secular eschaton soon?

Notes

1   Strictly speaking, I should have said something like "the laws of reality." The laws of nature coincide with the laws of reality only if nature coincides with reality: that is, if naturalism is true. If naturalism is false – because, say, there exists a God who has plans for humanity that are not constrained by the laws of nature – it may be that something awaits us in the future that belongs to none of the possible futures that are consistent with the present and the laws of nature. If God exists, "the laws of reality" will be just that set of propositions that supervene on the divine nature. If God does not exist but naturalism is nevertheless false – if naturalism is false for some other reason than that there is a God – the laws of reality would supervene (or at least partly depend) on the nature or natures of whatever beings it is whose existence is not a part of the natural order. (For I suppose that naturalism is false if and only if there are beings – not abstract entities, but beings with causal powers – whose existence is not a part of the natural order.) In the text, I shall, for the sake of simplicity, use the phrase "the laws of nature" to mean "the laws of reality."

2   For present purposes, "There is a probability of 0.57 that it will be the case that p" may be understood to mean, "In 57 percent of the physically possible futures that are continuous with the present, it will be the case that p." This conception of the probability of future events would not do for most purposes. It has the consequence that if the world is deterministic, then, for any p, the probability that it will be the

case that p is either 0 or 1; and it has the consequence that only in certain special cases (the case of a proposition asserting that an eclipse will take place at a given moment, for example) would it be possible to know or even make any reasonable guess about whether the probability of a proposition about the future was 0 or 1. This consequence of our conception of probability of a proposition about the future, therefore, shows that this conception can hardly be the conception that is employed by insurance companies. It will do for our highly abstract and theoretical purposes, however. In fact, it will not only do, but is exactly the conception our purposes require.

A remark for conceptual puritans: "In 57 percent of the possible futures, p" is a colloquial way of saying, "The measure of the set of possible futures in which p is 0.57 times the measure of the whole set of possible futures."

3   For citations of Nietzsche's scattered remarks on *die ewige Wiederkunft*, see Arthur C. Danto, *Nietzsche as Philosopher* (New York: Macmillan, 1965), chapter 7.

4   Nietzsche believed that he himself would return eternally, and embraced this idea joyfully. The Greek atomists found this a horrible possibility and maintained that the "future duplicates" of Nietzsche (or whomever) that the cosmos produced would not be Nietzsche but rather people, as we should say today, qualitatively but not numerically identical with him. It seems plausible to suppose that if the Greek atomists had read Kripke on the essentiality of species-origins, they would have maintained that the human-like beings of future cosmic reorderings would not be human beings but would rather be members of infinitely many numerically distinct species with the same anatomical and physiological characteristics as human beings.

5   And possibly the Old Norse or "Odinic" religion. I say "possibly" because the Old Norse eschatology cannot be said with certainty to be historically independent of Christian eschatology.

6   Indeed, most, if not all, pagan mythologies contain stories about how the physical world came to be.

7   Apparently something like the Greek-atomist position (minus, perhaps, intermittent cosmic dissolutions and reorderings) was not uncommon during the so-called ages of faith – although of course it is not well represented in the written records of the period, which were mostly the works of clerics and monks. The following words were written around the year 1200 by one Peter of Cornwall, prior of Holy Trinity, Aldgate: "There are many people who do not believe that God exists ... They consider that the universe has always been as it is now and is ruled by chance rather than by Providence." Peter's manuscript is unpublished. Apparently he gives no explanation of what he means by "many people." These two sentences from his manuscript are quoted in Robert Bartlett, *England under the Norman and Angevin Kings, 1075–1225* (Oxford: Clarendon Press, 2000). I have taken them from a review of that book by John Gillingham, which appeared in *The Times Literary Supplement* (May 5, 2000), p. 26. I suppose the translation to be Bartlett's.

8   The Doomsday Argument is the work of several thinkers. The physicist Brandon Carter has the best claim to being its inventor. The most systematic exposition and defense of the argument is to be found in John Leslie, *The End of the World: The Science and Ethics of Human Extinction* (London and New York: Routledge, 1996). The presentation of the Doomsday Argument in the present essay is not based on this book, which I deliberately did not read till after I had finished a first draft of this

essay. I believe that nothing I say is inconsistent with Leslie's treatment of the Doomsday Argument. My presentation and defense of the argument (which is, of course, very abbreviated) contains nothing inconsistent with Leslie's. The main difference seems to me to be that I have made considerably more use of spatial analogies than Leslie does; but spatial analogies figure prominently in his treatment of the argument.

Like "the Big Bang," "the Doomsday Argument" is a dyslogistic name, coined by the intellectual opponents of its referent, and ultimately accepted by its proponents. As Leslie says, "[the more accurate name] 'anthropic argument suggesting that we have systematically underestimated the risk that the human race will end fairly shortly' would have been far too lengthy a label" (ibid., p. 194).

9   Suppose we have some evidence that is relevant to a thesis called Hypothesis. Call this Old Evidence. Suppose we acquire some relevant new evidence: New Evidence. Old Evidence and New Evidence together compose Total Evidence. How should we revise the "old" or "prior" or "antecedent" probability of Hypothesis (the probability of Hypothesis on Old Evidence) in the light of New Evidence? – that is, how are we to calculate the probability of Hypothesis on Total Evidence, given that we know the probability of Hypothesis on Old Evidence? Bayes's theorem is an answer to this question. Very roughly speaking, it tells us that the new probability of Hypothesis is a function of its antecedent probability and the degree to which adding Hypothesis to Old Evidence raises the probability of New Evidence. More exactly, Bayes's theorem tells us that the probability of Hypothesis on Total Evidence is equal to the probability of Hypothesis on Old Evidence multiplied by a certain ratio, the ratio of

The probability of New Evidence on (Old Evidence plus Hypothesis)

to

The probability of New Evidence on Old Evidence alone.

10   In these "hotel room" examples, I have glossed the fact that the sea may be invisible from a hotel-room window (for at least two obvious reasons) even if the hotel is close to the sea. No point of principle is affected by this fudge.

11   $0.01 \times 0.5 \ / \ [(0.99 \times 0.0002) + (0.01 \times 0.5)] = 0.9615384$.

12   Does this seem intuitively to be too high? Try the following game with playing cards (or do something equivalent with your computer or a table of random digits). Take 10 cards, ace to 10. Draw one at random and discard the higher cards. Then draw a card at random from the remaining cards. Do this a large number of times and record your results. You will find that you "end up with" the ace about 30 percent of the time. (And the deuce about 20 percent of the time, the trey about 15 percent of the time, the four about 10 percent of the time . . . and the 10 about 1 percent of the time. The sum of the 10 percentages is of course 100 (or would be but for my rounding off).

13   You can see that the odds my reasoner has calculated are *about* right if you consider the case in which the probability of the expected event is exactly $\frac{1}{3}$. Suppose someone wanted to bet that a thrown die would land either three or six. It's two to one that a thrown die won't land three or six: "won't" is twice as likely as "will." If you want

to bet that a die will land either three or six, a rational bookie will agree to give you any odds less than two to one: he'll agree to pay you $1.99 on each dollar you bet (or any smaller sum) if you win. Agreeing to pay a bettor $2.00 on the dollar in a bet that a die will land three or six would be a waste of a bookie's time, for, in an eternity of such bets, he'd simply break even. (The 12-cent difference – $2.12 versus $2.00 – is due to the difference between the probabilities 0.3333 ... and 0.32000 ...)

14 The sum of the first n integers (1, 2, ... , n) is $n(n + 1)/2$.

15 30 percent rather than 32 percent because of the "graininess" of the present example. In this example, I am placed within a randomly chosen 100-mile segment of a river, and not at a randomly chosen *point* on the shore of a river.

16 For an extended discussion and evaluation of these scenarios (I can think of none he doesn't consider), see chapters 1 and 2 of Leslie's *The End of the World*.

17 One of Verne's characters – I think in *From the Earth to the Moon* – does speculate, in a rather jocular fashion, that the world may end when an enormous boiler, heated to a pressure of 10,000 atmospheres, explodes. That wouldn't actually be possible, or not without fantastic innovations in materials engineering: a boiler the size Verne's character imagines, and made of any material *we* could imagine, would instantly collapse under its own weight. But there was an "unknown" possibility, a possibility now actual, the possibility of a device just as apt to destruction as the impossible device Verne put into his character's mouth.

18 In modern English, "doom" is hardly more than a romantic word for "death" and our understanding of "doomsday" reflects this sense of "doom." The original meaning of "doom," however, was something like "judgment," and the original meaning of "doomsday" – as in "Domesday Book" – was "day of judgment."

Suggested Further Reading

Bostrom, Nick (2002) *Anthropic Bias: Observation Selection Effects in Science and Philosophy*. New York: Routledge.

Edwards, Paul (ed.) (1992) *Immortality*. New York: Macmillan.

van Inwagen, Peter (1997) *The Possibility of Resurrection and Other Essays in Christian Apologetics*. Boulder, Colo.: Westview Press.

Zimmerman, Dean (1999) The Compatibility of Materialism and Survival: The "Falling Elevator" Model. *Faith and Philosophy*, 16, 194–212.

Chapter 12

The Many-Sided Conflict Between Science and Religion

Philip Kitcher

In 1882, when Charles Darwin died, his family planned to bury him in the local churchyard.[1] Their wishes were overridden by English popular opinion, and Darwin was awarded a large public funeral in Westminster Abbey. On that occasion, the dean of St Paul's delivered a eulogy in which he explicitly contrasted the initial reception of *The Origin of Species* with the view of the 1880s: the theory of evolution was no longer seen as a threat to religious belief. So the Anglican church made its peace with Darwin.

During the last 120 years many people have thought differently. Contemporary creationists often pose the question "Which nineteenth-century thinker has had the most baneful influence on subsequent thought?" – and answer it by identifying the bearded scientist who lies at Westminster. (An odd choice, one might think, given Marx's comments on the dormitive powers of religion, and Nietzsche's announcement of the death of God.) The conflict between Darwin and religion has become emblematic of the relations between science and religion. When the issues are so narrowly focused, it's not hard to motivate compatibilism, of the sort to which Anglicans have long been partial. Once upon a time I advocated compatibilism.[2] But I have lapsed. The relations between science and religion need to be considered from a broader perspective, and, when they are, the easy peace of 1882 no longer seems sustainable.

To introduce my theme, I'll start from a general view about large-scale change in the sciences. Since the publication of Thomas Kuhn's monograph on *The Structure of Scientific Revolutions*,[3] historians and philosophers have become aware that resolution of the debates that seem to have marked the most important revolutions in our understanding of nature was extremely complicated. Kuhn destroyed once and for all the myths that the triumph of Copernicanism in the early modern period was delayed only because its opponents were blind to the force of observations and reasoned arguments, and that Lavoisier won the day for his "new chemistry" by performing experiments that were resisted only because of the stubbornness of his adversaries. We have become used to the idea that, in these and kindred episodes, the eventual losers were able to put forward sophisticated reasons for their favored positions, and that the controversy was only closed when a wide range of considerations had been explored.[4] To cite a familiar slogan: in revolutionary science there is no "instant rationality."

The power of Galileo's *Dialogue Concerning the Two Great World Systems*[5] results from his confrontation of Aristotelian geocentrism with a diverse set of difficulties. Time and again, Simplicio, the spokesman for Aristotle, is forced to admit that he has no developed answer to the challenge at hand. Yet, in the style of one of the children's toys that bob back up when knocked sideways, Simplicio optimistically suggests that the investment of more time and talent in the Aristotelian program will solve the trouble. Similarly, in the 1780s, defenders of phlogiston chemistry must concede that they have no articulated accounts of the composition of substances, equipped to satisfy all the constraints Lavoisier's experiments compel them to accept – but they propose to continue the search for the missing analyses. Given any individual challenge, these responses are quite correct. Scientific theories always face unsolved problems, and it is eminently reasonable for a theorist not to overreact at the first sign of trouble. As the challenges mount, however, there comes a point at which reiteration of the theme is quixotic, and even pathetic – as Pope Urban's official readers undoubtedly saw when they read the lines Galileo had put into Simplicio's mouth.

A similar point applies, I believe, to conflicts between science and religion. So long as one focuses on a single area of difficulty, the religious believer has a natural response: there are things here beyond our understanding, points that logic and empirical knowledge cannot settle. Trouble arises when one recognizes the range of contexts in which optimism has to be invoked, and it is then natural to think of the faithful apologist as analogous to Simplicio or to the latter-day phlogistonians.

Darwinism and the Problem of Evil

Back then to Darwin, who can serve as the starting point for a much broader inquiry. No doubt it was easier in 1882, at the ebb of the fortunes of Darwin's idea of natural selection, to soften the impact of evolution. Sophisticated churchmen had, after all, long accepted the thesis of an ancient earth on which successive ecologies had appeared. Now they understood the history of life as a process of descent with modification in which all organisms were related. So long as they could resist the claim that natural selection has been the chief means of modification, they could conjure up a deity who set the entire enterprise in motion, and who probably intervened at crucial steps – for example in the speciation event that gave rise to *homo sapiens*.

Contemporary theists are not so lucky. Rehabilitated in the early twentieth century, natural selection offers us a mechanism for evolutionary change that doesn't seem particularly attuned to the predilections of a wise and beneficent creator. As Richard Dawkins points out, evolutionary arms races are prevalent in nature: antelopes and cheetahs are subject to opposed regimes of selection;[6] if genetic variations arise that favor improved evasion on the part of antelopes, cheetahs will starve; on the other hand, if there are mutations favoring increased cheetah speed, the antelopes will be eaten. When we envisage a human analogue presiding over a miniaturized version of the arrangement – peering down on his creation – it's hard to equip the face with a kindly expression. Conversely, it's natural to adapt Alfonso X's famous remark about the convolutions of Ptolemaic astronomy: had a benevolent creator proposed to use evolution under natural selection as a means for attaining his purposes, we could have given him useful advice.

Darwin was completely aware that his account of the history of life offered a ready explanation for the nastiness of nature: citing the same example that fascinates contemporary biologists as different as Dawkins and Stephen Jay Gould, he points out that we need no longer wonder at "ichneumonidae feeding within the live bodies of caterpillars."[7] This is only one instance in which the challenge to religious sensibilities is continuous with Hume's recapitulation of the ancient problem of evil. One Darwinian contribution to that problem lies in undermining appeals to the omnipresence of design in nature – the apparent fit between organism and environment testifies not at all to the beneficence of the deity but simply reflects the past operation of natural selection. Another lies in the depiction of a vaster canvas on which animal suffering can be displayed.

In fact, after Darwin, we can distinguish three distinct versions of the problem of evil. The first is the classic difficulty. The presence of evil is logically incompatible with the existence of an omnipotent, omniscient, and completely benevolent deity. Any such deity would, in virtue of its benevolence, eliminate evil insofar as it was able; because of its omnipotence and omniscience it would eliminate evil insofar as it wished to; thus a deity with all three attributes would eliminate evil entirely; the presence of evil in the world signals the absence of any such being. There is a well-worn way of dealing with the problem. Pain and suffering exist because, without them, human virtue would be logically impossible. Human vice exists, because, if it did not, human freedom, and hence genuine human virtue, could not exist. The presupposition of this attempted solution is that even an omnipotent and omniscient deity could not create beings who would freely always choose to do the good. Generations of philosophers of religion have tried to defend this presupposition by offering refined accounts of human freedom and the logical limits of omniscience. With scholastic ingenuity and nice distinctions, they struggle to maintain the bare possibility that even an omnipotent being might have to allow human wrongdoing as the price of freedom.[8]

The second variant of the problem of evil focuses specifically on instances of non-human suffering that would seem easily eliminable without disturbing any of the higher purposes alleged in the line of solution to the first problem. Throughout the history of life billions of animals have suffered painful and unnecessarily extended deaths. A world in which those deaths were swifter or less agonizing would leave the genealogy of organisms intact, preserving the supposed higher purposes of human virtue and freedom.[9] A creator with the traditional attributes would thus not produce the world we actually inhabit. To this argument, the standard response is to appeal to a purpose for the excess pain, one that is invisible from our limited human perspective. Once again, there is a scholastic struggle to explain why our normal canons of appraising hypotheses should be suspended here, so that we don't simply eliminate the suggestion of a hidden rationale.

The third version of the problem arises once we recognize that the idea that human beings and non-human animals might suffer for broader ends is difficult to reconcile with the assumption of divine justice. Few theists would be satisfied with the image of their deity as some monstrously consistent utilitarian who sacrifices the interests of some of its creatures in order to promote some broader good. Divine justice seems to require that the animals who suffer themselves be compensated, that the suffering is not simply instrumental to the wonders of creation but redeemed *for them*. Appreciation of the point has driven some apologists to propose that the holocaust victims benefitted because their suffering made possible a closer awareness of and relation to the deity.[10] Whatever moral sensitivies may be trampled in this characterization, it is surely vulnerable to an obvious point. If such extreme suffering really serves a genuine purpose that redeems it, then divine justice has to be squared with the recognition that many of us have been "deprived" of the opportunity for the wonderful rewards at which the theist gestures. If ordinary lives, free from acute torment, suffice for the state of union with the deity, then the suffering of the victims is not necessary and hence unredeemed. If, on the other hand, extreme agony is needed to attain a state of such transcendent quality that it compensates for the dreadful suffering, then those of us who do not experience such agony have been unjustly treated. The theist evidently has some delicate accounting to do.

We have then a long history, about 3 billion years of life, that has produced at the extreme end of one of many lineages a species whose special characteristics are supposed to give point to this apparent shaggy dog story. The principal mechanism that has guided the process is one that generates conflict, and sometimes acute suffering. Whether we focus on human life or on the lives of all sentient organisms, there are at least three difficulties in squaring the occurrences we observe with the alleged attributes of the deity. The conflicts generated by fusing Darwinian insights with classical philosophical concerns about evil and suffering pose severe research problems for traditional theists, whose confrontations with these issues frequently seem to resemble the flailings of seventeenth-century Aristotelians or late-eighteenth-century phlogistonians.[11]

The Appeal to Religious Texts and Traditions

Perhaps my judgment is too harsh. After all, if the theist could identify some independent justification for belief in a deity, then it would be reasonable to proclaim that there must *be* answers to the questions, even though they haven't yet been articulated. Of course many believers think exactly this, holding that their favored texts and traditions (whether oral or written) provide the needed justification. At this point other scientific studies generate new difficulties.

For more than two centuries, scholars have attempted to reconstruct the ancient worlds in which major religious texts were produced and the even more distant worlds of the events they purport to describe.[12] One of the main twentieth-century contributors to the study of the four Gospels offers a succinct account of the similarity between these kinds of investigations and those in the natural sciences.

> Geology attempts to reconstruct the history of the past by a highly scientific applica-tion of the method of observation. Facts over as wide a range as possible are collected, sifted, and compared, in order that hypotheses may be framed which will satisfactorily account for the observed phenomena. The critical investigations pursued in this volume are of a precisely similar character.[13]

The parallel with geology is apt. For like Darwin's great inspiration, Charles Lyell, the students of religious texts use present observations of the processes that occur in religious, social, and political life to probe the events of the distant past.

The conclusions they draw are often disconcerting. I'll draw on a tiny example. Luke's moving version of the events surrounding the birth of Jesus diverges from that offered by Matthew in many respects: Luke has Joseph and Mary traveling from Nazareth to Bethlehem, Matthew locates them in Bethlehem all along; Matthew has wise men and no shepherds, Luke has shepherds but no wise men (the Christianity with which I grew up solved the problem in the obvious way by combining everything). Furthermore, it's hard to reconcile the dates. Herod, a main character in Matthew's story died about 10 years before the appointment of the Roman official whom Luke takes to have been an administrator at the time of the nativity. But I want to focus on a different detail. Luke has to solve the problem of having the birth take place in Bethlehem, even though he views Mary and Joseph as inhabitants of Nazareth. His solution is offered in a passage that Christians are thoroughly familiar with

> And it came to pass in those days, that there went out a decree from Caesar Augustus, that all the world should be taxed. And this taxing was first made when Cyrenius was governor of Syria. And all went to be taxed, every one into his own city. And Joseph also went up from Galilee, out of the city of Nazareth, into Judea, unto the city of David, which is called Bethlehem; because he was of the house and lineage of David.[14]

The overwhelming evidence is that this is complete fiction.

For not only are there no records of a census or a general taxation at this time, but, even if there had been one, this is surely not the way in which it would have been conducted. We know something about Roman attitudes towards the religious lore and ethnic traditions of the Jews – at best, they saw them as barbaric enthusiasms. We also know something about the ways in which Romans obtained population counts and how they levied taxes. Instead of moving the population around, they quite sensibly dispatched their own trusted officials. Luke invites us to think of Cyrenius as having done something quite mad. In the interests of administering some kind of census or taxation, he encourages a mass migration so that there can be conformity to the ethnic principles of the natives.

Consider, for another example, the depiction of Pilate offered by the Gospels. The story of the Roman official offering to release Jesus and encountering a baying Jewish mob is thoroughly familiar, and has surely played a significant role in Christian anti-Semitism. But the action Pilate contemplates – releasing a prisoner for the local religious festival – is quite unprecedented in Roman administration of Judea, or any other province with indigenous zealotry. It's also incompatible with what we know of the man, some of whose repressive activities are documented, and who was, apparently, recalled because of protests against his harsh treatment of the Jews. There is, of course, a much simpler explanation for the presence of these stories. The canonical Gospels were written as the expression of a broader Hellenistic Jesus movement, after it was clear that the movement was unlikely to flourish as a reform of Jewish religion and after the Roman grip on the eastern Mediterranean had tightened. The evangelist who first recorded the story, Mark, chose a strategy of appeasing the Romans and making scapegoats of the Jews. It was probably sound politics, but I concur completely in the judgment of the Jesus Seminar: "That scene, although the product of Mark's vivid imagination, has wrought untold and untellable tragedy in the history of the relation of Christians to Jews. There is no black deep enough to symbolize adequately the black mark this fiction has etched in Christian history."[15]

These are not isolated examples. Two centuries of intense scholarship on the writings of early Christianity and on the spread of the Jesus movement have stripped away the stories that form the backbone of the religion, leaving us with an itinerant speaker, put to death by the Romans, whose oracular sayings we can still find morally insightful. Philology, archeology, history, political science, and sociology combine to yield a scientific hypothesis that places the historical Jesus in the company of Socrates, Hillel, and the Buddha – excellent company, to be sure – but that should leave us reasonably skeptical about his divinity, or about any connection to a deity.[16]

Matters are no different when we turn to the other major monotheistic religions. Scientific understanding of the Hebrew Bible interprets it as a collection of legends, some of them common to various tribes in the ancient Near East, some of them peculiar to the Jewish tradition, variously reformulated and retold by different sources, with emphases attuned to political struggles, particularly with respect to lines of rightful descent in kingship and in the priesthood.[17] Because the accounts of its origin are so much more detailed and explicit, the case of the Koran is especially clear. There's little reason to doubt that we have a tolerably accurate version of what the Prophet recited to his associates after his various excursions to the desert. What's at issue, of course, is the relation between the content of those recitations and the actual events in the desert, and, for all the reassurances that the Koran offers its readers, it cannot simply be read as self-authenticating. Muhammad may have said just the things that have been passed down to us, but there is more than one explanation for how he came to say them.

The effects of scientific study of religious texts have long been evident to those who have taught seminary students, and it's hardly surprising that religious fundamentalisms oppose such study with almost as much zeal as they lavish on Darwin. Julius Wellhausen's famous letter of resignation presents the problem poignantly:

> I became a theologian because I was interested in the scientific treatment of the Bible; it has only gradually dawned upon me that a professor of theology likewise has the practical task of preparing students for service in the Evangelical Church, and that I was not fulfilling this practical task, but rather, in spite of all reserve on my part, was incapacitating my hearers for their office.[18]

Thus if the considerations about pointlessness, evil, and suffering in a Darwinian world place an epistemological burden on the theist, it appears that appealing to the authority of texts and religious traditions cannot bear that burden.

The Evolution of the World's Religions

But it gets worse. The difficulties of relying on religious texts and traditions don't simply emerge from the revelations of scientific studies of individual instances. As our understanding of the diversity of world religions increases, it's hard for believers to avoid seeing themselves as participants in one cultural lineage among many. Just as each draws on the supposed authority of the tradition in which she stands, so must she recognize that others, with quite different, even incompatible, doctrines, do just the same. By what right can anyone maintain the privileged character of her tradition and its deliverances?

Muslims, Jews, and Christians, for all their squabbles, agree on many things. Each believer must appreciate, however, that had she been acculturated within one of the aboriginal traditions of Australia, or within a society in central Africa, or among the Inuit, she would accept, *on the basis of cultural tradition*, remark-ably different views. How is the symmetry broken? How does the believer show that her favored tradition is privileged?

The variety of belief across cultures is sometimes invoked to undermine our confidence in the findings of the natural sciences. Critics of the idea that we can claim approximate truth for our views about heredity or about chemical reactions point out that people in other cultures think differently. On what basis do we think of ourselves as right and them as wrong? How can the special status of Western science be maintained without committing a kind of cultural imperialism that imputes to other societies a failure of full rationality?

Although these are serious questions, I think that there is a straightforward answer in the scientific case. We are able to use our own views about chemical composition and about hereditary transmission to make extraordinarily precise predictions and exceptionally delicate interventions across a wide and increasing range of contexts. The cultural alternatives have no similar power: there is, for example, no Melanesian theory of genetics that will enable the breeding of fruit flies with some male and some female tissues or the manufacture of bacteria that will churn out large quantities of a desired protein. Such alternatives are lacking not because the Melanesians are irrational or stupid. Part of the explanation may lie in their not having formulated these problems, or in their not being interested in solving them. Another part surely stems from the institutionalization of natural science in the West in the seventeenth and eighteenth centuries, a process that has coordinated individual endeavors in ways that now flower in practically successful research.

Much more could be said to articulate this line of response. But this is not the occasion for saying it.[19] Instead, I want to point out an important disanalogy between the import of religious and scientific diversity. Reflecting on the sciences, we can specify a criterion for breaking the symmetry: the appeal to success in prediction and intervention at which I have gestured. Nothing similar is available in the religious case. There's no special triumph of one tradition to which believers within that tradition may point to display their special privilege.

An obvious way to address the difficulty is to focus on points of agreement among all religious traditions. Perhaps the believer can isolate a core doctrine, shared worldwide, and take this, at least, as genuine religious knowledge.[20] Comparative studies of religion have made it abundantly clear how difficult it is to find common features – hence the frustratingly vague definitions of "religion" that invoke some "acceptance of the transcendent." Certainly, if religions are to be counted as authoritative only insofar as they agree, the faithful will be hard pressed to vindicate the notion of a personal deity.

But there's a deeper point, one that cuts not only at the inclusive strategy just indicated but at any method of relying on sacred texts and traditions. Why have religions flourished in all – or, at least, almost all – of the societies that historians and anthropologists have discovered? The religious answer is that all these groups have had an appreciation, however dim or partial, of the fundamental religious phenomena. Studies of the spread of religious movements in contemporary and historical societies enable us to offer a scientific rival. Religions spread within societies when they offer the members of those societies things that those members want; they spread across societies when they encourage social cohesion, and when they enable a society to deal successfully with its neighbors. Religious doctrines don't have to be true to be good at doing these things. Truth (like Mae West's goodness) may have nothing to do with it.[21]

Consider some examples. Detailed sociological studies of conversions to the Unification Church have revealed that the Moonies were highly attracted by the companionship that church membership offered – indeed the studies revealed that a good recruitment strategy was to seek out the lonely in urban areas.[22] Similarly conversions to Christianity in the Greco-Roman world were plainly facilitated by the perceptions of upper-middle-class pagan women that the lives of their Christian counterparts were better than their own: husbands were more faithful and less abusive.[23] An intriguing conjecture proposes that, in an urban world marked by filth and recurrent outbreaks of plague, the Christian injunction to comfort the sick would have raised survival rates at times of epidemic, simply because of the good effects of giving water and other forms of basic care; outsiders thus saw that Christians recovered more frequently, and may have attributed this to divine concern for their well-being.[24]

I suggest taking an evolutionary perspective on the history of religions. Societies have bequeathed their forms of culture to the extent that those societies have maintained themselves, spawned new societies, and attained cultural domination over other groups. For most religious believers, most of the religious doctrines held throughout human history must count as false, if not absurd; there are simply too many contradictory stories in the vast diversity of world religions. From the evolutionary perspective, there is nothing surprising in this. Provided that a bundle of religious claims satisfies the needs of a group, promotes the harmonious interactions within that group, and indirectly helps either in generating new descendant groups or taking over others, it will become prevalent. There are abundant reasons for thinking that packages of religious doctrine are especially good at doing these things: acts of great courage and sacrifice have often been encouraged in the name of religious rewards. For another example, we can turn to the use of religion to back the rules of the tribe. A common theme in the explanations offered by hunter-gatherers for their maintenance of the totem rules, is that, even when apparently alone, they are observed by a being "who, from his residence in the sky watches the actions of men" and who "is very angry when they do things that they ought not to do, as when they eat forbidden food."[25] To the extent that a crucial problem in the evolution of sociality is that of making defection or cheating unattractive, the idea of an all-seeing deity with punitive powers is a brilliant invention.

From the cultural evolutionary perspective I've sketched there's a simple explanation for the prevalence of religions across the cultural lineages we know. Societies that failed to invent some package of religious ideas were at a selective disadvantage in the business of reproducing their cultures, because their rivals could mobilize techniques of social persuasion that preserved group integrity, promoted the formation of descendant groups, and led to successful absorption of neighbors. Each of us stands in the most recent generation of one of these cultural lineages. Contemporary Judaism, contemporary Christianity, contemporary

Islam, like the beliefs of contemporary hunter-gatherers, or of the Nuer, exist because they are modified descendants of socially successful myth-making originating at some distant point in the past. At least in outline, we have an explanation that treats all religious traditions symmetrically, identifying them as differentially successful and equally false.

The Appeal to Religious Experience

Perhaps, however, the idea of relying on text and tradition to take up the epistemological burden was a misstep. Religious believers might do better to try to ground their claims in the special experiences they have. Just as detailed historical studies of the New Testament were beginning to threaten conventional pieties, the Protestant theologian Schleiermacher delivered his famous brief on behalf of religious experience.[26] A century later, after most of the arguments I've condensed were troubling devout intellectuals, William James and his diligent student Starbuck undertook to provide a scientific investigation of the phenomena.[27] Their contemporary descendants might hope to find in religious experiences a justification for religious belief, one that can survive the scrutiny of any psychological inquiry.

If the statistics are to be believed, a large number of people have had some form of religious experience. But perhaps we should be a little worried about the statistics, since there seem to be quite remarkable swings from year to year, decade to decade.[28] Of course, the content of the experiences varies quite a bit: some hear voices in the fields, some feel the imprint of the wounds inflicted at the crucifixion, others have a sense of some "transcendent presence" with them throughout a long period, and yet others see the Virgin in a window in Brooklyn.

I have no doubt that the overwhelming majority of these reports are perfectly sincere. The important issue for the conflict between religion and science is why they occur. The preferred religious explanation is that the visionaries have, at least temporarily, a special ability to discern aspects of reality that our ordinary experience cannot disclose. The obvious scientific rivals invoke psychological and sociological causes – stimulation of normal sensory channels, against particular psychological backgrounds, induces people to assimilate their current experiences to the religious framework supplied by their culture, or by some culture with which they are familiar. Thus a storm on the road to Damascus may have caused a psychologically troubled Jewish tentmaker to resolve conflicts in his desires by representing his environment in the categories of the religious movement he was persecuting.[29]

How can we decide between religious and scientific understandings of such episodes? Let's start by reminding ourselves of the ways in which we come to recognize others as having ways of gaining knowledge that outstrip our own. Some children are able to determine with enormous speed whether or not numbers are prime, other people have absolute pitch, and yet others are able to report reliably on the type and vintages of wines. In all such cases, of course, we have independent ways of checking, and these are employed before anyone is attributed the pertinent ability. Throughout the history of Western religions, the search for analogous ways of checking has been important in the assessment of self-described visionaries: the medieval procedures for certifying anchorites and anchoresses involved elaborate comparisons of the contents of their alleged experiences with the orthodox articulation of church doctrine. But, at this stage of our inquiry, that approach to checking won't do. The import of my earlier arguments was that reliance on texts and traditions is epistemologically suspect, and indeed the turn to religious experience is attractive precisely because it promises a way of independently vindicating the claims of a religious tradition. So we can't hope to emulate the straightforward ways in which we credit others with special knowledge-generating abilities.

As with the validation of religious texts and traditions, the full force of the problem emerges in recognizing the wide diversity of religious experiences. William James rightly entitled his book *The Varieties of Religious Experience*, but from the perspective of contemporary studies in comparative religion, his range of examples was, understandably, narrow. The visions of Jews, Muslims, and Christians differ in ways we might view as fundamental until we attend to the reports offered by the Yoruba, the Inuit, and Australian aborigines about their own religious experiences.[30] To propose that the religious experiences of those whose lives are full of encounters with goddesses, ancestors, and totemic spirits are to be understood in psychosocial terms while those reported by Western monotheists are accomplished representations of religious truth invites obvious and unpleasant questions about why the psychosocial explanation shouldn't be accepted more broadly. To maintain that all the religious experiences are completely correct is evidently impossible: the reports of visionaries are massively inconsistent.

But there's an obvious intermediate strategy. Perhaps we can suppose that all sincere religious experiences disclose some aspect of the divine – they represent the "element of ultimacy" that is the essence of religion. On this account, there is a genuinely religious apprehension at the core of the world's varied religious experiences, but this is overlain and colored in each case by the social and psychological constructions of individuals and rival cultural traditions. Challenged to explain what this common element is, champions of religious experience may be reduced to gesturing at some transcendent source of order and meaning – for more substantive characterizations are likely to distinguish among the varieties of religious experience – but at least they can claim to have salvaged some minimal epistemic role for the episodes they endorse.

There are three main concerns about this strategy. First, it hardly delivers what believers want: the born-again Christian for whom Jesus is a constant living presence is unlikely to be greatly reassured by the suggestion that, while the rich content about a personal redeemer is a psychosocial construction, the core of the experience is an accurate sense of the transcendent. Second, if the core religious experience is genuinely ineffable, then the position is vulnerable to an objection that has been apparent ever since Hegel. A bare, unconceptualized given – whether in sensation or in some more recherché kind of experience – cannot serve as the foundation for knowledge. In the context of religious experience, the point has been thoroughly developed by Wayne Proudfoot, and it is, as far as I can see, devastating.[31]

The third difficulty is more strictly scientific than philosophical. My presentation has made it sound as though the episodes we are to assess for their knowledge-generating power might equally be explained in terms of a special ability to descry parts of reality or understood in psychosocial terms as delusions. The evidence from neurophysiology and psychology is currently fragmentary, but there are obvious suggestions about the contexts in which religious experiences occur and about the pedigree of the states induced. It's hardly surprising that a psychologist as astute as James should have recognized that an overwhelming number of the examples about which he knew should have occurred at times when people were obviously and profoundly troubled, and, much as he wished to arrive at a clear validation of religious experience, he conscientiously recognized the possibility that the supposed consciousness of some "transcendent element" sprang from psychological mechanisms he was unable to identify clearly. Almost a century later, studies of the frequency with which religious experience seems to occur to various kinds of people or to increase after the administration of known hallucinogens reinforce suspicions that subjects of religious experience are temporarily in states like those that permanently – and tragically – disconnect some people from surrounding reality. To say this is not to endorse the ethical legitimacy of some infamous experiments, nor is it to suggest that we can offer a scientific explanation of the psychological mechanisms, nor is it even to pretend that we have strong reasons for the hypothesis that religious experiences are delusional.[32] Rather we should recognize clearly that we don't know what to make of certain parts of human experience. Given the extent of our ignorance in this area, supposing that religious experiences can somehow be assimilated to the categories and doctrines of ancient doctrines that have descended to us by a lengthy process of cultural descent with modification is a blind leap into space.

Faith

And that, you might think, is just the point. My approach has been to survey the ways in which many scientific disciplines bring difficulties for the religious believer on a number of fronts. Throughout, I've been pitting scientific evidence against religion, as if the believer claimed to know – and, of course, sometimes, in unguarded moments, theists will use this vocabulary ("I know that my redeemer liveth"). Many religious people surely find that type of formulation irritating (to understate), and would insist that conflicts between science and religion are resolved, across the board, because the believer isn't in the business of weighing evidence. Acceptance of religious doctrines and precepts is a matter of faith.

This line of escape presupposes that it is valid, at least on occasion, to adopt views that are not supported by the evidence. The presupposition can be questioned, and indeed it was questioned more than a century ago by a talented British mathematician, who is little known because he died young. William Clifford belonged to a group of late-Victorian intellectuals who saw a different conflict between science and religion, one that left no moral justification for leaps of faith. [33] The heart of Clifford's claim is that our beliefs are consequential: in light of what we believe we act, and in acting we affect the well-being of others. We owe it to those who will be touched by what we do to form accurate beliefs, and we can only discharge our responsibility if we apportion assent to the evidence. In Clifford's famous example, the shipowner whose wishful thinking leads him to send out an unsound ship has made a moral lapse when he disregards available evidence.

Mathematicians aside, most people remember Clifford because he provoked the most celebrated essay of one of America's most celebrated philosophers. William James responded that Clifford's view was too narrow. In "The Will to Believe," he argued that Clifford had ignored a particular kind of choice people have to make. On some occasions, we find ourselves confronting options that are "forced, live, and momentous" – there is no way to avoid making a decision, there is no possibility of resolving our situation by gaining evidence, and the decision will make an important difference to our lives. Under such circumstances, James contended, there's nothing to do but jump, and, of course, he commended affirming doctrines that seem likely to improve our lives.[34]

In some ways, Clifford provided James with an easy target. For it's not hard to see that the agnosticism he favored has practical consequences like those of firm rejection of religious precepts: for the conduct of human lives, there seem to be only two alternatives; the choice seems both forced and momentous. Further, the evangelical rhetoric employed by Clifford and his contemporary descendants – like Richard Dawkins – encourages the view that scientism has itself become a religion, that religious faith is opposed by a rival, and less consoling, faith. But I think we can free his position from these defects, and that, when we do so, the fundamental point is sound.

Imagine a half-hearted believer. She makes the leap James recommends, but, having leapt, she is firmly aware of what she has done. Should the doctrines of her religion command of her something that she believes to be impermissible – by the lights of moral principles she independently accepts – she will override the religious commandment in favor of the secular prohibition. Nor will she treat the religious doctrine as a shortcut in the hard task of deciding what kinds of actions are morally correct, what kinds unjustifiable. She approaches these questions by reflecting on a variety of cases and on a range of moral theories that try to account for judgments about such cases. She regards her moral conclusions as fallible, but she thinks she will do better to pursue her reflective methods than to allow her favored religion to dictate what should and should not be done. As I said, she is firmly aware that, in adopting her religion, she has leapt beyond the evidence.

Contrast her with a more earnest character, one who adopts a religion on the basis of faith and then lets the doctrines adopted determine what is to be done. To the extent that this person has any independent views about moral matters, he takes them to be superseded by the chosen religious stance. In Kierkegaard's famous phrase, his faith expresses itself in a "teleological suspension of the ethical."[35] Should he come to believe that he has been divinely commanded to kill his son, he will take steps to do so; should he come to think that believers in other religions must be suppressed by force, he will undertake the suppression. Even if his life never brings conflict between the dictates of his religious principles and the actions he would have pursued had he tried to engage in serious reflective inquiry about moral matters, it will still be true of him that he *would* have subordinated carefully considered moral judgments to his faith in any situation of conflict.

The heart of Clifford's argument is that this earnestness, this zeal, is morally unjustified. Actions taken because of submission to principles adopted on blind faith can – and throughout human history have – brought intense suffering to many people. When such actions conflict with the conduct recommended by systems of morality that would have been adopted under a more reflective and wide-ranging inquiry, then both the actions and the attitudes underlying them are culpable.

With the half-hearted believer matters are different. Her religion is carefully contained, allowed to play no substantive role in her psychological life. This kind of faith can coexist with the scientific critique. But it is pertinent to ask if a faith so attenuated is worth fighting for. If it's true that "a difference, to be a difference, must make a difference," then the distinction between the half-hearted believer and her agnostic counterpart is slight indeed. Both Clifford and James would have emphasized, I think, the unimportance of not being earnest.

Conclusion

I have given a whirlwind tour of the many fronts on which hostilities between science and religion erupt. Vastly more could be said about each of them. But I want to close by recapitulating my main theme. The troubles of religion – signaled in twentieth-century strategies of evasion that invoke "objects of ultimate concern," "grounds of being," and "the performative character of religious discourse" – arise not because of forced capitulation in a single arena. Rather, the difficulties are everywhere, kept out of view, I believe, only because of a myopic perspective. Pose the issue solely as a conflict between monotheistic religion and Darwin, and the believer, while on the defensive, can still hope to find an escape. As we look more broadly, that hope diminishes until, I believe, it evaporates.

From the perspective I have commended, each contemporary human being stands at the tip of a long cultural lineage in which religious beliefs have played a prominent and often socially useful part. Our incomplete scientific knowledge provides us with a view of aspects of nature and of our own history that enables us to understand these beliefs for what they are. We can admire the works of art and literature they have inspired, we can view them sometimes as reinforcing moral claims that are warranted on independent grounds, but we should also see that they are wild extrapolations from our evidence and that they should not be earnestly adopted on blind faith. To take that attitude is, I trust, compatible with recognizing our profound ignorance about many aspects of our universe. The humanism I favor recognizes the limits and shortcomings of our knowledge; it simply denies that we can make up for these shortcomings by committing ourselves to consequential views that are at odds with what evidence we have.

Notes

1 An earlier version of this essay was delivered as a Templeton Lecture at Columbia University.

2 See the final chapter of Philip Kitcher and Patricia Kitcher, *Abusing Science: The Case Against Creationism* (Cambridge Mass.: MIT Press, 1982). My coauthor should not be held responsible for the fuzzy compatibilism of that chapter; she always urged a more resolute line.

3 Thomas Kuhn, *The Structure of Scientific Revolutions* (Chicago: University of Chicago Press, 1962).

4 Here I draw on my own reinterpretation of revolutionary episodes that Kuhn described differently (perhaps ambiguously). See my *The Advancement of Science* (New York: Oxford University Press, 1993), chapters 6 and 7.

5 Galileo, *Dialogue Concerning the Two Great World Systems*, trans. Stillman Drake (Berkeley: University of California Press, 1967).

6 Richard Dawkins, "God's Utility Function," *River Out of Eden* (New York: Basic Books, 1995).

7 Charles Darwin *On The Origin of Species* (London: John Murray, 1859; reprint, Cambridge, Mass.: Harvard University Press, 1964), p. 472.

8 For a contemporary formulation of the problem, see John Mackie, "Evil and Omnipotence," *Mind*, 64 (1955), pp. 200–12. The most strenuous defender of the "free will defense" has been Alvin Plantinga; see, for example, *The Nature of Necessity* (Oxford: Oxford University Press, 1974), chapter 9; and also *God, Freedom, and Evil* (Grand Rapids, Mich.: Eerdmans, 1977).

9 See William Rowe, "The Problem of Evil and Some Varieties of Atheism," *American Philosophical Quarterly*, 16 (1979), pp. 335–41. Rowe's formulation has attracted a number of attempts at rebuttal. See for example, Stephen Wykstra "The Humean Obstacle to Evidential Arguments from Suffering: Avoiding the Evils of 'Appearance,'" *International Journal for Philosophy of Religion*, 16 (1984), pp. 73–93.

10 Marilyn McCord Adams, "Horrendous Evils and the Goodness of God," *Proceedings of the Aristotelian Society*, supplementary volume 63 (1989), pp. 297–310. When I heard Adams make an oral presentation of this line of argument, several members of the audience found it so insensitive to the sufferings endured in the death camps that they left in moral protest.

11   Philosophers will know that there is an enormous literature on the part of Christian apologists, one that deals in fine distinctions of types of possibility. None of that literature really addresses all three of the problems in their full force. It is best seen, I believe, as the last gasp of a desperate scholasticism.

12   For a classic historical review of the first hundred years of the research, see Albert Schweitzer, *The Quest of the Historical Jesus* (Baltimore, Md.: Johns Hopkins University Press, 1998).

13   B. H. Streeter, *The Four Gospels* (London: Macmillan, 1926), p. 23.

14   Luke 2:1–4. Because of the beauty of its language, I have cited the Authorized (King James) version. Nothing turns on the choice of translation.

15   Robert W. Funk and the Jesus Seminar, *The Acts of Jesus* (San Francisco: Harper, 1998), p. 153.

16   For valuable work in this general tradition, see Dominic Crossan, *The Historical Jesus* (San Francisco: Harper, 1992); Helmut Koester, *Ancient Christian Gospels* (Philadelphia: Trinity, 1990); Elaine Pagels, *The Origins of Satan* (New York: Vintage, 1996); and Bart D. Ehrman, *Jesus: Apocalyptic Prophet of the New Millennium* (New York: Oxford University Press, 1999). I regard these works as providing evidence for my conclusion, even if the authors would prefer not to draw it.

17   An accessible introduction, presenting both consensus views and original, more controversial hypotheses, is Richard Elliott Friedman, *Who Wrote the Bible?* second edn. (New York: Harper, 1997). My argument does not depend on Friedman's extremely interesting novel proposals, but on the points he shares with other Biblical scholars.

18   Quoted in Friedman, *Who Wrote the Bible?*, p. 165.

19   I have addressed these points in "A Plea for Science Studies," in *A House Built on Sand*, ed. Noretta Koertge (New York: Oxford University Press, 1999); a more extensive treatment of some of the issues is provided in my "Real Realism: The Galilean Strategy," *Philosophical Review*, 110 (April 2001), pp. 157–97.

20   This approach is adopted by many of the contributors to Philip Quinn and Kevin Meeker, eds., *The Philosophical Challenge of Religious Diversity* (New York: Oxford University Press, 2000). Despite their obvious integrity, most Christian authors seem to me to make their task easier by ignoring the religions of Africa, Melanesia, Polynesia, and indigenous America.

21   I borrow this line from Michael Levin. See his article "What Kind of Explanation is Truth?," in *Scientific Realism*, ed. Jarrett Leplin (Berkeley: University of California Press, 1984).

22   See John Lofland and Rodney Stark "Becoming a World-Saver," *American Sociological Review*, 30 (1965), pp. 862–75.

23   Rodney Stark, *The Rise of Christianity* (San Francisco: Harper, 1997), chapter 5.

24   This hypothesis was first proposed by William H. McNeill in *Plagues and Peoples* (New York: Doubleday, 1977), pp. 108–9; it is developed by Stark, *The Rise of Christianity*, chapter 4. For other valuable perspectives on the spread of early Christianity, see Wayne Meeks, *The First Urban Christians* (New Haven: Yale University Press, 1983); Henry Chadwick, *The Early Church* (London: Penguin, 1967); W. H. C. Frend, *The Early Church* (Minneapolis: Fortress Press, 1982), and W. H. C. Frend, *The Rise of Christianity* (Philadelphia: Fortress Press, 1984).

25   See Edward Westermarck, *The Origin and Development of the Moral Ideas* (London: Macmillan, 1908) vol. 2, p. 671.

26 Friedrich Schleiermacher, *On Religion* (Cambridge: Cambridge University Press, 1988). Originally published in German in 1799.

27 William James, *The Varieties of Religious Experience* (New York: Longmans, 1902).

28 See Benjamin Beit-Hallahmi and Michael Argyle, *The Psychology of Religious Behaviour, Belief, and Experience* (London: Routledge, 1997), chapter 5.

29 For an elaboration of this view of Paul's conversion (which I find interesting but by no means established), see John Shelby Spong, *The Letters of Paul* (New York: Riverhead Books, 1998), preface, esp. xxvi–xxxvi.

30 I have learned about religious experience in different groups from Benjamin Ray, *African Religions* (Upper Saddle River, N.J.: Prentice-Hall, 2000), Steven Katz, ed., *Mysticism and Philosophical Analysis* (New York: Oxford University Press, 1978) and Stephen Katz, ed., *Mysticism and Sacred Scripture* (New York: Oxford University Press, 2000), especially from Katz's own informative contributions to these volumes.

31 See Wayne Proudfoot's classic study, *Religious Experience* (Berkeley: University of California Press, 1985).

32 See the discussion of the "Marsh Chapel miracle" in Beit-Hallahmi and Argyle, *The Psychology of Religious Behaviour*, 85ff. For a range of attempts to provide a psychological explanation of religious experience, see Bernard Spilka and Daniel McIntosh, eds., *The Psychology of Religion: Theoretical Approaches* (Boulder, Colo.: Westview Press, 1997). Particularly suggestive is the attempt by Wayne Proudfoot and Phillip Shaver to draw on attribution theory (Spilka and McIntosh, chapter 11), although, with the current fragmentary evidence, it seems to me premature to opt for any specific psychological mechanism. What is abundantly clear, however, is that there are many potential rivals that are at least as plausible as the believer's favored hypothesis. Philosophical attempts to salvage a justification for religious belief, such as those of Alvin Plantinga (*Warranted Christian Belief*, New York: Oxford University Press, 2000) and of William Alston (*Perceiving God*, Ithaca: Cornell University Press, 1999), while sometimes ingenious (Alston) and usually scholastic (Plantinga), show a notable failure to confront either the diversity of religious experience or the psychological findings.

33 William K. Clifford, "The Ethics of Belief," in *Lectures and Essays* (London: Macmillan, 1886).

34 William James "The Will to Believe," in *The Will to Believe and Other Essays in Popular Philosophy* (Cambridge, Mass.: Harvard University Press, 1979).

35 Søren Kierkegaard, *Fear and Trembling* (Harmondsworth: Penguin Books, 1985).

Suggested Further Reading

Gould, Steven Jay (1999) *Rocks of Ages: Science and Religion in the Fullness of Life*. New York: Ballantine.

Newman, John Henry (1982) *The Idea of a University*. Notre Dame: University of Notre Dame Press. Originally published London: B. M. Pickering, 1873.

Polkinghorne, John (1998) *Belief in God in an Age of Science*. New Haven: Yale University Press.

Polkinghorne, John (2000) *Faith, Science, and Understanding*. New Haven: Yale University Press.

Chapter 13

Theism and the Foundations of Ethics

William E. Mann

A normative ethical theory is a theory that tells us what is right and what is wrong. Somewhat more fully and precisely, a normative ethical theory specifies what is obligatory, what is forbidden, and what is permissible and why. We do not suffer from the lack of normative theories. There are deontological theories, consequentialistic theories, perfectionistic theories, and more. (For a contemporary sampling, see LaFollette, 2000.)

Among those theories one will find examples putatively based on various religious traditions. Contemporary philosophers have tended, for the most part, to look askance at such theories. Set aside for the moment those religious traditions, like austere versions of Buddhism, that depend on no gods. One source of philosophical antipathy towards normative theories based on theistic grounds is an argument that has its roots in Plato's *Euthyphro*. Supposing that the religious tradition in question is monotheistic, we can ask whether something is obligatory, for example, because God declares it to be obligatory, or whether God declares it to be obligatory because it *is* obligatory. Choose the first option and you appear committed to the view that whatever God declares as obligatory is obligatory just in virtue of his declaring it so. Had God capriciously declared that torture is obligatory, then torture would henceforward have been obligatory. The first option also appears to carry with it the implication that we are motivated to do what is obligatory out of fear: to transgress a divinely sanctioned obligation is to court divine wrath.

Choose the second option and other unpalatable consequences await you. On the second option the moral economy is already in place independent of God's declarations. Thus if torture is forbidden, then God would be mistaken or lying, were he to declare torture permissible or obligatory. So God, even on his best behavior, can function only as an educator and enforcer of a moral order over which he has no legislative control. Education and enforcement are important functions. There is no reason, however, to think that these functions cannot be discharged successfully by humans. The second option thus assigns no moral role unique to God.

The dilemma generated by these two options must be confronted by those who attempt to base a normative theory on their theistic convictions. In the remainder of this essay I shall sketch a case for one kind of monotheistic normative theory that provides a response to the dilemma. The theory is not one to which every monotheistic ethicist need give assent. It does, however, incorporate many of the features that are central to theism.

Constraints on Theory

What should one expect of *any* adequate normative theory? To what extent can a theistic theory meet these expectations? I begin by sketching briefly some criteria in answer to the first question. At the end of this essay I will return even more briefly to the second question.

An adequate normative theory should provide a rationally defensible, systematic, and coherent account or explanation of why the obligatory is obligatory, the forbidden is forbidden, and the permissible is permissible. One would expect that *rational defensibility* entails some fairly substantial universality condition. That is, the theory should specify a normative principle (or set of normative principles) that applies impartially and unexceptionably to all people. Utilitarianism and Kantianism are famously universal. One would also expect that rational defensibility includes some sort of consonance between the normative theory and our pre-theoretical intuitions about many cases. (One such intuition fuels the universality condition, namely, that persons, the primary subjects of concern of normative theory, do not differ from each other just insofar as they are persons.) It may well be that an adequate normative theory leads us to revise some of our judgments about right and wrong. But it is extremely hard to envision the possibility that an adequate normative theory would imply that all or even most of the pre-theoretical intuitions of reasonable, well-informed people were in error. A *systematic* account is one that provides unified justification for normative judgments made about a wide variety of cases. Our pre-theoretical intuitions might form what appears initially to be a laundry list of opinions about right and wrong. It might be that some of the intuitions remain unconnected to the others, even after the application of a normative theory. Nevertheless, an adequate normative theory should show us, in a convincing way, the *simile in multis* among seemingly diverse cases. Unconnected intuitions may then be regarded as a symptom either of an incomplete theory or of an insufficiently integrated set of intuitions. If the former, then the theory needs revision; if the latter, the intuitions need revision. *Coherence* includes but is not confined to logical consistency among the theory's principles. A normative theory that unequivocally implied that taking a life is always wrong and always not wrong would be incoherent in virtue of being inconsistent. A theory that implied that whenever motorists are driving on the right side of the road, they should shift to the left side, and whenever they are driving on the left side, they should shift to the right side, may pass the test of logical consistency but is surely incoherent nonetheless.

In addition to the conditions just mentioned, an adequate normative theory should provide agents with a guide to action and judges with criteria for appraisal of agents' performances. A normative theory's action-guiding aspects are pro-spective, telling an agent what ought to be done or avoided in situations of choice. Appraisal is primarily retrospective, an after-the-fact activity in which the agent or others may engage. Because the agents to whom normative theories are addressed are (or include) humans, an adequate theory must take into account actual human psychology. This requirement entails at a minimum that a theory's action-guiding principles should be *cognitively perspicuous* and connected to human motivational structure. Moral principles so complicated that they could be learned and applied only with great difficulty might be usable in the task of appraisal by a sophisticated judge with time to spare, but they would be virtually useless as a guide to action. But even a simple, easily learned principle can be difficult to apply correctly in making a decision. This point can be illustrated by considering the difference between act- and rule-utilitarianism. Act-utilitarians insist on the applicability of the utilitarian principle directly to individual choice situations: an act is right if and only if no other alternative act available to the agent has better consequences on balance. Rule-utilitarians argue that in many cases, especially cases involving the pressure of time, partial ignorance, and emotional bias, the agent's attempt to apply the utilitarian principle directly to a decision is apt to result in the wrong choice, by the lights of the utilitarian principle itself. Instead we should depict the situation differently. There is a set of succinct moral rules – rules like *Do not lie, Keep your promises*, and so on – the following of which tends to produce optimal results in the long run. These are the rules that should guide our action. The utilitarian principle then serves as the principle that validates the set of optimal, succinct moral rules. In sum, the rule-utilitarian claims that this version of utilitarianism pays sufficient respects to the limitations of human cognition. (This is the beginning, not the end, of a debate between act- and rule-utilitarians. For my purposes I need not endorse either side.)

Suppose that we have a normative theory that passes with flying colors the constraints of rational defensibility, systematicity, coherence, and cognitive per-spicuity. Even so, the theory might leave us cold. Suppose the theory says that I ought to do x. Why should I care about doing x? Different sorts of theories give different sorts of answers. Utilitarians enjoin me to bring about optimal con-sequences, taking into account everyone affected by my action. But why should I want to act that way, especially in circumstances in which what is optimal for others comes at a cost to me, a cost I can avoid paying by choosing an alternative action? Kantians claim that I should act only on that maxim that I would be willing to see become a universal law of human behavior; that so to act is the expression of complete practical rationality. Why should I care to act in that way? The response that my question is a kind of logical impertinence – asking for a reason for being rational presupposes my acceptance of rationality as dispositive

– misses the question's point. The question is not about reasons but about motives. Granted that reason reigns in the realm of rationality, what is supposed to *move* me to act as reason bids? Even if I am not prepared to become an expatriate from the realm, I can assure you that there are occasions when my desires urge me to be a scofflaw. Kantians do not deny the motivational power of desires. They are committed, however, to regarding as irrational every case of a person's acting on desires that are contrary to what reason dictates. Thus the burden on Kantians is to offer an account of practical reason according to which its proper functioning elicits motivation sufficient to eradicate or submerge any desires to the contrary.

The question posed in the previous paragraph expresses the concern that an adequate normative theory be *motivationally realistic*. It is not simply that once one understands the theory, one will see its point; one must in addition find the point attractive. And the "one" in question here must be a human person, fully equipped with the desires, emotions, and foibles to which humans are subject. A normative theory that ignores these conative aspects of human psychology might be an intellectually entertaining edifice, but who could or would want to dwell in it?

Further reflection may lead one to add further constraints on the notion of an adequate normative theory. I suspect, however, that one will not be led to abandon any of the constraints of rational defensibility, systematicity, coherence, cognitive perspicuity, and motivational realism.

On Making the Rules

Recall that the second option of the *Euthyphro*-inspired dilemma with which this essay began was the proposition that God declares something to be obligatory because it is obligatory, not vice versa. This option has the consequence that God plays, at best, a supporting role in our morality play: despite the room the option leaves him as educator and enforcer, he would seem to have delegated the education in and enforcement of moral norms to other, earthly actors. Perhaps the play has a final judgment scene, in which God has the last words to say about our fates. Even so, on the second option God's judgment would only be a matter of holding us accountable to norms of conduct, none of which were of his making. The dilemma's first option ascribes to God a much more central role, but we saw that it also appears to be vulnerable to two objections, one about divine arbitrariness, the other about ignoble human motivation. Nonetheless, I shall attempt a defense of this option, arguing that, properly understood, it has responses to the objections.

Let us express the first option's central thesis vaguely as the thesis that God makes the moral rules. If pressed to be more explicit about what the notion of "making" amounts to here, many theists, past and present, claim that making is achieved by *commanding*. Theists have biblical warrant for adopting this conception. In Exod. 20:1–17 God's revelation to Moses on Mount Sinai consists of 10 commandments: when Moses repeats them in Deut. 5:6–21, he appends to them the so-called Great Commandment – perhaps as a supplement, perhaps as a summary – to love God "with all your heart, and with all your soul, and with all your might" (Deut. 6:5). When a lawyer asks Jesus what the Great Commandment is, Jesus recites it and adds that there is a second like it, to love your neighbor as yourself (Matt. 22:39). Following this Biblical tradition we might suppose that any normative theory that accepts the thesis that God makes the moral rules is a "divine command theory." I suggest, however, that we not take the phrase too seriously, allowing that it might be both too wide and too narrow. Too wide, because it would be premature to foreclose the possibility that some divine commands are not intended by God to be morally binding. "Let there be light" expresses a command but imposes no obligations. Somewhat more controversially, one might argue that God's commandment to Abraham to sacrifice his son does not make the sacrifice obligatory or even permissible, because God had no intention that Abraham carry out the command. (See Wierenga, 1983, p. 390.) Too narrow, because commands properly speaking are but one kind of communicative device speakers can use to direct behavior. (I presuppose that God does communicate with humans: see Wolterstorff, 1995.) Included in the family of imperatives are requests, recommendations, warnings, instructions, and invitations. A flexible divine command theory should allow for the possibility that God might use any of these devices – and for that matter non-imperative devices – to lay moral obligations and prohibitions upon humans. To put it another way, such a theory should be sensitive to the fact that the way in which divine authority makes itself known can vary as background and context varies. When the scribes and Pharisees ask what should be done with the woman caught in adultery, Jesus says, "Let him who is without sin among you be the first to throw a stone at her" (John 8:7). But Jesus and his audience know full well that no member of the crowd is without sin. Thus what appears on the surface as an imperatival granting of permission is intended by Jesus and understood by the crowd to be an injunction *not* to stone the woman.

There are philosophers, however, who subscribe to the thesis that God makes the moral rules, but who do not accept divine commands as the entities that make the moral rules. Mark Murphy (1998) has recently argued for a view according to which a person's being morally obligated to do something depends on God's *willing* that the person act so, not on God's commanding that the person act so. Two questions are certain to arise here. What is divine willing? How does a will-based theory differ from a command-based theory? On a view like Murphy's, divine commands are the vehicles that typically *convey* obligations, but they do not *make* the obligations *obligatory*; God's will is responsible for that. It is clear that much rides here on an understanding of the notion of God's willing. For example, one can understand the notion in such a way that it would follow that the will of an omnipotent being is unimpedible; whatever God wills, happens. This notion is too strong for Murphy's purposes. For if God's will makes the moral rules and if God also unimpedibly wills universal compliance with them, then none of us would ever sin. (Murphy makes a similar point, relying alternatively on God's omniscience and rationality. See Murphy, 1998, p. 16.) But if God were not to will universal compliance with his rules, then the rules would appear to lack the important characteristic of universality and their promulgator would correspondingly appear to be capricious.

In contrast, a notion of willing as mere desiring is too weak. It seems possible that even an omniscient and perfectly rational being could have conflicting desires. (The desire for A conflicts with the desire for B if the realization of A precludes the realization of B and vice versa.) If divine desires were sufficient to create moral obligations, then conflicting divine desires could easily impose inconsistent obligations, and thus a normative theory based on God's desires alone risks the charge of incoherence.

It could be argued that insofar as he is perfect, God is immune from conflicting desires, so that inconsistent obligations cannot arise in this way. It is not clear, however, how an argument from perfection to absence of conflicting desires is supposed to go. If conflicting desires entail indecisiveness, that might constitute a reason for thinking that a perfect being would not have them. But it is not obvious that indecisiveness is the inevitable outcome of conflicting desires, especially when one desire outweighs the other. One might try to exploit the point about desires having different weights and argue, alternatively, that conflicts of desires can only arise in agents with incomplete knowledge or defective reasoning abilities: an omniscient and perfectly rational being would see where the weight of reason falls in any situation and desire accordingly. Aside from the fact that this maneuver makes the dubious presupposition that there are no cases in which reason finds two incompatible alternatives in exact rational equipoise, it fails to address the issue at hand. The fact – if it be a fact – that God always tailors his desires to fit the contours of reason does not show that he cannot have conflicting desires. On the contrary, if God's will is exquisitely responsive to reasons, he will, one presumes, see what is attractive, say, about alternative B and to that extent desire B, even if it should happen that reason awards higher marks to alternative A.

Perhaps we need not speculate so extravagantly about divine psychology in order to come up with a defensible conception of will that steers a middle course between the overly strong conception of an unimpedible will and the insufficiently strong conception of a mere wish. Murphy appeals to a medieval distinction between one's antecedent will and one's consequent will (Murphy, 1998, p. 18). As a first approximation we can think of the distinction as the difference between what one simply wants and what one wants, all things considered. I simply want a drink from that tall, frosty tumbler of clear liquid. Tell me that it is laced with prussic acid and, all things considered, I will not want the drink. To illustrate the distinction this way might lead one to think that an essential component of the distinction is temporal sequence involving a change of desire: at first I wanted the drink, then I came to believe that it was poisoned, and then I rejected it. But the distinction need neither be sequential nor involve a change of mind. Suppose that someone invites you to play chess. You are a good player and enjoy the challenge of a good competitor. You know nothing about the skill of your opponent. You enjoy winning chess games. But you also want (antecedently) your opponent to play cleverly, even if that should result in your losing. As the game progresses it becomes evident that your opponent is not very skilled. Your desire now (consequently) is to defeat your opponent as quickly as possible so that you may return to reading your novel. Still, you continue to want, somewhat forlornly and against the evidence, your opponent to play well: you value a good game over a good novel but a good novel over a boring game. Your consequent desire has not supplanted your antecedent desire; if anything it may have amplified it. And although your opponent may not be able to thwart your consequent will, to win the game quickly, he is certainly apt to frustrate your antecedent will, that he should play adroitly. (It is important for theological reasons to insist that the antecedent-will/consequent-will distinction need not involve stages of change on the part of the willing agent. Thomas Aquinas, for example, wants to apply the distinction to God's willing activity while also holding that because God is eternal, there is no successiveness in God's mind. See the passage cited in Murphy, 1998, p. 18.)

Murphy proposes to identify the source of moral obligation with God's antecedent will, not God's consequent will. We are to suppose, for example, that it is God's antecedent will that no one commit adultery, and that that will makes adultery forbidden. Just as your bootless chess opponent can thwart your antecedent will, so human adulterers can thwart God's. God's consequent will, on the other hand, has the sort of unimpedibility that we would expect of an omniscient, omnipotent being. You will checkmate your opponent no matter what he may do. In similar fashion, we may suppose, God will bring his all-things-considered plans to fruition, no matter what creatures may do.

What rides on the distinction between a divine command theory and a divine will theory? They are species under the same genus and they can be expected to converge in many cases. What difference could it make whether murder is wrong because God's command forbids it or because God's will does? The differences should emerge when we consider cases in which the two theories might part ways. Might there be cases in which God commands something that he does not will? Conversely, might there be cases in which God wills something that he does not command? In either case, which creates the obligation, the command or the will?

We saw earlier that some philosophers have taken the case of God's commandment to Abraham to sacrifice his son to be an example of the first possibility. (Adams, 1999, p. 260 demurs, claiming that "the case it poses should not be taken as a relevant possibility in theistic ethical theory." Adams's rejection seems to be based on epistemological grounds: "[A]ny reason for believing that God does not ... want us to do something will virtually always be a reason, of approximately equal strength, for believing that God has not commanded us to do it.") Were we to admit the case, the question would remain: is Abraham obligated to sacrifice his son, as the divine command dictates, or to refrain, as the divine will requires? It seems clear that divine command theorists would choose the first option and divine will theorists would choose the second.

Robert Adams welcomes the possibility of cases in which God wills something that he does not command. They provide room, within a divine command framework, for *supererogatory* actions, actions that are "beyond the call of duty," morally praiseworthy yet not morally obligatory (Adams, 1999, pp. 260–1). In a straightforward manner Adams's theory can describe supererogatory actions as actions God wants us to perform but does not command.

The situation with divine will theory is not as straightforward. Suppose there are cases in which God wills something but does not command it or reveal it in any other way. If God's antecedent will invariably creates moral obligations, then it would follow that God's creatures would have obligations for which they are liable, by divine reckoning, yet about which they are completely ignorant. This situation would be deplorable. (I avoid describing the situation as unjust or as a violation of creatures' rights. If injustice and infringement of rights can only arise as a *consequence* of violations of moral norms created by God, as both divine command theorists and divine will theorists must maintain, the norms themselves cannot be unjust or in violation of anyone's rights.) If a civil authority punished people who acted in ways contrary to the authority's desires, even though the desires had never been publicized, we would regard the authority as tyrannical. If, in order to avoid this possibility, a divine will theorist claims that divinely willed but wholly unexpressed obligations do not or cannot exist, the claim appears to concede too much to divine command theory. If communicative expression is necessary for obligatoriness to take effect, it is hard to see how God's will can play the role advertised by divine will theory. God's will may propose, but it appears as though God's commands would actually dispose.

This quandary is a quandary only for a divine will theory that accepts the proposition that God's antecedent will always creates moral obligations. Philip Quinn has recently argued that divine will theory need not accept the proposition. Quinn's argument is prompted by a desire to accommodate supererogation within a divine will theory, but the distinction Quinn invokes, if it is viable, will also dissolve our putative quandary. Quinn claims, in effect, that God's antecedent will might be at least two-sorted. Quinn suggests that one way to make room for supererogatory actions is to allow that "obligatory actions are actions God both wants us to perform and antecedently intends that we perform, while supererogatory actions are actions God wants us to perform but does not antecedently intend that we perform" (Quinn, 2002, p. 461). One can extend Quinn's distinction to dissolve alleged cases of unrevealed obligations by maintaining that some of the actions God wants us to perform may never be revealed but are not obligatory; the obligatory actions are always wanted, intended, *and* publicized by God.

Still, it would be fair to ask why, on this account, the intentional, obligation-creating aspects of God's antecedent will *are* always made known to creatures, and to expect an answer that avoids pinning the obligation-creating function on the communicative acts by which God's will is made known. There is, moreover, another worry about Quinn's distinction between antecedent desires and antecedent intentions. A divine antecedent intention that creates an obligation would be an intention that a creature perform an action. Adams notes that "An intention is normally an intention to do something oneself," and that when we speak of an agent intending that someone or something else, *X*, do something, that implies an intention on the agent's part "to do something to see to it, or at least make it significantly more likely, that *X* will do what was intended" (Adams, 2002, p. 484). Desires need not have this agentive feature. Quinn is correct to distinguish intentions from desires, but the worry is that intentions, especially the intentions of an all-knowing, all-powerful being, are too *peremptory* for Quinn's purpose. A rational agent can have conflicting desires. Conflicting intentions, in contrast, betoken agent irrationality. Why so? The answer seems to lie in the fact that an intention is a kind of resolution that something shall be done, a resolution that takes desires as inputs and determines which desires are to be satisfied. A conflict of intentions leaves their author in the unenviable position of being committed to do and to refrain from doing something. (For more on this and other differences between desires and intentions, see Mann, forthcoming.) Applying this to the case of God, I must say that it seems as though if God has antecedent intentions, they are logically posterior to God's antecedent desires. In short, Quinn's divine antecedent intentions appear to be functionally indistinguishable from God's consequent will. In particular, just as God's consequent will is unimpedible, so, it would seem, are his antecedent intentions. If this is so, then when Quinn says that God both wants and antecedently intends that creatures perform certain actions, and that God's wanting and intending are what makes the actions obligatory, it follows that no one ever sins. Thus I am inclined to think, pending further clarification from divine will theorists on the connections among God's antecedent will, its communication, and supererogation, that a divine command theory is preferable to a divine will theory.

Love

To someone waiting to be convinced that there can be a viable theistic normative theory the choice between divine command theory and divine will theory can seem quaint at best. Either account must be prepared to respond to these critical issues. First, there is the *feasibility problem*. The content of the commandments that are supposed to be fundamental are to love God and to love our neighbors as ourselves. What is being commanded here such that it is the sort of thing that can reasonably be commanded? Order me to close the window and I would know how to go about complying immediately. Tell me to translate Aristotle's *Metaphysics* from Greek into Korean and I know what would be required for me to comply, but you had better anticipate a long wait. Now command me to love you, or to love someone else. Lovable as you or they may be, I might be unsure about how to take steps to fulfill your command. Love is famously involuntary. Although your command does not formally violate the principle that ought implies can, love for another particular person may just be psychologically inaccessible to me. Second, there is the *character problem*. How do commands like these reflect on the personality of the commander? Pleading for another's love can be pathetic, but commanding another's love appears to be pathological, a sign of overbearing arrogance or something worse. Third, there is the *aptness problem*. Why should we *love* God and our neighbors? It certainly might be prudent to hew closely to the line drawn by an omnipotent being, but prudent servitude is not the same thing as love. And being nice to one's neighbors is a good policy to follow, but being nice to them does not require loving them.

One way to handle these problems is to offer a minimalist account of love. According to it, you should not think of the love that is being commanded as a complex emotional state, process, or relationship. Think instead of the two Great Commandments as merely dictating constraints on behavior: we should act *as if* we loved God and our neighbors. Immanuel Kant heads in this direction vis-à-vis the second Great Commandment: "*Love* is a matter of *feeling*, not of willing, and I cannot love because I *will* to, still less because I *ought* to (I cannot be constrained to love); so a *duty to love* is an absurdity. But *benevolence* (*amor benevolentiae*), as conduct, can be subject to a law of duty" (Kant, 1991, p. 203). Perhaps the clearest recent statement of the minimalist account is from André Comte-Sponville: "Only actions can be commanded; therefore the commandment requires not that we love but that we act *as though* we loved – that we do unto our neighbor as we would unto our loved ones, and unto strangers as we would unto ourselves. The commandment prescribes not feelings or emotions, which are not transferable, but actions, which are" (Comte-Sponville, 2001, p. 97). The minimalist account resolves the feasibility problem by claiming that what is being commanded is something that can sensibly be commanded, namely, actions, not attitudes. The aptness problem is resolved by maintaining that love is not what is required, but rather *as-it-were love*. As for the character problem, the minimalist account can finesse it by maintaining that the Great Commandments are misstated: "You shall love God with all your heart," should really be "You shall act as if you love God with all your heart," and one salient way of doing that is to act as if you love your neighbor as yourself. Understood in this way, the personality of the author of the commandments can be seen to be relatively benign, in fact, downright beneficent, although perhaps with a touch of self-importance or personal insecurity.

But if it would have been so easy to state the commandments correctly, why are they worded as they are? There is the psychological phenomenon that sometimes mimicking a certain kind of attitude leads the mimicker to acquire the attitude. If I want to become brave, Aristotle says, I should act as the brave person acts. More to the point, Smith's feigned concern for Jones's welfare, initially motivated by greed, if practiced long enough, may ironically ensnare Smith into genuine concern for Jones. The minimalist is poorly served by this phenomenon, for it suggests that love-like behavior towards God and neighbor, even if valuable in its own right, is to be valued primarily as a means to achieving what the Great Commandments overtly demand of us – *love* of God and neighbor. Moreover, the phenomenon undermines the claim that "only actions can be commanded." Commands can legitimately take attitudes as their object: ask any parent bent on instilling the correct attitudes in their children. It is just that some commands cannot be obeyed directly and immediately. But then neither can your command to me to translate Aristotle's *Metaphysics*. One should not take the difficulty (at least on some occasions) in complying with such commands as a reason for rejecting their feasibility. Within a page of declaring that a duty to love is an absurdity, Kant goes on to say:

> So the saying "you ought to *love* your neighbor as yourself" does not mean that you ought immediately (first) to love him and (afterwards) by means of this love do good to him. It means, rather, *do good* to your fellow man, and your beneficence will produce love of man in you (as an aptitude of the inclination to beneficence in general). (Kant, 1991, p. 203)

The concession deflates much of what he had said earlier.

Thus there is a response to the feasibility problem that does not lead to the minimalist account. But the character and aptness problems remain. Resolution of the character problem would seem to require reflection on the nature of God, more specifically, on God's personality. Resolution of the aptness problem can hardly proceed without an examination of the notion of love. I propose to begin with the latter project, and to interweave the former into it as we proceed.

The philosophical literature on love is immense. Any attempt to survey it adequately would require a book. I propose instead to organize our examination around the fact that classical Greek has three terms all loosely translatable as "love," *eros, philia*, and *agapē*. (For a similar ordering see Comte-Sponville, 2001, pp. 222–90.) We should not suppose that the original, common usages of these terms bear the philosophical sophistication that we will see attached to them. The terms were appropriated early on by philosophical and religious traditions to emphasize different features arguably exhibited by the phenomenon of love. Taking them in the order given, *eros, philia, agapē*, we will see a sort of dialectical escalation of the conditions said to be important to a theistic conception of love.

Eros

Desire – paradigmatically, sexual desire – is central to the notion of *eros*. In the *Symposium* Plato lobbies for a vision of *eros*, chastened by reason, that impresses this otherwise unruly, arational drive into the service of the quest for wisdom.

Erotic lovers begin, typically, by loving a particular person's body. Under the tutelage of reason they can come to realize that what they love about a person's body is its beauty. In general, it is a thing's beauty that makes it naturally attractive. Now the beauty of particular bodies is a low-level beauty. Insofar as rational lovers are attracted to beauty, and more strongly attracted the more beautiful they realize a thing to be, they will find themselves engaged in a pursuit of higher and still higher orders of beauty (the beauty of souls, well-crafted laws, knowledge), culminating in the Form of Beauty Itself, eternally and perfectly beautiful, the cause of beauty in all other things. Plato provides a complementary vision of the nature and function of the Form of the Good in the *Republic*, according to which the Good both confers truth on things so that they can be known and empowers our souls so that we can acquire knowledge. Although the Good is superior to truth and knowledge (superior, Plato says, in *beauty*), the Good is itself an object of knowledge. The interconnections between the two Forms are so intimate (for example, it is necessarily the case that everything good is beautiful and vice versa) that were it not for Plato's assurance that they are two, one might think they were one and the same. Like Beauty Itself, the Good is an end point of a lover's quest: the lover is a lover of wisdom.

The Form of the Good, then, determines what shall be members of the domain of truths while it enables souls to grasp those truths. Inasmuch as the Good and its works are transcendently beautiful, they are pre-eminently attractive and pre-eminently fitting objects of *eros*. The erotic pursuit of truth and the Good results in the lover's "giving birth in beauty," that is, producing virtuous works in the lover and in others. So for Plato, *eros*, when harnessed by reason, motivates us to pursue the beauty of truth up to its transcendent font, the Good, and to replicate, insofar as it is in our power, the beauty of goodness in ourselves and others.

An impressive array of traditional theistic themes naturally radiates from this Platonic core when Beauty and the Good are replaced by God. Many theists maintain, for example, that everything that is good is good because it is an image of supremely good God. Many theists maintain further that everything that exists is good to some degree because it has been created by God, from whom no evil can flow. Philosophically minded theists have sometimes described God as the cause of truth, including even – perhaps especially – necessary truth (Mann, 1997), and the illuminator of souls, thereby making human understanding possible. It is tempting to assimilate the contemplation of Beauty Itself into the beatific vision of God, who has been described by some influential theists as Beauty Itself (Sherry, 1997). Finally, theists generally agree that genuine love for God can only emanate from a virtuous soul, one inclined, among other things, to love others inasmuch as they are created in God's image.

Adams's *Finite and Infinite Goods* is surely the most ambitious and profound recent attempt to launch a theistic normative theory from a Platonic base. On Adams's conception, as on Plato's, the good is the fundamental evaluative notion. Badness is conceptually parasitic on goodness. The badness of a thing is either a deficiency of or an opposition to the good, not anything that has any independent ontological status (Adams, 1999, pp. 102–4). And the normative notions that give rise to networks of obligation, namely, wrongness and rightness, are similarly parasitic on the good but are in addition social in character, specifying what transactions among persons are forbidden (because they oppose the good in some way), permissible (because they are not forbidden), or required (because it is forbidden that they not be done). (Adams, 1999, pp. 231–2. It will have occurred to the perceptive reader that, consistent with Adams's divine command theory, the social unit in which obligations can arise can be very small. In the account of creation given in Genesis 2, God commands Adam, before Eve has been created, not to eat the fruit of the tree of the knowledge of good and evil.) The most distinctive feature of the notion of the good that Adams develops is that it is a kind of *excellence*. This feature is not at home in instrumental, utilitarian, well-being, or desire-satisfaction conceptions of the good. (In fact, we are probably most familiar with evaluative excellence in non-moral domains, such as aesthetics and sports.) But it does comport well with the Platonic conception of *eros* tracking excellence through its images up to its maximal, transcendent source.

It is no part of Plato's or Adams's case that we can fully fathom now all the glory of this transcendent source. Quite the contrary: holiness, divine transcendence, or the Good Itself, as Adams puts it, "screams with the hawk and laughs with the hyenas. We cannot comprehend it. It is fearful to us, and in some ways dangerous" (Adams, 1999, p. 52). It is enough that we understand that God is supremely good, not what all the entailments of supreme goodness are. This understanding of God allows its believer to reply to the arbitrariness objection to the thesis that God makes the rules. If God is supremely good, his own goodness will prevent him from issuing commands whose obedience would irremediably oppose the good. (Questions can arise here whether God's inability to issue such commands threatens to invalidate his omnipotence or freedom. I think not, but I will not argue the case here.) We can see now one reason Adams has for maintaining that the good is more fundamental than the right. God's commands determine what is right and what is wrong, but God's commands do not determine what is good, except in the sense that his creative fiats determine what good creatures shall exist.

Love modeled on Platonic *eros* provides its defender with straightforward answers to the aptness and character problems. Recall that the nub of the aptness problem was a request for an explanation for why love is the attitude we should take towards God and our neighbors. We should love God because God is supremely worthy of love. We should love our neighbors because they image the goodness of their creator. The character problem challenged the psychological character of someone who commands another's love. In addition to the general consideration that not all imperatives need be construed as commands, there is the point that it is plausible to believe that God, conceived as supreme goodness, would want to communicate to his creatures the message that their ultimate happiness, a happiness in comparison to which all other conceptions of happiness pale, rests in the beatific vision of the divine.

Philia

Despite these affinities between Platonism and theism, there is one striking difference. Plato's Forms of Beauty and the Good richly repay their lovers' labors but they do not reciprocate their lovers' love. Beauty Itself is far more beautiful than the most exquisite landscape or portrait, but every bit as impersonal. Theists insist that God is personal, a being to whom emotions, beliefs, desires, and intentions can be ascribed. More than that, they insist that God can and does love his creatures. The notion of love as *eros* seems ill-suited to characterize this love. Plato insists that *eros* entails a need or lack on the part of the lover along with a kind of vulnerability. According to Plato, one cannot love what one already has. The only sense that Plato attaches to the notion of loving what one possesses is that one wants to continue to possess the object of one's love when there is a liability that it can be removed in the future. Plato's gods lack nothing and nothing can be taken away from them; thus they love nothing. Furthermore, if, as Adams maintains, *eros* admires excellence, we need an account of why perfect God would love creatures conspicuous for their lack of excellence.

Adams's analysis of *grace* addresses the sort of concern just expressed. Grace is "love that is not completely explained by the excellence of its object" (Adams, 1999, p. 151). It is thus important for Adams that love – even perfectly rational love – be allowed discretionary leeway vis-à-vis the value of its objects. It may be that Mozart's music is superior to Haydn's, but I would not wish to be told that I should always choose to listen to Mozart over Haydn. Still, as the title of Adams's book reminds us, the gap between the goodness of God and the goodness of creatures is not like the smallish gap between Mozart and Haydn; it is infinite. So we must face the questions, (a) why infinitely good, infinitely self-sufficient, and infinitely competent God would create and sustain us when he could have created better creatures and (b) how it might be that, despite the observation noted in (a), God does love us.

About (a) I shall say little except to report that for all I know, God *has* created beings more excellent than we are. Moreover, *any* finite being that infinitely good God creates will be, not just less excellent than God, but less excellent than *infinitely* many kinds of beings God could create. As for (b), we need, as preamble, to sort out some attitudes that most theists would not like to believe characterize God's love for us.

Ed is a breeder of golden retrievers. He takes an interest in their overall health because he wants to compete successfully against rival breeders for pet-shop business. Ed's retrievers are benefitted by Ed and Ed prizes their health. Knowing just this much, however, we have no reason to believe that Ed loves his retrievers. Ed tends to his retrievers, we might suppose, solely because he sees them as means to an ulterior end about which he does care, his own well-being. Were we to discover that God's concern for us is analogous to Ed's concern for his retrievers – for example, that God supports our passing show solely for its contribution to the divine recreation – we should conclude that God does not love us. Kindly treatment towards others is compatible with enlightened self-interest. By itself, kindly treatment is not love.

Jo cares about the welfare of domesticated animals, believing that it is what humans owe to the species they have made unfit for survival independent of humans. She works tirelessly on projects sponsored by humane societies. She lives more austerely than she might otherwise in order to further these projects. Her will bequeaths her estate to the American Society for the Prevention of Cruelty to Animals. But for all of that, Jo does not have pets. She believes that she can accomplish more for the welfare of domesticated animals if she is not encumbered by the burden of responsible pet ownership. Jo's behavior is motivated differently from Ed's: it is a specimen of detached benevolence. "Benevolence" because Jo wants domesticated animals to flourish for their sakes, not hers. "Detached" because Jo does not want to become involved with the creatures she benefits.

I think it is clear that Jo does not love animals. In general, if x benefits y at a cost to x, it does not follow that x loves y. If God's attitude towards us is like Jo's attitude towards animals *and nothing more*, we should conclude once again that God does not love us. And if our treatment of our neighbors completely emulated Jo's treatment of domesticated animals, we would not love our neighbors. I shall assume that justification of the latter claim provides justification for the former. Suppose that all humans were to adopt the stance towards all humans, including themselves, that Jo adopts towards domesticated animals. Think of the benefits. We would witness a large-scale, voluntary, and more equitable distribution of the world's resources. In human affairs tolerance and peaceful coexistence would be more pervasive than now. The world would be a utilitarian utopia. Yet it would also be devoid of love. In its place we would find detached universal benevolence, with each of us striving to behave as Lord Shaftesbury would behave, except that our behavior would be aimed at a population of like-minded Shaftesburys.

What is missing? One thing that distinguishes human love from detached benevolence is love's focused selectivity. Suppose that Jo has only enough resources to provide for five of six puppies from the same litter. Al, who shares Jo's ideals, will provide for the sixth. It would be pointless to ask Jo *which* five should be supported by her funds and which one by Al's. It would satisfy all that Jo cares about if one simply assigned one of the numbers between one and six to each puppy, cast a die, and allocated Al's funds to the puppy whose number comes up. Contrast Jo's attitude with Vi's. Confronted with a litter of puppies, Vi invariably lavishes attention on the one puppy who responds most enthusiastically to her presence. Vi has thus had several pets whose companionship has enriched her life as she has enabled them to flourish.

Jo and Vi are similar in one respect. It is important to them not merely that domesticated animals flourish but that they be *agents* of animal flourishing; their desire in this respect is agent-centered. Yet they differ in another respect. Vi's desire, we may say, is "object-focused" whereas Jo's is "object-diffuse." The only properties that affect Jo's decisions are properties relevant to an animal's ability to flourish. Given any two animals whose prospects for flourishing are equal, it is a matter of indifference to Jo which animal should receive her support when only one can. Vi counts such properties, but she also, consciously or unconsciously, attaches great importance to some properties, such as enthusiastic response, that from the point of view of detached benevolence are irrelevant. Vi may even be led on some occasions to choose a puppy whose prospects for flourishing are less good than another's.

Object-focusing distinguishes detached benevolence from a conception of love that theists should seek, for the feature of object-focusing makes it explicit that love, as opposed to detached benevolence, involves the desire to enter into and sustain a relationship between lover and beloved (cf. Adams, 1999, p. 139). Even so, agent-centered and object-focused love can be directed towards many kinds of things. The beloved might be a person, an animal, an artwork, or a vintage wine. Thus the nature of the relationship will vary depending on features of the beloved. Theists should be primarily concerned to explore a concept of love in which both lover and beloved are personal agents.

In an extended sense, *philia* means fondness or affectionate regard, attitudes that can be held towards a wide variety of things. But in books 8 and 9 of the *Nicomachean Ethics* Aristotle examines what is surely the dominant sense of *philia*, namely, friendship. *Philia* is founded on the phenomenon of one's wishing good to a person for that person's own sake. For *philia* to be instantiated there must be reciprocation of one's goodwill, mutual recognition of that mutual goodwill, and mutual action based on that mutual recognition. These conditions restrict *philia* to beings whose mental life is rich enough to have cognition, self-awareness, desires, and intentions. (As Aristotle laconically observes, it is absurd to suppose that one can befriend wine.) *Philia* promises the theist what *eros* does not deliver, a conception of love that is distinctively and necessarily *inter*personal.

The promise is hollow, however, if there is anything about *philia* that precludes a *philia* relationship between God and humans. The major threat would appear to be the radical inequality of the two parties. There can be friendships between unequals if the inequality is not extreme. For example, *philia* encompasses relationships between parent and child, in which, according to Aristotle, parents merit greater love from their children than they owe to their children. But can such a relationship exist between two beings, one of whom, as many theists maintain, is infinitely superior to the other? Two problems arise here, one for human participants in the putative *philia* relationship, the other for the divine participant. If, as many theists claim, God is omnipotent and utterly self-sufficient, then our wishing good to God for God's sake might seem to be droll at best: how could God *fail* to achieve the good? On the divine side of the relationship there is the disturbing thought that there must be precious little of worth in us to inspire God to want to befriend us.

Let us consider the second problem first. It receives powerful articulation from Jonathan Edwards. Here is Edwards at his friskiest:

The God that holds you over the pit of hell much as one holds a spider, or some loathsome insect, over the fire, abhors you, and is dreadfully provoked; his wrath towards you burns like fire; he looks upon you as worthy of nothing else, but to be cast into the fire; he is of purer eyes than to bear to have you in his sight; you are ten thousand times so abominable in his eyes as the most hateful venomous serpent is in ours. (Edwards, 1995, pp. 97–8)

One might try to lighten the message by pointing out that the people loathsome in God's eyes are the sinners. But, alas, in Edwards's eyes we all are sinners. Edwards's analogy, however, is not particularly apt. Spiders and serpents are not of our making, nor are our encounters with them typically of our choosing. Because some of them are dangerous and it is not always easy to discriminate between the dangerous and benign varieties, prudence dictates a default policy of blanket avoidance. In contrast, theists generally insist that God created us and freely chooses his encounters with us, and that while we may disappoint God, we certainly pose no threat to him.

Return to the case of Vi. Vi does not judge her dogs by the same standards she uses to judge her human friends. Conversely, she does not hold her human friends up to the same standards she expects of her dogs. She simply enjoys the company of both, rejoicing in what they are and in what they may become. She thrives vicariously in their flourishing. She wishes them good for their own sakes. What reason can be given for thinking that, unlike the relationships Vi has with her human friends, Vi cannot enter into *philia* relationships with her dogs? That both parties to a friendship must be rational agents? The claim is not obvious, but even if true, it would not rule out *philia* relationships between God and humans. Still, there is the issue of the infinite distance in goodness separating us from God. Theists, I think, are entitled to ground their resistance to Edwards's hellfire in the very source of that infinite distance, that is, God's infinite goodness. One dimension of infinite goodness is infinite *bounty*, a capacity and willingness to care for all creatures great and small, and to care in a way that is not necessarily proportioned to their greatness or smallness. Moreover, infinite knowledge, power, and goodness confer upon their possessor an infinite capacity for object-focusing. I lack sufficient knowledge, power, and goodwill to muster the object-focusing required to enter into *philia* relationships with very many others. God is under no such limitations. Object-focusing, writ large, seems to capture much of what has been traditionally conveyed by the notion of divine *providence*.

Theists may reasonably suppose, then, that infinitely bounteous, infinitely providential God desires to enter into *philia* relationships with us. We can, however, spurn the offer of friendship. This possibility of rejecting what God has to offer addresses the problem raised a while ago, namely, what the point of wishing good to God could be. If God prizes friendship with us, then there is a way in which God can fail to achieve a good, a good that depends on our willingness to affiliate ourselves with God.

Agapē

In discussing *eros* and *philia* I have dwelt mostly on the implications these notions have for love between God and humans, leaving aside, for the most part, the implications the notions have for love among humans. The imbalance in attention was excusable on grounds that we were antecedently familiar with erotic and friendship relations among humans. What was less clear is whether and how *eros* and *philia* apply to the divine. What remains to be discussed is the injunction to love one's neighbors as oneself. Consider first the question of the identity of the "neighbors" one is obligated to love. When asked this question, Jesus responded with the parable of the good Samaritan (Luke 10:29–37). A natural interpretation of the parable is that one's neighbors are just anyone in need, including, as the parable takes pains to illustrate, strangers one will encounter only once. But of course the point of the parable is not that one is obligated to love only strangers and then only when they are in need. It is rather that one's love must extend *even* to strangers in need when there is no prospect of reciprocation. And the Samaritan's actions are depicted as obligatory, not supererogatory: at the end of the parable Jesus simply says, "Go and do likewise."

Quinn has recently argued that neither *eros* nor *philia* captures this conception of love (Quinn, 2000). Although Quinn does not call this conception *agapē*, the term seems apt, especially in light of the frequency with which *agapē* and its relatives appear in New Testament Greek. Endorsing Søren Kierkegaard's *Works of Love*, Quinn ascribes to *agapē* impartiality and immutability, features conspicuously absent from human-to-human instances of *eros* and *philia*. Impartial *agapē* is a love of absolutely everyone, not just the few to whom we may be attached erotically or by ties of friendship. ("For if you love those who love you, what reward have you? Do not even the tax collectors do the same?" Matt. 5:46.) Moreover, unlike *eros* and *philia*, immutable *agapē* is a love not subject to variation, no matter what vicissitudes should befall the beloved.

Quinn follows Kierkegaard (1995) in emphasizing the demandingness of *agapē* conceived in this way. "The stringency of the obligation to love is likely to give offense. In that respect, it resembles the requirements of impartial benevolence or utility maximization in secular moral theories, which are criticized for setting standards impossibly high or not leaving room for personal projects" (Quinn, 2000, p. 59). In another respect, it is likely to give *more* offense than its secular ilk, since it sets an even higher standard. The demands of impartial benevolence or utility maximization are typically satisfied when an agent performs the action that best realizes the one or the other. It is not the business of theories stressing impartial benevolence or utility maximization to pry into the intentions and motives harbored by the agent. Such states of mind are of secondary interest at best, relevant, say, to predictions about the agent's long-range tendencies to act benevolently or maximally. In the picture that accompanies *agapē* in the New Testament, however, the agent's states of mind are crucial. For example, it is sufficient for a charge of adultery that a man look at a woman lustfully (Matt. 5:28). The duty laid upon one by this agapēistic picture is not simply to conform one's *actions* to God's commands but also to conform one's *will* (cf. Mann, forthcoming). It seems, then, that in order successfully to discharge the obligation imposed by *agapē*, one would need superhuman powers of what I have been calling object-focusing, saintly doses of compassion and forgiveness, and mastery, direct or indirect, over one's desires and intentions. Perhaps the acquisition of these powers is what is intended by the command that "You, therefore, must be perfect, as your heavenly Father is perfect" (Matt. 5:48). Perhaps in turn Quinn had something like these implications in mind in saying that the stringency of *agapē* is likely to give offense. What *agapē* offends against is the principle that "ought implies can:" we are commanded by God to be perfect; we are thus under an obligation to perfect ourselves; perfecting ourselves entails acquiring *agapē*; acquiring *agapē* calls for developing abilities and character traits beyond our capacity to develop.

This predicament will probably be a litmus test for one's allegiance to the principle that "ought implies can." It would carry us beyond the confines of this essay to deal adequately with that issue. I will conclude by gesturing to one maneuver that many theists have adopted. Of course, they will say, we are not able *by ourselves* to perfect ourselves. But it need not follow that we must either deny the "ought implies can" principle or take ourselves to be under no obligation to perfect ourselves. Consider this analogy. Dot is a lifeguard on duty, who spots Vic in danger of drowning. Dot is obligated to try to save Vic's life. But no matter how hard Dot might try, she would not succeed by herself: a shark would fatally attack Vic before she could reach him. Dot knows that, as always, Ace is patrolling the area. Ace is a shark hunter with unparalleled skills. Yet Ace's ways are inscrutable: sometimes Ace responds to the threat of shark attacks, sometimes he does not lift a finger. In particular, Ace's actions appear to be causally independent of Dot's. Now suppose Dot reasons as follows. "If I try to save Vic and Ace does not dispatch the shark, then I cannot succeed. So in that case, the principle that ought implies can entails that I am under no obligation to try. I could go through the motions of trying to save him. But if Ace does not intervene, then going through the motions would be futile. Moreover, I was never obligated to put on a show of pretending to try to save him; I was supposed to be obligated to genuinely try. Now I feel lucky and lazy today. I am not going to try to save Vic, and I will bet that Ace will not dispatch the shark. If that is so, then there is no obligation that I will have failed to fulfill."

In reaction to Dot's reasoning, it seems plausible to say that she is obligated to try to save Vic, even in the case in which Ace does nothing to intervene on her behalf. One can hold this intuition while not surrendering the "ought implies can" principle, if one is willing to make the following maneuver. The obligation picked out by "ought" is the obligation to try to save Vic. The ability picked out by "can" is not the ability to save Vic *sans phrase*. It is rather the ability to save Vic *if there are no sharks present*, or *if Ace exercises his expertise*. These abilities, though conditional, are not capricious. For one thing, they are abilities that many people lack. Dot's conditional ability is grounded in her having sufficient swimming strength and lifesaving skills to succeed (were it not for the shark). For another, in an intuitive sense but one which is hard to make precise, the conditions that have to be met are not outlandish given the real-world circumstances. There are nearby possible worlds – in which the shark prowls elsewhere or in which, if the shark is on the scene, Ace decides to intervene – wherein Dot succeeds in saving Vic. But the defender of the "ought implies can" principle must not allow the conditionality of the "can" to infect the "ought:" Dot's obligation is to try to save Vic, period, *not* to try to save Vic *provided that* there are no sharks present or *provided that* Ace exercises his expertise. In short, the "ought" in this case is unconditional while the "can" is (non-capriciously) conditional.

In similar fashion, a theist can preserve the "ought implies can" principle by claiming that the obligation to perfect ourselves is unconditional while the ability is conditional, in particular, conditional on divine grace, an integral part of God's love. If the obligation to perfect oneself entails an obligation to extend *agapē* to all others, even our enemies, it turns out that our ability to love our "neighbors" depends on God's ability to love us.

Summing Up

I suggested earlier that an adequate normative theory must be rationally defensible, systematic, coherent, cognitively perspicuous, and motivationally realistic. What are the prospects for the theory sketched here?

Recall that two components of rational defensibility are universality and some significant degree of consonance with our pre-theoretical intuitions about what is right and what is wrong. Universality is vouchsafed (perhaps to an uncomfortable degree) by the agapēistic interpretation of who our neighbors are. The theory can also provide an account of consonance. For example, reflective humans hold the intuition that cruelty is wrong. The theory provides a natural validation of that intuition: cruelty violates the commandment of neighborly love. It is easy to multiply examples, and this fact goes some considerable way to accounting for the theory's systematicity. Because the theory contains two normative principles, one might worry that they could conflict, thus exposing the theory to a charge of incoherence. Could there be a case in which what is required by love for God conflicts with what is required by love for neighbor? Defenders of the theory have strategies at their disposal to defuse the worry. One strategy, for example, is to insist that the two principles are lexically ordered, that is, that in cases of apparent or potential conflict, the command to love God always takes precedence over the command of neighborly love. The two principles appear to be perspicuous, or at least not any less perspicuous than other, rival moral principles. Finally, in building on the phenomenon of love, tempered by reason, the theory builds on a powerful human motivating factor.

The theory I have sketched is a theory according to which God makes the most general moral rules, the normative rules that determine what actions are obligatory, what are forbidden, and what are permissible. I have argued that God's commands do the making, not God's will. The theory would not, however, suffer shipwreck were it to be shown that a divine will theory is on balance preferable. For what would remain on either account are the injunctions to love God and one's neighbors, injunctions promulgated by perfectly good God. I have structured my exposition of the injunctions around the trio of *eros*, *philia*, and *agapē* because of the influence those terms have had in the philosophical discussion of love. The theory should be of some interest to theists and to non-theists willing to investigate a distinctively theistic normative theory.

References

Adams, Robert M. (1999) *Finite and Infinite Goods: A Framework for Ethics*. New York: Oxford University Press.

Adams, Robert M. (2002) Responses. *Philosophy and Phenomenological Research*, 64, 475–90.

Comte-Sponville, André (2001) *A Small Treatise on the Great Virtues*. New York: Metropolitan Books.

Edwards, Jonathan (1995) Sinners in the Hands of an Angry God. In J. E. Smith, H. S. Stout, and K. P. Minkema (eds.), *A Jonathan Edwards Reader* (pp. 89–105). New Haven: Yale University Press. Original work published in 1741.

Kant, Immanuel (1991) Metaphysical First Principles of the Doctrine of Virtue. In M. Gregor (trans.), *The Metaphysics of Morals* (pp. 179–279). Cambridge: Cambridge University Press. Original work published 1797.

Kierkegaard, Søren (1995) *Works of Love*, trans. H. V. Hong and E. H. Hong. Princeton: Princeton University Press. Original work published in 1847.

LaFollette, Hugh (ed.) (2000) *The Blackwell Guide to Ethical Theory*. Malden, Mass.: Blackwell.

Mann, William E. (1997) Necessity. In P. L. Quinn and C. Taliaferro (eds.), *A Companion to Philosophy of Religion* (pp. 264–70). Oxford: Blackwell.

Mann, William E. (forthcoming) Abelard's Ethics: The Inside Story. In J. Brower and K. Guilfoy (eds.), *The Cambridge Companion to Abelard*. Cambridge: Cambridge University Press.

Murphy, Mark C. (1998) Divine Command, Divine Will, and Moral Obligation. *Faith and Philosophy*, 15, 3–27.

Quinn, Philip L. (2000) Divine Command Theory. In Hugh LaFollette (ed.), *The Blackwell Guide to Ethical Theory* (pp. 53–73). Malden, Mass.: Blackwell.

Quinn, Philip L. (2002) Obligation, Divine Commands and Abraham's Dilemma. *Philosophy and Phenomenological Research*, 64, 459–66.

Sherry, Patrick (1997) Beauty. In P. L. Quinn and C. Taliaferro (eds.), *A Companion to Philosophy of Religion* (pp. 279–85). Oxford: Blackwell.

Wierenga, Edward (1983) A Defensible Divine Command Theory. *Noûs*, 17, 387–407.
Wolterstorff, Nicholas (1995) *Divine Discourse*. Cambridge: Cambridge University Press.

Suggested Further Reading

Beaty, Michael; Fisher, Carlton; and Nelson, Mark (eds.) (1998) *Christian Theism and Moral Philosophy*. Macon, Ga.: Mercer University Press.

Helm, Paul (ed.) (1981) *Divine Commands and Morality*. Oxford: Oxford University Press.

Idziak, Janine Marie (ed.) (1979) *Divine Command Morality: Historical and Contemporary Readings*. New York: The Edwin Mellen Press.

Outka, Gene, and Reeder, John P. (eds.) (1973) *Religion and Morality: A Collection of Essays*. Garden City, N.Y.: Anchor Books.

Quinn, Philip L. (1978) *Divine Commands and Moral Requirements*. Oxford: Clarendon Press.

Chapter 14

Religion and Politics

Philip L. Quinn

Like oil and water, according to a cliché, religion and politics do not mix. Or, more precisely, when they do, the results are often deplorable. Behind the cliché stands a fund of historical experience. There are inquisitions, crusades and jihads, forced conversions, and colonialist exploitations carried out in the name of religious values. On the contemporary scene, there are divisions along religious lines that foster violence in Northern Ireland, the Balkans, Lebanon, Israel, northern Africa, India, Indonesia, and elsewhere. To be sure, religion is never the sole cause of such violent conflicts, and often enough cynical politicians manipulate religious differences to advance agendas that are strikingly at odds with deep religious values. Yet subsequent experience has only served to render more poignant Lucretius's old lament, *tantum religio potuit suadere malorum* ("Religion has been able to persuade to such great evils," Lucretius, 1951, 1, 101)!

The history of early modern Europe was not exceptional. The Reformation shattered the fragile unity of medieval Christendom, and the Wars of Religion followed. Exhaustion more than anything else brought violent conflict to an end. Religious toleration became a *modus vivendi*; it is now supported by settled habits in Western liberal democracies, with residual violent conflict more or less confined to the geographical or cultural peripheries. But such habits are hostages to circumstances. I am writing this essay in the immediate aftermath of the attacks on the World Trade Center and the Pentagon. There has been sporadic violence directed against mosques and Muslims in the United States, though most voices that have spoken out so far have urged toleration. Things could get worse, however; settled habits might be unsettled by events.

Religious toleration becomes an issue for political philosophy when one asks whether there are theoretical grounds to support habits of religious toleration. Is it possible for religious toleration to become more than a more or less stable *modus vivendi* in a religiously diverse liberal democracy? What normative principles of morals or politics underwrite the practice of religious toleration? John Locke and John Stuart Mill, leading lights of the British liberal tradition in political philosophy, have argued for the practice of religious toleration. On the European continent, Pierre Bayle and Immanuel Kant have offered somewhat different arguments to justify that practice. The first main section of this essay will be devoted to a critical examination of some of their arguments. What I hope to show is that it is far from clear that the practice of religious toleration currently rests on firm normative foundations. The philosophical project of justifying that practice has not been brought to completion; there is more work for philosophers to do in this domain of inquiry.

Of course there is room for skepticism about the value of this philosophical project. A philosophical argument for the practice of toleration is not likely to convert religious fanatics or religiously inspired terrorists. If settled habits of toleration were lost, the practice would probably not endure, even if philosophers were armed with good arguments for it. I think there are at least two things worth saying in response to such worries. First, the philosophical project of justifying the practice of religious toleration has some intrinsic theoretical value. Utilitarians are sometimes criticized for holding a theory that frequently cannot in practice tell us what we ought to do because we often cannot calculate the consequences of all the alternative actions available to us in a situation in which we must act. A good reply is that it would be of theoretical interest to know that actions are morally right just in case they maximize utility even if this knowledge left us without a straightforward decision procedure for ethics. Similarly, it would be theoretically interesting to have knowledge of arguments that justify the practice of toleration even if such knowledge left us without a sure way to convert the intolerant. And second, a philosophical justification for the practice of religious toleration would most likely have limited practical value even if it were not a panacea. Such a justification could, for example, form part of a pedagogy aimed at inculcating and maintaining habits of toleration in the citizens of a liberal democracy even if it could not convert the intolerant or sustain those habits all by itself. For reflective democratic citizens are likely to accept the process of habituation and its outcomes if they know the habits it implants in them are good or at least have assurances that the relevant experts have such knowledge. A philosophical justification could therefore help to stabilize and perpetuate the practice of religious toleration. So important theoretical and practical values are at stake in the philosophical project of finding solid foundations for religious toleration.

Fear of religious conflict is part of what motivates several contemporary liberal political philosophers to propose exclusions of religious discourse from the American public square. The proposed exclusions vary in scope and severity. Robert Audi and John Rawls have recently argued forcefully for moral exclusions of religious reasons from the politics of liberal democracies. Their arguments have not gone unchallenged. Nicholas Wolterstorff and I, among others, have criticized such proposals on a variety of grounds. The second main section of this essay will focus on the current debate about political liberalism's proposals. I shall argue against the views of Audi and Rawls, but I shall also criticize some of the counterarguments set forth by Wolterstorff.

It should not be at all surprising that attempts to exclude religion from the political realm or even to limit its role in political discourse will be resisted by religious believers. Religious world-views are typically regarded by those who adhere to them as comprehensive. They are supposed to regulate the whole of the believer's life, not just a part of it. Moreover, such world-views are also typically regarded as ultimate. As Paul Tillich puts it, religious faith is a matter of ultimate concern. Its values are not supposed to be compromised or subject to trade-offs. Comprehensiveness and ultimacy combined often lead religious believers to think that the political order under which they must live is bound to be defective unless it endorses their religious values. These values cannot be relegated to the private sphere without loss. Even if believers think they must live with such a loss because the only alternative would be violent conflict, they will wish to express their religious values and try to win others over to them in public political discourse. But liberal democracies whose citizens are religiously diverse are bound to find the injection of religion into public political discourse at best somewhat risky and at worst downright dangerous. For the paths to salvation or liberation and the social arrangements that would most encourage people to follow those paths differ widely from one religion to another. A liberal democracy simply cannot, under conditions of religious diversity, fully endorse the religious values of all its citizens. What is more, the deepest commitment of liberal democracies is to viewing their citizens as free and equal. Where there is disagreement, neither can they fully endorse the values of one religious world-view rather than another without departing from the commitment to freedom and equality of citizens. So liberal democracies will wish to minimize the intrusion of religious values about which there is disagreement into politics. Even expression of them in public political discourse is apt to seem a threat. In an imaginary liberal democracy in which all citizens regarded religion as a wholly private matter, religion could be excluded from politics without loss. In an equally imaginary liberal democracy in which all citizens shared the same religious world-view, religion could inform politics without risk. In actual liberal democracies, it is not the case that all citizens see religion as an entirely private matter; nor is it the case that all citizens share the same religious world-view. A choice between loss and risk or some mixture of the two seems inevitable. So much is at stake for both religion and liberal democracy in the debate about excluding religious reasons from public political discourse.

Religious Toleration

One of the interesting arguments in Locke's *A Letter Concerning Toleration* focuses on the issue of toleration by the state or commonwealth of religions or churches. His strategy is to define functions that do not necessarily overlap for the commonwealth and the churches. The commonwealth is defined as "a society of men constituted only for the procuring, preserving and advancing their own civil interests" (Locke, 1824, p. 10). Civil interests include life, liberty, health, and private property. A church is "a voluntary society of men, joining themselves together of their own accord in order to the public worshipping of God, in such a manner as they judge acceptable to him, and effectual to the salvation of their souls" (Locke, 1824, p. 13). Churches are to be tolerated provided their forms of worship do not adversely affect the civil interests that are the commonwealth's sole concern. The Lockean principle governing this sort of toleration is the following:

> Whatsoever is lawful in the commonwealth, cannot be prohibited by the magistrate in the church. Whatsoever is permitted unto any of his subjects for their ordinary use, neither can nor ought to be forbidden by him to any sect of people for their religious uses ... But those things that are prejudicial to the commonwealth of a people in their ordinary use, and are therefore forbidden by laws, those things ought not to be permitted to churches in their sacred rites. (Locke, 1824, p. 34)

Locke gives the example of taking bread or wine, either sitting or kneeling. Since the commonwealth should not regulate this activity when a person engages in it at home, it should not regulate it when it is a part of religious worship. Thus the state should tolerate diverse forms of eucharistic practice. But the state should not tolerate human sacrifice of the sort practiced in Aztec religious rituals, because this form of worship adversely affects the civil interest of its victims in their lives. And, to mention a more controversial case, if ingesting peyote adversely affects some civil interest of people, perhaps, for example, their health, and laws against it in the United States are therefore justified, Native Americans should be forbidden to use peyote in their religious rituals.

This Lockean argument has recently been the target of criticism by Paul J. Griffiths. He defines a religion as "a form of life that seems to those who inhabit it to be comprehensive, incapable of abandonment, and of central importance" (Griffiths, 2001, p. 7). Given this definition, religious interests cannot be neatly separated from Lockean civil interests. As Griffiths points out, "much of what is taken by inhabitants of particular religious forms of life to be required of them as such is in fact directly relevant to and does in fact directly impinge upon the interests of the Lockean state, as it also does upon the interests of the European and American democracies at the turn of the millennium" (Griffiths, 2001, p. 108). He offers as an example the many Christians and Jews who find it impossible to reconcile the legality of abortion with what is required of them by their religious identities. The Lockean state cannot therefore be tolerant of all aspects of all religious forms of life; it cannot be entirely neutral on all political questions to which religious forms of life propose answers. Griffiths concludes that "toleration of all religious proposals from a position of religious neutrality is impossible, unless religion is defined in such a way as to eviscerate it and thereby to make it effectively unrecognizable to faithful Jews, Buddhists, Muslims,

Christians, and most others who inhabit forms of life that seem to them comprehensive, unsurpassable, and of central importance" (Griffiths, 2001, p. 111).

Griffiths is no doubt correct in thinking that absolute religious neutrality is impossible, but this conclusion is no objection to the Lockean argument he is discussing. It is an argument about the extent to which the state should tolerate diverse forms of religious worship or ritual. It does not address the broader question of the extent to which the state should tolerate practices that are required or recommended by some religious forms of life but are not matters of worship or ritual. And even within its narrow scope, Locke's argument does not pretend to occupy a position of absolute religious neutrality. Its principle prohibits to churches in their rites things that are prohibited to people in their use outside religious contexts. The Lockean state is not committed to toleration of ritual human sacrifice or rites involving torture. If it were, it would be deeply repugnant. So Lockeans will agree with Griffiths that absolute religious neutrality is impossible and unrestricted toleration of religious practices is undesirable. His criticism of Locke's argument therefore misses the mark.

It also seems to me that Griffiths presents a misleading picture of the consequences of accepting his definition of religion. To return to his example, the religious identities of many Christians and Jews do indeed require them to hold that abortion is a grave moral wrong. But it is possible to think that one's religious morality is comprehensive, incapable of abandonment or unsurpassable, and of central importance without also thinking that the state ought to impose that morality on all the citizens of a religiously diverse democracy in which many people dissent from key components of one's moral code. Many Christians and Jews who consider abortion a grave moral wrong do in fact think that the state ought not to impose this tenet of their morality on their fellow citizens by means of a legal prohibition. They find it possible to reconcile their religious identities with the legality of abortion. To be sure, some of them may reckon it a loss that they do not live in a religiously homogeneous society and may view acquiescence in a situation in which abortion is legally permitted as a mere *modus vivendi*. However, it would be extremely uncharitable to claim that such people are not faithful Christians or Jews simply because they oppose having crucial moral prohibitions from their religious forms of life legally imposed on others who do not participate in them. Recourse to a definition of religion that eviscerates it or renders it unrecognizable to those who take their religious forms to life to be comprehensive, unsurpassable, and of central importance is not needed to make room for devoutly religious people who can reconcile their religious identities with the legality of abortion. These definitional marks of religion do not entail that all the faithful would prefer to use the power of the state to enforce their morality on others or to work toward a theocracy.

I think the vulnerability of this Lockean argument lies in its attempt to offer a functional definition of the state. Locke's claim that the commonwealth is constituted solely for the procurement, preservation, and advancement of civil interests, as he understands them, obviously does not provide a descriptively adequate definition of historical or contemporary political realities. There have been and still are theocratic states constituted at least in part to procure, preserve, and advance distinctively religious interests such as obedience to God's laws or the salvation of souls. To be sure, many liberals hold that Locke's definition specifies the *proper* functions of a state; they may say that the commonwealth *ought to be* constituted only to procure, preserve, and advance such interests as life, liberty, health, and property. But theocrats will disagree. And a normative dispute of this sort cannot sensibly be settled by a definitional stipulation. Any definition that might be proposed would beg the question against some parties to the dispute. If a Lockean account of the proper functions of a state is to be vindicated, it must emerge as the conclusion of substantial normative argument in political theory. It cannot appear, as it does in the present context, as an unsupported definitional premise in an argument for tolerating diverse forms of religious worship.

Another argument from Locke's *Letter* addresses the issue of toleration of religious belief. It is encapsulated in the following passage:

> The care of souls cannot belong to the civil magistrate, because his power consists only in outward force: but true and saving religion consists in the inward persuasion of the mind, without which nothing can be acceptable to God. And such is the nature of the understanding, that it cannot be compelled to the belief of anything by outward force. Confiscation of estate, imprisonment, torments, nothing of that nature can have any such efficacy as to make men change the inward judgment that they have framed of things. (Locke, 1824, p. 11)

Let us spell this argument out in a bit more detail. Suppose the state, personified in the quotation as the civil magistrate, has as an end bringing all its citizens into the true and saving religion. In order to do so, it must insure that they are all inwardly persuaded of the correct religious doctrines. Suppose too that the citizens differ among themselves about which religious doctrines are correct. What is the state to do? The only means at its disposal is the application or threat of outward force directed against those of its citizens who are inwardly persuaded of incorrect religious doctrines. But even if the state is willing to persecute such citizens, such a policy of coercive action cannot succeed in achieving the state's end, because outward force cannot compel change in belief. So persecution in order to bring citizens into the true and saving religion is instrumentally irrational. The state must in any case put up with incorrect religious beliefs if some of its citizens have them; it would be pointless to persecute rather than to tolerate diversity of religious belief.

Locke holds that outward force cannot compel belief because he thinks that belief is not subject to voluntary control. He insists that "speculative opinions, therefore, and articles of faith, as they are called, cannot be imposed on any church by the law of the land; for it is absurd that things should be enjoined by laws, which are not in men's power to perform; and to believe this or that to be true, does not depend upon our will" (Locke, 1824, pp. 39–40). The law might enjoin me to recite the words of a certain creed every day, for the words I utter are under my voluntary control and so this recitation is in my power to perform. What would be absurd, according to Locke, is a law enjoining belief in the creed thus recited. Yet my recitation would not be acceptable to God unless I were inwardly persuaded of the truth of this creed. If the state coerced me into daily recitation of the creed of true and saving religion but I lacked belief in it, the state would not have brought me into that religion. The state can coerce lip-service; it cannot coerce genuine faith.

Jeremy Waldron has made two objections to this Lockean argument. The first attacks its assumption that belief is not subject to voluntary control. He grants that belief is not normally subject to direct voluntary control. If I am looking at a green tree, there is no act of will I can now perform that will make me believe I am looking at a red fire engine. If I do not believe that Jesus rose from the dead, there is no act of will I can now perform that will immediately bring it about that I believe the Christian doctrine of the resurrection. He points out, however, that belief is often subject to indirect voluntary control because we can control within limits the sources of belief we attend to or take notice of. Suppose it highly likely that we will believe the doctrines of the true and saving religion if we read its sacred books and take part in its holy rituals often enough. The state could then increase the number of citizens who eventually wind up accepting the true and saving faith by coercing everyone to read those books and participate in those rituals. Perhaps if the state compels me to recite its creed every day under threat of legal punishment, I will in a few years come wholeheartedly to believe its central dogmas. Thus intolerance can under some conditions be an effective means to religious ends. As Waldron puts the point, "since coercion may therefore be applied to religious ends by this indirect means, it can no longer be condemned as in all circumstances irrational" (Waldron, 1988, p. 81). Of course this is a lesson we might also have learned from Pascal. His advice to the libertines who were persuaded by his wager argument of the rationality of betting on the existence of God but found themselves lacking belief in God was that they should start by attending masses and using holy water. And the lesson applies to guarding the citizens against falling into heresy as well as to converting them to orthodoxy. If an attractive heresy is likely to seduce citizens who read its scriptures and celebrate its rites away from the true and saving religion, banning those scriptures and rites will be a rational means to the state's religious end. Hence this Lockean argument for the irrationality of religious intolerance fails.

Waldron's other objection is moral. Even if the argument were successful, it would, he thinks, recommend toleration for the wrong reason. Its complaint is that intolerance is irrational to engage in, not that it wrongs its victims. On his view, "what one misses above all in Locke's argument is a sense that there is anything *morally* wrong with intolerance, or a sense of any deep concern for the *victims* of persecution or the moral insult that is involved in the attempt to manipulate their faith" (Waldron, 1988, p. 85). I agree that there is something morally wrong with intolerance. When it is addressed to religious inquisitors, however, I do not think this charge is likely to be dialectically effective unless it has argumentative support it does not get from Waldron's essay. For they are apt to trot out the familiar paternalistic reply that their actions actually confer benefits on those affected by them. They often appeal in such replies to some other-worldly good such as the soul's salvation that is supposed to depend upon correct religious belief and practice and to outweigh vastly the this-worldly evils of persecution or manipulation. And it is not obvious how to respond to such appeals without begging the question against their claim that there are such great other-worldly goods.

John Stuart Mill's *On Liberty* contains a utilitarian argument for toleration. As we shall see, the paternalism of the inquisitors gives rise to a problem for this argument, which is only to be expected, since utilitarians endorse paternalism when it maximizes utility. Unlike Jeremy Bentham, Mill does not define utility reductively in terms of pleasure and pain. He says: "I regard utility as the ultimate appeal on all ethical questions; but it must be utility in the largest sense, grounded on the permanent interests of man as a progressive being" (Mill, 1948, p. 16). But he does exclude one sort of consideration from his weighing up of costs and benefits, noting explicitly that "I forgo any advantage which could be derived to my argument from the idea of abstract right, as a thing independent of utility" (Mill, 1948, p. 16). So violation of a moral right to freedom of religious belief or worship will not count for Mill as a separate cost in arriving at conclusions about the balance of costs and benefits of intolerant actions or practices.

Friends and foes of religious toleration are likely to disagree about its costs and benefits because of factual disagreements about its consequences. Consider a dispute between an atheist and a theist. The atheist will say that divine punishments visited upon unbelievers because their unbelief offends God are not to be counted as a cost of tolerating atheism, since, there being no God, there are no such punishments. Some theists will insist that there are divine punishments for atheism which must be reckoned as a cost of tolerating it. A utilitarian argument addressed to both parties in this dispute cannot take sides in it; it must remain neutral if it is to be persuasive to both parties. So such an argument can appeal only to costs and benefits that are acknowledged to be on common ground between the disputing parties.

It seems that Mill is trying to abide by such a constraint. David Lewis attributes to him a rule of neutralism, not because he explicitly states and defends it, but because he never violates it. According to this rule, both parties are invited to assent to a common list of costs and benefits.

> This common list is supposed to have decisive weight in favour of toleration. One or the other side may have in mind some further costs and benefits that obtain according to its own disputed opinions, perhaps including some that count in favour of suppression; but if so, these considerations are supposed to be outweighed by the considerations on the neutral common list. (Lewis, 2000, p. 162)

Mill's list is summarized at the end of the second chapter of *On Liberty*. The costs and benefits it cites apply to religious freedom but also to wider freedoms of thought and expression.

There are four items on the list. First, suppression risks loss of truth, for "if any opinion is compelled to silence, that opinion may, for aught we can certainly know, be true." Second, even suppression of error inhibits efforts to move from partial truth to the whole truth, because "it is only by the collision of adverse opinions that the remainder of the truth has any chance of being supplied." Third, even if the received view happens to be the whole truth, "unless it is suffered to be, and actually is, vigorously and earnestly contested, it will, by most of those who receive it, be held in the manner of a prejudice, with little comprehension or feeling of its rational grounds." And fourth, in addition "the meaning of the doctrine itself will be in danger of being lost, or enfeebled, and deprived of its vital effect on the character and conduct: the dogma becoming a mere formal profession, inefficacious for good, but cumbering the ground, and preventing the growth of any real and heartfelt conviction, from reason or personal experience" (Mill, 1948, p. 65). For the sake of argument, let us suppose that all the items on this list are indeed common ground in the dispute about toleration. If we wish, we can even add to it. For example, surely everyone would agree that paying for the system of thought-police and prisons needed to enforce it would be a cost of suppression.

Even so, as Lewis observes, the expanded list will not give Mill what he needs. It will not provide a balance in favor of toleration that outweighs considerations that count in favor of suppression according to the disputed opinions of the foes of toleration. In order to make this point vivid, Lewis imagines a utilitarian inquisitor. He accepts the items on the expanded list but complains that the tally is incomplete. It omits the crucial cost of tolerating religious heresy: the eternal damnation of the heretics. From the inquisitor's point of view,

> that is something infinitely worse than any evil whatever in this life; infinitely more weighty, therefore, than the whole of the neutralist tally. Further, damnation is not just a matter of pain . . . Damnation is harm along exactly the dimension that Mill wanted us to bear in mind: it is the utter absence and the extreme opposite of human excellence and flourishing. (Lewis, 2000, p. 168)

The inquisitor believes that heresy is contagious. He thinks people are likely to be seduced by its charms. He need not believe that he can eradicate heresy once and for all. But he does think he can stop it from spreading and thereby save some who would otherwise be damned. Nor need he believe he can save the heretics by forced conversion. He thinks he can prevent many of those who are not yet heretics from being infected. So he concludes that the balance of costs and benefits is overwhelmingly in favor of suppressing heresy. Thus Mill's argument fails. This is of course not a failure of utilitarianism as such; it is only a failure of utilitarianism constrained by the rule of neutralism. However, if utilitarian argument is not thus constrained, it will not persuade the utilitarian inquisitor or, more generally, be dialectically effective even against foes of toleration who are themselves utilitarians.

The arguments for religious toleration examined so far do not make a solid case for it. If we suppose that they are typical of what classical British liberalism has to offer, it does not provide a strong intellectual bulwark against intolerance. An interesting fact about these arguments is that they do not appeal to epistemological considerations. Classical arguments found in a continental European liberal tradition deploy an explicitly epistemic strategy in defense of religious toleration. My next task is to scrutinize two such arguments.

One of them is to be found in the impassioned defense of religious toleration in Pierre Bayle's *Philosophical Commentary on These Words of Jesus Christ "Compel Them to Come In."* It is easy to understand Bayle's passion. His older brother Jacob, who was a Protestant minister, had been imprisoned by French Catholic authorities and tortured in an unsuccessful attempt to compel him to renounce his religious loyalties. Shortly before Jacob died in prison in 1685, the Edict of Nantes was revoked, and thereafter the persecution of Protestants in France grew in intensity. The words of Jesus referred to in Bayle's title come from the parable of the great dinner in Luke's Gospel. According to this story, when the invited guests make excuses for not coming to the dinner party and even poor folk from the neighborhood do not fill all the places, the angry host says to his servant: "Go out into the roads and lanes, and compel people to come in, so that my house may be filled" (Luke 14:23). Starting at least as far back as Augustine, some Christians had used this verse as a proof-text to provide Biblical warrant for forced conversions. Bayle's book contains a battery of arguments against interpreting this verse in such a way that it can be used to support that sort of religious persecution. His most interesting argument combines moral and epistemological considerations.

According to Bayle, the general principle on which the argument rests is "*that any particular dogma, whether advanced as contained in Scripture or proposed in any other way, is false, if repugnant to the clear and distinct notions of natural light, principally in regards to morality*" (Bayle, 1987, p. 33). As the reference to clear and distinct notions of natural light indicates, Bayle is working with a Cartesian epistemology in which the epistemic status of deliverances of the natural light is so high that it guarantees their truth. Given the principle that a doctrine is false if contrary to the natural light, what he needs to show is that the words "Compel them to come in," when interpreted as commanding forced conversions, yield a claim contrary to the natural light. He does not appeal to general religious skepticism for support at this point. On the contrary, he insists "that by the purest and most distinct ideas of reason, we know there is a being sovereignly perfect who governs all things, who ought to be adored by mankind, who approves certain actions and rewards them, and who disapproves and punishes others" (Bayle, 1987, p. 35). We also know in the same way that the worship we owe this supreme being consists chiefly in inner acts of the mind; even when the adoration we ought to render to a perfect being also involves exterior signs, it must include interior mental acts. Bayle supposes that these mental acts depend upon the will and cannot be compelled. He says:

> It is evident then that the only legitimate way of inspiring religion is by producing in the soul certain judgments and certain movements of the will in relation to God. Now since threats, prisons, fines, exile, beatings, torture, and generally whatever is comprehended under the literal signification of compelling, are incapable of forming in the soul those judgments of the will in respect to God which constitute the essence of religion, it is evident that this is a mistaken way of establishing a religion and, consequently, that Jesus Christ has not commanded it. (Bayle, 1987, p. 36)

At this point, however, a difficulty that Locke's second argument encountered also confronts Bayle. It may be, for example, that since religious beliefs are not under the direct control of the will, people threatened with religious persecution cannot become converts simply by deciding to do so. But even if this is the case, compelling outward practice may in the long run be an effective means to inducing inward belief. Compulsion may after all be indirectly capable of forming in the soul the judgments which constitute the essence of religion. Like Locke, Bayle is vulnerable to empirical confutation on this point.

However, Bayle has, as I see it, the resources to bypass the vexed question of whether compulsion is an effective means to establishing a religion or at least to minimizing the effects of heresy. He can appeal directly to moral considerations. Early in the book he announces that he is "relying upon this single principle of natural light, *that any literal interpretation which carries an obligation to commit iniquity is false*" (Bayle, 1987, p. 28). Though he grants that the literal interpretation of the words "Compel them to come in" supports the practice of forced conversion, it is open to him to hold that it is morally wrong to use compulsion to produce the inner acts that are essential to religion. So the following argument is available to Bayle. According to the literal interpretation of Luke 14:23, Jesus has commanded the use of compulsion to produce the inner acts essential to religion. This command carries with it an obligation to use compulsion for that purpose, because commands of Jesus are divine commands and so impose obligations. But the obligation to make such a use of compulsion is an obligation to commit an iniquity, since it is morally wrong to use compulsion for this purpose. Hence the literal interpretation of Luke 14:23 is false, and so Jesus has not commanded the use of compulsion to produce the inner acts essential to religion.

But is the moral principle that it is wrong to use compulsion to produce the inner acts essential to religion itself a deliverance of the natural light? Probably not. What is more, I think Bayle himself could not consistently even hold that it is true unless it is subject to an important qualification. This is because he allows for special dispensations from divine moral laws. Indeed, he believes that God can and sometimes does dispense from the Decalogue's prohibition on homicide. There are, he affirms, circumstances that "change the nature of homicide from a bad action into a good action, a secret command of God, for example" (Bayle, 1987, p. 171). The cases he has in mind are, of course, the Biblical stories in which God commands homicide. The most famous of them is the *akedah*, the binding of Isaac, recounted in Genesis 22; according to that story, which served as a basis for Kierkegaard's notion of the teleological suspension of the ethical, God commanded Abraham to slay his son Isaac. So Bayle has left a loophole open to religious inquisitors. He cannot consistently deny that they may be right if they claim they have been dispensed by God from the principle that it is morally wrong to use compulsion to make converts or claim they have received a secret divine command to employ compulsion for this purpose. But inquisitors do not typically offer private divine dispensations or secret divine commands as epistemic grounds for their intolerant activities. Perhaps this is because they suppose that even their fellow believers would assign such claims a very low epistemic status, viewing them as utterly incredible at best. One might think, however, that the mere possibility of such private dispensations or secret commands is enough to preclude the principle that it is always wrong to use compulsion to make converts from being a deliverance of the natural light.

In my opinion, though at this point I go beyond anything explicit in Bayle's text, his best strategy would be to conduct the argument without making any dubious appeals to the Cartesian natural light. The epistemic credentials of two conflicting claims are to be assessed and then compared. One is a moral principle to the effect that intolerant behavior of a certain kind is wrong; the other is a conflicting religious claim. The epistemic principle called upon to adjudicate the conflict is that, whenever two conflicting claims differ in epistemic status, the claim with the lower status is to be rejected. In the case of particular interest to Bayle, the moral principle is that using compulsion to produce the inner acts essential to religion is wrong. Though it may not be evident by the natural light, it is an intuitively plausible principle. And even if, strictly speaking, it needs to be qualified by a *ceteris paribus* clause to allow for such possibilities as secret divine commands, potential violations of such a clause are not at issue in the present context. So the epistemic status of the moral principle is fairly high. The conflicting religious claim is that employing compulsion to produce the inner acts essential to religion is obligatory because Jesus commanded it. Considerations Bayle dwells on in the *Philosophical Commentary* can be deployed in assessing the epistemic status of the religious claim. For instance, after arguing that Luke 14:23 should be interpreted in the light of its context, Bayle contends that reading the verse in a way that supports forced conversion "is contrary to the whole tenor and general spirit of the Gospel" (Bayle, 1987, p. 39). Considerations of this sort show that the epistemic status of the religious claim is lower than that of the moral principle. The religious claim is, therefore, to be rejected. The Baylean case succeeds.

An advantage of this strategy is that it allows the friends of religious toleration to focus on the specific grounds for intolerance offered by their opponents and to attack them one by one. A corresponding limitation is that a particular application of it, even if it is successful, eliminates only one ground for religious intolerance. Hence repeated applications will have to succeed in order to build a cumulative case against the full array of grounds invoked by the foes of religious toleration.

Kant presents an epistemic argument against the religious inquisitor in the context of the doctrine of conscience he develops in *Religion within the Boundaries of Mere Reason*. According to that doctrine, conscience is a state of consciousness that is itself a duty. For any action I propose to perform, I must not only be of the opinion that it is morally right or think it probable that it is right; I have a duty to be aware of being epistemically certain that it is morally right before I proceed to perform it. If I act in the absence of such an awareness, I act unconscientiously and hence violate this duty, even if the action I perform is, in fact, right and so I violate no further duty in performing it. Kant applies his doctrine of conscience to an inquisitor whose religious faith is so firm he is willing to suffer martyrdom for it, if need be, and who must judge the case of someone, otherwise a good citizen, charged with heresy. If the inquisitor condemns the heretic to death, Kant wonders, does he act with a lack of conscience and thus consciously do wrong? Kant builds it into the case that the inquisitor "was indeed presumably firm in the belief that a supernaturally revealed divine will (perhaps according to the saying, *compellite intrare*) permitted him, if not even made a duty for him, to extirpate supposed unbelief together with the unbelievers" (Kant, 1996a, p. 203). Thus Kant's inquisitor is, as it were, a target of Bayle's arguments, since *compellite intrare* is, of course, Latin for the "Compel them to come in" of Luke 14:23.

Kant's famous response to the inquisitor of his example deserves to be quoted in full:

> That to take a human being's life because of his religious faith is wrong is certain, unless (to allow the most extreme possibility) a divine will, made known to the inquisitor in some extraordinary way, has decreed otherwise. But that God has ever manifested this awful will is a matter of historical documentation and never apodictically certain. After all, the revelation reached the inquisitor only through the intermediary of human beings and their interpretation, and even if it were to appear to him to have come from God himself (like the command issued to Abraham to slaughter his own son like a sheep), yet it is at least possible that on this point error has prevailed. But then the inquisitor would risk the danger of doing something which would be to the highest degree wrong, and on this score he acts unconscientiously. (Kant, 1996a, pp. 203–4)

And in *The Conflict of the Faculties*, Kant returns to the *akedah*, which is alluded to in the second parenthetical remark in the passage just quoted, in order to say more about Abraham's epistemic situation. He there insists that "Abraham should have replied to this supposedly divine voice: 'That I ought not to kill my good son is quite certain. But that you, this apparition, are God – of that I am not certain, and never can be, not even if this voice rings down to me from (visible) heaven," (Kant, 1996b, p. 283).

According to Kant, then, Abraham cannot be epistemically certain that the voice he hears comes from God, and so he cannot be certain that killing his son is morally right. If he proceeds to slay Isaac, he violates the duty of conscience to have an awareness of such certainty and so acts unconscientiously. Moreover, Abraham can be certain that killing his son is morally wrong unless, allowing for the most remote possibility, God does command it. If he proceeds to sacrifice Isaac, he also runs the very great risk of wrongly doing so. Therefore, if Abraham proceeds to kill Isaac, he surely violates a duty to act conscientiously and most likely also violates a duty not to kill his son. Similarly, Kant's inquisitor cannot be epistemically certain that scripture actually records a divine command to eliminate unbelievers along with their heresies. So if he condemns the person accused of heresy, he surely violates a duty to act conscientiously and most likely also violates a duty not to kill people on account of their religious faith.

If we set aside the complications introduced into the picture by Kant's doctrine of conscience, I think we may fruitfully view Kant as working with the argumentative strategy I outlined in my discussion of Bayle. The inquisitor can be almost certain that it is morally wrong to kill people on account of their religious faith; he falls short of complete certainty only because he allows for the remote possibility of a divine command to do so. But the inquisitor cannot be even close to certain that it is morally right or even obligatory to kill unbelievers because God decrees it, since he cannot achieve anything close to certainty that scripture contains such a divine command. Hence the claim that it is morally right or even obligatory to kill unbelievers is to be rejected.

Difficulties with Kant's use of this strategy resemble those that arise in the case of Bayle. Kant has an extremely optimistic view of our ability to attain epistemic certainty about principles of moral wrongness. Suppose we grant that it is certain that killing people for their religious faith is wrong and so conclude with Kant that it is not right for the inquisitor to kill heretics. What of other sorts of religious persecution at the inquisitor's disposal? Consider, for instance, exile, which in a passage I quoted Bayle offers as an example of compulsion. Is it really epistemically certain that sending people into exile or, more generally, excluding them from a political community on account of their religious faith is morally wrong? Is it certain that the magistrates of Calvin's Geneva would have done wrong if they had expelled Catholics from the city under conditions in which the exiles were compensated for lost property? Is it certain that the elders of a contemporary Amish farming community would do wrong if they excluded those of other faiths from their community? Perhaps Kant would hold that these claims are certain too, but I doubt that they are. So I think the strategy I am discussing will not serve to rule out all the forms of religious intolerance I oppose if it can only be successfully employed with principles of moral wrongness that are epistemically certain or very nearly so.

But if we deploy the strategy with principles of moral wrongness that fall considerably short of epistemic certainty, we must worry about the possibility that it will in some cases support intolerance. As traditionally conceived, God is very powerful. It would thus seem to be well within God's power to communicate to us a sign that confers on the claim that God commands some intolerant behavior, for example, issuing threats to heretics, a fairly high epistemic status. Let us grant that Kant's inquisitor cannot be epistemically certain that scripture contains a divine command to persecute heretics because of the facts about transmission and interpretation he cites. Suppose we also concede to Kant that someone who hears a voice commanding persecution that resounds from the visible heaven cannot be absolutely or apodictically certain that it is divine speech. It does not follow that hearing such a voice cannot confer on the claim that God has commanded what the voice is taken to command a fairly high epistemic status. Therefore it seems possible for even sense perception to bestow on the claim that intolerant behavior is obligatory because it is divinely commanded an epistemic status higher than that of a conflicting principle of moral wrongness that falls considerably short of certainty. In that case, according to the argumentative strategy under considera-tion, it is the moral principle that is to be rejected. What is more, if there is a kind of religious experience that is distinct from but analogous to sense perception, such religious perception could also contribute to elevating the epistemic status of the claim that intolerant behavior is obligatory because divinely commanded to a level above that of a conflicting moral principle that is less than certain. And, of course, there might be a cumulative case argument from a variety of considera-tions that confers fairly high epistemic status on a claim that intolerant behavior, having been divinely commanded, is morally obligatory. So if we apply our strat-egy to cases in which the moral principle we appeal to has an epistemic status considerably less than certainty, we cannot guarantee in advance that it will not lose out in competition with a religious claim about an obligation to persecute imposed by divine command that has somehow managed to achieve a higher epistemic status. In short, even if this strategy is effective against the worst sorts of religious intolerance, it may not serve the purpose of defending the com-prehensive regime of toleration favored by contemporary liberals.

The result of our examination of some classical arguments for religious tolera-tion will surely seem disappointing to those in search of theoretical grounds for the tolerant habits now widespread in liberal democracies. There are powerful objections to the arguments constructed by Locke and Mill. And the epistemic strategy deployed by Bayle and Kant may lack the power to defend the full array of tolerant practices favored by contemporary liberals. The arguments we have inherited from the early modern champions of religious toleration leave its prac-tices resting on rather shaky philosophical foundations.

Exclusions of the Religious

It may at first seem odd that early modern liberals argued for a political order more inclusive and tolerant of religious diversity than most states of their era while some contemporary liberal theorists advocate the exclusion of religion from the political life of the liberal democracies of which many of us are citizens. I think the impression of oddity vanishes, however, once we realize that both groups of liberals are motivated by fear of the threat religious conflict can pose to the stability of a political order. Of course these contemporary liberal theorists do not wish to deprive people of religious liberty or to engage in religious persecution, but they do want religion kept out of politics. An example is Richard Rorty who, in a brief discussion of Stephen Carter's *The Culture of Disbelief*, endorses what he describes as the happy, Jeffersonian compromise that the Enlightenment reached with the religious, which "consists in privatizing religion – keeping it out of what Carter calls 'the public square,' making it seem bad taste to bring religion into discussions of public policy" (Rorty, 1994, p. 2). And Rorty's fear makes itself manifest when he goes on to attribute to liberal philosophers the view that "we shall not be able to keep a democratic political community going unless the religious believers remain willing to trade privatization for a guarantee of religious liberty" (Rorty, 1994, p. 3). But it is obvious that many religious believers do not regard the proposed privatization of religion as happy and demonstrate by their behavior that it is not a compromise they accept. Excluding religion from the public square strikes them as unreasonable and unfair. What do liberal theorists who want to keep religion out of the public square have to say in defense of the proposed exclusion?

Robert Audi's fullest response to this question occurs in his *Religious Commitment and Secular Reason*. The motivating fear behind his exclusionary proposal becomes apparent when he remarks that "if religious considerations are not appropriately balanced with secular ones in matters of coercion, there is a special problem: a clash of Gods vying for social control. Such uncompromising absolutes easily lead to death and destruction" (Audi, 2000, p. 103). Audi explains what he has in mind when he speaks of secular considerations by giving an explicit definition of secular reasons. He says: "I am taking a secular reason as roughly one whose normative force, that is, its status as a prima facie justificatory element, does not evidentially depend on the existence of God (or on denying it) or on theological considerations, or on the pronouncements of a person or institution *qua* religious authority" (Audi, 2000, p. 89). Two principles of moral obligation he advocates show that the balance of considerations he favors is heavily tilted in the direction of the secular. The first is the principle of secular rationale. It says that "one has a prima facie obligation not to advocate or support any law or public policy that restricts human conduct, unless one has, and is willing to offer, adequate secular reason for this advocacy or support (say for one's vote)" (Audi, 2000, p. 86). The second is the principle of secular motivation. It says that "one has a (prima facie) obligation to abstain from advocacy or support of a law or public policy that restricts human conduct, unless in advocating or supporting it one is sufficiently *motivated* by (normatively) adequate secular reason" (Audi, 2000, p. 96). In these two principles, Audi tells us, we are to understand a prima facie obligation to be "one that provides a reason for action which is strong enough to justify the action in the absence of conflicting considerations, but is also liable to being overridden by one or more such considerations" (Audi, 2000, p. 92).

A curious feature of Audi's view is that he admits that one may be within one's rights in violating his two principles. This would not be puzzling if he had in mind only legal rights derived from the constitutional guarantee of free exercise of religion. But he makes it clear that he is thinking of moral rights. He claims explicitly that "there are ideals of moral virtue that require of us more than simply acting within our moral rights" and goes on to explain that the ideals he has in mind are "what might be called *involuntary ideals*: their non-fulfillment (under the conditions to which they are relevant) subjects citizens in a liberal democracy to criticism, even if in various cases one may avoid it because of, say, a stronger conflicting demand" (Audi, 2000, p. 85). And he seems to think that the difference between his involuntary ideals and the prima facie obligations specified by his two principles is largely a terminological matter. He says: "In the main I shall speak here of prima facie obligations; but given that I recognize a moral right to act in ways that fall short of the relevant standards, the terminology of ideals may at times be preferable provided we distinguish between voluntary and involuntary ideals" (Audi, 2000, p. 86). This seems to me a mistake. Even if there are involuntary ideals whose non-fulfillment makes citizens liable to criticism, it does not follow that someone who fails to live up to them is liable to criticism of the same kind or severity as that to which someone who violates a non-overridden prima facie obligation is liable. Someone who violates a prima facie obligation that is not overridden is appropriately criticized or blamed as a wrongdoer. But someone who merely fails to live up to an ideal only deserves criticism as an underachiever or for falling short of some lofty level of excellence. If Audi has in mind only ideals of good citizenship, it is misleading of him to frame his principles in the vocabulary of moral obligation. Since he does frame them in that vocabulary not only in his book but also in several earlier published papers, I shall assume it is his intention that they be understood as genuine principles of prima facie moral obligation, not as mere ideals.

In a previous discussion of Audi's views, I argued that his principles would, if scrupulously followed by all citizens of a religiously pluralistic democracy such as the United States, "have the effect of excluding some religious believers from full participation in political debate and action on some important issues" (Quinn, 1997, p. 139). Consider a person sufficiently motivated to take part in peacefully advocating more restrictive abortion laws and to vote for candidates for political office who support such laws solely by the belief that God has made it known through the teaching authority of the Catholic Church that almost all abortions are wrong. Suppose she also thinks that all cogent secular reasons support more liberal abortion laws than those she favors and so neither has nor is willing to offer any secular reason at all for her advocacy and votes. Her advocacy and votes will, therefore, violate both of Audi's principles unless the obligations they specify are overridden in her case. Assume for a moment they are not overridden. Then she can come into compliance with those principles only by either ceasing her advocacy and refraining from voting for the candidates she prefers or coming to have, to be willing to offer, and to be sufficiently motivated by adequate secular reasons for her advocacy and votes. Thinking as she does that there are no adequate secular reasons for her actions, however, she will also think that the latter alternative is not open to her. She will thus conclude that she can comply with the principles only by ceasing her advocacy and refraining from voting for the candidates of her choice. I think she is under no obligation to perform such actions in her circumstances.

Could Audi's two principles be defended by supposing that the prima facie obligations they specify are overridden in the case of my advocate of more restrictive abortion laws? If we say that they are overridden whenever someone who relies only on religious reasons does not have, is not willing to offer, and is not sufficiently motivated by adequate secular reason for advocacy and votes, then the principles will be vacuous. But the kinds of overriding considerations Audi cites when he gives examples are not present in the case of my advocate. For instance, he mentions circumstances in which secrecy is necessary as an overrider for the obligation to be willing to offer secular reason. So this line of defense does not look promising. In addition, it is not the tack Audi takes. His response to my argument goes as follows:

> We should also distinguish *full* participation in debate from *unrestricted* participation. I can participate fully in political debate – even dominantly – whether or not I use all my arguments or express all my sentiments. To be sure, if I have only religious considerations to bring to such a debate . . . then the rationale principle may lead me not to use them in certain ways. I may, for instance, point out their bearing, but I may not advocate coercive legislation on the basis of them. (Audi, 2000, pp. 108–9)

However, this seems to me a merely terminological ploy. I am happy enough to put my point in his terms; my claim is that conscientious adherence to his two principles would exclude some religious people from unrestricted participation in political debate and action on some important issues.

The complaint I base on this claim is that Audi's two principles impose a heavy burden on religious people that non-religious people are not required to bear. This seems almost blindingly obvious. Perhaps its force will become apparent if we consider the principle that is obtained by replacing the word "secular" with the word "religious" in Audi's rationale principle. The resulting principle of religious rationale says that one has a prima facie obligation not to advocate or support any law or public policy that restricts human conduct, unless one has, and is willing to offer, adequate religious reason for this advocacy or support (say for one's vote). Secular humanists and atheistic naturalists would rightly object that this principle would impose an unreasonable and unfair burden on them. So too would a principle of religious motivation. Unless Audi's secular principles differ from the parallel religious principles because secular reason has justificatory force that religious reason lacks, religious believers can, by parity of reasoning, rightly object that Audi's principles impose such a burden on them. But Audi neither argues for nor endorses the view that there are systematic differences in epistemic efficacy between secular and religious reason. Thus he cannot block the objection that his exclusion of the religious is unreasonable and unfair. The objection therefore succeeds.

A different exclusionary proposal is embodied in the doctrine of public reason developed by John Rawls in *Political Liberalism* (1993) and later revised in "The Idea of Public Reason Revisited" (1997). For Rawls, public reason is connected with an ideal conception of citizenship for a constitutional democratic regime. It is not an ideal for the whole of life of a democratic citizen; it is only meant to regulate a citizen's participation in political affairs. And even within the political sphere, the limits it imposes apply only to questions of constitutional essentials and questions of basic justice. Yet it is not a supererogatory ideal, asking only for conduct above and beyond the call of duty. It "imposes a moral, not a legal, duty – the duty of civility – to be able to explain to one another on those fundamental questions how the principles and policies they advocate can be supported by the political values of public reason" (Rawls, 1993, p. 217). What sorts of normative constraints do this ideal and the duty of civility it imposes actually involve? They are constraints on the content of public reason aimed at securing explanations "in terms each could reasonably expect others might endorse as consistent with their freedom and equality" (Rawls, 1993, p. 218).

The content of public reason includes substantive liberal principles of justice and guidelines for inquiry that "specify ways of reasoning and criteria for the kinds of information relevant for political questions" (Rawls, 1993, p. 223). They are the parts of a liberal political conception of justice. The substantive principles of justice and the guidelines for inquiry in turn specify political values of two sorts. The substantive principles give rise to values of political justice, which include equality of political and civil liberty and equality of opportunity. The guidelines give rise to values of public reason, which include political virtues such as reasonableness and a readiness to honor the duty of civility. Only political values of these two sorts can be appealed to in justifications that honor the duty of civility. Since the aim of public reason is to justify laws and policies regarding constitutional essentials and basic justice to all citizens of a pluralistic constitutional democracy, in making our justificatory arguments "we are to appeal only to presently accepted general beliefs and forms of reasoning found in common sense, and the methods and conclusions of science when these are not controversial" (Rawls, 1993, p. 224), and "we are not to appeal to comprehensive religious and philosophical doctrines – to what we as individuals or members of associations see as the whole truth – nor to elaborate economic theories of general equilibrium, say, if these are in dispute" (Rawls, 1993, pp. 224–5). In short, common sense's deliverances and uncontroversial science lie within the bounds of public reason, while comprehensive doctrines, both religious and secular, as well as disputed science lie outside those bounds. This is exactly how one would expect Rawls to draw the boundary line around public reason, since he wants it to provide a shared public basis for political justification.

Are citizens who wish to live up to the Rawlsian ideal always supposed to remain within the bounds of public reason when matters of constitutional essentials and basic justice are at stake? In *Political Liberalism*, Rawls distinguishes between the exclusive view and the inclusive view of public reason. According to the exclusive view, "reasons given explicitly in terms of comprehensive doctrines are never to be introduced into public reason" (Rawls, 1993, p. 247). He suggests that the exclusive view would be appropriate for the highly idealized case of a society more or less well ordered by a single set of substantive principles of justice and untroubled by deep political disputes. However, he acknowledges that the inclusive view is better suited to less idealized cases. On that view, citizens are allowed, in some circumstances, "to present what they regard as the basis of political values rooted in their comprehensive doctrine, provided they do this in ways that strengthen the ideal of public reason itself" (Rawls, 1993, p. 247). An example he discusses indicates how the inclusive view's proviso might be satisfied. It involves a nearly well-ordered society in which there is a serious dispute about the application of one of the shared principles of justice. Suppose religious groups dispute about whether the principle of fair equality of opportunity, as applied to education, supports state aid to parochial schools. Rawls imagines that religious leaders might, by introducing portions of their comprehensive doctrines into the public forum, try to show how those doctrines affirm shared political values. If they succeeded, they would, Rawls thinks, strengthen the ideal of public reason and thereby satisfy the proviso of the inclusive view. He holds that the inclusive view seems correct because it "is more flexible as needed to further the ideal of public reason" (Rawls, 1993, p. 248).

But he changes his mind on this point. In "The Idea of Public Reason Revisited," he replaces the inclusive view with the wide view of public political culture. Like the inclusive view, the wide view is specified in terms of a proviso, but its proviso is more permissive than that of the inclusive view. According to the wide view, "reasonable comprehensive doctrines, religious or nonreligious, may be introduced in public political discussion at any time, provided that in due course proper political reasons – and not reasons given solely by comprehensive doctrines – are presented that are sufficient to support whatever the comprehensive doctrines are said to support" (Rawls, 1997, pp. 783–4). As Rawls is aware, the new proviso gives rise to questions. When must proper political reasons be given in order to satisfy the proviso's stipulation that they be given in due course? Must the same people who introduce their comprehensive doctrines into political discussion satisfy the proviso? How constraining the wide view turns out to be will depend on the answers to such questions. However, Rawls professes not to be able to provide much help in answering them. He believes the details of how to satisfy the proviso "must be worked out in practice and cannot feasibly be governed by a clear family of rules given in advance" (Rawls, 1997, p. 784). As I see it, Rawls moves from the inclusive view to the wide view at least in part because he wants to address the concerns of some religious people that his brand of political liberalism is unduly exclusive of the religious. But there is only so far he can go in this direction while remaining loyal to his liberalism's core aspiration to political justification to all citizens on questions of constitutional essentials and basic justice. Reasons drawn from comprehensive doctrines that divide us must ultimately be redeemed in terms of political values we share as free and equal citizens. So even after the wide view's proviso is in place, ultimate political justification still must be in terms of shared political values and so must be conducted within the limits of public reason.

It seems to me we can detect behind this aspiration a muted form of fear of conflict. In the introduction to *Political Liberalism*, Rawls tells us that its central question may be put this way: "How is it possible that there may exist over time a stable and just society of free and equal citizens profoundly divided by reasonable though incompatible religious, philosophical, and moral doctrines" (Rawls, 1993, p. xviii)? The fear of conflict prompts the worry about stability. Incompatible comprehensive doctrines, even when all are reasonable, are potential sources of conflict and hence are potentially destabilizing. It is to his credit that Rawls sees that this holds, not only for religious comprehensive doctrines, but also for secular comprehensive doctrines, and so treats doctrines of the two sorts in the same fashion. In this respect, he is considerably more insightful than Audi.

The views of Rawls and Audi can usefully be compared on two other points. One is a point of difference. In one respect, Audi is more permissive than Rawls. Rawlsian public reason excludes both religious and secular reasons drawn from comprehensive doctrines, while Audi's principles of prima facie obligation exclude only religious reasons. In another respect, Rawls is more permissive than Audi. The limits of public reason apply only when matters of constitutional essentials and basic justice are at stake, while Audi's principles apply, more broadly, whenever laws or public policies that restrict human conduct are at issue. The other point of comparison is one of similarity. Both Rawls and Audi include in the normative machinery they employ both ideals and deontology – duty, in the case of Rawls, and obligation, in the case of Audi. It is as if both of them want to have their cake and eat it too. They can appeal to ideals of citizenship in order to highlight the excellence built into their conceptions of the good liberal citizen. And they can appeal to duty or obligation in order to make it seem that such excellences are demanded or required of us.

Rawls is quite clear about ways in which the ideal of public reason is supposed to constrain discussion in the public forum. It asks citizens to submit to the discipline of working up and being prepared to defend a political conception of justice. And it also asks them to submit to the discipline of using their political conceptions as filters on argument that make the route from their comprehensive doctrines to ultimate political justification indirect. According to Rawls,

> What we cannot do in public reason is to proceed directly from our comprehensive doctrine, or a part thereof, to one or several political principles and values, and the particular institutions they support. Instead, we are required first to work to the basic ideas of a complete political conception and from there to elaborate its principles and ideals, and to use the arguments they provide. (Rawls, 1997, pp. 777–8)

We must proceed by way of political conceptions because in public reason we aim at justification in terms of values all citizens can reasonably be expected to endorse and political conceptions rather than comprehensive doctrines are sources of such values. Bearing the yoke of this discipline will not be equally easy for all citizens. Is it too much to ask of the religious citizens of a liberal democracy?

Nicholas Wolterstorff thinks it is. Published in 1997, his criticism of Rawls is directed against *Political Liberalism*; it does not take into account "The Idea of Public Reason Revisited," which was only published in that year. Yet one of Wolterstorff's main arguments applies as directly to the views of the later paper as it does to those of the earlier book. Its sole premise is this: "It belongs to the *religious convictions* of a good many religious people in our society that *they ought to base* their decisions concerning fundamental issues of justice *on* their religious convictions" (Wolterstorff, 1997, p. 105). The conclusion he infers immediately from that premise is this: "Accordingly, to require of them that they not base their decisions and discussions concerning political issues on their religion is to infringe, inequitably, on the free exercise of their religion" (Wolterstorff, 1997, p. 105). And in the sentence immediately following the one that states this conclusion, which serves as a kind of gloss on it, he makes it clear that his argument is aimed at views common to the earlier book and the later paper by Rawls. Speaking of the religious people referred to in the argument, Wolterstorff says: "If they have to make a choice, they will make their decisions about constitutional essentials and matters of basic justice on the basis of their religious convictions and make their decisions on more peripheral matters on other grounds – exactly the opposite of what Rawls lays down in his version of the restraint" (Wolterstorff, 1997, p. 105).

I think this is a bad argument. Its premise is undoubtedly true: there surely are many religious citizens of liberal democracies whose religious convictions include the belief that they should base their political responses to fundamental questions of justice on their religion. Its conclusion, however, is ambiguous. If there were a legal requirement that they not do so, it would clearly infringe on the free exercise of their religion. But Rawlsian political liberalism proposes no such legal duty; its duty of civility is a moral rather than a legal duty. Rawls himself is explicit about how this distinction bears on constitutionally protected liberties. He says that the duty of civility is not a legal duty because "in that case it would be incompatible with freedom of speech" (Rawls, 1997, p. 769). By the same token, the duty of civility would be incompatible with the free exercise of religion if it were a legal duty. So if the conclusion of the argument is to make contact with Rawls, it must be taken to claim that morally requiring religious citizens not to base their political activity on their religion is an infringement of the free exercise of their religion. Thus interpreted, however, the conclusion is false, and so the argument is invalid. Morally prohibiting religious citizens from basing their political activity on religious grounds would no more infringe their free exercise of religion than would morally prohibiting them from treating gays and lesbians disrespectfully on religious grounds. In both cases, the free exercise clause constitutionally protects conduct that violates proposed moral requirements, and as long as religious citizens have effective legal freedom to violate such requirements there has been no infringement of the free exercise of their religion. Hence Wolterstorff's argument fails to show that Rawlsian political liberalism treats religious citizens inequitably or unfairly.

Yet despite the fact that I think Wolterstorff's attack on Rawls fails, I also believe that the constraints of Rawlsian political liberalism, even when it is understood in terms of the wide view of public political culture, impose excessive burdens on many citizens. Some of them are the religious citizens Wolterstorff mentions; others are non-religious citizens whose secular comprehensive doctrines require them to base their decisions concerning fundamental issues of justice on those doctrines. As I see it, Rawlsian political liberalism does ask too much of such citizens. I conjecture that my disagreement with Rawls on this issue stems from differences in the way we view the problem of stability for a pluralistic liberal democracy. I share with Robert Adams the view that "Rawls underemphasizes the combative aspects of a democratic polity and tends to overestimate the level of theoretical agreement in political ethics needed for an attainably just society" (Adams, 1993, p. 112). It also seems to me quite plausible that what principles of constraint on political argument, if any, are needed to prevent dangerous conflict will vary from one society to another depending on such contingent factors as historical experience, cultural traditions, and likely future development. And, though this is an empirical matter about which I could be mistaken, it seems to me that the stability of the liberal democratic political order of the United States at present is not seriously threatened by the presence of conflicting yet reasonable comprehensive doctrines, even though the constraints proposed by Rawls are not widely observed by ordinary citizens. I conclude that those constraints impose an excessive burden because they are necessary neither in order to respond to a serious threat of instability nor for the sake of an attainably just society.

I do, however, see something deeply attractive in the Rawlsian ideal of public reason; this is its aspiration to justification on questions of constitutional essentials and basic justice in terms of political values every reasonable citizen might reasonably be expected to endorse. Probably, given prevailing circumstances in the United States at present, it is unrealistic to expect all reasonable citizens to accept the yoke of discipline required to live by it. It is evidently not always a serious objection to an ideal that it is unrealistic. But I think it is a serious criticism of an unrealistic ideal that it purports to impose moral duties. Rawls clearly conceives of his ideal of public reason as imposing a moral duty, the duty of civility. According to a somewhat different conception of moral ideals, however, they urge or advise conduct that is morally excellent but above and beyond the call of duty. I am on record as holding that "on this conception, I am prepared to subscribe to the ideal of public reason, understood as including the wide view of public political culture, despite its restrictions, as a political ideal in our present circumstances" (Quinn, 2001, p. 124). Conceived in the way Rawls thinks of it, as imposing a duty of civility, I am not willing to subscribe to it except in hypothetical circumstances. I would subscribe to it, for example, if there were an overlapping consensus on a single liberal political conception of justice among all the reasonable comprehensive doctrines present in my society. In these circumstances, compliance with the duty of civility would not be excessively burdensome for any reasonable citizen. And I might subscribe to it if there were an overlapping consensus on a family of liberal political conceptions among all those doctrines. As things actually are, I do not subscribe to it. My conclusion is that religious citizens in the United States presently do not act contrary to duty and are not guilty of wrongdoing if, chafing at even the modest constraints implied by the wide view of public political culture, they choose not to live within the limits of Rawlsian public reason.

References

Adams, Robert M. (1993) Religious Ethics in a Pluralistic Society. In G. Outka and J. P. Reeder, Jr. (eds.), *Prospects for a Common Morality* (pp. 93–113). Princeton: Princeton University Press.

Audi, Robert (2000) *Religious Commitment and Secular Reason*. Cambridge: Cambridge University Press.

Bayle, Pierre (1987) *Pierre Bayle's Philosophical Commentary*, trans. A. G. Tannenbaum. New York: Peter Lang. Original work published 1686.

Griffiths, Paul J. (2001) *Problems of Religious Diversity*. Oxford: Blackwell.

Kant, Immanuel (1996a) *Religion Within the Boundaries of Mere Reason*. In I. Kant, *Religion and Rational Theology*, trans. A. W. Wood and G. Di Giovanni. Cambridge: Cambridge University Press. Original work published 1793.

Kant, Immanuel (1996b) *The Conflict of the Faculties*. In I. Kant, *Religion and Rational Theology*, trans. A. W. Wood and G. Di Giovanni. Cambridge: Cambridge University Press. Original work published 1798.

Lewis, David (2000) Mill and Milquetoast. In D. Lewis, *Papers in Ethics and Social Philosophy* (pp. 159–86). Cambridge: Cambridge University Press.

Locke, John (1824) *A Letter Concerning Toleration*. In J. Locke, *The Works of John Locke*, vol. 5. Oxford: G. and J. Rivington et al. Original work published 1689.

Lucretius (1951) *De Rerum Natura*. In R. E. Latham (trans.), *On the Nature of the Universe*. Baltimore: Penguin Books.

Mill, John Stuart (1948) *On Liberty*. In J. S. Mill, *On Liberty, Representative Government and the Subjection of Women*. Oxford: Oxford University Press. Original work published 1859.

Quinn, Philip L. (1997) Political Liberalisms and their Exclusions of the Religious. In P. J. Weithman (ed.), *Religion and Contemporary Liberalism* (pp. 138–61). Notre Dame, Ind.: University of Notre Dame Press.

Quinn, Philip L. (2001) Religious Citizens within the Limits of Public Reason. *The Modern Schoolman*, 78, 105–24.

Rawls, John (1993) *Political Liberalism*. New York: Columbia University Press.

Rawls, John (1997) The Idea of Public Reason Revisited. *The University of Chicago Law Review*, 64, 765–807.

Rorty, Richard (1994) Religion as Conversation-Stopper. *Common Knowledge*, 3, 1–6.

Waldron, Jeremy (1988) Locke: Toleration and the Rationality of Persecution. In S. Mendus (ed.), *Justifying Toleration* (pp. 61–86). Cambridge: Cambridge University Press.

Wolterstorff, Nicholas (1997) The Role of Religion in Decision and Discussion of Political Issues. In R. Audi and N. Wolterstorff, *Religion in the Public Square* (pp. 67–120). Lanham, Md.: Rowman and Littlefield.

Suggested Further Reading

Carter, Stephen L. (1993) *The Culture of Disbelief*. New York: Basic Books.

Greenawalt, Kent (1995) *Private Consciences and Public Reasons*. Oxford: Oxford University Press.

Heyd, David (ed.) (1996) *Toleration: An Elusive Virtue*. Princeton: Princeton University Press.

Mendus, Susan (1989) *Toleration and the Limits of Liberalism*. London: Macmillan.

Neuhaus, Richard J. (1986) *The Naked Public Square*. Grand Rapids, Mich.: Eerdmans.

Perry, Michael J. (1997) *Religion in Politics: Constitutional and Moral Perspectives*. Oxford: Oxford University Press.

Index